Marx, Engels, and Marxisms

Series Editors
Marcello Musto
York University
Toronto, ON, Canada

Terrell Carver
University of Bristol
Bristol, UK

The Marx renaissance is underway on a global scale. Wherever the critique of capitalism re-emerges, there is an intellectual and political demand for new, critical engagements with Marxism. The peer-reviewed series Marx, Engels and Marxisms (edited by Marcello Musto & Terrell Carver, with Babak Amini and Kohei Saito as Assistant Editors) publishes monographs, edited volumes, critical editions, reprints of old texts, as well as translations of books already published in other languages. Our volumes come from a wide range of political perspectives, subject matters, academic disciplines and geographical areas, producing an eclectic and informative collection that appeals to a diverse and international audience. Our main areas of focus include: the oeuvre of Marx and Engels, Marxist authors and traditions of the 19th and 20th centuries, labour and social movements, Marxist analyses of contemporary issues, and reception of Marxism in the world.

More information about this series at
http://www.palgrave.com/gp/series/14812

August H. Nimtz

Marxism versus Liberalism

Comparative Real-Time Political Analysis

August H. Nimtz
Department of Political Science
University of Minnesota
Minneapolis, MN, USA

ISSN 2524-7123   ISSN 2524-7131   (electronic)
Marx, Engels, and Marxisms
ISBN 978-3-030-24945-8   ISBN 978-3-030-24946-5   (eBook)
https://doi.org/10.1007/978-3-030-24946-5

Cover illustration: Artwork by Natalie Johnsen Morrison

This Palgrave Macmillan imprint is published by the registered company Springer Nature Switzerland AG.
The registered company address is: Gewerbestrasse 11, 6330 Cham, Switzerland

SERIES FOREWORD

THE MARX REVIVAL

The Marx renaissance is under way on a global scale. Whether the puzzle is the economic boom in China or the economic bust in "the West," there is no doubt that Marx appears regularly in the media nowadays as a guru, and not as a threat, as he used to be. The literature dealing with Marxism, which all but dried up twenty-five years ago, is reviving in the global context. Academic and popular journals and even newspapers and online journalism are increasingly open to contributions on Marxism, just as there are now many international conferences, university courses and seminars on related themes. In all parts of the world, leading daily and weekly papers are featuring the contemporary relevance of Marx's thought. From Latin America to Europe, and wherever the critique of capitalism is reemerging, there is an intellectual and political demand for a new critical encounter with Marxism.

TYPES OF PUBLICATIONS

This series brings together reflections on Marx, Engels and Marxisms from perspectives that are varied in terms of political outlook, geographical base, academic methodologies and subject matter, thus challenging many preconceptions as to what "Marxist" thought can be like, as opposed to what it has been. The series will appeal internationally to intellectual communities that are increasingly interested in rediscovering the most powerful critical analysis of capitalism: Marxism. The series editors will ensure that authors and editors in the series are producing overall an eclectic and stimulating yet synoptic and informative vision that will draw a very wide and diverse audience. This series will embrace a much wider range of scholarly interests and academic approaches than any previous "family" of books in the area.

This innovative series will present monographs, edited volumes and critical editions, including translations, to Anglophone readers. The books in this series will work through three main categories.

Studies on Marx and Engels

The series will include titles focusing on the *oeuvres* of Marx and Engels which utilize the scholarly achievements of the ongoing *Marx–Engels Gesamtausgabe*, a project that has strongly revivified the research on these two authors in the past decade.

Critical Studies on Marxisms

Volumes will awaken readers to the overarching issues and world-changing encounters that shelter within the broad categorization of "Marxist." Particular attention will be given to authors such as Gramsci and Benjamin, who are very popular and widely translated nowadays all over the world, but also to authors who are less known in the English-speaking countries, such as Mariátegui.

Reception Studies and Marxist National Traditions

Political projects have necessarily required oversimplifications in the twentieth century, and Marx and Engels have found themselves "made over" numerous times and in quite contradictory ways. Taking a national perspective on "reception" will be a global revelation, and the volumes of this series will enable the worldwide Anglophone community to understand the variety of intellectual and political traditions through which Marx and Engels have been received in local contexts.

Toronto, Canada   Marcello Musto
Bristol, UK   Terrell Carver

TITLES PUBLISHED

1. Terrell Carver & Daniel Blank, *A Political History of the Editions of Marx and Engels's "German Ideology" Manuscripts*, 2014.
2. Terrell Carver & Daniel Blank, *Marx and Engels's "German Ideology" Manuscripts: Presentation and Analysis of the "Feuerbach chapter,"* 2014.
3. Alfonso Maurizio Iacono, *The History and Theory of Fetishism*, 2015.
4. Paresh Chattopadhyay, *Marx's Associated Mode of Production: A Critique of Marxism*, 2016.
5. Domenico Losurdo, *Class Struggle: A Political and Philosophical History*, 2016.
6. Frederick Harry Pitts, *Critiquing Capitalism Today: New Ways to Read Marx*, 2017.
7. Ranabir Samaddar, *Karl Marx and the Postcolonial Age*, 2017.
8. George Comninel, *Alienation and Emancipation in the Work of Karl Marx*, 2018.
9. Jean-Numa Ducange & Razmig Keucheyan (Eds.), *The End of the Democratic State: Nicos Poulantzas, a Marxism for the 21st Century*, 2018.
10. Robert Ware, *Marx on Emancipation and the Socialist Transition: Retrieving Marx for the Future*, 2018.
11. Xavier LaFrance & Charles Post (Eds.), *Case Studies in the Origins of Capitalism*, 2018.
12. John Gregson, *Marxism, Ethics, and Politics: The Work of Alasdair MacIntyre*, 2018.
13. Vladimir Puzone & Luis Felipe Miguel (Eds.), *The Brazilian Left in the 21st Century: Conflict and Conciliation in Peripheral Capitalism*, 2019.
14. James Muldoon & Gaard Kets (Eds.), *The German Revolution and Political Theory*, 2019.

TITLES FORTHCOMING

Gustavo Moura de Cavalcanti Mello and Mauricio de Souza Sabadini (Eds.), *Financial Speculation and Fictitious Profits: A Marxist Analysis.*
Michael Brie, *Rediscovering Lenin: Dialectics of Revolution and Metaphysics of Domination.*

ACKNOWLEDGMENTS

As a work in progress for almost two decades, this book benefits from invaluable input from many sources, not the least, the undergraduate students in a political theory topics course at the University of Minnesota I taught twice between 2017 and 2018 who read drafts of it at various stages. Their questions and responses helped tremendously in clarifying my claims and making them more accessible. Owing in part to their positive feedback the course is now certified for a regular departmental offering.

Most input from colleagues and friends focused on specific chapters. Sergio Valverde was the exception. As well as his informed commentary on every chapter—his expertise on Hegel was particularly useful in revising Chap. 2, the Marx–Engels/Tocqueville comparison—his enthusiasm for the project was motivating. Chapter 2 continues to benefit from invaluable feedback on an earlier version from Ron Aminzade, the late Roger Boesche, Mary Dietz, Lisa Disch and Lansiné Kaba. Thanks to Rob Nichols and Nancy Luxon for their positive reaction to the revised version. Especially appreciated is the feedback, once again, from Mary Dietz, her suggestions and commendation for Chap. 3, the Marx–Mill comparison.

A special thanks to Bob Holt, whose work along with late colleague John Turner attracted me to Minnesota to be a member of the department's renowned comparative politics subfield many years ago. That a comparative politics sensibility informs the book is no accident. Bob's critical, thoughtful and challenging feedback regarding my Lenin–Weber and Lenin–Wilson comparisons required me to sharpen my claims. The response of another comparative politics colleague, Phil Shively, was encouraging. Ron Aminzade's sociology lens and Andrew Zimmerman's history lens on Weber were particularly helpful.

Chapter 4, the Lenin–Wilson comparison, garnered the most feedback. Exceptionally valuable were the suggestions of Alex Anievas about the international relations literature and the questions Ron Krebs posed about the research question itself. And I'm indebted to Ron for suggesting to Nicauris Heredia Rosario, one of the graduate students who organized the Minnesota International Relations Colloquium in 2018–2019, that they invite me to present the chapter. The comments and questions were helpful, including one from my sister Sanna Towns. Others contributed to the final draft, including Martin Sampson, Kyle Edwards, Ash Eberle—especially her editorial input—Gary Prevost and Geoff Mirelowitz. Bob Braxton deserves special mention; his graduate seminar paper planted the idea of a Lenin–Wilson comparison. I should mention long-time friend and distinguished historian Allen Isaacman; along with suggestions, he assured me about five years ago that the project would be original.

Thanks also to the two anonymous peer reviewers, especially the one who offered detailed constructive criticisms—making, I think, for a better book. I am grateful as well to Marcel Musto and Terrell Carver for including the book in their Palgrave Macmillan series "Marx, Engels and Marxisms." Without the faith that Michelle Chen, acquisitions editor at Palgrave Macmillan, had in the project from our initial conversation this book would not have been possible. Her colleagues at Palgrave Macmillan, including John Stegner, are also to be commended. Though all of the mentioned assistance has been immensely invaluable, I am, of course, ultimately responsible for what eventually found its way into the book.

Last, but not least, many thanks to my companion and very talented comrade Natalie Johnsen Morrison whose painting "The Reds and the Yellows," done specifically for the book, adorns the cover. There aren't, as she correctly points out, many communist women artists—which she works to rectify.

Contents

CHAPTER 1

Introduction

Not one of us possesses the breadth of vision that enabled [Marx], at the
very moment when rapid action was called for, invariably to hit upon
the right solution and at once get to the heart of the matter ... at a
revolutionary juncture his judgment was virtually infallible.
Engels, 1884

Thanks to the current occupant of the White House, "socialism" is on the
U.S. public agenda in a way it hasn't been for at least a half-century or
even longer. In October 2018, the Trump administration's Council of
Economic Advisers (CEA) issued a seventy-page report entitled "The
Opportunity Costs of Socialism." "Coincident with the 200th anniversary
of Karl Marx's birth, socialism," it began, "is making a comeback in
American political discourse. Detailed policy proposals from self-declared
socialists are gaining support in Congress and among much of the electorate."[1] The report purports to show how such proposals are misguided and
counterproductive. In his State of the Union Address to Congress in
February 2019, President Trump vowed that "we renew our resolve that
America will never be a socialist country." "Socialism," hence, will
undoubtedly be a central target in his 2020 reelection campaign. The
president's pledge isn't unwarranted. Among Democratic Party presidential hopefuls is Senator Bernie Sanders, a declared "socialist." A leading
Republican Party strategist makes a convincing case that Sanders, nineteen
months before the 2020 election, "is a real contender."[2] The last time that

© The Author(s) 2019
A. H. Nimtz, *Marxism versus Liberalism*, Marx, Engels,
and Marxisms, https://doi.org/10.1007/978-3-030-24946-5_1

was even remotely possible for a self-professed socialist was a century ago, in the case of Socialist Party candidate Eugene V. Debs, from a prison cell.

The background to all of this is the continuing fallout from the Great Recession, "secular stagnation" as some defenders of capitalism term it or, in the language of some Marxists, the global crisis of late capitalism. In March 2019, Jamie Dimon, CEO of J.P. Morgan Chase, the country's largest bank, said that while his "company is doing fine, it is absolutely obvious that a big chunk of [people] have been left behind. ... Forty percent of Americans make less than $15 an hour. Forty percent of Americans can't afford a $400 bill, whether it's medical or fixing their car. Fifteen percent of Americans make minimum wages, 70,000 die from opioids [annually]. ... So we've kind of bifurcated the economy."[3] Not surprisingly, therefore, "only 37% of Americans ... think the country is going in the right direction while 56.4% think it's on the wrong track," according to a poll in April 2019.[4] This is the reality that made possible not only the Trump election victory in 2016 but also the Brexit vote in Britain in 2016 and later the "gillets jaunes" protests in France in 2018–2019. Marx once said that a drowning person will grab hold of a twig in hope of salvation.

This book is a needed intervention into the discussion/debates about this unprecedented reality. One of the two most frequent charges levelled at socialism is that it has never worked, beginning with the Soviet Union. But that assumes, as the CEA report does, that socialism was once instituted and/or is in place somewhere. Although not a priority for this book, the charge is serious and needs to be addressed, which I do in the Conclusion. Suffice it to say here that nothing in any of the utterances of Karl Marx, Frederick Engels or Vladimir Lenin supports the claim that socialism ever existed in the Union of Soviet Socialist Republics—probably, except for the Holy Roman Empire, the most misnamed state in history. It was Joseph Stalin in 1936 who first so declared. The burden of proof is on those who think Stalin—who lied about almost everything—knew better than Marx, Engels and Lenin to explain why.

The other major accusation about socialism is that it is an authoritarian and inherently antidemocratic project owing exactly to what unfolded in the Soviet Union, the sanguinary Stalinist counterrevolution, as some of us call it. Insinuated is that socialism was born with a fatal flaw that paved the way to Stalinist outcomes not only in the USSR but elsewhere as well. This recent example of the innuendo is typical. "Given the violent tenor of Marx's writings, his hatred of the bourgeoisie and of capitalism, his contempt for other socialist theoreticians who disagreed with him, and his delusions about the possibility of creating a utopia dominated by a morally superior proletariat, he would have sanctioned Lenin's brutality." And this is in an account that claims to be sympathetic to Marx.[5] Often accompanying the charge is the suggestion that the Marxist socialist project lacked the assumed democratic groundings of the alternative liberal project. But how accurate is the charge and its companion thesis? Is it true that the original Marxist project came with a democratic deficit unlike the liberal alternative? This question more than any other drives this inquiry. Implicit in the question is the need for some sort of comparison between the Marxist and liberal enterprises in their original incarnations to make a determination—immanently political projects that had political consequences. But what kind of comparison?

If politics is the art of knowing what to do next, then the test of political perspective is making decisions about unfolding events—in real time. After the fact, or in hindsight, we can all look or make ourselves look smart, to be the proverbial Monday morning quarterback. Figuring out "what is to be done" in the moment is the real challenge—before all the data has come in. Real-time political analysis, what this book seeks to make a case for as a method, is, then, about the political judgments and actions that flow from them as developments are under way.[6] Engels's assessment of his partner to a fellow comrade a year and a half after his death in 1883 comes close to capturing what this inquiry is about. "Not one of us possesses the breadth of vision that enabled [Marx], at the very moment when rapid action was called for, invariably to hit upon the right solution and at once get to the heart of the matter … at a revolutionary juncture his judgment was virtually infallible."[7] But were there any liberal rivals similarly talented that Engels might have ignored or not known of? That's in part the task at hand.

More concretely, this book examines how a "materialist conception of history," a Marxist perspective, compares to alternative varieties of liberal perspectives when subjected to real-time analysis. How well did either do in representing the events in motion? How good was either in informing actions to be taken? If predictive in anyway, how accurate were the forecasts? Have the claims stood the test of time? Most importantly, how did either perform for advancing the democratic quest?

To this end, I have selected four key moments in modern history about which leading Marxists and liberals made political judgments as they were in motion and for which there are ample archival data. So that the comparison is fair, I've selected liberals who engaged not just in analysis but in practice—some indication that they too like the Marxists tried to varying degrees to shape the outcome of the events under examination—after all, what politics is about. Unlike historians—who someone once accused of being vultures because "they feed off the past"—political people aren't just dispassionate observers of the world in which they live; they seek to be protagonists of history. This is, hence, a study in comparative real-time political analysis—unique as far as I can tell.

The four cases under the microscope: Karl Marx and Frederick Engels versus Alexis de Tocqueville on the Revolution of 1848 in France; Marx versus John Stuart Mill on the U.S. Civil War; Vladimir Lenin versus Max Weber on the Russian Revolution of 1905; and, lastly, Lenin versus Woodrow Wilson on the October Revolution of 1917 and the end of World War I. I supplement in appendices to the Marx–Mill and Lenin–Weber comparisons, respectively, the campaign for electoral reform in Britain in 1866–1868 and the impact of the October Revolution in Germany. Both additions confirm and enrich the findings in the main body of the relevant chapters.

This is the first time seminal figures in liberalism in many of its varieties have been subjected to real-time political analysis in comparison to their Marxist counterparts—an incredible fact in and of itself.[8] Clearly, others have thought about doing so, or, better, actually pretended to having done so. This is particularly true when it comes to Mill and Tocqueville. Graeme Duncan's 1973 *Marx and Mill: Two Views of Social Conflict and Social Harmony*, for example, suggests such a comparison but actually doesn't deliver.[9] The reader would hardly know from his account that real-time politics and acting on them was at the center of Marx's life. For Duncan and many others trained like him in the academy, it's all about texts.[10] But to treat Marx simply as an author is unpardonable. And if Duncan could be so myopic about Marx, it's no surprise, then, that he ignored Mill's most politically consequential moment, or, what could have been, in relation to the U.S. Civil War.

As for Tocqueville, the literature, sometimes, is suggestive but unfulfilling. Consider most recently, the Ewa Atanassow/Richard Boyd 2013 collection.[11] Two of its essays imply or hint at a comparison. Nestor Capdevila's "Democracy and Revolution in Tocqueville: The Frontiers of Democracy" brings Marx into the conversation but only at the end and almost cursorily—and without even mention of either's involvement in the European Spring. The same is true with Atanassow's "Nationhood—Democracy's Final Frontier?." That Marx *and* Tocqueville were first and foremost political activists, as I hope to show, is evidently unimportant to those who prioritize texts and ideas as determinant in politics. But "ideas," the young Marx concluded, "cannot carry out anything at all." Tocqueville, to be seen, would have been sympathetic to Marx's dictum.

James Kloppenberg's 2016 *Toward Democracy*, an otherwise magisterial survey of the ideas—but not the struggles—about the millennial-old democratic quest, ends in the mid-nineteenth century with the European Spring and the U.S. Civil War, the foci of my Chaps. 2 and 3. The heroes in both events for him are Tocqueville, Mill and Abraham Lincoln; to his credit, Tocqueville gets a question mark—at the least as I hope to show.[12] Marx is brought in, as is common with these kinds of treatments, again, cursorily, stereotypically and only to score points for liberalism. It never occurred to Kloppenberg, who operates only in the realm of ideas, that the tendentious claims he makes about Marx's democratic bona fides, in invidious comparison to the others, could be tested against the others in real time, the 1848 revolutions and/or the Civil War. Real-world politics, the effective test for political ideas, is not, however, what Kloppenberg does.

Even a left-leaning tome, Domenico Losurdo's 2011 *Liberalism: A Counter-History*, missed the mark.[13] Though apparently sympathetic to the spirit of Marx's politics, he too succumbs to the text-only treatment of Marx, and, inexcusably, the pre-communist Marx texts to draw critical conclusions about him. Because Marx, Tocqueville and Mill all figure significantly in his critical look at liberalism he would have been on surer footing had he subjected all three to real-time political analysis, again, in relation to the European Spring and the Civil War. The terrain upon which to interrogate liberalism is real-time politics. The test for politics of any kind in the nineteenth century, the scope of Losurdo's book, is its two most consequential contests for advancing the democratic quest.

Sheri Berman's recently published *Democracy and Dictatorship in Europe* betrays another failing in the literature, in particular regard to Tocqueville. While Berman cites approvingly Tocqueville as an authority on 1789, he is nowhere to be found in her account of the events of 1848. She correctly points out that the "crushing of the June Days and the renewed appeal of the 'forces of order' in France encouraged counter-revolution elsewhere in Europe."[14] But by not at least noting Tocqueville's counterrevolutionary role in that "crushing," as detailed in Chap. 2 of this book, is to give him a free pass. The silence of liberals like Berman regarding Tocqueville's sanguinary conduct in the drama of 1848 is deafening—not for the first time. And when compared to Marx and Engels, as done here, it's understandable. The contrasts with the two communists aren't flattering for the hero of many liberals. A worker in the streets of Paris during the "June Days"—to be as attention-grabbing as possible—could be forgiven for wanting to either shoot or knife to death the author of *Democracy in America*.

The Lenin–Weber comparison in Chap. 4 regarding the 1905 Russian Revolution isn't one, I admit, that would have automatically come to mind for even the most informed. Feedback I got on the drafts I shared with others was often one of surprise and sometimes incredulity. Only a close reading of Lenin could have revealed it as a potentially fruitful comparison. And, alas, too few of those who pretend to know Lenin—friend and foe alike—actually take the time to read him. But to not take advantage of the fact that two of the most influential figures in modernity both examined—in real time—what proved to be the "dress rehearsal" for arguably the most consequential event in the twentieth century, the 1917 Russian Revolution, would have been inexcusable for a project such as this. And that Lenin and Weber both read one another, unlike in the Marx/Engels–Tocqueville and Marx–Mill comparisons, makes for an even more instructive case study. Berman, too, is noticeably silent about Weber's counterrevolutionary role in revolutionary Germany following the October Revolution—distilled in the appendix to Chap. 4.

The Lenin–Wilson comparison, Chap. 5, on the other hand, isn't farfetched. Arno Mayer's still valuable 1959 tour de force and insufficiently heralded book *Political Origins of the New Diplomacy, 1917–1918* raised that possibility for the first time in the mainstream literature.[15] But absent in a meaningful way in what was otherwise a real breakthrough piece of scholarship is Lenin's voice, the other leading protagonist in all of those still resonating events. It's not enough to hear Wilson. Without the actual declarations of Lenin and other Bolsheviks such as Leon Trotsky, Wilson's utterances and actions, as I hope to demonstrate, were incomprehensible. Politics may explain why Mayer minimized if not silenced Lenin. The context in which the book appeared is in the midst of the Cold War whose orthodoxy imposed limits on what could be discussed in the academy, and not just behind the Iron Curtain.

Four decades later, another mainstream academic covered a large portion of the terrain as Mayer had done, specifically, the diplomacy for ending World War I. Adam Tooze's highly acclaimed *The Deluge*, stands on, without sufficient acknowledgment, Mayer's work.[16] But unlike Mayer, Tooze offers a tendentious social democratic rendering of the Bolshevik leader. There is a time-worn cottage industry, Leninology and textbook Leninism, that is based on either ignoring what Lenin actually said, or selectively reading him, as in Tooze's case, or, in one spectacularly egregious example, putting words into his mouth.[17] This book seeks to correct that decades-old practice.

In anticipation of the centenary of World War I, a spate of books have appeared, one of which has a title that looked promising, Arthur Herman's *1917: Lenin, Wilson, and the Birth of the New World Disorder*.[18] Well-written and, thus, accessible, Herman is no fan of Wilson—quite critical as the subtitle of the book suggests. But neither is he enamored with Lenin. His portrait is unapologetically tendentious—just the latest rendering from the bin of the long-established Leninology enterprise. Herman at least recognized that both Lenin and Wilson were not only aware of one another but sought, unlike in the other comparisons, to influence the actions of each other, making for an even more instructive comparison of all the four case studies.

This is a sampling of the literature I'm aware of that justifies the need to do a project like this, again, comparative real-time political analysis—apparently, the first of its kind. Readers, of whatever degree of information and persuasion, can decide for themselves if they think the effort and their reading of it was worth the time. I'm willing to bet that they'll feel rewarded for the effort. I certainly was in researching and writing the project. If it motivates others to do the same with other historical figures, as I suggest in the Conclusion, then it has certainly been worth doing.

Chapter 2, "The European Spring, 1848–1851: Marx and Engels versus Tocqueville," begins with the relevant biographical background of all three protagonists to understand how they read and responded to that mid-nineteenth-century democratic wave. The price Tocqueville's family paid for its aristocratic origins in the reign of terror of the French Revolution forever marked him. It foretold better than his authorship of his two-volume *Democracy in America* how he would respond to the upheaval that instituted France's Second Republic in February 1848. Also determinant was the prior decade-long experience as a leading figure in France's National Assembly and, thus, France's political establishment. An aristocratic liberal rather than a republican is the appropriate label for Tocqueville given his support to constitutional monarchy before February. Ironically, his *Democracy in America* and related narratives were more determinant in understanding Marx's political trajectory—key in the communist conclusions he reached by 1844. Engels came to similar conclusions by a different route. All three protagonists anticipated the February Revolution through different perspectives. Despite those differences, the Marx–Engels team was often in agreement with Tocqueville about the causes and course of the Revolution. What they most differed on was how to respond; class and class orientation was above all determinant. While Marx and Engels did all they could from afar to encourage the revolt, Tocqueville on the scene and with governmental power did all he could, as already noted, to crush the rebellion, in blood. As well, he enabled the imposition of a dictatorship to consolidate the defeat of Europe's first proletarian revolution—what a reading of his *Democracy* would not have anticipated.

The Marx–Engels/Tocqueville comparison offers many rewards but not the least is that it allows for an assessment of the world's first social democratic government that issued from the February Revolution—what most commentators, pro and con, have in mind in thinking about, at least in America, "socialism." Never before had a government sought to address the problem of unemployment, unique to the new mode of production rooting and extending itself for the first time in one corner of the globe. Once a jobs program was instituted, the first of its kind, the question then became whether the right to work should be enshrined in the constitution—issues that continue to resonate today. How Marx and Engels versus Tocqueville responded is especially instructive.

Chapter 3, "The United States Civil War: Marx versus Mill," begins, unlike Chap. 2, with a much more abbreviated treatment of the relevant biographies of the protagonists—understandably for Marx given the details provided in the prior chapter. Mill, on the other hand, unlike Tocqueville the politico, was first and foremost an intellectual. Thus, the focus is on those rare moments in his biography when he actually related to political developments, especially revolutionary ones that offered an opportunity to compare and contrast him with Marx. Thus, the opening section in the chapter hones in on the French theater of the 1848 Revolutions. How the two responded, in terms of time and energy, anticipated their responses to the Civil War, the most consequential contest for the global democratic quest after the French Revolution. By the time the War arrived in April 1861, Marx and Mill were on the same political page about wanting to end the rule of the slavocracy in America. But, unlike Mill, Marx, in residence in London, had a coterie of comrades in America, an ersatz party, working to make that possible. Marx swung into action immediately in defense of the Union cause, preparing for the "struggle in the press" to defend the Lincoln administration from Britain's overwhelmingly pro-Confederacy press. Beginning in September 1861, he was able to publish numerous articles in various venues, including the leading U.S. newspaper that Lincoln read religiously. Not until February 1862 did Mill get into print something on behalf of the Union cause. In the end, he wrote only two pro-Union articles though having far more potential than Marx for getting published in Britain as the country's leading intellectual.

Also distinguishing Marx and Mill were their intended audiences in defense of the Union. When opportunities to get published dried up, Marx turned his attention to organizing the English working class for the Union cause against London's inclination to support the Confederacy. Mill, on the other hand, sought to sway mainly the opinion of the English elite. In the end, the English working class proved to be more decisive in enabling the Union cause—certainly what Lincoln thought. Marx, simply put, correctly prioritized the English working class in aiding and abetting the demise of the world's last remaining bulwark of slavery.

The different class orientations of the two protagonists were glaringly on display within a year after the end of the Civil War around the issue of electoral reform in Britain. It coincided with Mill's decision to become active in politics for the first time, running for and winning a seat in Parliament. Whether to support household or universal male suffrage, with Mill favoring the former and Marx the latter, exposed their essential differences. Along the way, Marx did all he could to limit Mill's influence in the working class—unbeknownst to Mill. Unlike the comparison in the second chapter, at least one of the protagonists in the third, Marx, was conscious about going head to head against the other, Mill—adding another layer of richness to the real-time analysis.

Chapter 4, "Two Takes on the Russian Revolution of 1905: Lenin versus Weber," also begins with relevant biographical details for understanding how the two protagonists read and responded to what proved to be "the dress rehearsal" for the October 1917 Russian Revolution. Weber, six years Lenin's senior, was primarily an academic but one who considered himself to be a "bourgeois nationalist scholar" and, thus, obligated to advance Germany's "national interests." Owing to a years-long bout of depression, his academic output was limited before 1905 except for his famous *Protestant Ethic and the Spirit of Capitalism* in 1904; it anticipated who he looked to for advancing democracy, the bourgeoisie. Lenin, on the other hand, a faithful student of Marx and Engels and the lessons they drew about 1848, prioritized the working class in alliance with the peasantry for instituting democracy in Russia for the first time. Those very different orientations determined how they responded to the 1905–1906 upheavals in Russia.

By the time Weber turned to the Russian developments in 1905, Lenin had given attention for at least half a decade to the prospects for a democratic revolution, including whether Russia's fledgling liberal movement would play a decisive role. That movement was the main concern of Weber's two-volume highly detailed account. Notably different, therefore, in their narratives is the role of the toilers in the streets, the strike movement—virtually absent in Weber's account whereas of decisive importance in what Lenin wrote. Both Lenin and Weber were in basic agreement about the fecklessness of Russian liberals in the revolution's defeat. Whereas for Weber that was the end of the story, for Lenin it was confirmation that he was correct in advocating for the alternative worker–peasant alliance. Most instructive for this book is that not only Lenin but Weber as well read the 1905–1906 events through the lens of the European Spring of 1848, specifically, the German edition, but with very different conclusions. The comparison permits a preliminary answer to one of the most consequential questions of the twentieth century: why wasn't there a liberal alternative to the Bolsheviks in Russia?

The appendix to Chap. 4 reveals that Weber could be as much a politico—with his own idiosyncrasies—as Lenin. With Germany's "honor" at stake in the Great War, Weber actively defended it even if that meant contravening the facts that the social scientist once extolled. It pitted him against Lenin in a way that the 1905–1906 theater could not—activist against activist. While Lenin was doing all he could, beginning with the February 1917 Revolution, to stimulate a similar overturn in Germany, Weber exerted as much energy to make sure that didn't happen. From then until Weber's death in 1920, their democratic credentials, or lack thereof, were tellingly counterposed. The Lenin–Weber comparison in the appendix offers another opportunity in real-time analysis in which at least one of the protagonists, Weber, was in conscious competition with the other—also enriching the comparison in the main body of the chapter.

"The October Revolution to the End of the 'Great War': Lenin versus Woodrow Wilson," Chap. 5, is the only one of the four comparisons in which both protagonists knew they were directly contesting one another in real time—making it, therefore, the richest of the four. And with a richer archival record owing to it being the most recent in time that's even more the case. It too begins with relevant biographical background, what

Lenin and Wilson drew on from their pasts to make sense of and to respond to the Guns of August that exploded in 1914. Lenin, once again, stood on the shoulders of his mentors, Marx and Engels. Wilson, without the benefit of such a head-start program, had to improvise. Once the 300-year-old Romanov dynasty came to an ignominious end in the February Revolution, Wilson could now justify U.S. intervention in the war in alliance with the Entente powers, to "make the world safe for democracy." But wanting to keep Russia in the war put him in diametrical opposition to Lenin who did all he could to extricate Russia from the bloodbath. Wilson's stance epitomized the politics of unintended consequences; it enabled Bolshevik ascent in October 1917. Armed with state power, Lenin immediately sought to make peace a reality, putting Wilson in the awkward position of seeming like a warmonger. His Fourteen Points speech to Congress in January 1918 was his attempt to take the moral high ground away from the Bolsheviks. Lenin and the Bolsheviks strategically used Wilson's contradictory position to make him resort to an irresolute response to the Bolsheviks in power—wanting their demise but not willing to mount a full-scale U.S. invasion to ensure their overthrow. The diplomatic *pas de deux* that Lenin engaged in with Wilson, and Wilson with Lenin, is the reason why, again, the fourth comparison is the richest. And at stake for their global political projects was which of them had better democratic bona fides.

In the Conclusion, I employ a series of questions to varying degrees to interrogate the materials presented in the four chapters. What are the broad and key conclusions to be drawn from the four real-time politics comparisons? How do the claims that Marx, Engels and Lenin made about the historical moments under examination—the French edition of the European Spring, the American Civil War, the Russian Revolution of 1905, the Bolshevik Revolution of 1917 and the end to World War I—compare and contrast to those of Tocqueville, Mill, Weber and Wilson? To what extent are their readings of the events in agreement and disagreement? Which of them had a more accurate reading of the events and made better forecasts? How did their theoretical/political views influence their responses? How do the four comparisons reveal key differences between Marxist and different varieties of liberal real-time politics? Most important, to what extent, if any, did their actions advance the democratic quest that was posed in all four moments? Can, lastly, a case be made for a superior theoretical purchase of either perspective for doing real-time politics? There are admittedly many details in the narrative that the reader might get lost in as one reviewer of the manuscript noted. A suggestion: beginning with the first part of the Conclusion that addresses each comparison can be the best way to avoid that potential problem. Also of importance are the epigrams that introduce each chapter. Far from being decorative, they purport to distill the essence of the four comparisons. The reader is advised, therefore, to return to the epigrams to ensure that they have understood after a reading what the chapter tries to convey.

In the second part of the Conclusion, attention turns to subsequent historical developments after the Great War. If it's true, as I show, that Marx, Engels and Lenin had better democratic credentials than their liberal cohorts, then how to explain all of the horrors later done in their names? I begin with a Marxist explanation of why socialism never came to be in the Soviet Union. Then, I speculate, in what can only be a cursory way, on a Marxist versus liberal real-time political reading of the consequences of that fact, specifically, the lead-up to World War II. The readings and actions of two influential figures, Leon Trotsky and John Maynard Keynes, a Marxist and a liberal, are a potentially fruitful comparative real-time political analysis as is done in the four cases in the book. Along the way, I distill Trotsky's most original contributions to Marxist theory, his explanations for the triumph of both Stalinism and fascism. A second potentially instructive comparative real-time analysis—again, only a sketch—could be Cuban president Fidel Castro versus U.S. president John Kennedy between 1961 and 1963. Now that Cuba is once again squarely in the crosshairs of Washington, the inquiry could have currency.

Finally, in the last section of the Conclusion, are there—in the spirit of real-time politics—lessons from the four comparisons for contemporary politics, for making sense of the unprecedented political moment in which we live? Is there a way out of the crisis that weighs increasingly on the world's toilers, the same crisis that put in the White House its current occupant?

The inspiration for this book is what I discovered while doing the research and writing for my 2000 book, *Marx and Engels: Their Contribution to the Democratic Breakthrough*.[19] I knew beforehand about their democratic practice that I sought to document with convincing evidence. What I didn't know was how singular their contribution had been. To prove my point, I decided to compare and contrast their readings and actions with someone more often identified with democracy, Tocqueville, also an influential actor in the drama of 1848–1851. The evidence made clear, as the reader will see in Chap. 2 (an updated version of the original chapter in my *Marx and Engels*) that the democratic qualifications of the two founders of modern communism were more deserved than those of the renowned author of *Democracy in America*. Tocqueville's revealing account of his role in the French theater of the European Spring, his *Souvenirs*, supplied invaluable evidence for my claim. I boldly claimed, as a result, that no two individuals in the nineteenth century did more to advance the millennial-old quest than Marx and Engels. Evidence regarding other liberal alternatives, I admit, was lacking. I'm now able to make a more convincing case. The Marx–Mill comparison in Chap. 3, as the reader will see, reveals that the two communists also had better democratic bona fides than the renowned author of *On Liberty*.

In a couple of instances in my *Marx and Engels*, I stated or at least suggested that only in another volume could the fate of their project be addressed, specifically, the counterrevolutionary outcome of the Russian Revolution. My 2014 two-volume *Lenin's Electoral Strategy* was the first down payment on that promise. I was able to make a convincing case for Lenin's democratic credentials. As one reviewer put it, "Nimtz's well-researched and historically informed analysis of Lenin's position will be an extremely important intervention in Lenin studies, and, without exaggeration, will, I think, definitively settle the issue of Lenin's close connection to the tactical positions of Marx and Engels, not to mention Lenin's deep commitment to the democratic horizon, whether tactically in terms of bourgeois representative assemblies or ideally in the deep democratic practices associated with working-class self-governance."[20] I contended that there was no smoking gun in Lenin's biography, certainly before the Bolshevik ascent to power in October 1917, to account for the revolution's betrayal as Trotsky termed it. Historical contingency, rather, best explained that tragic outcome which still resonates. But to really be convincing about Lenin's "democratic practices," I would have had to do with him as I did with the Marx–Engels versus Tocqueville comparison in the earlier book, namely, compare and contrast Lenin to some liberal light. I didn't do that, nor, I must confess, did I even consider doing so. Now I can say that it's been done—what the comparisons with Weber and Wilson constitute. No two liberals, in all their variations, are a better match for a real-time comparison with Lenin for assessing democratic capabilities. Both were enormously influential then and later and, by chance for this exposition, both competed with Lenin in real time in the arena for advancing democracy. It's hard to imagine more fitting and consequential scenarios—the October Revolution, its impact on ending the Great War and Germany's transition to republican government for the first time—for doing such a test.

Lenin, as instantiated in Chaps. 4 and 5, had no liberal rival who contributed more to the democratic quest than the Bolshevik leader—which will probably be the biggest surprise for the reader. To learn, for a teaser, that Woodrow Wilson praised Bolshevik leaders for acting in "the true spirit of modern democracy" in his famous Fourteen Points address to Congress in January 1918 is not what today's eyes are accustomed to reading. The contrast with the denunciation of "socialism" by the current occupant of the White House in his State of the Union address to Congress almost exactly a century later couldn't be more striking. Reading Lenin in real time, I show, permits a more accurate portrait of him than the stereotypical image rendered through the lens of all that was done later in his name—in hindsight. Again, the advantages of real-time political analysis.

NOTES

1. https://www.whitehouse.gov/briefings-statements/cea-report-opportunity-costs-socialism/.
2. Karl Rove, "Bernie Sanders Could Win This Time," *Wall Street Journal*, April 18, 2019, p. A15.
3. https://www.cnbc.com/2019/03/18/jamie-dimon-says-weve-split-the-us-economy-leaving-the-poor-behind.html.
4. Ibid.
5. Scott L. Montgomery and Daniel Chirot, *The Shape of the New: Four Big Ideas and How They Made the Modern World* (Princeton: Princeton University Press, 2015), p. 117. Marx—maybe a sign of the times—is elevated into the pantheon of the four key "thinkers" for today, along with Adam Smith, Charles Darwin, Thomas Jefferson and Alexander Hamilton.
6. This is similar to Raymond Geuss's point on "the importance of timing in political action. Successful action … often depends on making a delicate judgment about what is realistically possible at what point in time … the moment that must be seized now because it will never recur—seeing when the time is ripe for action and grasping opportunities that will not present themselves again. An ability to pick the crucial moment when action can be successful is an important constituent of one of the skills a good politician exhibits." Raymond Geuss, *Philosophy and Real Politics* (Princeton, NJ: Princeton U.P., 2008), pp. 31–2.
7. *Marx-Engels Collected Works* (New York: International Publishers, 1995), vol. 47, p. 202 (hereafter *MECW, 47*, p. 202).

8. I'm aware that "liberalism" can be a contested label. Without getting into the debate, I think a convincing case can be made for the four figures employed in this examination. Helena Rosenblatt's recent and useful book, *The Lost History of Liberalism: From Ancient Rome to the Twenty-First Century* (Princeton, NJ: Princeton U.P., 2018), includes all four in her understanding of the label's historical usage.

9. *Marx and Mill: Two Views of Social Conflict and Social Harmony* (New York: Cambridge, U.P., 1973).

10. In my *Marx and Engels: Their Contribution to the Democratic Breakthrough* (Albany, N.Y.: SUNY Press, 2000), pp. 301–3, I elaborate on the academy's time-worn practice of depoliticizing Marx; basically, a mirror image of itself.

11. Ewa Atanassow and Richard Boyd, eds., *Tocqueville and the Frontiers of Democracy* (New York: Cambridge U.P., 2013). An earlier example, to be discussed in Chap. 1, is J.P. Mayer's *Alexis de Tocqueville: A Biographical Study in Political Science* (New York: Harper & Brothers, 1960).

12. James T. Kloppenberg, *Toward Democracy: The Struggle for Self-Rule in European and American Thought* (New York: Oxford U.P. 2016), chapter 14.

13. Domenico Losurdo, *Liberalism: A Counter-History* (London: Verso, 2011).

14. Sheri Berman, *Democracy and Dictatorship in Europe: From the Ancien Régime to the Present Day* (New York: Oxford University Press, 2019), p. 97.

15. Arno Mayer, *Political Origins of the New Diplomacy, 1917–1918* (New Haven: Yale U.P, 1959).

16. Adam Tooze, *The Deluge: The Great War, America and the Remaking of the Global Order, 1916–1931* (New York: Viking Press, 2014).

17. I'm referring to Bertrand Wolfe's *Three Who Made a Revolution*, a work that introduced Lenin to many an aspiring scholar for more than the last half-century. Wolfe's blatantly doctored rendering of one of his texts may have been the origin of the all so common portrait of Lenin as an ogre in mainstream circles. For details, see my *Lenin's Electoral Strategy*, vol. 1 (New York: Palgrave Macmillan, 2014), pp. 190–3. Neither has Marx escaped such machinations. The prize-winning political scientist Adam Przeworski performed a similar sleight of hand on one of his texts; see my "Marx and Engels's Electoral Strategy: The Alleged versus the Real," *New Political Science*, vol. 32, no. 3 (September 2010).

18. Arthur Herman, *1917: Lenin, Wilson, and the Birth of the New World Disorder* (New York: HarperCollins, 2017).

19. Nimtz, *Marx and Engels*.

20. Bradley J. McDonald, *Perspectives on Politics* vol. 13, no. 4 (December 2015), pp. 1133–5.

CHAPTER 2

The European Spring, 1848–1851: Marx and Engels versus Tocqueville

And yet [Bonaparte's coup d'état] is inevitable, unless resisted by an appeal to revolutionary passions, which I do not wish to rouse in the nation.
Tocqueville, 1851

By [resisting Bonaparte] it [the Party of Order] would give the nation its marching orders, and it fears nothing more than that the nation should move.
Marx, 1852

If the French Revolution of 1789 inaugurated the modern era, as is widely recognized, its second edition secured its place in history. The 1848–1849 revolutions that commenced in Paris in February 1848 put in place, if haltingly, the prerequisites for republican rule in France; not for the last time a revolutionary process would extend over decades. The "European Spring," as it would come to be known, commenced the definitive end to a centuries-old institution, absolute monarchy. That the mass upheavals that began in 2011 to put an end to decades-long despotic rule in North Africa and the Middle East—and that continue to reverberate—are called the "Arab Spring" is no coincidence.[1] Three participants in those mid-nineteenth-century developments would come to exercise enormous influence afterward—two exactly because of the seismic character of what had taken place and whose lessons they distilled.

© The Author(s) 2019
A. H. Nimtz, *Marxism versus Liberalism*, Marx, Engels, and Marxisms, https://doi.org/10.1007/978-3-030-24946-5_2

Comparing how Alexis de Tocqueville, on one side, and Karl Marx and Fredrick Engels, on the other side, read and responded to the European Spring in real time is the aim of this chapter. How did their readings compare and contrast? Which were more accurate? Most importantly, which of the readings and actions were more consequential in advancing the democratic quest? The focus here is on the French theater. Marx and Engels operated in Germany for the first thirteen months of its revolution. Only when forced to retreat from the German battlefield could they turn their attention to France. To understand how all three read and responded to the French events, a summary of the relevant elements of their backgrounds that they brought to them is necessary. Consistent with the sensibility of real-time analysis—the past makes the present smarter—it's appropriate to begin with Tocqueville, almost a generation older than Marx and Engels.

The Aristocratic Liberal Politician

Alexis de Tocqueville (1805–1859) was a true scion of the nobility with a pedigree that went back to the eleventh-century monarch William the Conqueror. Like many other French aristocrats, Tocqueville's family fell victim to the Reign of Terror that accompanied France's first experiment with republican government in 1789. His great grandfather who had unsuccessfully defended Louis XVI from the guillotine met the same fate shortly afterward in 1794 as well as four other immediate family members. The lucky ones spent brief periods in prison like his father and mother from which the latter never recovered emotionally. The Terror understandably marked Tocqueville for the rest of his life.[2]

Tocqueville was nine years old when the Bourbon restoration, enabled by Napoleon's counterrevolution in 1799, took place in 1814 with the installation of Louis XVIII. His brother Charles X succeeded him in 1824. The thoroughly reactionary character of his rule, despite formally being a constitutional monarch, probably disabused the young aristocrat of any longing for the *ancien régime* if he had any. Thus, he seemed to have welcomed its overthrow through a popular three-day revolt in July 1830 and replacement with Louis-Philippe of the Orléans line of the Bourbon dynasty. Because the new ruler had the support of the emergent bourgeoisie the possibility for reforms seemed likely.

Like many other intellectuals of his class Tocqueville sought an alternative to the stale world of absolute monarchy but without the agita of revolution, a subject to which he had given considerable attention in his studies. But was that possible? Could, in other words, democracy be instituted without a revolution? Perhaps there was an answer elsewhere such as on the other side of the Atlantic. Under the pretext of studying the penal system in the United States Tocqueville departed for the new world with his friend and intellectual companion Gustave de Beaumont (1802–1866) in April 1831. The most consequential result of their nine-month tour of the country was Tocqueville's *Democracy in America*, its first volume published in 1835. Though of lesser renown, Beaumont's historical novel about an ill-fated interracial romance in America, *Marie, or Slavery in the United States*, would come to have unanticipated importance as will be seen later.

The central claim of *Democracy* is that "an absolute and immense democracy" is what "we find in America."[3] The reason was due to "the equality of condition" in place there.[4] No evidence for that claim was more important than that "universal suffrage has been adopted in all the states of the Union."[5] His second volume, published in 1840, highlighted two other factors that enabled the "absolute democracy," "public associations" and "religious matters" and "beliefs," Christianity specifically. As for why "equality of condition" existed in the United States, it was a "providential fact."[6] For Tocqueville the deist, providence, therefore, explained America's good fortune. And the country was especially blessed in one particular way. "The great advantage of the Americans is that they have arrived at a state of democracy without having to endure a democratic revolution, and that they are born equal instead of becoming so."[7] Not surprisingly, the quite violent seven-year war that brought the republic into existence got at best cursory treatment.[8] Tocqueville is probably the author of the sanitized version of U.S. state origins. I leave aside the veracity of Tocqueville's main claims, disputed, to be seen, by the real-time sources Marx consulted about America. Important here is that it is in *Democracy* that his abhorrence of the revolutionary road to democratic transformation is first made public—in anticipation of his response to 1848.

Only at the end of the first volume of *Democracy* did Tocqueville address the all too obvious exceptions to his claim of America being "an absolute and immense democracy"—"the Indians and the Negroes. ... These topics are collaterally connected with my subject without forming a part of it; they are American without being democratic, and to portray democracy has been my principal aim."[9] In a footnote, Tocqueville recommended Beaumont's book: it "should have a surer and more lasting success among those readers who above all else, desire a true picture of actual conditions."[10] He was right. One of those readers would be the young Marx whose newfound method required "a true picture of actual conditions." In the second volume of *Democracy*, the more sober of the two about the United States, Tocqueville speculated on the future. "If ever America undergoes great revolutions, they will be brought about by the presence of the black race on the soil of the United States; that is to say, they will owe their origin, not to the equality, but to the inequality of condition."[11] In this, Tocqueville was remarkably prescient. But everything he had said in volume one of *Democracy* about the "black race" leaves little doubt that he would not have welcomed such an explosion.

Despite all the acclaim that greeted volume one of *Democracy* when it appeared in 1835, the 30-year-old Tocqueville never considered an intellectual vocation. "That is entirely opposed to my way of judging the things that matter in life."[12] To a friend, "I have always valued action above everything else."[13] The success of the book was rather a stepping-stone to a political career, what others of his family and class had done—fulfilling in his view the civic duties of the aristocracy. His eyes were on the lower house of the National Assembly, the Chamber of Deputies. There were four constituencies he considered contesting. He settled on his home district in Normandy. The platform he ran on in his first election campaign in 1837 accepted the legitimacy of the Louis-Philippe regime, called for France to move toward "progressive paths" while "rejecting," not surprisingly, "revolution altogether."[14] He lost the contest and attributed it to class baiting in the rural areas owing to his aristocratic origins about which he interestingly wrote: "In the minds of these coarse men there was something like the instinctive repugnance Americans feel for men of color."[15] His cousin, Louis-Mathieu Molé, the prime minister, appeared to have tipped the scales against him.

Tocqueville wasn't discouraged by his loss. He successfully contested another election two years later in 1839 against an incumbent who was widely seen as a duplicitous pretender in opposition to the regime. He actively campaigned on a platform of independence from both the government, again, headed by his cousin Molé, and the semi-reform-minded opposition. He won an election in which only three percent of males in France could vote and only ten percent of that number, owing mainly to property/income qualifications, were eligible to take office.[16] Democracy in France, unlike in America, was very much an elite affair—what Tocqueville knew better than anyone.

The reality of being an independent in a parliamentary setting where parties were needed to enact policies required Tocqueville to be transparent about his politics as he confided to a fellow deputy:

> My mind is attracted by democratic institutions but I am instinctively aristocratic because I despise and fear mobs. At the most fundamental level, I passionately love freedom, legality, respect for rights, but not democracy. I hate demagoguery, the disordered action of the masses, their violent and unenlightened intervention in public affairs. … I belong neither to the revolutionary nor the conservative party. But, when all is said and done, I incline towards the latter rather than the former because I differ from the conservatives over means rather than ends, while I differ from the revolutionaries over both means and ends.[17]

As a dispassionate observer of what was in place on the other side of the Atlantic, Tocqueville might be mistaken for having been in "love" with "democracy." Back home, however, the story was different. Nothing better anticipated his course in 1848 than this self-description. His conscious decision to choose a "left center" seat in the semicircular arrangement of the Chamber, where he sat for all of his thirteen-year tenure there, wasn't inconsistent with his characterization of his politics. The reality of elite politics in Restoration France did indeed place him to the left of center; 1848 would be different.

His very first speech in the Chamber was revealing. The issue was European imperialist rivalry in North Africa and the Middle East as the decrepit Ottoman Empire was coming apart. Tocqueville advocated for a robust intervention into the fray to defend France's glory, if not the Napoleonic version then that of the *ancien régime* and its once glorious empire in North America before being downsized by archrival Britain. "Any government which cannot wage war," to avoid a similar outcome in the Near East, "is a detestable government."[18] His assertive, if not aggressive, nationalism caused the once warm relations he had had with the English intellectual John Stuart Mill, also a nationalist (to be seen in the next chapter), to cool; their friendship had originated in Mill's enthusiastic review of *Democracy*.

It was in Algeria that Tocqueville would most display and realize his vision for French overseas glory, making him a leading architect of its imperialist project in Africa. In 1847, the Chamber assigned him to draw up a report and make recommendations on French rule in the colony. It called for an uncompromising war against the rebel Algerian leader Abd el-Kader. The tone was set at the beginning: "We must admit ... as a demonstrated truth, that our domination of Africa must be firmly maintained."[19] The report made clear that the indigenous population must be treated as conquered subjects and at no time should the impression be given that they "are our compatriots and our equals."[20] The only nod to democracy that Tocqueville made in the report was his advocacy of liberal democratic rights for the French settlers in Algeria. As André Jardin, Tocqueville's most authoritative biographer, notes, the "unequal society thus envisaged hardly seemed to conform to that divine plan for equality among men described in the *Democracy*." Tocqueville was motivated, he concludes, by imperialist leanings that had their roots in the feudal absolutist world of Louis XIV. "This aspect of his character has sometimes been overlooked by those who see Tocqueville only as he appears in the *Democracy*."[21] And because providence and religion figured significantly in Tocqueville's explanation of sociopolitical reality—the product of his *Democracy*—Islam was determinant in his understanding of Algeria. After a detailed reading of the Qur'an, he concluded that Islam "is the principal cause of the decadence so visible today in the Muslim world. ... I therefore regard it as a form of decadence rather than a form of progress in relation to paganism itself."[22] Religion gave him an ideological rational to defend French imperialism in Africa and elsewhere. There is nothing to suggest that Tocqueville ever changed his views on Algeria.[23]

Tocqueville's orientation toward the center left in the Chamber of Deputies was most pronounced from 1842 to 1846 when a more conservative government was in office. He feared, rightly, that liberty and freedom, his ideals, were under threat in the name of the need to avoid revolution—also his desire. He tacked to the left "not in order to adopt the 'color' of the left, but to impose his own."[24] Odilon Barrot was the recognized leader of the constitutional left opposition to whom he made overtures for an alliance; "left" in such a constrained electoral system had, understandably, nothing to do with republicanism, let alone revolution. Tocqueville had come to recognize that his lack of sufficient oratorical and people/political skills limited whatever hopes he may have had for heading a government. What he thought he could best do was to be an expert adviser to the center left. His renown as author of *Democracy* gave him, he thought, the capital to do so. To be noted in his maneuvering, as Jardin instructively points out, "in Tocqueville's eyes, universal suffrage was *not* [my italics]," despite what *Democracy* might have suggested, "the characteristic mark of democracy."[25] The defense of freedom and liberty could be done, therefore, without the input of the "lower classes" in their immense majority.

To advance his perspective in the Chamber, Tocqueville realized that he needed to impact public, that is, elite opinion. Hence, his decision to purchase a newspaper in 1844 with the help of his wealthy brother. Its name, *Le Commerce*, made clear its intended audience. But the paper, he announced, wouldn't be "'so ridiculous as to speak in the name of a new party'." Rather, it would be another venue for "'the great national party which has ceaselessly worked, through all the vicissitudes of a half century of revolution to establish political liberty and equality before the law'."[26] Without the mooring of a party, however, the project floundered within a year and despite Tocqueville's always informed contributions to the organ. His attempt for it to be an alternative voice to both the constitutional and center left failed. In another revealing moment, he explained to one of his allies what he had tried to do: "I have broken with part of my family ... to embrace the cause and the idea of '89. Having made such great sacrifices for my opinions ... I will uphold these doctrines as long as I am in the Chamber, with all my power and all my strength, at all costs, even if I should be the only one to do so."[27] Tocqueville's complicated relation to 1789 was all so evident here.

The August 1846 elections to the Chamber gave Tocqueville cause for optimism. Though conservatives made significant gains, the fact that the center left also did while Barrot's constitutional left suffered losses was in his opinion promising. The new crop of center left deputies, "the newcomers," was heartening, perhaps the solution to the decade-long and now boring pas de deux of the establishment left with Louis-Philippe. He spelled out his hopes in a letter to a possible ally:

> A party that took it upon itself as its principal mission to work politically and actively for the moral and material well-being of the lower classes, without indulging their prejudices or inflaming their passions, would assume a new role that would be at the same time a great one.[28]

Yet, Tocqueville wasn't willing to give voice to "the lower classes" in the governance process; it could be indulgent and inflammatory. When the topic of expanding the suffrage arose in the Chamber, he "did not take part directly in the discussions on parliamentary reform and electoral reform." As Jardin explains, he "was more in favor of the latter than he had once been … but he would have liked to balance the extension of the electoral body somewhat by instituting a two-stage vote."[29] Only after the overthrow of Louis-Philippe would he endorse electoral reform, making him a "latter-day republican" as those like him came to be known. Again, Tocqueville never pretended to being a democrat, certainly in his homeland.

The premise that informed Tocqueville's efforts was the assumption that the leading protagonist in French politics was its middle class whose interests he sought to represent. Only when it was too late did he come to recognize that a new actor was about to contest for taking political center stage—the Parisian proletariat. Fortunately, for the sake of real-time political analysis, he left an account of how he read and responded to that new chapter in France's contentious political history, his *Souvenirs* or *Recollections*.

The Making of Two Communists

Like Tocqueville, Marx and Engels were products of the French Revolution of 1789. But unlike him, they began their political careers as democrats, radical democrats to boot, owing exactly to that seismic event. Trying to realize the promise of 1789 is what led them to communism—aided and abetted inadvertently by Tocqueville; thus, the decision to go first with him for introducing both sets of protagonists for this real-time political comparison.

Even with its limitations, Restoration France offered more political liberties than its neighbor to the East. Only in Germany's most western provinces where Napoleon's armies had been were there traces of what 1789 had promised. While respectively thirteen and fifteen years Tocqueville's junior, Karl Marx (1818–1883) and Frederick Engels (1820–1895) were marked by 1789, especially because of having come of age politically in that part of Germany. Though neither could claim aristocratic origins like Tocqueville, both came from privileged backgrounds: Marx from an intellectual/professional middle-class milieu and Engels from the emergent German capitalist class. Like other youth of their generation, the burning question for the two was how liberal democracy could be planted on German soil. The proximity of relatively more liberal France was no doubt a determinant in their quest for an answer. That Marx was a Jew is of no little importance given that 1789 opened up new opportunities for those who so identified.

As a newly minted Ph.D. in philosophy in 1841, Marx hoped that he could get a teaching post at one of the German state universities. That would be unlikely, he quickly realized, given his radical democratic politics that he was unwilling to compromise. Thus his decision to become a cub reporter for a liberal organ in his home province of Rhineland-Palatinate, the *Rheinische Zeitung*. But he soon learned first-hand in 1842 about the heavy hand of absolute monarchy, the Prussian Hohenzollern dynasty that ruled over the province. State censorship of his articles about the oppression of the peasantry was evidence for him of the "essence" of the regime. "There is no confidence in the intelligence and goodwill of the general public even in the simplest matter. ... This fundamental defect is inherent in all our institutions."[30] How to explain and how to rectify?

Not surprisingly, given his education, Marx turned for an answer to Georg Hegel (1770–1831), the towering figure of German philosophy for his generation. Hegel stood on the shoulders of the best thinkers that not only Germany had to offer, Immanuel Kant for sure, but also France and England, especially, for the latter, political economists like Adam Smith and David Ricardo. Marx, in other words, began his political quest with a much more informed and sophisticated intellectual base than Tocqueville did thirteen years earlier—generational privilege.

However much Hegel had served as a mentor, Marx began to see his shortcomings, particularly his politics. Most problematic was his advocacy of constitutional monarchy as the alternative to absolute monarchy—a solution, Marx charged in 1843, that was an obstacle to the "sovereignty of the people," or "true democracy." He also criticized Hegel for not calling for "the *extension* and greatest possible *generalization* of *election*, both of the right to *vote* and the right to *be elected*. This is the real point of dispute concerning political *reform*, in France as in England."[31] Thus, at the same moment Tocqueville was enabling constitutional monarchy in France and an electoral system that was far from having universal suffrage, Marx—again, thirteen years his junior—was roundly denouncing such arrangements. He also offered his first criticisms of liberals in the democratic quest. That liberal opponents to the regime embraced Hegel's position was evidence that they were "by no means equal to the task" to defend not only freedom of the press but any other political liberties.[32] The failure of the liberal owners of the *Rheinishe Zeitung* to put up a fight when it was banned was further proof for Marx of liberal vacillation. Within a year, he would argue, without being specific, that the only answer to Prussian despotism was the "impending revolution."

In criticizing the regime, Marx also engaged in a debate with the left, specifically, the Young Hegelians. One of their favorite topics was the critique of religion that Marx found unsatisfactory. "I requested ... that religion should be criticized in the framework of criticism of political conditions rather than that political conditions should be criticized in the framework of religion ... for religion in itself is without content, it owes its being not to heaven but to the earth, and with the abolition of distorted reality, of which it is the *theory*, it will collapse of itself."[33] For Tocqueville, religion was indeed the frame to explain politics—exactly what Marx was criticizing. Providence and Christianity explained democracy in America while Islam, as he was arguing at almost the same time, was "the principal cause of the decadence so visible today in the Muslim world." The religion question revealed, therefore, the very profound epistemological/methodological gulf between Tocqueville and Marx.

Marx soon realized that criticism was unconvincing if it wasn't accompanied by a solution. To do so required, as he chided the Young Hegelians, "less vague reasoning, magniloquent phrases and self-satisfied self-adoration, and more definiteness, more attention to the actual state of affairs, more expert knowledge." More concretely, as he explained two years later in *The Germany Ideology*, "one has to 'leave philosophy aside' ... one has to leap out of it and devote oneself like an ordinary man to the study of actuality, for which there exists also an enormous amount of literary material, unknown, of course, to the philosophers." In pursuit of his new course, Marx made clear that he was burning bridges: "Philosophy and the study of the actual have the same relation to one another as onanism and sexual love."[34]

The U.S. "actuality" provided the most important insight. If America, as he would conclude, was the best that political democracy had to offer, then clearly something else was required for "human emancipation." When Tocqueville wrote in a footnote in *Democracy* that Beaumont's *Marie*, unlike his volume, would be more appealing to "those readers who above all else, desire a true picture of actual conditions" in America, little did he know how prescient he had been. *Marie*, also published in 1835, provided just the kind of "expert knowledge" and "literary material" to which the young Marx was referring and not just for the reality of race in America. Almost a third of the novel consisted of appendices with valuable observations about race—both Blacks and Indians—class, religious, and gender issues.[35]

It was in Marx's 1843–1844 articles, "The Jewish Question," that the U.S. case revealed its importance for the analytical-cum-political break-through he was about to make.[36] In addition to Beaumont's *Marie*, the articles were informed by Tocqueville's *Democracy* and a two-volume account by an English traveler to the United States published in 1833, Thomas Hamilton's, *Men and Manners in America*. Despite their title, the articles are basically about the requisites for political democracy and, thus, the lessons from America. Though *Democracy* gets only minor billing in them, one of its major findings figured significantly in Marx's argument. The religiosity of the country that Tocqueville noted and explained, unlike anything in Europe, was telling for Marx. Religion for him, like for the Young Hegelians, was a "defect" in a society because it fostered sectarianism, "the separation of man from man." That widespread religiosity, with its accompanying sectarian practices that both Hamilton and Beaumont reported on, particularly with regard to race, not only existed but seems to have been fostered by the most politically democratic state in the Atlantic world, was probably the first sign for Marx that the United States was no paragon for "human emancipation."[37] Tocqueville's own tendentious attitudes about non-Christians could have been more evidence for Marx's critique of religion.

Marx's notebooks reveal his close reading of Hamilton's volumes that offered a more sober portrait of America than Tocqueville's with many details about class and racial inequality. Contra Tocqueville's claim, for example, that "universal suffrage has been adopted in all the states of the Union," Hamilton's account made clear that was not the case; Virginia's electoral laws had fairly high property qualifications for who could vote and be elected. Yet his data on the states that had abolished property qualifications allowed Marx to make one of his key observations about the significance of private property for political democracy. The prohibition of property qualifications did not, however, abolish private property, it "even presupposes it." The secular state, therefore, "allows private property, education, occupation, to *act* in *their* way … to exert the influence of their *special* nature. Far from abolishing these *real* distinctions, the state only exists on the presupposition of their existence."[38] As long as inequalities in wealth—as well as education and occupation—persisted, Marx noted, there would be inequalities in access to the electoral process including the "right to be elected." Two-hundred years earlier in the context of the English Civil Wars, Gerrard Winstanley, the Digger or True Leveler, had reached a similar conclusion.[39] The U.S. case revealed, again, that "political emancipation was not human emancipation" or "true democracy."

Another topic that captured Marx's attention in Hamilton's account was the recently formed Workingmen's party in New York City, the first of its kind anywhere. Their demand for "equal and universal education" is noteworthy: "It is false, they say, to maintain that there is at present no privileged order, no practical aristocracy, in a country where distinctions of education are permitted. ... There does exist then—they argue—an aristocracy of ... knowledge, education and refinement, which is inconsistent with the true democratic principle of absolute equality."[40] Could this have been the inspiration for Marx's earlier-cited point about how social distinctions such as education "*act* in *their* way ... to exert the influence of their *special* nature"? Marx's soon to be taken path to the proletariat for the solution to the democratic quest may have had its origins in what Hamilton reported.[41] Though Tocqueville was in New York within months of Hamilton's visit in 1831, there is nothing in his account about the Workingmen's Party.

In pointing out the limitations of political democracy in the United States, Marx was in no way dismissive of what was in place on the other side of the Atlantic. To the contrary; political democracy was far superior, he knew, to what existed in Hohenzollern Germany. His main point about the United States was that its democracy, "political emancipation," was not "true democracy" or "human emancipation." Rather the United States was a work in progress and not the "absolute democracy" that Tocqueville claimed. The combination of what Tocqueville, Beaumont and Hamilton reported revealed that something else was required for "true democracy." That something else is what his attention would then turn to. In other words, Marx had yet to reach communist conclusions.[42]

Unlike Marx, Engels came to radical democratic and communist conclusions by another route. He too had to grapple with Hegel but did so as a self-taught scholar. So telling about the bourgeoisie in that era is that his father, a factory owner, saw no need for his son to get a university education. Being a bookkeeper, a career to be learned on the job, was deemed more practical. Engels, essentially a high school dropout, had to pursue his intellectual proclivities on his own time, hanging out with the university crowd and attending lectures to learn what they were absorbing. Having been raised in a pious protestant family, Engels had to grapple more with, unlike Marx, the religion question and, hence, the debates among and with the Young Hegelians. Like Marx, he thought German liberals or at least some of them were committed to fight for liberal democracy. He too, however, began to doubt their resolve.

Most consequential for his partnership with Marx is that Engels knew first-hand about the other major influence, in addition to the French Revolution, on him and Marx—the industrial revolution. Because his family had part ownership in a textile factory in Europe's industrial heartland, Manchester, England, Engels's apprenticeship as a clerk there for two years from 1842 to1844 gave him the opportunity to experience industrial capitalism par excellence, what his cohorts in more backward Germany could only read about. An essay he had published in 1843, "Outlines of a Critique of Political Economy," is what convinced Marx to turn his attention to that literature in order to understand the basis of civil society and how it related to the secular state. On his way back from Manchester, Engels met with Marx in Paris where he was now in exile. Their ten-day meeting, in August/September 1844, to discuss what they had in common resulted in what is arguably the most consequential political partnership in modern history; with due apologies to John Reed, "Ten Days that Would Shake the World." That the subtitle of Marx's magnum opus *Capital* a quarter century later was essentially the same as the title of Engels's article is no coincidence.

In their first collaborative writing in 1844, *The Holy Family*, Marx and Engels declared that the proletariat

> cannot emancipate itself without abolishing the conditions of its own life [and, thus,] … without abolishing *all* the inhuman conditions of life of society today which are summed up in its own situation. … It is not a question of what this or that proletarian, or even the whole proletariat, at the moment *regards* as its aim. It is a question of *what the proletariat is*, and what in accordance with this *being*, it will historically be compelled to do. Its aim and historical action is visibly and irrevocably foreshadowed in its own life situation as well as in the whole organization of bourgeois society today. There is no need to explain here that a large part of the English and French proletariat is already *conscious* of its historic task and is constantly working to develop that consciousness into complete clarity.[43]

Only the working class, hence, had the interest and capability to bring about "true democracy" and "human emancipation"—what would distinguish Marx and Engels from others who called themselves communists.

The other key issue in *The Holy Family* addressed the all-important question in modern politics—the role of intellectuals in movements of the masses. They criticized the Young Hegelians for thinking, as Marx and Engels had once believed, that as philosophers they were "the spiritual weapon" of the masses—its brain. And the problem with such a perspective is that the "brain" begins to "see itself incarnate not in a *mass*, but exclusively in a *handful* of chosen men." But history revealed, such as the French Revolution, that it was the "great mass" that was the true mover for human advancement. The "great mass" now was the proletariat as demonstrated by the "French and English workers." Intellectuals who thought like the Young Hegelians could never be the source for real transformation. "*Ideas,*" Marx emphasized in making his point, "can never lead beyond an old world order but only beyond the ideas of the old world order. Ideas *cannot carry out anything* at all. In order to carry out ideas men are needed who can exert practical force."[44] At the very beginning of his joint venture with Engels, Marx was, therefore, skeptical about any liberatory project that relied on the goodwill of "a handful of chosen men" such as intellectuals.

Of the two now self-proclaimed communists, only Engels had had direct experience and contact with organized workers—which allowed them to make the previously quoted claim about that "large part of the English … proletariat already *conscious* of its historic task." His two years in Manchester brought him in contact with the Chartists, the first working-class political organization, at least in Europe—and what mostly informed their declaration about the revolutionary potential of the proletariat. The Chartist six-point program for political rights for the working class including universal manhood suffrage, composed in 1838 (more about this in Chap. 3), was decisive in their decision to privilege the proletariat above and beyond any other social layer. Engels's *The Condition of the Working Class in England*, published in 1845, brought the Chartists to the attention of aspiring German communists. Not only did Engels write about the Chartists but he sought to forge ties between them and workers movements on the continent. Through his articles in their organs, he introduced to them, even before the formation of their partnership, "Dr. Marx," a member of the German "communist party." Engels, hence, took the lead on what would later be called proletarian internationalism. He and his partner's enthusiastic embrace of the Chartist program in 1845 stands in telling contrast to Tocqueville's unwillingness in that moment—before 1848—to support meaningful electoral reform in France.

When the Prussian army brutally suppressed a strike of silk weavers in Silesia in June 1844, it laid bare the class nature of the state and about which Marx and Engels drew their most important political conclusion. Only if the proletariat organized itself politically and took state power could it liberate itself. That was the only piece still missing in their road to communism.

Marx's six-week visit to Manchester and London with Engels in July–August1845 reinforced his decision to prioritize the working class. He could now put faces on his claims about the revolutionary potential of the working class. Not only was it an opportunity to see advanced capitalism with his own eyes but, even more importantly, to meet the proletarian fighters about whom Engels had been writing and talking. Their discussions resulted later that year in the first international workers organization, the Society of Fraternal Democrats. In addition, the visit was an opportunity to use the libraries there for research for what would eventually be his magnum opus. It was Engels, by the way, who more than anyone insisted that Marx get down to writing and completing *Capital*, a quarter of a century away. If Beaumont's partnership with Tocqueville was consequential in varying ways for the latter, that was even more the case for Marx with the union he forged in 1844 with Engels—until the very end and beyond.

All of the aforementioned practical experiences and theoretical insights were distilled in Marx's famous three-page "Theses on Feuerbach" of 1845. They are a critique of the best that philosophy had to offer Marx at that stage in his trajectory—the materialist perspective of German philosopher Ludwig Feuerbach (1804–1872). The thread that runs through all of Marx's kernels of wisdom is the need to bring human actions into "the materialist doctrine," particularly *"revolutionary practice"*—for both the "educator" and "society" as a whole. And, as if in summation of his argument—an actual line precedes it unlike for the others—the famous 11th or last thesis: "The philosophers have only *interpreted* the world in various ways; the point is to *change* it."[45] Nothing better encapsulates what would distinguish the once doctorated philosophy student from the world in which he had come of age intellectually than the 11th thesis. The real world of politics and political activity was now his calling. The "Theses" were like a divorce settlement—at least as he saw it.[46] Tocqueville, as noted, also valued action above intellectual inquiry, which makes, therefore, for a fair comparison of the two sets of protagonists for their responses to 1848.

Marx and Engels's *The German Ideology*, written between 1845 and 1846, was a more collaborative project than *The Holy Family*. It was both a final settling of accounts with German intellectual traditions and, more significantly, a detailed declaration of what the Marx–Engels team stood for. Though never published in their lifetime, it was written, as they later said, "for self-clarification." Its key claims would soon find their way into subsequent publications such as Marx's 1847 critique of the French anarchist, Joseph Proudhon, *The Poverty of Philosophy*. One point worth noting is his critique of Proudhon's assumption that "*Providence* is the locomotive" that drove toward the default position of social organization— "equality," not unlike how Tocqueville explained the U.S. reality. "Providence, providential aim, this is the great word used today to explain the march of history. In fact, this word explains nothing," Marx countered. "It is at most a rhetorical form, one of the various ways of paraphrasing facts."[47] Again, the deep theoretical divide between Marx and Tocqueville. As well as for *The Poverty of Philosophy*, core ideas in *The German Ideology* would inform Marx and Engels's most famous publication on the eve of the European Spring, to be discussed shortly.

One dimension of the tome is worth mentioning because it allows for a comparison with Tocqueville. *The German Ideology* broadcast their new method of analysis, "the materialist conception of history," as they called it, or historical materialism. "Actuality" had revealed how more productive modes of production had displaced less productive ones. And that process strengthened the fighting capacity of the exploited layers of society and, thus, historical redemption. The capitalist mode of production, despite all its warts, was on balance; in other words, an advance for the class struggle of the oppressed against the oppressors. With that set of assumptions, it's not surprising, therefore, that Engels—it's not clear what Marx's position was—applauded French imperialism in Algeria; history's way of clearing the less productive modes of production away with the more productive ones and, thus, defensible. In that sense, it could be argued that Engels, at least, was on the same page with Tocqueville about the "civilizing mission" of French imperialism as some have argued.[48] To the extent that both Marx and Engels might have subscribed to the civilizing mission of capitalism, events in France would soon dispel them of such illusions. "Blowback" from the colonial project came to haunt the working class in France and would, thus, force them to revisit at least some of the claims of their historical materialist perspective as will be seen.

Marx's critique of constitutional monarchy took on new meaning when the Louis-Philippe regime, due to pressure from Berlin, expelled him, wife Jenny and daughter Jenny from France in February 1845. His writings, even from afar, increasingly alarmed the Hohenzollern absolutist monarchial regime of Frederick IV. Just as Tocqueville was enabling the Louis-Philippe government, Marx was being victimized by it. Relocated to Brussels, Marx set out to do, with the assistance of both Jenny and Engels, what was implied in the 11th of the Feuerbach theses, party building. If Tocqueville could never see the need for a political party to advance his perspective, Marx and Engels thought just the opposite.

The first fruit of the party-building efforts of the "Marx party" as it came to be known was the Committees for Communist Correspondence, formed in 1846, with Brussels as its headquarters, the Marx household specifically. Its purpose was to foster communication between communist currents in various countries and to build a communist party in Germany. That brought the Marx–Engels team to the attention of the League of the Just, a German worker's current in exile in London, Paris and Brussels. The League invited the duo to join them, to which they agreed. Both sides had conditions for the union: for the Marx–Engels team that the League abandon its semi-clandestine mode of operation and change its name to the League of Communists; for the League that the two intellectuals draft a document that stated the program and aims of the new organization. Thus, the birth of the *Manifesto of the Communist Party*.[49] Marx, working with two drafts by Engels, finally completed the writing of the forty odd-page document on January 24, 1848. Exactly a month later, it came off the press in London, the same day that Louis-Philippe abdicated to the demands of a mass uprising that erupted two days earlier in Paris and, hence, the commencement of the European Spring. Seldom in history has a writing been so timely.

COMPARING MARX, ENGELS AND TOCQUEVILLE IN REAL TIME

The upheaval in Paris on February 22 began to be emulated elsewhere, not only in Europe, in at least fifty locations, but as far as South America.[50] It reached Berlin on March 18. From April to the following May 1849, Marx and Engels were deeply immersed in the German events, having literally been on the barricades. The imminent defeat of the German revolution forced them to withdraw from the field. In London, in July 1850, Marx began a number of assessments of the European Spring, one now known as *Class Struggles in France*. Almost at the same time, Tocqueville, a participant in the French edition of the revolutionary wave, began his account of what had already largely taken place, his *Souvenirs* or *Recollections*. *Class Struggles* and *Recollections* not only begin about the same time but end within months of one another less than a year later. Comparing the two accounts ensures that Marx and Engels who, unlike Tocqueville, wrote subsequent analyses about what had transpired in France, do not have the unfair advantage of hindsight. What's being compared, then, are two accounts written about the same time about the same events that had already occurred—hence, a fair comparison.[51] For the sake of closure, later writings of all three are employed in a more limited manner.

Unlike for the three other cases in this book, the mainstream literature on the 1848 revolutions acknowledges contrasting Marxist and liberal accounts, Marx and Tocqueville specifically. As Roger Price notes, both Marx's and Tocqueville's "views have exercised a substantial influence on writing about the revolution by both historians and sociologists ever since."[52] Another advantage in comparing the two is that both individuals, as political people and activists, are regarded even today as alternative poles of attraction that influence, not surprisingly, how their two accounts are received. Thus, for the Tocqueville partisan and anti-Marxist J. P. Mayer, "Tocqueville's understanding of the structure of the historic process was perhaps subtler than that of Marx. ... Tocqueville was a realistic sociologist; in comparison Marx was a Utopian."[53] His 1960 *Alexis de Tocqueville: A Biographical Study in Political Science* comes close to being the only text in the mainstream literature that might be considered to be a comparison of both towering figures.[54] But it's selective and invidious when it comes to Marx, and virtually silent in comparing the two about the drama of the 1848 Revolution. A systematic comparison of *Class Struggles* and *Recollections* as is done here for the first time reveals that Marx, contra Mayer, had a superior grasp of political reality and more accurately anticipated the political outcome in France.

Comparing the two texts, it could be argued, is unfair. *Class Struggles*, though a little more than a third of the length of *Recollections*, was an explicit political analysis of the French Revolution of 1848 whereas Tocqueville's book was more of a private memoir. Unlike Marx's account, it was never intended to be published but, as Tocqueville explained, only a "mental relaxation for myself and not a work of literature." Yet therein lies an important difference between the two men and their works that justifies a comparison. As a communist, Marx was obligated to draw a balance sheet on the 1848 revolutions and to disseminate those lessons in order to influence subsequent events. Tocqueville, albeit a participant in the revolution—on the other side of the barricades as an officer in the national guard and Minister of Foreign Affairs in one of the governments—felt, on the other hand, no similar compulsion. Reflecting on the upheaval was for him a private affair.[55] Marx and Engels, who had to scrape for every penny to publish their accounts, had no such luxury. Thus, their approach to writing about 1848 was quite different from that of Tocqueville. Almost every paragraph in *Class Struggles* is pregnant with political analysis whereas *Recollections* requires the reader to wade through what is often interesting, sometimes fascinating and never boring narrative to find proportionately fewer political insights.

On the Eve of Revolution

From the beginning of both accounts, the degree of agreement is noteworthy. On the eve of the February Revolution both agreed that the monarch Louis-Philippe represented not the aristocracy but rather the bourgeoisie. For Tocqueville he was "the head of the bourgeoisie" and for Marx the bourgeoisie's "crowned scapegoat" who ruled on their behalf. Like Marx and Engels, Tocqueville accurately predicted not only the Revolution but also its social content. In a draft of what was to have been "a programme in the form of a manifesto" for his parliamentary caucus in October 1847, Tocqueville wrote that revolution was once again on the agenda.

> The French Revolution [of 1789], which abolished all privileges and destroyed all exclusive rights, did leave one, that of property. Property holders must not delude themselves about the strength of their position, or suppose that, because it has so far nowhere been surmounted, the right to property is an insurmountable barrier; for our age is not like any other. ... Soon the political struggle will be between the Haves and the Have-nots; property will be the great battlefield. ... Do you think it is by chance, or by some passing caprice of the human spirit, that on every side we see strange doctrines appearing ... which all deny the right of property[?] ... Who can fail to recognize in this the last symptom of the old democratic disease of the times, whose crisis is perhaps approaching?[56]

And in a speech to the Chamber of Deputies on January 29, 1848, Tocqueville tauntingly asked his colleagues if they hadn't noticed that the

> working classes ... passions have changed from political to social? Do you not see that opinions and ideas are gradually spreading among them that tend not simply to be the overthrow of such-and-such laws, such-and-such a minister, or even such-and-such a government, but rather to the overthrow of society, breaking down the bases on which it now rests? ... such opinions ... must sooner or later ... bring in their train the most terrifying of revolutions?

Tocqueville's insights were consistent at one level of analysis with Marx and Engels's *Manifesto*—the presumption that a new form of class struggle was now on humanity's agenda, that between the proletariat and the bourgeoisie.

As well as the similarities, the differences in the forecasts of Tocqueville, Marx and Engels are noteworthy. Engels highlighted, in a November 1847 article on the reform movement in France, specifically, the campaign for the "extension of the suffrage," the differences between the "Liberals," "Democrats" and "Radicals." Only the "Radicals" supported universal suffrage and a republican form of government and only one paper, *Réforme*, "understands not merely Political Reforms, which will, after all, leave the working classes as miserable as before—but Social Reforms, and very definite ones."[57] Tocqueville not only failed, as already noted, to support meaningful electoral reform, but he "opposed *every* concrete proposal made to reform suffrage during the July Monarchy."[58] He found his way to republicanism only after the February Revolution, a "latter-day republican" in the parlance of the period.

Working-class participation in the reform movement, Engels noted, alarmed the regime more than middle-class involvement. Workers, however, were engaged in a far more important task—"the study of those questions of social economy. ... Within a month or two, six thousand copies of M. Louis Blanc's work on "The Organisation of Labour" [which advocated for state-financed worker cooperative production] have been sold in the workshops of Paris. ... They read likewise a number of other works upon these questions; they meet in small numbers of from ten to twenty, and discuss the different plans propounded therein."[59] Engels unreservedly endorsed proletarian self-education since he and Marx had concluded a few years earlier that only if the oppressed prepared for their liberation by becoming conscious of their tasks would they likely succeed. What Engels detailed explains why Tocqueville feared the "strange doctrines" and "ideas … spreading among" the workers.[60]

Engels assured his readers that French proletarian self-education did not in the least imply that "the revolutionary ardour of the people is decreasing. … On the contrary, the necessity of a revolution, and a revolution more thoroughgoing, more radical by far than the first one, is deeper than ever felt by the working people here." Rather than being provoked into a premature confrontation—"the government desires a riot, they provoke it by every means"—workers, Engels argued, wanted to know how to "guarantee the stability of their conquest; that will destroy not only the political, but the social power of capital that will guarantee their social welfare, along with their political strength." Workers at the appropriate moment, he predicted, would take to the streets because "a collision between the people and the government will be inevitable." Regarding the middle-class reformers, it was his "fear" that "most … will hide themselves in the darkest corner of their houses, or be scattered like dead leaves before the popular thunderstorm. Then it will be all over with Messrs Odilon Barrot, de Beaumont and other Liberal thunderers, and then the people will judge them quite as severely as they now judge the Conservative Governments." Most significant for this comparison is that Barrot and Beaumont were key members in the faction that Tocqueville belonged to—the "moderate republicans" as he called them.[61] The outcome for Tocqueville's ersatz party came remarkably close to Engels's forecast.

Engels, therefore, also accurately foresaw the revolution as well as its class content. However, unlike Tocqueville, he provided a more nuanced analysis that took into account the different shadings within Tocqueville's "Haves and Have-nots." He recognized from the outset that the most ardent republicans were a minority on France's political spectrum. This no doubt explains his call for revolutionary restraint on the part of the working class—a sober recognition of the chances for working-class success given the relationship of political forces. With sharper foresight, Engels, in a key insight, noted that unlike the 1832 Reform Bill in England, the extension of the suffrage to the "small bourgeoisie" in France would be to the disadvantage of finance capital. The petit-bourgeoisie, who were "so much oppressed and squeezed by the large capitalists, … would be obliged to have recourse to direct aggressive measures against the moneylords, as soon as they get the suffrage." Marx's and Engels's more nuanced analysis equipped them better than Tocqueville for understanding, therefore, why big capital was quite content with Louis-Bonaparte's overthrow of France's Second Republic at the end of 1851.

What most distinguished Engels's analysis, on the eve of the revolution, from Tocqueville's was its employment of class as resting on economic categories and dynamics. Tocqueville's "Haves and Have-nots" were generic whereas those of Marx and Engels were specific to the capitalist mode of production. Private ownership of the means of production and *not* property per se as Tocqueville implied was the basis, Marx and Engels argued, of the social as well as political "power of capital."[62] As the *Manifesto* stated, "the distinguishing feature of Communism is not the abolition of property generally, but the abolition of bourgeois property." It was the varieties of capitals, financial versus industrial capital, which the more imprecise "haves and have-nots" distinction failed to capture. The dynamics, also, of the capitalist mode of production were different from previous economic systems. Glaringly absent in Tocqueville's forecast was any discussion about the economic crisis that racked the working classes and the petit-bourgeoisie on the eve of the revolution—for Marx and Engels of grave importance in trying to forecast a rise as well as an ebbing of the revolutionary tide and in explaining the particulars of February.

Explaining the February Revolution

Marx and Tocqueville differed sharply on the class character of the revolt. For Marx, what February did was to *"complete the rule of the bourgeoisie"* by instituting a bourgeois republic. It "finally brought the rule of the bourgeoisie clearly into view, since it struck off the crown [i.e. Louis-Philippe's downfall] behind which capital kept itself concealed."[63] Because the proletariat had played a decisive role in its success the result was a *"republic surrounded by social institutions,"* a bourgeois republic that instituted some social programs. For Tocqueville, however, it was just the opposite: "the real and only party defeated was the bourgeoisie."[64] The winners were the propagators of "those socialist theories ... that later kindled real passions, embittered jealousies, and finally stirred up war between the classes. ... Socialism will always remain the most essential feature of the February Revolution."[65] Subsequent events made it clear that Marx had made a more accurate call at the outset of the revolution. For Tocqueville to still characterize February as a socialist overturn two years later when he wrote his account reveals—in addition to his political biases—his limitations as a political analyst.

Earlier in *Recollections* Tocqueville upbraided "all those absolute systems that make all events of history depend on great first causes linked together by the chain of fate and thus succeed, so to speak, in banishing men from the history of the human race."[66] February was due rather to, Tocqueville argued, what in current social science parlance is called relative deprivation—the gap between raising the expectations of the masses, the product of 1789 and increased "prosperity," and their inferior social situation.

> Inevitably they were bound to discover sooner or later that what held them back in their place was not the constitution of the government, but the unalterable laws that constitute society itself; and it was natural for them to ask whether they did not have the power and the right to change these too, as they had changed the others. And to speak specifically about property, which is, so to speak, the foundation of our social order, when all the privileges that cover and conceal the privilege of property had been abolished and property remained as the main obstacle to equality among men and seemed to be the only sign thereof, was it not inevitable, I do not say that it should be abolished in its turn, but that at least the idea of abolishing it should strike minds that had no part in its enjoyment?[67]

Also propelling rising expectations were "economic and political theories, which were beginning to attract notice and which tended to encourage the belief that human wretchedness was due to the laws and not to providence and that poverty could be abolished by changing the system of society." The real culprit for the outbreak was, as Tocqueville wrote in a letter soon after February, socialist ideology:

> The crisis from which the workmen in large manufactories were suffering ... lasted a very short time, and though severe was not unexampled. It was not want, but ideas, that brought about that violent Subversion; chimerical ideas on the relations between labour and capital, extravagant theories as to the degree in which government might interfere between working men and employer. ... I repeat, we have to contend with ideas rather than with wants.[68]

Implied in Tocqueville's insistence on an idealist over a materialist explanation of February was that placing limits on ideas and their dissemination could prevent future revolts—in anticipation of the antidemocratic policies he would advocate after the June uprising.

Tocqueville was correct in a broad historical sense in pointing to the rising expectations of France's working classes because of 1789 to explain the February Revolution. However, to speak of "prosperity" or overall improvement in the standard of living of workers and peasants in France in the late 1840's was problematic. In pointing to the particulars of the economic crisis that peaked in 1848 as the more immediate background factor to explain the February uprising, Marx and Engels offered a more credible explanation. Though not inconsistent with Tocqueville's explanation, their argument provided the specifics for understanding the actual timing of events—for example, why 1848 and not 1846. The ups and downs of the business cycle, the uniquely boom-and-bust character of this new mode of production into which France's working population was being inexorably integrated was the dynamic factor that fueled their sense of relative deprivation.

Tocqueville's class biases were on unmistakable display in his explanation of February. He could easily oppose "absolute systems" to explain "human wretchedness"—"providence" did a better job for him—while confidently embracing "the unalterable laws that constitute society itself ... property, the foundation of our social order." The claim that poverty "was the work of laws and not of Providence" was as Irving Zeitlin convincingly argues, "a proposition whose validity Tocqueville continued to deny all his life."[69] Tocqueville the insightful social observer, as his admirers often claim, gave way to Tocqueville the liberal aristocratic politician. Yet, what makes Tocqueville so interesting as a social commentator, specifically, in making sense of February, was his ability to grasp the principal dilemma of class society. For the dispossessed, it was understandable—but certainly not agreeable for him and his class—why the "socialist" alternative, as he understood it, would be more attractive than a social system based on private ownership of the means of production.

Tocqueville's introduction to *Democracy in America* drew attention to a "universal" fact—the "gradual development of the principle of equality. ... Would it, then, be wise to imagine that a social movement the causes of which lie so far back can be checked by the efforts of one generation? Can it be believed that the democracy which has overthrown the feudal system and vanquished kings will retreat before tradesmen and capitalist?"[70] His point that the end of feudal privileges, the result of 1789, had exposed the class reality of bourgeois society as never before was completely consistent with what Marx and Engels wrote in the opening pages of the *Manifesto*: "the modern bourgeois society that has sprouted from the ruins of feudal society has not done away with class antagonisms … it has simplified class antagonisms." Bourgeois democracy in the form of republican rule not only placed the proletariat on the best terrain to carry out its fight for "true democracy" but revealed in the clearest light its true enemy, the bourgeoisie itself.

The redeeming feature of February for Marx and Engels, therefore, was that it removed the monarchist fig leaf on bourgeois rule in France. While they could have agreed with Tocqueville that by the mid-nineteenth century or six decades after 1789 the contradictions of the property question were being posed in a way as never before—the *Manifesto* itself was testimony to that fact—that was a long way from concluding that a particular revolt, such as February, actually instantiated that new reality. Whereas Tocqueville, as well as many revolutionary republicans, mistakenly believed that working-class rule was instituted in February, Marx and Engels, however, saw the overturn as only the prelude to what took place in June—the struggle for proletarian hegemony.[71] To confuse the two revolutionary processes, the fight for political democracy with the socialist revolution, or, to assume that February was June was politically costly. Since Tocqueville was on the other side of the barricades, the costs were not as high to his side as they were to revolutionary republicans as subsequent events revealed; the latter were unprepared to defend the June uprising, with many of them actually opposing it because they assumed its goals had already been achieved in February. At the level of political and social analysis, Tocqueville's statement about a general trend, though not incorrect, failed to see the complexity of the way that tendency actually unfolded. Marx and Engels, on the other hand, writing about the events as they were occurring and afterward, Marx's *Class Struggles* and, later, his *Eighteenth Brumaire*, provided a far more accurate and insightful reading of political reality.

Tocqueville concluded his explanation of the reasons for the February uprising with a discussion on the prospects for socialism, providing one of his most profound insights about the course of human history:

> Will socialism remain buried in the contempt that so justly covers the socialists of 1848? I ask the question without answering it. I am sure that in the long run the constituent laws of our modern society will be drastically modified. But will they ever be abolished and replaced by others? That seems impracticable to me. I say no more, for the more I study the former state of the world, and indeed even when I see the modern world in greater detail,

when I consider the prodigious diversity found there, not just in the laws but in the principles of the laws and different forms that the right of property has taken and, whatever anybody says, still takes on this earth, I am tempted to the belief that what are called necessary institutions are only institutions to which one is accustomed, and that in matters of social constitution the field of possibilities is much wider than people living within each society imagine.[72]

To entertain the possibility that nothing is written in stone when it comes to social organization echoes what was fundamental in Marx's and Engels's "materialist conception of history." That Tocqueville could find himself in agreement with a basic premise of the founders of revolutionary communism says more about all three of them as keen social observers rather than political allies.[73] As the subsequent course of the 1848 Revolution revealed, Tocqueville was an active opponent of everything that Marx and Engels stood for. While he may have been "tempted" to consider a socialist alternative, his actions, especially from June onwards, made clear that he was an active defendant of class rule. However, as astute social observers, Tocqueville, Marx and Engels had an advantage that many of their twentieth-/twenty-first-century sympathizers did not, namely, the opportunity to witness the transition from the feudal to the capitalist mode of production with their attendant political forms. The period of history in which they all came of age politically may have impressed them with the fact that "in matters of social constitution" nothing is permanent, including the "right of property." Tocqueville's analysis betrayed his aristocratic contempt for the bourgeoisie, explaining, perhaps, why he could objectively speculate on its circumscribed future; the class from which he originated had now met or was on its way to meeting a similar fate. But again, less we be taken in by Tocqueville the latter-day acclaimed observer of social reality, the operative word is speculation.

Toward the June Revolution

In the run-up to the June Revolution, Marx and Tocqueville were both critical of the policies of the provisional government—but from different sides of the class divide. In Tocqueville's opinion, "there have been more mischievous revolutionaries than those of 1848, but I doubt if there have been any stupider."[74] Among the stupidities was the alienation of the peasantry. His rural department of La Manche in Normandy revealed trepidations among the property owners, regardless of the size of their holdings, about the future course of the revolution after February, concerns that tended to solidarize them. "Ownership constituted a sort of fraternity linking all who had anything, the richest were the elder brothers and the less prosperous the younger; but all thought themselves brothers, having a common inheritance to defend. As the French Revolution [1789] had divided up ownership of the land *ad infinitum*, the whole population seemed part of one vast family."

Most problematic was the failure of the provisional government to take steps to win over the peasantry under the new scenario of universal manhood suffrage—only for the second time since 1792 and unique to France. "They forgot," Tocqueville charged, "that their predecessors [in the 1789 revolution] at the same time that they gave every peasant a vote did away with tithes, abolished the *corvée* and other seignorial privileges, and divided the nobles' land among their former serfs, whereas there was nothing similar that they could do. By establishing universal suffrage they thought they were summoning the people to support the revolution, whereas they were only arming them against it." With insight that Marx would have appreciated, Tocqueville faulted the provisional government for not having the foresight to provide debt relief for small farmers. "In France every farmer owns some part of the soil, and most of their small holdings are encumbered with debt; therefore the creditor rather than the noble was their enemy, and it was he who should have been attacked."[75] The neglect of the small peasantry resulted in pro-republican forces losing big to conservatives in the May elections. The rural vote was decisive.

Marx would have agreed with much that Tocqueville wrote about the provisional government's ineptness toward the peasantry. But he had more to say on the issue that was politically superior to Tocqueville's otherwise keen observations. Benign neglect, for example, wasn't the sole reason for the Revolution's loss of support in the countryside. The imposition of a tax on the peasantry was, in his opinion, the government's undoing. "Whereas the Revolution of 1789 began by shaking the feudal burdens off the peasants, the Revolution of 1848 announced itself to the rural population by the imposition of a new tax, in order not to endanger capital and to keep its state machine going."[76] The tax, Marx argued persuasively, was the regime's attempt to placate the bourgeoisie, finance capital specifically—the creditors of the small peasantry. Rather than tax the bourgeoisie to cover needed state expenditures, the provisional government decided to squeeze small peasants.

Debt relief for small peasants, a proposal that Marx and Engels put forward in their program for the German theater of the European Spring, was not the panacea that Tocqueville took it to be.[77] On numerous occasions, Marx pointed out that the French Revolution of 1789 proved that land reform without the end of the market or capitalist property relations would simply result in a new subjugation for the peasantry, this time to capitalist creditors rather than landlords of old. Precisely because Tocqueville upheld, in practice certainly, the sanctity of private property and thus, by implication, capitalist property, he could only offer a palliative to small peasants and not a cure as Marx and Engels proposed. The subsequent history of capitalist property relations in the countryside have profoundly confirmed their prognosis that under capitalism peasants would be converted into rural debt slaves. The provisional government's policies effectively ruled out an alliance between workers and peasants—the only coalition that could have successfully defended the gains of the February Revolution.[78] Increasingly, the peasantry began to regard Parisian workers, the government's most loyal supporters, as its class enemy because of the tax—paving the way for the Revolution's demise.

Explaining the June Days

Given the ineptness of the provisional government, Tocqueville confessed that his side should have taken advantage of the situation soon after February:

> I had always thought that there was no hope of gradually and peacefully controlling the impetus of the February Revolution and that it could only be stopped suddenly by a great battle taking place in Paris. I had said that immediately after the 24th February, and what I now saw persuaded me that the battle was not only inevitable but imminent, and that it would be desirable to seize the first opportunity to start it.

For Tocqueville, then, his side should have found a pretext to provoke the proletariat into a fight. He got his wish in June when the government ended the public works program, the most important of the social policies, in the eyes of Parisian workers, ushered in by February.

The abolition of the world's first public works program for the unemployed was for Marx a direct provocation. "The workers were left no choice; they had to starve or let fly. They answered on June 22 with the tremendous insurrection in which the first great battle was fought between the two classes that split modern society. … The Paris proletariat was *forced* into the June insurrection by the bourgeoisie. This sufficed to mark its doom." To understand Marx's point, it is well to recall Engels's counsel of revolutionary restraint to France's proletariat so that it allow itself sufficient time to prepare for a fight—a luxury it was not afforded. For Marx, then, it was no surprise that the workers who fought "with unexampled bravery and ingenuity" did so nevertheless "without leaders [and] without a common plan."[79] Their defeat, hence, was inevitable.

Tocqueville's description of the June revolt was strikingly similar to Marx's. It was, as he put it, the "greatest" insurrection in French history—owing to the number of participants—as well as the "strangest, because the insurgents were fighting without a battle cry, leaders, or flag, and yet they showed wonderful powers of co-ordination and a military expertise that astonished the most experienced officers." While Marx attributed the lack of leadership to inadequate preparation, Tocqueville, reflecting his opposition to the insurrection, blamed the insurgents for being too radical. That for Tocqueville "prevented any man of standing from putting himself at its head."[80] While true that no leader ever emerged, due in part, as Tocqueville recognized, to the imprisonment of key republican figures a month earlier, Marx and Engels had never placed their hope in any "man of standing"—and why, exactly, the need for adequate preparation. They showered praise on those revolutionaries that did step forward to provide leadership such as Joachim René Kersausie (1798–1874), who Engels, writing in real time, said would go "down in history as the *first commander-in-chief of barricade fighting*."[81]

Unlike Marx and Engels who were in Cologne at the time, Tocqueville had the advantage of being on the scene of the insurrection. His *Recollections* provided the kind of detail that only someone present could describe—especially for understanding it from the perspective of the insurrection's opponents. Yet Tocqueville's picture was markedly inferior to what Marx and Engels provided to the readers of the *Neue Rheinische Zeitung*, the newspaper they edited, as the revolt was unfolding and in its immediate aftermath based on reports and other news from Paris. Engels's details on the "purely military description of the struggle" still constitute primary source material.

Tocqueville also agreed with Marx on the class character of the uprising: "Another point that distinguished it from all other events of the same type during the last sixty years was that its object was not to change the form of the government, but to alter the organization of society. In truth it was not a political struggle (in the sense in which we have used the word 'political' up to now), but a class struggle, a sort of 'Servile War'."[82] Based on what he actually witnessed, Tocqueville concluded "that the whole of the working class backed the revolt, either actively or in its heart. ... In fact the spirit of insurrection circulated from end to end of that vast class and in all its parts, like blood in the body." Tocqueville was also most informative about the class composition of the insurgents' opponents. The "volunteers" who came to Paris from his own home district were "landowners, lawyers, doctors and farmers, my friends and neighbours. ... The same was true almost everywhere in France. The most stick-in-the-mud little squire from the backwaters and the elegant, useless sons of the great houses all remembered that they had once formed part of a warlike ruling class, and all displayed dispatch and energy, such vigor there is in these old aristocratic bodies." Tocqueville's frankness about the class character of the June days, which corroborates Marx's interpretation, is what some modern-day analysts of the events deny.[83]

What Marx and Tocqueville most disagreed on were the reasons for the insurrection. Like February, the June uprising for Tocqueville had its origins in "the theory of socialism." The revolt was "a powerful effort of the workers to escape from the necessities of their condition, which had been depicted to them as an illegitimate depression, and by the sword to open up a road towards that imaginary well-being that had been shown to them in the distances as a right. It was this mixture of greedy desires and false theories that engendered the insurrection and made it so formidable." Once again, Tocqueville resorted to his "socialist culprit" thesis to explain June. Since it was naive for workers to think that they could change the conditions and institutions under which they lived, they clearly must have been operating under some kind of "false consciousness," that is, "false theories." Marx the historical materialist rejected, of course, the "socialist theory" as culprit argument. The February Revolution revealed, he argued, the subjective as well as objective limitations of France's proletariat. "It makes no theoretical inquiries into its own task. The French working class had not attained this level; it was still incapable of accomplishing its own revolution."[84]

Working-class consciousness in June was still a work in progress. Though true, as he and Engels believed, that February inaugurated the era of socialist revolution, it was a mistake to conclude from that general proposition that the proletariat thought the same. The causes for the uprising were rather quite basic—survival. The ending of the public works program meant that thousands of Parisian workers would have no means of subsistence. This is what Marx meant when he wrote that the workers were forced into the revolt—"they had to starve or let fly."

Exactly because Marx and Engels, on one hand, and Tocqueville, on the other hand, were on different sides of the political divide, their descriptions of the June events often read like mirror class images of each other. Their agreement, for example, on the lumpenproletariat composition of the Gardes Mobiles—one of the components of the regime's security forces—is remarkable,[85] or their assessments of the outcome of the defeat of the June uprising. Those "fateful days," Tocqueville concluded, "did not quench the fire of revolution in France, but they brought to an end, at least for a time, what one might call the proper work of the February Revolution. They delivered the nation from oppression by the Paris workmen and restored it to control of its own fate."[86] Marx's conclusion, again not inconsistent with Tocqueville's, was written from an opposite class vantage point as well as being richer and more precise.

> In the National Assembly all France sat in judgment upon the Paris proletariat. The Assembly broke immediately with the illusions of the February Revolution; it roundly proclaimed the *bourgeois republic*, nothing but the bourgeois republic. ... The proletarians ... had to be vanquished in the streets. ... Just as the February republic, with its socialist concessions, required a battle of the proletariat, united with the bourgeoisie, against the monarchy, so a second battle was necessary in order to sever the republic from the socialist concessions, in order to officially work out the *bourgeois republic* as dominant. The bourgeoisie had to refute, arms in hand, the demands of the proletariat.[87]

Echoing, finally, Tocqueville's qualifier "at least for a time," Marx returned to the thesis that he and Engels had been arguing for since at least 1846: namely, that the bourgeois republic offered the proletariat the best terrain upon which to overthrow its adversary. The June defeat, then, only hastened the day for the showdown between labor and capital. About June, then, "we exclaim: *The revolution is dead—Long live the revolution!*"

In the midst of the June events and afterward, another side of Tocqueville revealed itself about which there is a deafening silence among his modern-day admirers. No longer content to be just an astute observer of history, Tocqueville sought in that moment to be one of its architects—

not unlike Marx and Engels, but from the other side of the barricades, literally. When it appeared at a crucial moment that the insurgents might prevail, Tocqueville put aside personal angst and did what had to be done to defend the "country's safety," or, as Marx put it, "to perpetuate the rule of capital, the slavery of labour." Although initially hesitant, he embraced the decision of the National Assembly to institute what he termed "a military dictatorship under General [Louis-Eugène] Cavaignac." Regarding his initial hesitation, he later wrote: "In that I made a mistake, which luckily was not imitated by many." Cavaignac, who had recently led France's conquest of Algeria, was given carte blanche powers, which Tocqueville enthusiastically endorsed, to employ the kinds of methods he had successfully used against Algerian peasants. As for the claims of some that Cavaignac partisans duped the Assembly into voting for the dictatorship, Tocqueville replied: "If they did use this trick, I gladly forgive them, for the measures they thus caused to be taken were indispensable to the country's safety."[88]

But beyond simply voting for Cavaignac's dictatorship, Tocqueville led the Assembly in going out into the battle zones to rally support for the general among the government's forces. When the faint-hearted in the Assembly began to vacillate on executing their vote, Tocqueville took the initiative. "'Gentleman,' I said, 'the Assembly may have been mistaken, but allow me to observe that, such a resolution having been publicly taken, it would be a disgrace for it to retreat, and a disgrace for us not to obey'."[89] Because of his resolve, the Assembly elected Tocqueville to be one of its sixty members to "disperse through Paris, informing the national guards of the various decrees just passed ... and thereby restoring their confidence. ... [W]e put on our sashes and went out." Almost exactly at the same time when Marx and Engels were leading the fight in Germany for solidarity with the insurgents in Paris through their newspaper, Tocqueville was doing all he could to insure that the revolt would be crushed—in blood.

Tocqueville's real-time account admits that the suppression of the revolt had been extraordinarily sanguinary: "The bloodiest days of the French Revolution compared to this are child's play."[90] His memoir two years later, however, made no mention of the brutality of the government's actions. True, it does reflect a degree of angst about what had occurred and fear—hindsight on Tocqueville's part—for what it portended. But as Marx put it sarcastically, "it is well-known how the bourgeoisie compensated itself for the moral anguish it suffered by unheard of brutality, massacring over 3,000 prisoners."[91]

In the Aftermath of the Revolution

The enthusiasm with which Tocqueville participated in the defeat of the insurgents anticipated not only his course in the coming months but also the direction of political developments in France. His actions following the June revolt—about which his *Recollections* are highly selective[92]— made clear that his merciless opposition to it was no momentary aberration. The "June Days," André Jardin notes, "disposed Tocqueville to adopt a conservative policy of order. ... He now voted against the limitation of the workday to ten hours, against the abolition of the salt tax [which was especially onerous for peasants], in favor of continuing to allow men called for military service to hire substitutes instead of making military service obligatory for all—and, of course, against amnesty for those convicted during the June Days."[93]

Tocqueville, as one of the eighteen Assembly members selected to draft the constitution—there were almost 900 representatives in the Assembly— played a key role in the final writing of the document.[94] In the debate on the right to work, his anti-working-class stripes were most visible. Prior to the June revolt an article in the draft preamble that obligated the state to provide workers with employment and assistance in times of need—one of the "social institutions," as Marx called it, of the February Revolution— was greeted with silence from Tocqueville. After June, when it was proposed that the state "recognizes the right of all citizens to education, work, and assistance" as a substitute for the earlier draft article, Tocqueville objected vehemently. He in fact led the charge that prevented its adoption in the final document.

> Tocqueville's speech on September 12 ... broadened the discussion; recognition of the right to work led to the socialization of society, and it was therefore socialism itself that he was denouncing. The latter, in its different forms, had three constant principles: the worship of material goods, the abolition of private property, and the suppression of individual liberty. It was as remote as possible from the values exalted by the French revolution. The revolution of 1848 would deny the ides of 1789 if it established socialism.[95]

The speech made quite a stir, published later as a pamphlet. In the opinion of one modern-day conservative Tocqueville partisan, it was "an impassioned defense of democracy against socialism and an account of their fundamental incompatibility."[96] Marx would have argued that the speech was rather "an impassioned defense" of bourgeois property rights vis-à-vis the rights of workers and a recognition of the "fundamental incompatibility" of the two sets of class interests.

Tocqueville's success in having the right to work clause excluded from the constitution was not, Marx opined, a surprise. Aside from the fact that the pre-June draft article was "the first clumsy formula wherein the revolutionary demands of the proletariat are summarized," and that the "right to work is, in the bourgeois sense, an absurdity, a miserable pious wish," the constitution itself simply "put on record the *existing* facts." Its final wording registered where real politics had taken place, on the barricades in June. Tocqueville's silence on the right to work issue before June, in contrast to his vehement opposition afterward, spoke volumes about the significance of the defeat Parisian workers had suffered. Prior to June the elites saw them as a real threat and, thus, the need for a concession to pacify them in some way. Tocqueville's silence about the concession suggested that he too was unwilling to challenge them. Only with their bloody defeat in June, that he helped to lead, could he now find his true voice. Tocqueville's success in deleting the right to work clause confirmed, again, "the *existing* facts" on the ground. He came close to admitting as much. When the draft committee was set up in May 1848, he wrote that the

> thing that most effectively deprived [it] of its freedom of mind was, one must admit, fear of outside events and the excitement of the moment. It is difficult to appreciate how much this pressure of revolutionary ideas affected even those minds least subject to such influence, and how it almost unconsciously drove them farther than they meant to go, and sometimes even in a different direction. There is no doubt that had the Committee met on the 27th June [i.e. after the defeat of the revolt] instead of the 16th May, its work would have turned out to be entirely different.[97]

"Pressure," in other words, explained the right to work and assistance concessions to the proletariat in the pre-June 24 draft of the constitution. Tocqueville's honesty about "outside events and the excitement of the moment" on the legislative process is invaluable—a rare moment in the early history of the bourgeois legislative process. It confirmed, by a leading insider of continental Europe's then most exemplary liberal democratic parliament, what Marx and Engels were arguing for exactly at the same moment in the German theater where they were acting. Against those who claimed that what takes place inside the parliamentary arena is the be-all and end-all of politics, what they dismissed as "parliamentary cretinism" was rather the "fear of outside events and ... excitement" that were decisive in politics. The complementarity of both Marx's and Tocqueville's points for effective working-class utilization of parliamentary democracy can't be overstated.

Tocqueville played a leading role in the deliberations of the Assembly for two other constitutional issues: a unicameral versus a bicameral legislature, and the popular election of the president. On the former, he supported a bicameral body and his notes for the speech that he intended to give—illness prevented him from doing so—revealed his argument. A single body, he feared, basically, would concentrate too much power in the hands of the newly enfranchised masses: "it was necessary to 'fight the chronic disease of democracies—instability, capriciousness, and tyranny on the part of the legislative power,' and for that, to 'slow down popular movements. The ruling principle of democracy is that nothing is to be done despite the people and apart from the people, and not that the people can immediately realize every desire'."[98] The legacy of the February Revolution, however, still reverberated throughout France, in spite of June, and the Assembly gave in to popular sentiment and voted instead for a unicameral body—much to Tocqueville's distress.

Regarding the election of the president, fear of the masses, again, motivated Tocqueville. A popularly elected president he felt would be a check against a too powerful Assembly. Even before the June Days, that was his position; even more so after suffering the defeat on the bicameral question. "I was, I confess, much more concerned with putting a powerful leader quickly at the head of the Republic than with drafting a perfect republican constitution. At that time we were under the divided, vacillating rule of the Executive Committee [of the provisional government], socialism was at our doors, and we were drawing near to the days of June."[99] With his assistance the Assembly voted in favor of a popularly elected president, "and we know as well what followed from it—the election of Prince Louis-Napoleon as president of the French Republic [December 1848], his coup d'état [December 1851], and the authoritarian regime of the Second Empire [beginning December 1852]. Tocqueville was not the last to ironize over that institution he had taken such pains to ensure and define."[100] Unwittingly, perhaps, Tocqueville's contribution to constitutional government paved the way for its overthrow.

Because Montesquieu's separation of powers doctrine inspired the two constitutional arrangements that Tocqueville proposed, it is instructive to note Marx's opinion of a similar proposal raised in the context of the

German revolution. In that situation, the issue was whether there should be a sharing of power between the crown and the Prussian Assembly. Marx and Engels bitterly opposed such an arrangement—"the Montesquieu-[Jean Louis] Delolme worm-eaten theory of division of powers"[101]—because in their view its intent was to stifle the revolution and limit the extension of popular rule, democracy. The reason for Tocqueville's enthusiasm for separation of powers, to limit mass involvement in the decisions of the state, that is, the revolution, was exactly why Marx and Engels opposed it. Again, the mirror class image of the two political perspectives. Unlike Tocqueville, Marx, of course, understood that in the final analysis constitutions do not protect freedoms or prevent coup d'états from occurring—only the mobilization of the masses offered any real likelihood of guarantees. Tocqueville, of course, found such an option too distasteful.

Tocqueville, in hindsight mode, attributed the later constitutional crisis that preceded the coup d'état to a "big mistake" that he was in part responsible for—the enactment of a provision that made the incumbent president ineligible for reelection. "Our minds were not supple and quick enough to turn around and see that as soon as it was decided that the citizens themselves should choose the president, the ill was without remedy, and that any rash attempt to hinder the people in their choice would only increase it." Thus, the decision to institute the popular election of the president had let the genie in the person of the masses out of the bottle. The dilemma Tocqueville expressed was symptomatic of a larger contradiction surrounding the constitution that Marx ably explained:

> The fundamental contradiction of this constitution, however, consists in the following: The classes whose social slavery the constitution is to perpetuate, proletariat, peasantry, petty bourgeoisie, it puts in possession of political power through universal suffrage. And from the class whose old social power it sanctions, the bourgeoisie, it withdraws the political guarantees of this power. It forces the political rule of the bourgeoisie into democratic conditions, which at every moment help the hostile classes to victory.[102]

The granting of universal manhood suffrage created, therefore, an inherently unstable situation for the bourgeoisie. The newly obtained political rights of the working class aggravated the fundamental incompatibility between the interests of labor and capital. Bonaparte's coup, as Marx would argue later, was an attempt to resolve the contradiction—an essential feature of bourgeois democracy that has resonated ever since.

Although lukewarm in his support for the republic—"I ... was indifferent to the Republic"[103]—Tocqueville nevertheless felt it was worth protecting. Because he and his cohorts, acting increasingly as the organized moderate faction inside the Party of Order, namely, the conservatives, were not inclined to look to the masses for support; they chose to work from within, to attempt to influence Louis-Bonaparte, the newly elected president who took office in December 1848. They convinced themselves that given the many qualms they had about Bonaparte their insider tactic was the only way to maintain the republic. Thus, their decision to accept posts within the new government of long-time Assembly colleague Odilon Barrot; Tocqueville became Minister of Foreign Affairs. Not unbeknownst to him he walked into a major foreign policy fracas that eventually led to his resignation. Though the issue of French intervention in the Roman revolution occupied much of his time, he said little about it in *Recollections*.

Tocqueville's writer's block about the Roman venture may have had to do with its outcome—and unequivocal failure of liberal foreign policy. What happened, essentially, is that a French expeditionary force in the late spring of 1849 intervened in the Roman revolution by overthrowing the republican government and reinstalling the Pope. Tocqueville, whose tenure as Foreign Minister began in June, was put in the seemingly uncomfortable position of defending the government's actions in the newly elected legislative Assembly; prior to taking office, he had voted as an Assembly member for the appropriation to send the force. Nevertheless, his correspondence made clear that despite the "great misfortune" it might be to subject Rome "to all the horrors of war," especially since his predecessor had created the dilemma about which he had had misgivings, "to withdraw covered with shame ... would be a frightful disaster."[104] Liberal democracy abroad, in tones reminiscent of many a twentieth-/ twenty-first-century liberal foreign policy maker, could be sacrificed for imperial interests at home. In the choice between revolution from below versus order from above, the latter had clear priority. Tocqueville attempted to assuage his liberal angst by getting assurances from the Pope that he would institute liberal reforms—on which the latter eventually reneged. In the end, then, Tocqueville had little if anything to show to liberal admirers of his Roman actions, explaining perhaps the silences in *Recollections*.[105]

The Roman intervention was a clear violation of the new constitution. When Ledru-Rollin, leader of the left republican Montagne or Mountain faction in the Assembly and critic of France's actions, asked to see documents related to the venture, Tocqueville refused. A peaceful and poorly attended Mountain-led demonstration on June 13 against the government's actions gave the interior minister the needed excuse to declare a state of siege on the bogus claim that the protest was an attempt at another June uprising (in Lyons, the proletariat did stage a real but ultimately unsuccessful revolt).

Marx, who had just arrived in Paris from the barricades in Germany, wrote an article for a German organ about the June 13 events. The irresolute and inadequate response of the Mountain faction, he declared, undermined any confidence Paris's proletariat may have had in its leadership. The "chief actor in the drama of June 13 was not the *people*, but the 'Mountain'."[106] Because the Mountain and other left republicans had failed to support the uprising of the proletariat the previous June, "June 13, 1849 is only the retaliation for June 1848. On that occasion the proletariat was deserted by the 'Mountain', this time the 'Mountain' was deserted by the proletariat." Tocqueville's assessment of June 13 complements Marx's. "In June 1848, the army had no leaders; in June 1849, the leaders had no army."[107]

With Ledru-Rollin and his faction on the run and forced into exile, Marx—who too, for the second time, had to flee France—predicted that despite its victory, the counterrevolutionary alliance in the Assembly, in which he included Tocqueville's moderate faction, "will not only disintegrate, [but] its extreme faction will soon reach a point when it will seek to discard even the irksome semblance of the Republic, and then you will see *how it will be blown away with a single breath and there will be a repetition of the February, but on a higher level.*" The salutary result of June 13 for Marx was that it polarized the situation by removing from the scene Ledru-Rollin's petit-bourgeois left republicans, whose role had been to blunt the class struggle, and, hence, in his view, encouraging the counterrevolution to finally put an end to the republican experiment. Such a bid would propel the "people" back into the streets to make the revolution this time "permanent." By the middle of 1850 Marx and Engels concluded that "permanent revolution," that is, a socialist revolution, was not on the agenda in France or anywhere else in Europe.[108] On the other hand, Louis-Bonaparte's coup d'état in December 1851 did indeed remove the counterrevolution's republican fig leaf.

As for the Roman intervention itself, the event that provoked June 13, Marx explained in *Class Struggles* that Bonaparte's support for the papacy in opposition to the Roman Republic began almost immediately with his accession to office in December 1848 and was well known by the National

Assembly and, hence, by Tocqueville. The reason for Bonaparte's position was no mystery. "The Roman revolution was ... an attack on property, on the bourgeois order, dreadful as the June [1848] Revolution. Re-established bourgeois rule in France required the restoration of papal rule in Rome ... to smite the Roman revolutionists was to smite the allies of the French revolutionists."[109] Tocqueville, an arch defender of Catholicism, was probably more on board with Bonaparte's Roman policies when he accepted the Foreign Affairs portfolio than what he suggested in *Recollections*.

Toward the End of the Republic

The June 13 events gave the government the needed pretext to limit democratic space throughout the country—policies that Tocqueville enthusiastically embraced and implemented, and about which there is virtual silence among his modern-day fans. With pride, he recalled that "we introduced the following measures: a law to suspend the [political] clubs, another to suppress the vagaries of the press with even more energy than had been used under the Monarchy; and a third to regularize the state of siege." When an opponent of these measures in the Assembly charged that they established a "military dictatorship" Tocqueville quoted approvingly his chief minister's reply: "'Yes ... it is a dictatorship, but a parliamentary one. No private rights can prevail over the inalienable right of society to save itself. There are certain imperious necessities that are the same for all governments, whether monarchies or republics'." In Tocqueville's own words, "the only way to save freedom was to restrict it."[110] For Marx, June 13 "makes the *legislative dictatorship* of the united royalists [the conservative coalition] a *fait accompli*. From this moment the National Assembly is only a *Committee of Public Safety of the party of Order*."

Tocqueville justified his actions with the claim that the way to "save freedom," to "prevent the overthrow of the Republic and in particular to stand in the way of a bastard monarchy under Louis Napoleon [Bonaparte,] ... the most immediate danger," was to win over to his government's side the Party of Order. But Marx had argued, presciently, that the party was increasingly tilting toward the "extreme faction" that sought to "discard the irksome semblance of the Republic." Tocqueville was well aware that his anti-republican concessions to the conservatives enabled those who wanted to end the republic. Unlike Marx, whose approach to defending the republic was to mobilize the masses—something Tocqueville was incapable of doing—he thought he could convince them that his government would further their interests. "They wanted order energetically re-established; in that respect we were their men, for we wanted the same as they, and we did it as well as they could desire and better than they could have done themselves ... they wanted to use our victory [over the Mountain faction in June] to impose repressive preventive laws. We ourselves felt the need to move in that direction although not wishing to go as far as they."[111]

The imposition of a "parliamentary dictatorship" constituted, as Tocqueville rationalized it, necessary "concessions to the fears and legitimate resentments of the nation ... after such a violent revolution." The "nation" of course meant Tocqueville's conservative allies. And "such a violent revolution" is challenged by Tocqueville himself who had written only a few pages earlier that June 13 was far less violent than the previous June revolt. In spite of these concessions, Tocqueville recognized that "such measures, laws and language pleased the Conservatives but did not satisfy them. To tell the truth, nothing short of the destruction of the Republic would have contented them." This is exactly what Marx had foreseen a year earlier. Yet Tocqueville, caught in his own contradictions, continued to believe that the rightward direction of his government would save the republic—despite knowing the agenda of the conservatives. "The leaders of the majority [in the Assembly] wanted to make use of us to get rigorous measures taken and repressive laws passed, so that government would be comfortable for our successors; and at that moment our Republican opinions made us more fit for the task than the Conservatives. They counted on being able to bow us out afterwards and bring their substitutes onto the stage."[112]

What explains Tocqueville's persistence in courting the conservatives who were so transparent about wanting to dismantle the republic? Because, he argued, the faction that he and his cabinet colleagues belonged to— those who wanted "to establish a moderate republic"—were a minority in the Assembly, they had to ally with the conservative majority. "We have undertaken to save the Republic with the help of parties who do not love it. Therefore, we can rule only by making concessions—only one must never give away anything of substance. In this matter everything depends on measure. At this moment the best, and perhaps the only guarantee for the Republic is our continuance in office. Therefore we must take all honourable means to keep ourselves there." Tocqueville's rationale highlighted the fundamental difference between his politics and those of Marx and Engels. Whereas the latter looked to the "people's alliance" of peasants, the petit-bourgeoisie and the proletariat, with the latter at its head,[113] to ensure victory in the fight for democracy, Tocqueville, foreshadowing many a well-intentioned twentieth-/twenty-first-century liberal, placed his hopes in enlightened latter-day republicans like himself. Thus, the necessity of "our continuance in office." Smart political maneuvering on their part was the "only guarantee" against the counterrevolution. It was beneath Tocqueville's aristocratic liberal dignity to look beyond the parliamentary arena for the only majority, as Marx argued, that had a class interest to "save the Republic"—the masses. Marx's critique five years earlier of the Young Hegelians as "a handful of chosen men" who pretended to think and act on behalf of the masses was no less applicable to Tocqueville and his well-intentioned moderate republicans.

Because, as Tocqueville recognized, Louis-Bonaparte represented "the greatest and most permanent of dangers" to the Republic, it was, thus, necessary to humor him—"to charm, or at least to content his ambition"—as well as the conservatives. To that end, he promised Bonaparte that he and his party would seek to revise the article in the constitution—one that he had played a major role in having included in the document—"'which forbids the re-election of the President. ... We would gladly help you to get that done'." In a further suggestion to Bonaparte,

> I went on to hint that perhaps in the future, if he governed France quietly, wisely and modestly, confining himself to being the first magistrate of the nation and not its suborner or its master, it was possible that, when his mandate expired, he might be re-elected despite Article 45 by almost unanimous agreement, for the Monarchic parties would not see the limited prolongation of his rule as the ruin of their hopes [of reinstalling a monarch], and even the Republican party might feel that a government such as his was the best way of getting the country used to a Republic and ready to acquire a taste for one.[114]

Having once feared a strong executive, Tocqueville was now willing to enhance its power—all in the name of saving the Republic. He would later blame Bonaparte's coup on the excesses of the left. Never did it occur to him that he may have whetted with his hints and suggestions the future dictator's appetite for an unbridled executive. What his comments reveal, once again, as with his tact on the conservatives, was Tocqueville's aristocratically haughty assumption that he could personally and skillfully engineer democracy's institutionalization in France. With such talents who needed the masses to bring about democratic rule! Toward the end of *Recollections*, written around September 1851, he had convinced himself that Bonaparte "seemed to like me better and better." The "Roman expedition, in which … I firmly supported the President until his policy became exaggerated and unreasonable, finally put me in his good graces." Tocqueville was Exhibit A for those liberals who, as Marx noted, mistakenly thought they could use Bonaparte for their own purposes. His naïveté would be costly.

If the Roman venture allowed Tocqueville to be in Bonaparte's "good graces," it didn't ensure his tenure as a cabinet minister. Looking for a pretext to assert his power vis-à-vis the Assembly, Bonaparte charged the government with inadequate support for his Roman policies and called for its resignation. When returned unceremoniously to the Assembly as ordinary members in November 1850, Tocqueville and his astute cohorts were in shock and depressed. Bonaparte, in the meantime, began to look for a way to continue his presidency in spite of the constitutional prohibition. Tocqueville assisted him by leading an unsuccessful effort in the Assembly in July 1851, to revise the constitution.[115] Marx correctly foresaw that the majority Party of Order would be "compelled to prolong the power of the President." Though the majority of the Assembly had voted in favor of revision, it lacked the requisite three-fourths majority. Frustrated with the Assembly's resistance, Bonaparte took matters into his own hands. On December 2, 1851, the anniversary of the coronation of his uncle Napoleon I, he carried out a coup d'état that dissolved the Assembly, leaving him to rule unencumbered. Tocqueville and other Assembly members who staged a symbolic resistance were arrested and spent a night in jail. A year later Bonaparte had himself crowned as Napoleon III. Thus, the official and unceremonious end to the Second Republic and the beginning of the Second Empire.

Explaining Bonaparte's Coup d'État and the Aftermath

Marx painted in broad outlines more than a year earlier what actually occurred. He was especially perceptive about the course of the Party of Order, with whom Tocqueville's faction had aligned. "In its struggle with the people, the party of Order is compelled constantly to increase the power of the executive. Every increase of the executive's power increases the power of its bearer, Bonaparte … it strengthens the fighting resources of Bonaparte's dynastic pretensions, it strengthens his chance of frustrating a constitutional solution by force on the day of the decision."[116] Seven months prior to Bonaparte's coup, Marx thought, erroneously, that the Assembly would reach an accommodation with him. Yet the reason he offered accurately captured much of their sentiment, including Tocqueville's: they "would prefer the lesser of two evils. They would prefer an Empire or a Dictatorship of Napoleon, to a Democratic and Social Republic."[117] It was exactly such sentiment that facilitated Bonaparte's coup as subsequent events revealed.

Like Marx, Tocqueville anticipated the coup, if not its timing. A meeting with Bonaparte on May 15, 1851, left Tocqueville with the impression that "he is far from renouncing the possibility of a *coup d'état* on his own."[118] But, however much Tocqueville saw himself as a key player in shaping France's democracy, his liberalism prevented him from taking the necessary steps to prevent Bonaparte's actions. He allayed all doubts about his true loyalties in a letter written a few months before the coup:

> I believe that the Bonapartist current, if it can be turned aside at all, can be turned only by meeting a revolutionary current, which will be still more dangerous.
>
> The government which I should prefer, if I thought it possible, would be a republic; but, believing its continuance impossible, I should see without regret Louis Napoleon become our permanent ruler, if I could believe that he would be supported by the higher classes, and would be able and desirous to rule constitutionally. But ... I [do] not believe either of these things to be possible.
>
> His reelection, therefore, especially if illegal, may have disastrous consequences. And yet it is inevitable, unless resisted by an appeal to revolutionary passions, which I do not wish to rouse in the nation.[119]

Tocqueville's honesty was at least refreshing. He clearly recognized, then—what Marx had long argued—that only a "revolutionary current" could stop the "Bonapartist current." But he preferred to hold his nose and stomach a Bonapartist dictatorship rather than see, as he called them during the June revolt, the "greedy" masses in power. It recalls his earlier quoted self-reflection made sometime around 1840: "I belong neither to the revolutionary nor the conservative party. But, when all is said and done, I incline towards the latter rather than the former because I differ from the conservatives over means rather than ends, while I differ from the revolutionaries over both means and ends." Nothing foretold better, again, his course after 1848 than that decade-earlier self-admission.

With all its attendant horrors, Tocqueville began to have second thoughts about the Bonapartist option. Another letter two weeks after the coup revealed his doubts:

> What has just happened in Paris is abominable, in form and substance. ... As for the event itself, it was contained as an embryo in the February, like a chick in an egg. For it to emerge, all that was needed was enough time for the incubation. As soon as socialism appeared, one should have predicted the reign of the sword. One engendered the other. I had been expecting it for a long time, and even though I am filled with shame and sorrow for our country and great indignation over acts of violence and certain contemptible actions that exceeded all bound, I feel little surprise and no inner confusion. ... The nation, at this moment, is mad with fear of the socialists and a passionate desire to regain its well-being. It is incapable and, though I say it with much regret, unworthy of being free.[120]

However much Tocqueville deplored the new situation, he could not resist resorting to his "socialist" culprit thesis to explain the abomination. In what may be the first instance of blaming the victims of counterrevolution in the bourgeois era, Tocqueville faulted the tens of hundreds of slain Parisian proletariat in June 1848 for Bonaparte's coup. And if the specter of socialism was the blame, it was Tocqueville himself who first evoked the red scare in his famous speech on the right to work debate in the constituent assembly. Exactly because he had personally enabled "the reign of the sword" during and after the June uprising could he "feel no inner confusion" about what Bonaparte had done.

What Tocqueville was incapable of grasping is the possibility that his actions, as well as those of his "moderate republican" colleagues, may have paved the road to Bonapartism. This, in fact, was one of the central arguments in Marx's summary statement of the lessons of the revolution, *The Eighteenth Brumaire of Louis Bonaparte*, written about six months after Tocqueville had made his last entry in *Recollections* and about eighteen months after the last article in *Class Struggles*. (Unlike Marx, Tocqueville never completed a balance sheet on the entire revolution; he apparently found it easier to turn his attention to the 1789 revolution which resulted in his unfinished *The Old Regime and the French Revolution*, published in 1856.[121]

Firstly, the state of siege of Paris that Tocqueville had enthusiastically supported in June 1848, Marx noted, was the "midwife" for the constituent assembly and its product, the republican constitution. "If the Constitution is subsequently put out of existence by bayonets [i.e. Bonaparte's coup], it must not be forgotten that it was likewise by bayonets, and these turned against the people ... that it had to be brought into existence."[122] A precedent was, therefore, established and it was only a matter of time before the "sabre and musket" would get the idea after subsequent state of sieges of "saving society once and for all by proclaiming their own regime as the highest and freeing civil society completely from the trouble of governing itself"—a permanent military state of siege led by Bonaparte.

Secondly, the actions of Tocqueville and the majority in the Assembly during the course of the June 1849 events also played into Bonaparte's hands, Marx argued. By failing to uphold the constitution in the face of Bonaparte's violation of it with his Roman intervention, by defeating the motion of the Mountain faction that called for Bonaparte's impeachment because of the violation, and by violating the parliamentary immunity rights of the Mountain members with their arrests and banishment, the parliamentary republic politically undermined itself vis-à-vis the presidency. "By branding an insurrection [the June 13 demonstration] for the protection of the constitutional charter an anarchic act aiming at the subversion of society, it precluded the possibility of its appealing to insurrection should the executive authority violate the Constitution in relation to it."[123]

Marx also pointed to the dismissal of Tocqueville and his fellow ministers as "a decisive turning-point" in Bonaparte's strengthening of his office vis-à-vis the legislature. "No one has ever sacked lackeys with less ceremony than Bonaparte his ministers. ... With it the Party of Order lost, never to reconquer it, an indispensable post for the maintenance of the parliamentary regime, the lever of executive power." From then onward, the Party of Order, the conservative majority in the Assembly that Tocqueville's faction had blocked with, never really challenged Bonaparte's enlargement of the executive at the expense of the legislative power. It dared not do so, as Marx explained, because by "so doing it would give the nation its marching orders, and it fears nothing more than that the nation should move."[124] In other words, a real fight against Bonaparte would have required, as Tocqueville explained in his letter on the eve of the coup, "an appeal to revolutionary passions, which I do not wish to rouse in the nation." It was as if Marx had read Tocqueville's very own words.

Lastly, the failed attempt Tocqueville led to revise the constitution in order to allow Bonaparte to run again for the presidency also played into the latter's hands. The problem, as Marx correctly diagnosed—he stated as much in *Class Struggles* eighteen months earlier—was that Tocqueville's party, "caught in inextricable contradictions," had boxed itself in a no-win situation due in large part to the Assembly's prostration before Bonaparte for at least the two previous years. It couldn't afford a rejection of revision since this would provoke Bonaparte to use force to retain the presidency at the moment when his tenure ended in May 1852. Such a scenario would provoke "revolutionary anarchy" since Bonaparte would be lacking authority at that moment along with an Assembly that "for a long time had not possessed it [that is, authority] and with a people that meant to reconquer it." But Tocqueville's bloc lacked the three-fourths majority needed to make a revision as required by the constitution. Interestingly, Marx presented Tocqueville in a relatively favorable light by noting that he qualified the motion for revision with another one that stated that the Assembly "had not the right to move the *abolition of the republic*."[125] Marx didn't know, apparently, that about five weeks later Tocqueville proposed "an overall revision of the Constitution not excluding even the republican form itself."[126]

Though a majority voted on July 19 for revision, it lacked about 100 votes for the required three-fourths. In spite of the defeat, as Marx underscored, "the majority of parliament declared against the Constitution, but this Constitution itself declared for the minority and that its vote was binding." Thus, Bonaparte now had a rationale for his coup because "had not the Party of Order subordinated the Constitution to the parliamentary majority on May 31, 1850, and on June 13, 1849? Up to now, was not its whole policy based on the subordination of the paragraphs of the Constitution to the decisions of the parliamentary majority? ... At the present moment, however, revision of the Constitution meant nothing but continuation of the presidential authority, just as continuation of the Constitution meant nothing but Bonaparte's deposition [i.e. he had to step down since he could serve only one term]. Parliament had declared for him, but the Constitution declared against parliament. He therefore acted in the sense of parliament when he tore up the Constitution, and he acted in the sense of the Constitution when he dispersed parliament."

In other words, by voting to reject the motion to impeach Bonaparte for violating the constitution with his Roman intervention on June 13, 1849, and to rescind universal manhood suffrage on May 31, 1850—what Marx called the "coup d'état of the bourgeoisie"—the parliamentary majority of the Party of Order had effectively dismissed the constitution.[127] Bonaparte thus had a precedent for doing the same. Also, because the constitution stood above the parliamentary majority it allowed Bonaparte to rationalize his own standing above the parliament. The failure, therefore, to revise the constitution gave Bonaparte the pretext he had been looking for since his election in December 1848. Tocqueville, perhaps for different reasons, could have agreed with Marx's observation that "if ever an event has, well in advance of its coming, cast its shadow before it, it was Bonaparte's coup d'état."[128]

CONCLUSION

Political philosopher Alasdair MacIntyre characterizes Marx's and Tocqueville's perspectives on the events of 1848–1851 as rival theories for interpreting the behavior of major participants and "action-guiding interpretations of political transactions."[129] While true, more important than theory for interpretation is the matter of theory for political action. As he correctly notes, but unfortunately does not explore, "Tocqueville's diagnosis warrants in retrospect a very different response to one and the same situation warranted by Marx's diagnosis." It is indeed Tocqueville's response to the events, as opposed to the one that Marx advocated, that is of far more political significance—for some participants, in fact, a matter of life and death. It isn't enough to argue, as MacIntyre convincingly does, that Marx and Tocqueville acted and interpreted the events of 1848–1851 from different theoretical premises. There was more at stake than simply interpretation. What about the political consequences of their theories? The real test of theory, for Marx and Engels certainly, was its effectiveness as a weapon for political action. The course that Tocqueville pursued, based on his deepest-held beliefs, assumed that republican democracy could be achieved and maintained *without* mobilizing the "revolutionary passions" of the masses. For the two communists, it was just the opposite—a conclusion they had reached by at least 1844. Tocqueville, unlike Marx and Engels, was in a position to put his line to the test of the French reality. It failed miserably.[130]

It is instructive to note Marx's preface to the second edition of *The Eighteenth Brumaire* in 1869 in which he took to task Proudhon's analysis of Bonaparte's coup d'état. "Proudhon, for his part, seeks to represent the coup d'état as the result of preceding historical development. Unnoticeably, however, his historical construction of the coup d'état becomes a historical apologia for its hero. Thus he falls into the error of our so-called *objective* historians. In contrast to this, I demonstrate how the *class struggle* in France created circumstances and relations that made it possible for a grotesque mediocrity to play a hero's part."[131] In other words, the class struggle made Bonaparte's accession possible but not inevitable. Had Tocqueville's *Recollections* and other writings on the French events been available to him, Marx could have subjected them to the same criticism.

Three months prior to the February Revolution, Engels, to recall, anticipated the "moment … at which a collision between the people and the government will be inevitable" and predicted that most of the prominent upper-class reformers, a number of whom formed the faction that Tocqueville later affiliated with would "hide themselves in the darkest corner of their houses, or be scattered like dead leaves before the popular thunderstorm. Then it will be all over with Messrs Odilon Barrot, de Beaumont and other Liberal thunderers, and then the people will judge them quite as severely as they now judge the Conservative Governments." In one sense Engels's prediction was incorrect—aside from the fact that Tocqueville's pre-February reform credentials were highly questionable—because the faction did not take flight after February or June. They, in fact, stood toe to toe *against* the people—behind of course the sabers and muskets of the military. They were enthusiastic participants, with Tocqueville in the lead, in implementing measures that limited the political space for the masses. One could argue that another error in Engels's prediction is that while Tocqueville and his cohorts were "scattered like dead leaves" it wasn't at the hands of the people but rather by Bonaparte.

Yet the spirit if not the letter of Engels's prediction was confirmed by events. For in the final analysis Tocqueville and his colleagues did take flight from the defense of the republic. In Tocqueville's case, the record makes clear that he consciously rejected the only course he knew would defend the republic, mobilizing the revolutionary masses. In that sense, he and his faction took flight. A case can be made that he also hid himself—from politics. He retreated into his research not for the purposes of drawing a full balance sheet for public consumption on the events of 1848–1851, including his own role, but for his own edification. Five days before Bonaparte's coup Tocqueville wrote "that he welcomed the inevitable disaster which would free him from the world of politics. ... 'I can only savor in imagination the time when, far from public affairs ... away from political conversations ... I will try to isolate myself from my time and my country to live by myself and for myself.'"[132] In the end, Tocqueville's class privileges allowed him the luxury to withdraw from political reality.

Tocqueville's retreat from politics stood in stark contrast to how Marx and Engels responded to Bonaparte's coup. Socialist revolution, in their view, was on the political agenda for the first time. Marx dropped everything—including his work on what would eventually be *Capital*—to write a balance sheet on the French Revolution, *The Eighteenth Brumaire*. It proved to be his most detailed political analysis, a necessary communist task to prepare the proletariat for the next upsurge in the class struggle. Marx's and Engels's assessments of the French Revolution—the German Revolution as well—were politically superior to what Tocqueville produced. In the process, they accurately foresaw Tocqueville's own political course.

Some eyes and ears may assume from this exposition that Marx and Engels always got it right about the events of the European Spring. To the contrary. Socialist revolution as they thought proved not, for example, to be imminent. Their self-criticism of their actions in the German theater, the March 1850 "Address of the Central Authority to the Communist League," is even clearer.[133] Not only is it required reading in understanding their politics but crucial, I contend, in explaining Lenin's course in 1917 as I sketch in Chap. 4. The closest that Tocqueville ever came to admitting his mistakes—maybe—was in his *Souvenirs*. But unlike the March 1850 "Address" it was meant mainly to be a private reflection rather than a writing intended for public consumption. The differences, again, are telling.

*   *   *

Right after the February Revolution, Tocqueville wrote a new preface to his *Democracy in America* in which he held up the American republican experience as a model for Europe. While "almost all Europe was convulsed by revolutions; America has not had even a revolt." The lesson for revolutionary France was that "it was not force alone, but good laws, that give stability to a new government."[134] It was just that posture, what Marx and Engels called parliamentary cretinism, the mistaken belief that the legislative arena was the center of politics, that blinded Tocqueville to the possibility of the kind of upheaval that shook his exemplary republic to its very foundations twelve years later. In fact, it was the revolutionary force unleashed by the Civil War and its aftermath—applauded and enabled by Marx and Engels as seen in the next chapter—that qualitatively advanced the country's political democracy, what the young Marx understood better than Tocqueville.

In anticipation of the Civil War four years away, the defining moment in American history, black abolitionist Frederick Douglass in 1857—two years before Tocqueville's death—uttered his oft-quoted lines about what he called "a philosophy of reform":

> If there is no struggle, there is no progress. Those who profess to favor freedom and yet deprecate agitation are men who want crops without ploughing up the ground; they want rain without thunder and lightning. They want the ocean without the awful roar of its many waters.[135]

The first sentence could easily have come from Marx or Engels. To an interviewer's question "What is?," three years before his death in 1883, Marx, looking out at the sea, answered "in deep and solemn tone ... Struggle!"[136] As for the other lines in the speech, Tocqueville, probably unknown to Douglass, could easily have been the target of his all so potent and timeless critique.

NOTES

1. On how both sets of upheavals resembled one another, see Kurt Weyland, "The Arab Spring: Why the Surprising Similarities with the Revolutionary Wave of 1848?" *Perspectives on Politics,* Vol. 10, No. 4 (December 2012).
2. For details, see André Jardin, *Tocqueville: A Biography* (New York: Farrar, Straus, Giroux, 1988), chapter 1. His authoritative account informs the broad contours of this overview of Tocqueville's life. Hugh Brogan's *Alexis de Tocqueville: A Life* (New Haven: Yale U.P., 2006) provides more details on this and other topics. Another overview of Tocqueville is Arthur Kaledin's 100-page "thematic biography" in his *Tocqueville and His America: A Darker Horizon* (New Haven: Yale U.P, 2011).
3. Alexis de Tocqueville, *Democracy in America* [hereafter *DIA*], *Volume I: The Henry Reeve Text* (New York: Vintage Books, 1945), p. 343. This overview of Tocqueville benefits from criticism that Richard Boyd made

of some of the claims I made about him in my book *Marx, Tocqueville, and Race in America* (New York: Lexington Books, 2003). See Boyd's review in *Perspectives on Politics*, vol. 2, no. 3 (September 2004).
4. Brogan, p. 275, argues persuasively that "equality of status" would be a more accurate translation from the French.
5. Ibid., p. 206.
6. Ibid., p. 6,
7. *DIA*, volume 2, p. 108.
8. For what actually occurred, see Allan Kulikoff, "Revolutionary Violence and the Origins of American Democracy," *The Journal of the Historical Society*, vol. 2, no. 2(2002).
9. *DIA*, vol. 1, p. 343.
10. Ibid., p. 16. For a discussion on the relationship between *Democracy* and *Marie*, see Brogan, pp. 294–96.
11. Ibid., vol. 2, p. 270.
12. Jardin, p. 275.
13. Brogan, p. 312.
14. Jardin, p. 290.
15. Ibid., p. 291.
16. James T. Kloppenberg, *Toward Democracy: The Struggle for Self-Rule in European and American Thought* (New York: Oxford U.P., 2016), p. 595.
17. Quoted in Jack Hayward, *After the French Revolution: Six Critics of Democracy and Nationalism* (New York: New York U.P., 1991), p. 149. Jardin, p. 305, provides a more abbreviated version. To understand in a broader sense what he meant, see Roger Boesche, *The Strange Liberalism of Alexis de Tocqueville* (Ithaca, N.Y.: Cornell U.P.), 1987), and Alan S. Kahan, *Aristocratic Liberalism: The Social and Political Thought of Jacob Burckhardt, John Stuart Mill, and Alexis de Tocqueville* (New York: Oxford U.P., 1992).
18. Jardin, p. 313.
19. Alexis de Tocqueville, *Oeuvres Completes, III*, 1 (Paris: Editions Gallimard, 1962), p. 311.
20. Ibid., p. 324.
21. Ibid., pp. 335, 342.
22. Ibid., p. 322.
23. For another critical take, but from a different perspective, on Tocqueville on Algeria, see Cheryl B. Welch, "Colonial Violence and the Rhetoric of Evasion," *Political Theory*, vol. 31, no. 2(April 2003).
24. Jardin, p. 347.
25. Ibid., p. 352.
26. Ibid., p. 390.

27. Ibid., p. 396.
28. Ibid., p. 399.
29. Ibid., p. 400.
30. *Marx-Engels Collected Works* (New York: International Publishers, 1975–2004), vol, 1, p. 130 (hereafter, *MECW, 1*, p. 130). For details on Marx's and Engel's political trajectories, see my *Marx and Engels: Their Contribution to the Democratic Breakthrough* (Albany: SUNY Press, 2000), chapter 1.
31. *MECW, 3*, p. 120.
32. *MECW, 1*, pp. 137–38.
33. *MECW, 1*, p. 395.
34. MECW, 5, p. 236.
35. *Marie, ou l'Esclavage aux États-Unis* (Paris: Gosselin, 1835).
36. The first two of the five articles, the most well known, were written in 1843 (*MECW, 3*, pp. 146–74). Less referenced, but just as important for understanding Marx's argument are the three in *The Holy Family*, written in 1844 (*MECW, 4*, pp. 87–90, 94–9, 106–18). Because of what might be interpreted as anti-Semitic comments in the articles, a long-standing debate has been in place about Marx's views regarding Judaism and Jews. A recent example of the "anti-Semitic Marx" is Scott L. Montgomery and Daniel Chirot's *The Shape of the New: Four Big Ideas and How They Made the Modern World* (Princeton: Princeton University Press, 2015), p. 82. For the still most authoritative refutation of the anti-Semitic Marx claim, see Hal Draper's "Marx and the Economic-Jew Stereotype," https://www.marxists.org/archive/draper/1977/kmtr1/app1.htm.
37. Tocqueville's insight also found its way into the first collaborative writing of Marx and Engels, *The Holy Family*: "religion develops in its practical universality only where there is no privileged religion (cf. the North American States)." (*MECW, 4*, p. 116)
38. *MECW, 3*, p. 153.
39. Engels suggested as much in one of the infrequent references in the Marx–Engels corpus to the English Civil Wars, *MECW, 6*, p. 399.
40. Thomas Hamilton, *Men and Manners in America*, 2 vols. (Edinburgh: William Blackwood, 1833), pp. 226–27.
41. For details of Marx's reading of Hamilton, Beaumont and Tocqueville, see my *Marx, Tocqueville*, chapter 1.
42. Losurdo, pp. 318–22, rests his critique of Marx on the basis of what he wrote about political democracy in the United States in his five articles, "The Jewish Question," that is, before becoming a communist.
43. *MECW, 4*, p. 37.
44. *MECW, 4*, pp. 84–6, 119. Marx, as later revealed, authored most of the book.
45. *MECW, 5*, pp. 3–8.

46. I'm indebted to Sergio Valverde who reminded me (private communication) that Hegel continued to exercise a major influence on Marx, especially in *Capital*, such as in his analysis of value. For a defense of Hegel's speculative method, see his dissertation, "A Speculative Theory of Politics: Logic of the Party Form," University of Minnesota, 2017. Marx's aforementioned "onanism" jab was probably a polemical excess as often happens in such debates. Yet, Marx failed to complete his magnum opus exactly because of the priority he gave, unlike the world of philosophy that he critiqued, to "revolutionary practice" as detailed in Chap. 2; hence the significance of the eleventh Feuerbach thesis.

47. *MECW*, 6, p. 173.

48. Jennifer Pitts accuses without documentation "Marx to some degree ... [with] enthusiasm for empire" in the case of Algeria. See her "Empire and Democracy: Tocqueville and the Algeria Question" *Journal of Political Philosophy*, 2000, vol. 8, no. 3, p. 296. She would be on surer ground regarding Marx if she were referring to India and Mexico. I address in detail the issue in my *Marx, Tocqueville*, Chap. 2.

49. For an overview of Marx's and Engels's party-building activities, see my "Marx and Engels on the revolutionary party," *Socialist Register 2017*, eds. Leo Panitch and Greg Albo (London: The Merlin Press, 2016).

50. Weyland, pp. 917–8.

51. There is the correspondence of Tocqueville, unlike for Marx (who to be remembered was deeply engaged at the time in the German theater of the European Spring), about the events in real time; see Alexis de Tocqueville, *Selected Letters on Politics and Society*, ed. Roger Boesche (Los Angeles: University of California Press, 1985). If anyone of the two authors was at an advantage in their later accounts, Tocqueville is the likely candidate. A close reading of the letters reveals, however, that what he wrote in real time was not at significant variance with his *Recollections* written two years later.

52. Roger Price, *The Revolutions of 1848* (Atlantic Highlands, N.J.: Humanities Press, 1988), p. 64. For other comparisons, see Edward T. Gargan, *Alexis de Tocqueville: The Critical Years, 1848–1851* (Washington, D.C.: Catholic U.P., 1955) and Irving M. Zeitlin, *Liberty, Equality, and Revolution in Alexis de Tocqueville* (Boston: Little, Brown, 1971), particularly chapter 6. Also, Craig Calhoun, "Classical Social Theory and the French Revolution of 1848," *Sociological Theory* 7 (Fall, 1989). The emphasis here, however, is on their politics.

53. J. P. Mayer, "Introduction" to *Recollections: The French Revolution of 1848*, ed. J. P. Mayer and a. P. Kerr (New Brunswick, N. J.: Transaction Books, 1987), pp. xxxii–iii. This is the edition of the *Recollections* employed here.

54. J.P. Mayer, *Alexis de Tocqueville: A Biographical Study in Political Science* (New York: Harper & Brothers, 1960).
55. George Kelly's *The Human Comedy: Constant, Tocqueville, and French Liberalism* (Cambridge: Cambridge U.P., 1992), p. 235, argues that Tocqueville's writing of history as a private memoir represented a liberal retreat from politics. Jardin states that "we should not necessarily believe him when he declares they are not destined for the public. ... No doubt he did not intend to release them to the public during his lifetime. But his reflections on his age led Tocqueville to a concern for what posterity would think of him." (p. 453).
56. Tocqueville, *Recollections*, pp. 12–13.
57. *MECW, 6*, p. 380.
58. Alan S Kahan, *Aristocratic Liberalism: The Social and Political Thought of Jacob Burkhardt, John Stuart Mill, and Alexis de Tocqueville* (New York: Oxford U.P., 1992), p. 72.
59. Ibid., p. 381.
60. Another writing that Tocqueville may have had in mind was Proudhon's highly popular *Qu'est-ce que la propriété?*, published in 1840, which popularized the aphorism that "property is theft."
61. Though Tocqueville, according to Roger Boesche (in a private communication), once referred to himself as a "liberal of a new kind," and Engels referred on occasion to Tocqueville's faction as "Liberal," I employ, given the present-day debates that surround the usage of this term, Tocqueville's "moderate republican" label.
62. Marx's critique at the end of 1847 (*6*, p. 405) of Alphonse de Lamartine's praise of private property for not distinguishing between bourgeois and other forms of private property could just as well have applied to Tocqueville. Lamartine became the effective head of the government that issued from the February Revolution.
63. *MECW, 10*, pp. 54–5.
64. *Recollections*, p. 73.
65. Ibid., pp. 74–5. Because socialists did accede to positions of authority in some locales like Rouen in the aftermath of February it might explain Tocqueville's assessment. See Aminzade, *Ballots and Barricades: Class Formation and Republican Politics in France, 1830–1871* (Princeton: Princeton University Press, 1993), p. 182, for particulars.
66. Ibid., p. 62. As to which "absolute systems" he is referring to it is unclear. It's possible he may have had Marx and Engels in mind but it is doubtful since their *Manifesto* had yet to appear in French. A more likely candidate for Tocqueville's criticism was Lorenz von Stein, whose *Der Socialismus und Communismus des heutigen frankreichs*—a second edition came out in 1848—was certainly much better known among the circles that he frequented than the *Manifesto*.

67. *Recollections*, pp. 75–6.
68. Quoted in Irving Zeitlin, *Liberty, Equality and Revolution in Alexis de Tocqueville* (Boston: Little, Brown, 1971), pp. 106–7.
69. Ibid., p. 105.
70. *DIA*, p. 6.
71. See Peter McPhee, "The Crisis of Radical Republicanism in the French Revolution of 1848," *Historical Studies*, Vol 16, No. 162 (1974), which suggests that another explanation for the revolutionary republican view of February was its institution for the first time of universal manhood suffrage that for them meant the defense of the provisional government at all costs.
72. *Recollections*, p. 76.
73. For the anti-Marxist Daniel Mahoney, Tocqueville's conclusion is "one of the most intriguing and unsettling remarks in his *Recollections*." That his hero could envision the possibility of socialism is "unsettling" for Mahoney, who reveals a profound ignorance of what Marx and Engels actually advocated. Nevertheless, he is correct to criticize any interpretation of his remarks to mean that Tocqueville was "somehow open to Marx and his view of the social question." Another problem that Mahoney has is reconciling Tocqueville's remarks with his "Speech on the Right to Work" made to the Constituent Assembly on September 12, 1848. The latter in Mahoney's opinion makes it clear that Tocqueville was unequivocal in his opposition to socialism. Be that as it may, the fact is that two years later in his *Recollections* he certainly seemed to have equivocated. Mahoney should at least address this apparent discrepancy that could reasonably be interpreted to mean that in his private memoirs Tocqueville was less certain about his opposition to socialism than in his public remarks two years earlier. See his "Tocqueville and Socialism," *Tocqueville's Defense of Human Liberty: Current Essays* (New York: Garland Publishing, 1993), p. 179.
74. *Recollections*, p. 96.
75. Ibid., p. 97.
76. *MECW, 10*, p. 61.
77. For details, see my *Marx and Engels*, pp. 64–5, 102–7.
78. According to Ron Aminzade (private communication), Ledru-Rollin later admitted that his government's policies regarding the peasantry were wrong-headed.
79. *MECW, 10*, pp. 67–9.
80. *Recollections*, p. 144.
81. *MECW, 7*, p. 64.
82. *Recollections*, p. 136. See Craig Calhoun, "Classical Social Theory and the French Revolution of 1848," *Sociological Theory*, 7 (Fall, 1989),

p. 221, for a discussion about whether Tocqueville and Marx got it right about the class character of the revolt.

83. Calhoun, in the previous note, for example.
84. *MECW, 10*, p. 56.
85. Mark Traugott, *Armies of the Poor: Determinants of Working-Class Participation in the Parisian Insurrection of June 1848* (Princeton, 1985), disputes Marx's and Tocqueville's class characterization of the Gardes Mobiles.
86. *Recollections*, p. 165.
87. *MECW, 10*, pp. 66–7.
88. *Recollections*, pp. 147–8.
89. Ibid, p. 148. Tocqueville's real-time account of his actions is consistent with what he wrote two years later; see Boesche, p. 213.
90. Ibid, p. 214.
91. *MECW, 10*, p. 68. Charles Tilly, The Contentious French (Cambridge: Harvard U.P. 1986), p. 384, says that 1400 "died in the June Days." Mary Gabriel, *Love and Capital: Karl and Jenny Marx and the Birth of a Revolution* (New York: Little, Brown, 2011) writes that "an estimated fifteen hundred people died. ... Insurgents were hunted down and executed, three thousand in all. Up to fifteen thousand more people were arrested and forty-five hundred of those deported in packed convoys to Algeria" (p. 148).
92. Tocqueville acknowledged in a marginal note to the chapter in *Recollections* that covers this period that "[t]here is a great gap" in it. (p. 167).
93. Jardin, p. 416.
94. Brogan, pp. 451–61, provides fascinating details about Tocqueville's role which are not always flattering.
95. Jardin, p. 419. About a month before the debate on the right to work issue Proudhon, a member of the Assembly, caused quite an uproar—reported by the *NRZ*—by making a prolonged attack on private property. Along the way he exclaimed that "By recognizing in the Constitution the right to work, you have proclaimed the recognition of the abolition of property" (*7*, p. 323). Proudhon's heresy may be what Tocqueville had in mind in lambasting the constitutional proposal.
96. Mahoney, p. 186.
97. *Recollections*, p. 169.
98. Jardin, p. 419.
99. *Recollections*, p. 178.
100. Jardin, p. 420.
101. *MECW, 10*, p. 570.
102. *MECW, 10*, p. 79.
103. *Recollections*, p. 166.

104. Jardin, pp. 438–9.
105. Kelly's argument, in fn. 55, that *Recollections* was not the private memoir that its author claimed it to be, has merit. By failing to discuss the Roman betrayal Tocqueville was in all likelihood attempting to influence his image for subsequent generations.
106. *MECW*, *9*, p. 477.
107. *Recollections*, p. 211.
108. Regarding Marx's and Engels's rethinking of their views on the imminence of socialist revolution, see chapter 4 in my *Marx and Engels*.
109. *MECW*, *10*, pp. 92–3.
110. *Recollections*, p. 220.
111. Ibid, pp. 219–20.
112. Ibid., p. 223.
113. My *Marx and Engels*, chapters 3 and 4, provide details.
114. *Recollections*, pp. 225–6.
115. This followed discussions Tocqueville had with Bonaparte on May 15, 1851. It's not clear from his memoir if this was the same or a different meeting referred to earlier in which Tocqueville raised various options for the president for how to stay in office.
116. *MECW*, *10*, p. 142.
117. Ibid., p. 580. From Marx's article, "The Constitution of the French Republic Adopted November 8, 1848," the only thing he wrote on the French situation between his last article in *Class Struggles* and the *Eighteenth Brumaire*. It is also noteworthy because of its detailed analysis of the democratic limitations of the constitution, giving lie to the oft-repeated charge that he ignored such matters.
118. *Recollections*, p. 292.
119. *Correspondence and Conversations of Alexis de Tocqueville with Nassau William Senior*, quoted in Irving Zeitlin, *Liberty, Equality, and Revolution in Alexis de Tocqueville* (Boston: Little, Brown, 1971), p. 118.
120. Jardin, p. 461. Sixteen years earlier in his *Democracy*, Tocqueville asked if it was possible to have an alternative to the American path to republican democracy "in which the majority, repressing its natural instinct of equality, should consent, with a view to the order and the stability of the state, to invest a family or an individual with all the attributes of executive power? Might not a democratic society be imagined in which the forces of the nation would be more centralized than they are in the United States; where the people would exercise a less direct and less irresistible influence upon public affairs, and yet every citizen, invested with certain rights, would participate, within his sphere, in the conduct of the government?" Tocqueville answered affirmatively. Thus, his willingness to acquiesce in Bonaparte's coup may have reflected his earlier vision about an

alternative path to democracy via the investiture of "an individual with all the attributes of executive power."

121. In the "Foreword" to his *Old Regime*, Tocqueville suggested that his analysis of 1789 would serve to explain subsequent events such as 1830 and 1848. Since he died before doing a planned follow-up volume, it is not certain how specific he intended to be in an analysis of 1848. At best, *Old Regime* is an implicit critique of the bourgeoisie in 1848 as well as Bonaparte's Second Empire.

122. *MECW, 11*, p. 118.

123. Ibid., p. 135.

124. Ibid, p. 155.

125. Ibid, p. 168.

126. Jardin, pp. 458–9.

127. Though Tocqueville enthusiastically voted against the impeachment motion on June 13, he in fact helped lead the charge against it as the Assembly member who headed the Ministry of Foreign Affairs; he did not, apparently, vote to abolish universal manhood suffrage. He was clearly opposed to the decision, as he explained to Bonaparte in their meeting on May 15, 1851. "I regard that law ... as a great misfortune, almost as a crime. It has deprived us of the only moral force society possesses today, that is to say, the moral power of universal suffrage, without ridding us of the dangers of that voting system. We are left to face a multitude, but an unauthorized multitude" (*Recollections*, pp. 291–2). As noted earlier, Tocqueville was no partisan of universal suffrage before 1848. His apparent change of heart in 1851 should be seen in that light as well as his well-known fears about the "unauthorized multitude."

128. *MECW, 11*, p. 176.

129. Alasdair MacIntyre, "The Indispensability of Political Theory," *The Nature of Political Theory*, eds. David Miller and Larry Siedentop (Oxford: The Clarendon Press, 1983), p. 27.

130. Whether Marx's and Engels's line would have been more effective if given an opportunity for implementation in France is of course pure speculation. What is certain is that they strenuously tried to realize it in the German theater. Though unsuccessful, they had no hesitation in faulting the Tocquevillian counterparts in Germany who too feared the masses, doing all they could to hold their "revolutionary passions" in check. Tocqueville, who visited Germany in May 1849, viewed the situation there in a way that would have certainly placed him and the Marx–Engels team on the opposite sides of the barricades had he been able to carry out his line there.

131. *MECW, 21*, p. 57.

132. Gargan, p. 255.

133. https://www.marxists.org/archive/marx/works/1847/communist-league/1850-ad1.htm.
134. *DIA*, vol. 1, pp. ix–x.
135. https://blackpast.org/1857-frederick-douglass-if-there-no-struggle-there-no-progress.
136. *MECW*, *24*, p. 585.

CHAPTER 3

The United States Civil War: Marx versus John Stuart Mill

[W]hat will most help to give a better direction to public opinion is that persons of talent, the more known and respected the better, should put themselves forward.
Mill, November 1861

[S]imple justice requires … a tribute to the sound attitude of the British working classes, the more so when contrasted with the hypocritical, bullying, cowardly, and stupid conduct of the official and well-to-do John Bull.
Marx, February 1862

The 1848–1849 revolutions, specifically the French theatre, also captured the attention of John Stuart Mill, arguably England's foremost nineteenth-century intellectual and leading champion of liberalism and one-time friend of Tocqueville. Two decades earlier, he was enticed to breathe the air of revolution for the first time when France exploded in 1830. Not surprising, therefore, that he would be tempted to do the same when revolutionary whiffs blew anew from the same place at mid-century. But his response to France's edition of the European Spring contrasted strikingly to that of Marx and Engels. It anticipated their different responses a decade later to the most consequential struggle of the century for the democratic quest, the Civil War in the United States—the centerpiece of this chapter. While Marx, Engels and Mill were all on the same political page about the need to overthrow the slavocracy, their actions in the

© The Author(s) 2019
A. H. Nimtz, *Marxism versus Liberalism*, Marx, Engels,
and Marxisms, https://doi.org/10.1007/978-3-030-24946-5_3

realization of that goal, particularly Marx vis-à-vis Mill, also stood in stark contrast. Glaringly on display, in terms of who to look to for victory for the North and how much time and energy to expend to realize that end, were the implications of their more fundamental political differences. Post–Civil War British domestic politics, specifically, the struggle for electoral reform—treated as an appendix—exposed those differences once again; a fitting coda for the comparison.

THE FRENCH AND ENGLISH CONNECTIONS: PRELUDE TO A COMPARISON

Like Marx and Engels, John Stuart Mill (1806–1873) too was a product, both intellectually and politically, of the French Revolution of 1789.[1] But if Mill, as he revealed in his *Autobiography*, identified with the Revolution's moderate current, the Girondists, Marx's sympathies were closer to its radicals, Jacque Roux, the Enragé (the Enraged and not to be confused with the Jacobins)—foreshadowing their different allegiances for subsequent events.[2] One of Mill's first political writings was in defense of 1789 against Tory opponents. The Revolution of 1830 offered the twenty-four-year-old his first opportunity to become if not an actual participant then at least a close observer of the revolutionary process. But he returned from his brief visit to Paris "disillusioned by the failure of the middle class to embrace democratic reform and became less hopeful about the possibility of radical change. The failure of the middle class in the Revolution of 1830 led Mill to become more sympathetic to Saint Simonian elitism as a vehicle for reform."[3]

If France allowed Mill to indulge his revolutionary fantasies, England did not. "In truth, Mill was anti-revolutionary at home."[4] Less than a year after his return from Paris, mass and violent protests against the House of Lords veto of an electoral reform law created a near revolutionary situation in the south of England, especially in the Bristol region.[5] Mill's reaction to England's most revolutionary moment in his lifetime is telling. If things were to escalate to an English version of 1789, as he wondered in a letter to his close friend the Scottish author John Sterling in October 1831, "I have not made up my mind what would be best to do."

> I incline to think it would be best to lie by and let the tempest blow over. ... You will perhaps think from this long prosing rambling talk about politics, that they occupy much of my attention: but in fact I am myself often

surprised, how little I really care about them. The time is not yet come when a calm & impartial person can intermeddle with advantage in the questions & contests of the day. … The only thing which I can usefully do at present, & which I am doing more & more every day, is to work out *principles*: which are of use for all times, though to be applied cautiously & circumspectly to any: principles of morals, government, law, education, above all self-education. I am here much more in my element: the only thing that I believe I am really fit for, is the investigation of abstract truth, & the more abstract the better.[6]

It's hard to find a better description of the relative importance of politics and intellectual endeavors in Mill's life than this early self-admission. The preference for the "investigation of abstract truth" over "care" for "politics" indeed anticipated most of his subsequent course (also, arguably, modern political science).[7] Because there is no record, one can only speculate about what the then fourteen-year-old Marx and twelve-year-old Engels were thinking about those options. But given their subsequent trajectories it's most likely they were reaching very different conclusions.[8] What can be said with certainty is that at almost the same age that Mill made clear his choices, twenty-six, Marx, twenty-seven, concluded that only through action, "revolutionary practice," could men of ideas and "abstract thinking" learn and that they were then obligated "to change … the world," in his *Theses on Feuerbach* (1845). Seldom have two early career choices proven so prescient for outcomes.

Between 1835 and 1840, Mill wrote three major review articles that made him arguably Britain's leading authority on America. Mill's detailed and thoughtful treatments of Alexis de Tocqueville's two-volume *Democracy in America* disclosed that he was in broad agreement with his positive portrait of the liberal democratic experiment in place on the other side of the Atlantic. Tocqueville considered the reviews essential for understanding the book.[9] Yet, there was no interrogation of Tocqueville's claim that despite the reality of the "three races," the "Indian tribes" and the "black population," specifically, America was "an absolute and immense democracy." Neither did he address the issue in another review in 1836 of Gustave de Beaumont's *Marie, or Slavery in the United States*, and Thomas Hamilton's two-volume travel account *Men and Manners in America*, which provided details on the race question absent in at least the first of Tocqueville's two volumes published in 1835. Three years after Mill's 1840 review article of the second Tocqueville volume the young Marx read and took notes on the same three books. Instructively, however, there is hardly a hint in Mill's readings of Tocqueville, de Beaumont and Hamilton of what Marx read into them, findings that would impel him on to communist conclusions (see Chap. 1). Again, if America was the best that liberal democracy had to offer, then something else was required for "true democracy."[10] The *Manifesto* five years later would provide the answer. The very different intellectual and experiential backgrounds that the two brought to the texts no doubt explains their different readings.

When England's working-class Chartist movement mobilized in the latter half of the 1830s, one of its leaders asked Mill in mid-1842 for support. While professing deep "respect" for them and offering help if he could—supplying, for example, books for their library—Mill could not, however, fully embrace their six-point charter, after whom they were named, for electoral reform. If they were successful, it would mean "a legislature absolutely controlled by one class, even when that class numerically exceeds all others taken together," that is, the working class.[11] That he could not countenance—the "tyranny of the majority" that his friend Tocqueville also abhorred.[12] Mill never abandoned that stance. Five months later the twenty-two-year-old Engels arrived in Manchester, England's industrial center, to do an accountancy apprenticeship in his family's textile plant. Within weeks he connected with the Chartists and initiated a political relationship that he and his soon to be partner Marx gave utmost importance to. Unlike Mill they endorsed all of the Chartist demands and for many years pointed to them as the paragon of working-class political action. The example of the Chartists is in fact what convinced Marx and Engels that the proletariat had both the interest and capacity to make democracy real for the first time—the truly revolutionary class. Their two very different responses to the Chartists would distinguish thereafter, more than anything, Mill's politics from those of the two communists.

Six years later the European Spring erupted, the 1848 Revolutions, with Paris, once again, in the vanguard. Despite having, apparently, intimate knowledge of French politics, Mill was caught off guard.[13] To rectify that failure, he wanted, just as he'd done for the 1830 upheaval, to witness the latest upsurge first hand. But an accident that limited his sight and mobility made that impossible. Only from afar could he relate to the fast-breaking developments, mainly through correspondence and journalistic interventions. Some of his contacts were protagonists in the unfolding drama and, not surprisingly, partisans of the moderate wing of the revolution, the conscious heirs of Mill's beloved Girondists of 1789. One of them, Alphonse de Lamartine, actually headed the provisional government that issued from the deposition of the monarch Louis-Philippe in February. The moderate leadership enthused Mill; it could guarantee real electoral reforms that might even be a model for England. To the mayor of Paris who had been in the provisional government he sent a copy of his just published magnum opus but admitted that abstract *Principles of Political Economy* were not likely to be of much use in that turbulent moment. While hopeful, there were "dangers," as he explained to an English acquaintance: "Communism has now for the first time a deep root, and has spread widely in France, and a large part of the effective republican strength is more or less imbued with it. The Provisional Government is obliged to coquet with this, and to virtually promise work and good wages to the whole labouring class: how are they to keep their promise, and what will be the consequences of not keeping it?"[14]

His concerns about how the government would deal with the unemployment problem, the product of the economic depression—arguably capitalism's first—were well founded. Democratic governance as an end in itself, his priority, was not what motivated the Parisian proletariat to send the monarchy packing in February. Their impatience with the provisional government in solving the jobs crisis brought them back into the streets in June, a futile attempt to realize the first proletarian revolution in history. Mill denied, contrary to the evidence, its bloody suppression: "not one person has been shot, not one life taken, by the authority of government in consequence of the insurrection. ... The mildness and moderation of the sincerely republican party are as conspicuous in the present head of the government and his cabinet as in the provisional government and executive commission who preceded him."[15] His friend Tocqueville, as noted in the previous chapter, had a hand in the bloodbath. In hindsight, the insurgency's rout, though Mill didn't see it that way, was the beginning of the end of the Revolution.

Far more worrisome for Mill was the new constitutional arrangement that allowed for the first time in France, or anywhere in Europe, the election of the head of state through universal male suffrage. He was instinctively suspicious of plebiscitary democracy; it could enable a strong man—exactly what happened when Louis Napoleon Bonaparte staged a coup d'état in December 1851. But before that fateful outcome Mill took his most public stance in defense of the defunct February provisional government against typical Tory condemnation of revolutionary France; he was virtually alone in his defense amid the circles he inhabited. His fifty-page "Vindication of the French Revolution of February 1848" article appeared almost a year later in 1849. While offering a strong defense of the government's right to work policies—before they were abandoned and what provoked the June insurgency—his main focus was the political reforms and what they might have portended. But by the summer of 1851, about four months before the coup d'état, all of that was increasingly history. Mill had become pessimistic about the situation—"I am for the first time downhearted about French affairs"[16]—and his virtual silence about France after his article appeared became deafening. There wasn't even mention of Bonaparte's coup. Like Tocqueville—as noted in the prior chapter—Mill too seems to have had a bout of writer's block when it came to the Revolution's denouement.

Though Mill once had high hopes for the Revolution—"the whole problem of modern society ... will be worked out in France & nowhere else" he wrote in May 1849[17]—it's telling, however, how little of it figured into his literary output during its course. Of his thirty-one newspaper letters from the beginning of the Revolution to Bonaparte's coup only four dealt with the French developments. Of his sixty-three letters during the same time only five dealt in any sustained way with the upheaval. And his "Vindication" article only focused on about the first five months of the provisional government. The Revolution, in its first two years at least, had clearly been important for Mill but not a priority.

As for how Marx and Engels read the events in France in real time (actually in near real time since they had all they could handle as protagonists in the German theater of the European Spring) see the preceding chapter.[18] But worth highlighting here is how Marx's explanation for Bonaparte's coup differed from Mill's. While the latter thought that the plebiscite paved the way for the coup—again, his privileging of forms of democracy—Marx argued that it was the slaughter of the proletariat, the truly revolutionary party, in June 1848, and a subsequent crackdown on the left a year later (and about which Mill was silent) that set the stage for the coup. Both repressive acts emboldened the future dictator. In other words, moderates like Mill's friend Tocqueville who endorsed the repression because of their "fear of the mob" enabled Bonaparte's strongman proclivities.

Aside from different interpretations of the events, two other points are worth making. First, Marx and Engels considered what they were doing in Germany, trying to consummate its democratic revolution, would help advance the process in France. Their communist theoretical perspective presumed that the democratic revolution was internationally constituted. Mill made no such assumptions; the nation state was his unit of analysis. Thus, when a feeble Chartist-organized attempt on April 10, 1848, was made in London to echo in England what was taking place on the continent Mill could only offer a sardonic observation about its failure—the "demon revolution, or at least a noisy braggart that attempted to look like him, sneaked away at the sight of a special constable's staff."[19] He had had no hand in trying to make the action effective; nor would it have occurred to him to do so. Revolutions, again, were for other countries, not for his native England.

Second, when Marx and Engels did retire from the battlefield of revolution and settled in London—temporarily they mistakenly thought—they were now, like Mill, observers from afar, thus making for a fairer comparison between the two parties about their real-time analysis. But by the time Marx settled in London, September 1849, Mill, living only a few miles away in Blackheath, had ceased to say virtually anything publicly or in correspondence about the French theater. Marx, on the other hand, had a lot to say, the communist obligation to document the class struggle, both victories and defeats, so that the toilers could learn. His articles that eventually became known as *Class Struggles in France* and his magisterial *Eighteenth Brumaire of Louis Napoleon*, all written between then and the beginning of 1852, forever overshadowed anything Mill wrote about the European Spring. Of the eighty-two letters Marx wrote during that period eleven dealt substantively with the French events. And he composed all of that under the most trying circumstances—a political refugee in a new country, poverty and economic insecurity, and the challenges of trying to maintain a family, including the death of two children. That Marx could be far more productive in writing about the French theater than Mill who had none of those obstacles to deal with—trying to find a publisher was another one—is truly remarkable. And not to be forgotten was Marx's research, at the British Museum, usually from nine to seven when open, and lecturing at the same time on his political economy project.

Last but not least, Marx had leadership responsibilities for the now reconstituted Communist League in London—which required providing aid to other refugees—to prepare the party for a return to the continent in anticipation of a revival of Germany's democratic revolution. That never happened but the effort was not in vain; it planted the seeds for Marx's effective intervention in the next most consequential moment in the democratic quest. The size of their literary outputs about the French events, in sharp contrast, captures in part what so distinguished Marx from Mill. Theorizing about democracy was patently more enjoyable for Mill than partaking in the laboratory of the class struggle—the only arena in which, as Marx knew, the outcome of the democratic quest is decided.

PRELUDE TO THE "GENERAL CONFLAGRATION"

The firing on Fort Sumter, South Carolina, by troops of the Confederate Government of the United States on April 12, 1861, came as a surprise to virtually everyone. Marx, Engels and Mill were no exception. Mill, perhaps, had more prescience about the war that would do away with slavery than Marx and Engels because, as he explained years later in his *Autobiography*, he had "been a deeply interested observer of the Slavery quarrel in America, during the many years that preceded the open breach."[20] Mill's stinging rebuke in 1850 to the conservative Thomas Carlyle, a one-time acquaintance, about his racist views of blacks registered how attentive he had been to the slavery question. In denouncing an article Carlyle had recently written, Mill, in a long letter to the venue that had just published it, argued that the abolition of slavery in the British colonies bode well for the eventual demise of all tyranny and ideas like those of Carlyle employed in its justification. "There is, however, another place where that tyranny still flourishes, but now for the first time finds itself seriously in danger. At this crisis of American slavery, when the decisive conflict between right and iniquity seems about to commence, your contributor [Carlyle] steps in, and flings this missile, loaded with the weight of his reputation, into the abolitionist camp."[21] If Mill's arithmetic was faulty—it would take a decade for the "decisive conflict ... to commence"—his algebra was nonetheless elegant.

Mill premised his rebuke of Carlyle with historical perspective:

> The history of human improvement is the record of a struggle by which inch after inch of ground has been wrung from these maleficent powers, and more and more of human life rescued from the iniquitous dominion of the law of might. Much, very much of this work still remains to do, but the progress made in it is the best and greatest achievement yet performed by mankind, and it was hardly to be expected at this period of the world that we should be enjoined, by way of a great reform in human affairs, to begin *un*doing it. ... [T]he abolition of despotism, seems to be, in a peculiar degree, the occupation of this age; and it would be difficult to shew that any age had undertaken a worthier.[22]

What's interesting about Mill's claim is its similarity, in tone at least, to Marx's and Engels's better-known assertion two years earlier: "The history of all hitherto existing society is the history of the class struggle." But a close reading of their *Manifesto of the Communist Party* makes clear that though they too viewed history as a "record of a struggle" against "maleficent powers" by the subjugated, that is, the class struggle, unlike Mill they didn't see that record as one of only "progress."[23] As for the proletariat specifically, "now and then the workers are victorious, but only for a time." "Inevitable," or *unvermeidlich* in the original, appears only once in the document and is immediately followed by instructions for how to ensure victories for workers. If "progress" for workers was inevitable, there would have been no need for the *Manifesto*. A program along with organization and action and not just being on the right side of history was, in other words, necessary for advancing "progress"—what had already so distinguished the two communists from Mill. That difference would soon be on display once again.

Just as Mill was giving Carlyle his comeuppance, on paper at least, Marx and Engels were preparing to return to the barricades as actual protagonists in the age-old struggle for "human improvement." If Germany's edition of the European Spring had been aborted, its still enthusiastic partisans sought greener pastures to continue the struggle. Marx had even considered moving to the United States since it was there where he could still be published—where the *Eighteenth Brumaire* first saw light of day. He eventually decided not to do so but many of the members of what increasingly came to be called "the Marx party" made the trip to the other side of the Atlantic. The "forty-eighters," as many of them also came to be known, saw the fight against chattel slavery as a continuation of what they'd been engaged in just recently. Though he remained in Europe, Marx too had a presence in the United States. First, through correspondence he advised his ersatz party. And, second, as a correspondent—with the assistance of Engels as ghost writer—for the most popular and influential liberal organ in the U.S., Horace Greeley's *New York Daily Tribune*, he spoke to a newspaper readership that may have been the largest anywhere in the world. One of those devoted readers would become the sixteenth president of the Republic.

Even before the upheavals of 1848–1849, Marx tried to influence opinions in the United States. Specifically, he waged a struggle through publications and correspondence against a current in the German émigré community that had momentarily called itself "communist" but who downplayed the importance of abolishing slavery. His newly arrived at "materialist conception of history" argued that pre-capitalist social formations such as slavery were an obstacle to the full flowering of capitalism and, hence, the growth of the efficacious fighters for "true democracy," the proletariat.[24] In the midst of being on the barricades for the German theater of the European Spring, Marx criticized in his Cologne-based newspaper *Neue Rheinische Zeitung—Organ der Demokratie* antislavery work in the United States that "took no practical steps toward its abolition."[25] Once the "good fight" in Europe had ended, Marx could devote more time to developments on the other side of the Atlantic, particularly the "practical steps." And he did so while doing "the scientific work," that is, the research that would be the basis for his political economy publications.

From afar, Marx advised his co-thinkers in the United States on how to wage the struggle against slavery, especially after the Kansas–Nebraska Act of 1854 permitted its extension to previously non-slave territories. His primary contact was Joseph Weydemeyer, a "Marx party" member, as they came to be known from the beginning and "forty-eighter"—the de facto leader of the party in the United States. Their correspondence was intermittent, no doubt having to do with Marx busily researching and getting into print in 1859 the first fruit of the scientific work, his *Contribution to the Critique of Political Economy*—a decade after Mill published his *Principles of Political Economy*. Mill, to be remembered, was twelve years older than Marx.

It was the John Brown insurgency on October 16, 1859, that suggested to Marx and Engels that things might be coming to a boil in the United States. Referring to at least one slave uprising that had been spawned by Brown's abortive rebellion, Marx declared, and Engels concurred, "that the most momentous thing happening in the world today is the slave movement—on the one hand, in America, started by the death of Brown [Dec. 2, 1859], and in Russia, on the other." As for "Russia," they were referring to the increasing mobilization of serfs against their own form of servitude. There is no real-time mention of the Brown rebellion in the Mill corpus.[26]

Marx party members then began to mobilize to influence the outcome of the nomination of the Republican Party candidate for the increasingly decisive 1860 presidential election—and to make sure that its convention platform was "hostile to slavery." Founded in 1854 it was the first antislavery party in the country and, understandably, looked favorably upon by them. Lincoln, they mostly concluded, seemed to be the "lesser of two evils." They then worked assiduously for his nomination and election; they may, therefore, have played a crucial role in arguably the most consequential election in U.S. history.[27] Though the record doesn't reveal that Marx or Engels gave direction to that effort, the ersatz party members felt, correctly, that what they were doing in insuring Lincoln's nomination and election was consistent with all of the advice the two had supplied so far and would, therefore, have approved of their actions. It is unlikely that Lincoln knew it was the Marx party that had been so conscious and active among the German immigrants in his nomination and election. He did know that the Germans, especially those in Illinois, were crucial in his nomination.[28]

Nothing in the Mill corpus reveals that he was aware in real-time of any of this lead-up to the Civil War. Unlike Marx and Engels he didn't have or wouldn't have thought to cultivate a grouping such as the Marx party to play the role it did on the scene and to keep him informed. What Marx had, in other words, unlike Mill, was an ersatz party that allowed him to influence events. Mill, at best, could be only "a deeply interested observer" from afar. While Mill correctly anticipated that "the decisive conflict between right and iniquity seems about to commence," the Marx party had been voting with its feet for the abolition of slavery for at least a decade to make that possible, "the practical work." Nothing in Mill's constitution—given the priorities he'd chosen decades earlier—would have allowed him to do the same and, thus, be as consequential in the developments that unfolded. Mill certainly had many contacts in the United States, and potentially more venues for propagating his certainly progressive views. *On Liberty*, his most famous work, was published on the eve of the war in 1859 (the same year Tocqueville died). Notably absent in it is any mention of the institution that provoked the bloodletting. And the milieu in which Mill inhabited could never have acted as did Marx's comrades. It's not what they did.

THE "GENERAL CONFLAGRATION" BEGINS

When the slave owners in South Carolina decided on December 20, 1860, to secede from the Union to protest Lincoln's election, Engels, in Manchester, commented to Marx, in London, on its significance in the final paragraph of a letter dated January 7. It took, to be noted, about two weeks for news in the United States to get to London.

In North America things are also hotting up. With the slaves the situation must be pretty awful if the SOUTHERNERS are playing such a risky game. The least irruption of irregulars from the North might result in a general conflagration. At all events, one way or another, slavery would appear to be rapidly nearing its end and hence also cotton production.[29]

Engels's letter was typical in his correspondence with his partner. The first five paragraphs dealt with party matters in Europe; the next with current politics in Prussia and Austria—the context for his comments about the beginning of the secession of the Confederacy. Though prescient about a "general conflagration," and "slavery ... rapidly nearing its end" Engels had no idea of what would be involved in realizing that outcome.

If the Marx–Engels correspondence was rife with politics, locally and globally, that of Mill stood starkly in contrast. The first opportunity he might have had to recognize the significance of what was taking place on the other shores of the Atlantic was in his letter to Tocqueville's friend Gustave de Beaumont—author of one of the texts that had, as I argue in Chap. 1, a major impact on Marx and the communist conclusions he reached in about 1844. Dated January 15, 1860, a week after Engels's letter, it was strikingly devoid of any real-time politics. It was mostly about Tocqueville who had died in April 1859 and his significance as the author of *Democracy in America* and what was lost with his death. There is, maybe, a hint of what was happening in real-time politics when he wrote "toutes les misères de notre temps," but that's speculation.[30] Mill, apparently, could not bring himself to even allude to the subject that had made Tocqueville famous and what was taking place in its borders at that moment. The difference with the Marx–Engels team couldn't be more striking.

In the meantime, Marx party members in the United States immediately signed up for the Union army when the Confederacy fired on Fort Sumter in April—the "irruption of irregulars from the North." Their effective leader, Weydemeyer, Marx's closest contact in the United States, soon rose to the rank of colonel, the only communist to have done so in the history of the U.S. military.

Marx too had to shift gears; the completion of *Capital* competed now with the research and writing required for "the struggle in the press." In his first written acknowledgment of what was unfolding in the United States, a letter to his uncle Lion Philips in Holland on May 6, 1861, Marx noted: "Here in London there is great consternation over the course of events in North America." He was referring to the growing public debate in Great Britain about which side to take in the conflict. Ruling-class England, through its leading organs, was decidedly pro-Confederacy. Marx, very soon, would begin to look for opportunities to contest that opinion—hence "the struggle in the press."

Marx's next comments to his uncle revealed that he'd been following the conflict closely. He noted which states had seceded and those that hadn't, the violence involved and the implications: "these acts of violence have rendered *all compromise* impossible." And even more presciently he observed:

> There can be no doubt that in the early part of the struggle, the scales will be weighted in favour of the South, where the class of propertyless white adventurers provides an inexhaustible source of martial militia. In THE LONG RUN, of course, the North will be victorious since, if the need arises, it has a last card up its sleeve in the shape of a slave revolution.[31]

Lincoln's decision a year later to arm blacks, the "last card up [his] sleeve," free and unfree, to fight the slavocracy did probably prove to be decisive in the outcome of the war.[32] Marx then discussed the immediate challenge for the Union, "HOW TO GET THEIR FORCES TO THE SOUTH." Not only did he raise the issue but he went into great detail about what was involved in meeting the challenge—no doubt what Lincoln's generals were also doing. I beg the reader's indulgence to make my point.

> Even AN UNOPPOSED MARCH—in this season—of 15 MILES PER DAY, WOULD BE SOMETHING TRYING; but Charleston, the nearest attackable point is 544 miles from Washington, 681 from Philadelphia, 771 from New York and 994 from Boston, and the last three named towns are the main operational bases against the South. The distance of Montgomery, the seat of the SESSIONIST CONGRESS, from those same places is 910, 1050, 1,130 and 1,350 MILES RESPECTIVE[LY]. A cross-country march would therefore seem to be QUITE OUT OF THE QUESTION. (Use of the railways by the NORTHERN INVADERS would merely lead to their destruction.) Hence, all that remains is sea transport and naval warfare which, however, might easily lead to complications with foreign powers. This evening the English government is to announce in the Commons what ATTITUDE it intends to adopt in such an eventuality.[33]

I promise not to go into this kind of detail henceforth. I do so here only to underscore how seriously from the beginning Marx and his partner took the developments on the other side of the Atlantic.[34] Clearly, given what he wrote, Marx was reading intensely to get up to speed to understand what a Union victory required. And only someone who had once been on the barricades—in the German theater of the European Spring— would want to know such logistical specificity. Also remarkable is that the letter was written immediately after two months of travel in Europe to deal mainly with his persistently precarious financial situation.

About a month later, on June 9, Mill responded to a compliment from a publisher in Philadelphia about his recently published book *Representative Government*, saying that "it was flattering to any author" to receive such accolades. But he begged off, due to other commitments, he said, writing something on the topic that the publisher had requested. In what could have been his first opportunity to do so in writing, Mill, for whatever reason didn't see the need in his reply to express his awareness of the existential crisis the Republic was facing.

Only on August 18 did he do so. It was in response to an up-and-coming scholar who more than anyone would motivate Mill to engage with the Civil War. John Elliot Cairnes sent Mill a copy of a manuscript he'd written on the political economy of U.S. slavery. Mill was impressed because, unlike "nearly all the writing which has appeared in England about the American disruption," Cairnes argued convincingly that contra "English organs of opinion [that] cry out for a recognition of the secession, and for letting slavery alone" that wasn't possible. The problem was that "slavery will not let freedom alone. As you have shewn, more powerfully than had been done before, American slavery depends upon a perpetual extension of its field; it must go on barbarizing the world more and more, and the Southern states will never consent to a peace without half of the unoccupied country, and the power which it would give of unlimited conquest towards the south. Instead of calling on the North to subscribe to this, it would be a case for a crusade of all civilized humanity to prevent it." In no uncertain terms, therefore, Mill declared for the first time his opposition to most English ruling-class opinion on the War. He then advised Cairnes to "connect" the proposed article "with the present crisis, and make [it], in effect, a pamphlet on that." This, then, was Mill's first effort to challenge his own ruling elite on its not too subtle support for the slavocracy about which, as he told Cairnes, he "felt ashamed and grieved."[35] In his *Autobiography* years later, he admitted that he was taken aback by "the rush of nearly the whole upper and middle classes of my own country, even those who passed for Liberals, into a furious pro-Southern partisanship: the working classes, and some of the literary and scientific men, being almost the sole exceptions to the general frenzy."[36] But months would pass before Mill himself would take a public stance.

Meanwhile Marx and Engels launched a campaign to win support for the Union through their journalistic endeavors. They agreed on a division of labor; Marx would focus on the political economy of the War while Engels would employ his expertise in military matters to focus on that dimension. On June 12, three days after Mill's suggestion to Cairnes, Engels responded to Marx's request for an overview of the military situation. Basically, he argued, the North was in a more favorable position in terms of mustering the largest number of soldiers. "For everyman the South can still produce, the North will produce three or four. ... Man for man, there is no question that the people from the North are markedly superior to those from the South, both physically and morally."[37]

Marx and Engels had access for about the first year and a half of the War to the *New York Daily Tribune*, Marx alone to *Die Presse*, a liberal daily in Vienna, and Engels to the Manchester weekly *Volunteer Journal for Lancashire and Cheshire* for the duration. Marx's first, and one of his longest, articles in the *Tribune* was written on September 18. His main task was to challenge the self-serving views of organs like *The Economist* and *The Times*. Because the Lincoln administration hadn't declared so far that the war against the secessionists was to be one to abolish slavery but to only maintain the Union, its side, therefore, had no redeeming features to merit support. But that ignored, Marx pointedly wrote the official declarations of the slavocracy for the rebellion: "to fight for the liberty of slaving other people. ... If Anti-Slavery and idealistic England felt not attracted by the profession of the North, how came it to pass that it was not violently repulsed by the cynical confessions of the South?" As Marx knew and would later point out, British capital and its mouthpieces in the press gave backhanded support to the Confederacy exactly because they had a material interest in it being victorious—the continuous supply of the commodity upon which England's enormously important textile industry rested, cotton picked by slaves and, thus, cheap.

Marx's point about the Confederacy engaged in a "fight for the liberty of slaving others" comes close to what Mill wrote to Cairnes a month earlier about the fundamental problem with slavery in America—it "will not let freedom alone" because it was about "slaving others." Again, both Marx and Mill were clearly on the same political page.

But hadn't the North, charged *The Economist* and others, been complicit for decades in enabling "the peculiar institution"? To refute this claim Marx had to display a deep understanding of the Republic's history. "The progressive abuse of the Union by the slave power, working through its alliance with the Northern Democratic Party, is, so to say, the general formula of the United States history since the beginning of this century." Through a series of political compromises over the decades, such as the Missouri Compromise and the Kansas–Nebraska Act, the North was forced to be complicit in defending the slavocracy.[38] But, claimed Marx, "the attentive observer of history could not but see that every new advance of the slave power was a step forward to its defeat." Those victories of the slave power, in other words, were only one side of the story. The inattentive—operating at the level of appearances—failed to see "the violent clash of the antagonistic forces, the friction of which was the moving power of its history for half a century." Crucial evidence for Marx was "the formation of the Republican party" in 1854 and the "large vote" its presidential candidate John Frémont got in 1856, "palpable proofs that the North had accumulated sufficient energies to rectify the aberrations which United States history, under the slaveowners' pressure, had undergone, for half a century, and to make it return to the true principles of its development." Precisely because the Marx Party had been active in the accumulation of antislavery forces in the Republican Party could Marx know from afar what the bourgeois press in Britain didn't—the building resistance to the slavocracy. Also, unmistakably and pedagogically on display was Marx's dialectical materialist approach for political analysis— "the violent clash of antagonistic forces."

Marx also had to address the charge of the anti-Northern British press that the war was merely about the "limitation of the institution of Slavery to States where the institution already exists" and not about its abolition and, thus, not worthy of support. But *The Economist*, he instructively retorted, had published a series of articles in 1859 that argued that "by dint of an *economical law*, American Slavery was doomed to a gradual extinction from the moment it was deprived of its power of expansion."

He then quoted a Southern Congressman in a speech later that year in the House of Representatives who threatened secession if indeed that would happen. If *The Economist* and others were really sincere about being for abolition, then they should support the Lincoln administration which came into office on the platform of limiting the expansion of slavery because that would effectively be "a constitutional way" of ending the institution. Such a solution would avoid the other option, quoting the newspaper, of "'the desperate expedient of proclaiming Negro emancipation and summoning the slaves to a general insurrection' ... a thing 'the mere conception of which ... is repulsive and dreadful'." Marx obviously reveled in his sarcasm. Also to be noted is that contra Mill's claim about what Cairnes had written, namely, "you have shewn, more powerfully than had been done before, American slavery depends upon a perpetual extension of its field," someone else in *The Economist* in 1859 had already done so.

At the end Marx hinted, drawing extensively on a liberal organ, that the real motive of the anti-Northern press in Britain was its hope that the sectional conflict would debilitate the United States and, thus, "draw out of [their] side the thorn of American rivalry."[39] In other words, nothing more was at play in the overwhelming support of the mainstream bourgeois press for the Confederacy than short-term material interests.

In subsequent articles Marx would elaborate on many of the key points he made in his first public stance on the Civil War. Most significantly, the *Tribune* article appeared in the most widely read newspaper in the United States. That the paper's "occasional correspondent" in London was none other than Marx and that the president of the United States, Abraham Lincoln, was one of the newspaper's loyal readers was of an order of importance for this chapter that can't be overstated. In all likelihood it was from Marx that most U.S. citizens first learned about the duplicity of the English press regarding the War. That would not be of little importance three weeks after his article was published. Whether Mill would have a similar impact remains to be seen.

About a month later Marx wrote two major articles on the War for *Die Presse*. Unlike for the *Tribune*'s readership it required him to explain why the conflict erupted. The "*slave question*," he argued convincingly, was the basic reason. Again, the "economic law" of slavery required its expansion into new territories to survive. And every territory that entered the Union as a slave state strengthened via the Senate the power of the slave owners. The election of Lincoln on a platform that called for limiting slavery to where it already existed was seen as an existential threat to their interests. Thus their decision to play "*va banque* [go bank]," that is, risk everything by seceding and firing on Fort Sumter.[40]

In a companion article Marx took on the claim of British anti-Northern sentiment that the solution to the conflict was simply to let the South secede. With ample evidence, such as how the ratio of slave to free persons in states affected pro- or anti-Confederacy sentiment, he countered that "the war of the Southern Confederacy is in the true sense of the word a war of conquest for the spread and perpetuation of slavery. ... Were it to relinquish its plans of conquest, the Southern Confederacy would relinquish its capacity to live and the purpose of secession." And then Marx, the historical materialist, made his key point: "The present struggle between the South and North is, therefore, nothing but a struggle between two social systems, the system of slavery and the system of free labour. The struggle has broken out because the two systems can no longer live peacefully side by side on the North American continent." And most prophetically, "It can only be ended by the victory of one system or the other. ... Events themselves drive to the promulgation of the decisive slogan— *emancipation of the slaves.*"[41] Despite Lincoln's reluctance to see what had to be done, Marx, armed with his theoretical perspective, accurately foresaw the President's history-making action a year later—the issuance of the Emancipation Proclamation.

Marx's point to his uncle in May about sea transportation and the "complications with foreign powers" was more prescient than he probably realized. On November 8, three weeks after the appearance of his first *Tribune* article, the seizure of two Confederate officials by a U.S. warship from a British ship, the *Trent*, almost led to war between the Union and Britain. Given the already anti-Northern British press, Marx had to swing into action in defense of the Union to oppose the nationalistic war drums beating in England. That also meant counseling moderation on the other side of the Atlantic, especially since Lincoln's Secretary of State Seward, as he told *Die Presse* readers, operated with a "characteristic act of tactlessness by self-conscious weakness simulating strength."[42] To the *Tribune* readers—one of whom, again, was Lincoln—he pointed out on December 19 that the seizure of the two Confederate officials was likely a "violation of maritime law" and warned that war with Britain would "do the work of the Secessionists" and that the Union could not prevail against the "overwhelming maritime power" of England.[43] A month later the imbroglio was settled pacifically with the release of the two Confederates. Whether Marx's advice for moderation was consequential in any way can only be cause for speculation. More certain is that he acted as if he could affect what was potentially a decisive moment in the course of the War. On display was real-time analysis not just for its own sake but for political impact.

In what turned out to be Marx's last wartime dispatch to the *Tribune*—domestic news about the War increasingly crowded out international affairs that correspondents like Marx supplied—he was also strategic. His February 1, 1862, article, "English Public Opinion," revealed its purpose in the very second sentence: "It ought never to be forgotten in the United States that at least the *working classes* of England, from the commencement to the termination of the difficulty [the *Trent* affair], have never forsaken them ... despite the poisonous stimulants daily administered by a venal and reckless press, not one single public war meeting could be held in the United Kingdom during all the period that peace trembled in the balance ... simple justice requires to pay a tribute to the sound attitude of the British working classes, the more so when contrasted with the hypocritical, bullying, cowardly, and stupid conduct of the official and well-to-do John Bull."[44] Dan Doyle suggests that the reason Marx no longer had access to the *Tribune* after this dispatch is because of the increasingly obvious political intent of his reportage that publisher Horace Greely found unappealing.[45] He may be right given the thrust of the article. If so, it means that Marx was willing to sacrifice a relatively secure income stream in order to advocate his politics. His risk-taking may have paid off big time three years later—as will be seen—with regard to at least one of the *Tribune* readers.

By the time Mill finally wrote something on the War, Marx had already published 18 articles—with Engels sometimes as ghost writer—dealing directly or indirectly with the War. He probably wrote more because *Die Presse* published only about half of the articles he sent to it of which it can be assumed that a number were about the War.[46] And the Marx–Engels correspondence regarding the War was equally rich.[47] Keep in mind, again, that Marx was also doing research for and writing his magnum opus—and, as always, trying to keep a roof over the heads of his family. The War took a toll not only on his finances but on Engels's as well.

MILL TAKES A PUBLIC STANCE

Why did it take Mill so long to get something into print, in February 1862? As already noted in his letter to Cairnes in August 1861, he opposed the pro-Confederacy attitude of most of ruling-class England and felt it needed to be challenged. In November he told Cairnes: "It seems to me that what will most help to give a better direction to public opinion, is that persons of talent, the more known and respected the better, should put themselves forward ostensibly, and even what in different circumstances might be called ostentatiously, as champions of the right view of the subject."[48] So, why hadn't he written anything to rectify the situation given his standing in intellectual circles? His later *Autobiography* offers an answer. "I was on the point of adding my words to" the opposition of the few others who had spoken out "when there occurred, towards the end of 1861, the seizure of the Southern envoys on board a British vessel, by an officer of the United States." That engendered a chauvinistic response and

> war-like preparations actually commenced on this side. While this state of things lasted there was no chance of a hearing for anything favourable to the American cause; and moreover I agreed with those who thought the act unjustifiable and such as to require that England should demand its disavowal. When the disavowal came, and the alarm of war was over, I wrote, in January 1862, the paper, in *Fraser's Magazine*, entitled "The Contest in America." And I shall always feel grateful to my daughter that her urgency prevailed on me to write it when I did: for we were then on the point of setting out for a journey of some months in Greece and Turkey, and but for her, I should have deferred writing till our return.[49]

A real-time letter to Cairnes on January 20, 1862, confirms that it was the *Trent* imbroglio that caused writer's block on Mill's part.[50] But that explanation raises more questions than answers. Debate and controversy about the War in England broke out almost immediately as Marx's letter to his uncle in May noted. Mill suggested the same in his letter to Cairnes in August. But the *Trent* controversy began in the second week in November. Again, why hadn't Mill written anything before then as did Marx? A perusal of his correspondence reveals that the War simply wasn't on his radar. Unlike Marx he had other priorities, largely intellectual and personal. It's true that he was writing a major work, *An Examination of Sir William Hamilton's Philosophy*, but so was Marx. His admission that his step-daughter Helen had to convince him to get something into print before going on their European trip lends credence to this interpretation.

But more intriguing from the perspective of this inquiry is Mill's admission that he thought he couldn't get "a hearing for anything favourable to the American cause" as long as the *Trent* matter hadn't been settled amicably. If accurate and not just self-serving, then what was it about Mill that disinclined him to publicly challenge prevailing opinion? Fear of alienating friends or breaking with one's own circle? Shortly before his *Fraser* article appeared he wrote that it was "likely to be much attacked."[51] According to friend Alexander Bain, he expected that it would "give great offence, and to be the most hazardous thing for his influence that he had yet done."[52] The implications are significant because politics requires a willingness to make personal breaks if necessary. Just at the moment when Mill, arguably Britain's most respected intellectual, could have played a major role in the most consequential movement for the democratic quest in his lifetime—the overthrow of chattel slavery in the United States—he opted for silence. Luckily the *Trent* affair was settled amicably without him. But in the depths of the crisis that wasn't certain. A Union war with Britain, as Marx correctly noted, would have been manna from heaven for the slavocracy.

Perhaps the answer to Mill's passivity is what he admitted three decades earlier to a friend in the midst of the upheavals in Britain leading to the 1832 Reform Act. Again, he found it "best to lie by and let the tempest blow over … [because] in fact I am myself often surprised how little I really care about [politics]." The contrast to Marx's response couldn't, once again, be more striking. Marx employed every resource at his disposal to try to challenge ruling-class opinion in order to shape the outcome of the dispute. It's hard to imagine Karl Marx being reluctant to break personal ties if necessary to advance what he thought was in the interest of the class struggle. He had already burned many bridges to his class—committed "class suicide" as African revolutionary Amilcar Cabral once put it—and unlike Mill he had had two decades of the rough and tumble game of politics under his belt. And while it's true that he didn't have "as much to lose" in England as did Mill in terms of personal capital, can there be any doubt what he would have done if he thought necessary to do so? His willingness to risk a source of desperately needed income, from *Tribune* publisher Horace Greeley, in order to advance his political agenda suggests what the answer is.

Whatever the case for the delay, Mill's article "The Contest in America" appeared in the February 1862 issue of one of the leading British literary venues—after the *Trent* dispute had been settled. The eleven-page article began with the admission that he hadn't said anything until then because of the dispute; "we," that is, England, "had, indeed, been wronged." And if the United States had gotten away with the transgression it would have invited "a constant succession of insults and injuries from the same and every other quarter." And he recognized that going to war with the Union risked aiding and abetting "a powerful republic, devoted not only to slavery, but to pro-slavery propagation … [to] spreading slavery wherever migration or force could carry it." Mill said he "shudders" to think if war had occurred and how it would be seen by history: "England stepped in, and, for the sake of cotton, made Satan victorious." So after establishing his nationalist credentials Mill then got to the heart of the matter—what was so problematic with the pro-Confederacy sentiment of Britain's ruling elite. And on this dimension, that the slave owners weren't willing to be confined to the states where the institution existed but needed to disseminate it to keep it alive, he and Marx, as already seen, were in agreement.

Like Marx did in his first *Tribune* article in September 1861, Mill disputed the line of the pro-Confederacy crowd that the War wasn't about slavery. To the contrary, he pointedly noted. The secession was due solely to the fear of the slave owners that the election of Lincoln spelled the eventual end of the "peculiar institution." And for that reason, the South would have to be militarily defeated to end the institution; "it will require a succession of humiliations to bring them to that." As for whether the North would be victorious, "I cannot tell," Mill wrote. But they certainly had the greater potential for doing so, especially in "encouraging [the South's] slaves to desert"—what Marx called, it may be remembered, the North playing "the last card up its sleeve." In anticipation of the Emancipation Proclamation eight months away, "Congress will very soon make up its mind to declare all slaves free who belong to persons in arms against the Union." Most significantly, however, it would be Lincoln's executive order and not Congress that would make that possible; Congress would later act in passing the 13th amendment. A new constitutional order, Mill astutely pointed out, would be required, particularly getting rid of the infamous "three-fifths" compromise—what the 14th amendment would do.

Mill ended his first public pronouncement with an unabashed defense of war against the slave owners and in opposition to those in England calling for peace: "war, in a good cause, is not the greatest evil a nation can face. … As long as justice and injustice have not terminated *their* ever renewing fight for ascendancy in the affairs of mankind, human beings must be willing, when need is, to do battle for the one against the other."[53] Not for the first time, as already noted, that Mill struck a tone reminiscent of the opening lines of the *Communist Manifesto*. Though Marx had made similar arguments six months earlier, there is no reason to assume that Mill was aware of his articles in the *Tribune*. His own track record on the subject allowed him to reach similar positions independently of Marx.

Despite the fact that the article incurred the wrath of pro-Confederacy voices, as he anticipated, it helped, he later wrote in his *Autobiography*, "to encourage those Liberals who had felt overborne by the tide of illiberal opinion, and to form in favour of the good cause a nucleus of opinion which increased gradually, and after the success of the North began to seem probable."[54] In the opinion of one latter-day account, the article was "'the most far-seeing and challenging paper that had yet been written by an Englishman on the American question'."[55] Since Marx wasn't an "Englishman" the claim may be accurate.

Just as liberals were gathering their courage, after receiving the signal from their leading figure, the English working class, Marx told *Die Presse* readers—as he had told *Tribune* readers a couple of weeks earlier—was displaying its valor once again. English history, he argued, revealed that "extra-parliamentary demonstrations" had always played in one way or another a decisive role in key moments in the country's political history and that was no less the case this time—in staying the hand of Britain in intervening on behalf of the Confederacy. His report on an anti-interventionist working-class meeting in London provided more details.[56] Thus while Marx and Mill could agree on ends, the need to end slavery and slave owner power, they differed profoundly on means, specifically, which social force to look to for its realization. For Mill it was "persons of talent, the more known and respected the better." In other words, the milieu in which he operated. For Marx it was the working class. The most recent scholarship shows that it was a combination of reformist middle-class forces—none of whom seemed to belong to Mill's circles—and working-class anti-interventionist mobilizations that dissuaded the Liberal Lord Palmerston government from going to war with the Union.[57]

MARX CONTINUES THE "STRUGGLE IN THE PRESS"

Nine months would pass before Mill published anything else on the War. In the meantime Marx wrote ten articles dealing directly with it, including a major one with Engels, and all for *Die Presse*, the only organ he now had access to. He also continued his rich correspondence with Engels about the War and other matters, not the least being the writing of *Capital*. A number of important developments in the conflict took place that he addressed, all leading up to what proved to be the decisive moment in the War. Since all of them, except for the last, escaped Mill's attention—which is telling—the treatment here, in chronological order, will be largely cursory.[58]

The anti-interventionist movement in England continued to attract Marx's attention. He seized upon any evidence that showed it was having an impact. It should be noted that in addition to articles on the Civil War, Marx wrote a number of articles on the Hapsburg intervention in Mexico at that moment, encouraged by the dictator Louis Bonaparte in France and with implications for the American theater. Marx was clearly trying to get his *Die Presse* readers to emulate the "indestructible staunchness of the English popular masses" that had stilled the hand of British imperialism from intervening in the American theater, that is, to do the same vis-à-vis the Hapsburgs for their adventure into Mexico.

The progress of the War garnered, understandably, most of Marx's reportage. He applauded Lincoln's decision in February to demote the feckless General George McClellan from Commander-in-Chief to merely General of the Potomac Army. "*President Lincoln* never ventures a step forward before the tide of circumstances and the general call of public opinion forbid further delay. But once 'Old Abe' realizes that such a turning point has been reached, he surprises friend and foe alike by a sudden operation executed as noiselessly as possible"[59]—a characterization that accurately presaged Lincoln's most consequential decision a few months later.

When Washington and London signed the Treaty for the Suppression of the African Slave Trade in April, Marx approvingly reported that a "mortal blow has been dealt the Negro trade by this Anglo-American Treaty—the result of the American Civil War." And even more promising was a Congressional bill to criminalize the internal slave trade in the United States. It would "paralyse the trade that the states raising Negroes (border slave states) are carrying on with the states consuming Negroes (the slave states proper)."[60]

"The capture of New Orleans" in May, Marx and Engels reported, was "distinguished as an almost unparalleled act of valour on the part of the [Union] fleet."[61] But the optimism that came with the victory soon gave way to pessimism, especially on the part of Engels, as the Confederacy racked up a few victories or held Union armies to a stalemate. That turn of events provoked the only known political disagreement between Marx and Engels and lasted for a couple of years. It revealed that the historical materialist framework that both employed to read such developments as the War was not intended to be an "all-purpose formula of a general historico-philosophical theory"—as Marx would insist years later[62]—to explaining social reality. It required looking at the big picture, the less than obvious, the dialectic of developments, singularity and nuance. To his partner, whose pessimism stemmed from what had been happening on the battle-field, Marx wrote in September 1862: "It strikes me that you allow yourself to be influenced by the military ASPECT of things A LITTLE TOO MUCH."[63]

In a related article Marx pointed to the less than obvious developments in the War. Things had gone well for the South only because, in his opinion, Lincoln had been reluctant so far to do what was necessary for victory. His desire to appease the "'loyal' slaveowners" in the border states that were still in the Union prevented him from putting "a company of Negroes in the field" to address the need of more recruits for the War and, thus, inscribing "the battle-slogan of 'Abolition of Slavery!' on the star-spangled banner."[64] But because the situation was tottering on the edge between victory and defeat Lincoln would now be forced to do exactly that. "So far, we have only witnessed the first act of the Civil War—the *constitutional* waging of war. The second act, the *revolutionary* waging of war, is at hand."[65] Few forecasts in the Marx–Engels corpus proved to be as prescient.

When Lincoln issued the first edition of his Emancipation Proclamation, arguably the decisive moment in the War, about a month later, on September 22, 1862, Marx was understandably impressed. His method allowed him to make one of the most complimentary comments ever about the American experiment:

Lincoln is a *sui generis* figure in the annals of history. ... He gives his most important actions always the most commonplace form. ... His latest proclamation, which is drafted in the same style, the manifesto abolishing slavery, is the most important document in American history since the establishment of the Union, tantamount to the tearing up of the old American constitution. ... Lincoln's place in the history of the United States and of mankind will ... be next to that of Washington! ... Lincoln is not the product of a popular revolution. This plebian ... an average person of good will, was placed at the top by the interplay of the forces of universal suffrage unaware of the great issues at stake. The new world has never achieved a greater triumph than by this demonstration that, given its political and social organization, ordinary people of good will can accomplish feats which only heroes could accomplish in the old world![66]

Marx's articles revealed just how intimately familiar he was—assisted by his partner—with the details about the American theater and, thus, the research needed to be so informed. To fully appreciate what he was doing, it's useful to provide a glimpse of the broader quotidian context in which he worked at that moment. Marx, after all, was human with all of the baggage and obligations that come with that and to not do so would result in a partial portrait of what it meant for him to be political. His letter to Engels in June 1862 is touchingly revealing. After recounting the depressing challenges his wife Jenny had to deal with regarding their very precarious financial situation, he told Engels: "I feel all the more sorry for the unfortunate children in that all of this is happening during the EXHIBITION SEASON [London's version of the world's fair], when their friends are having fun, whereas they themselves live in dread lest someone should come and see them and realize what a mess they are in."

Yet, there was the other side to him, the multitasking Marx, as he explained further to Engels. "I myself, by the 'by, am working away hard and strange to say, my grey matter is functioning better in the midst of the surrounding *misère* than it has done for years. I am expanding this volume [second draft of *Capital*], since those German scoundrels estimate the value of a book in terms of its cubic capacity."[67] The more challenges, the more productive it seems that Marx was—perhaps a core characteristic.

MILL'S SECOND AND LAST PUBLIC STANCE

Mill, who was on vacation in Europe at the time of Lincoln's Emancipation Proclamation, was also impressed. It caused him to break away from his routine and to comment to correspondents on the significance of Lincoln's action:

> Mr. Lincoln's anti-slavery proclamation, which no American, I think, can have received with more exultation than I did. It is of the highest importance, & more so because the manifest reluctance with which the President made up his mind to that decided step indicates that the progress of opinion in the country had reached the point of seeing its necessity for the effectual prosecution of the war. ... In England, the Proclamation has only increased the venom of those who after taunting you so long with caring nothing for Abolition, now reproach you for your Abolitionism as the worst of your crimes.[68]

About a year later he commented incisively on Lincoln in a way he had not before:

> Mr. Lincoln appears to me a very favourable specimen of an American public man, and a credit to the nation which elected him, as he seems to be simply honest without any trick or charlatanerie. He is the 'rusticus abnormis sapiens' whom America has not taught us to expect to find among her politicians, even when they have commenced life as rail splitters. That which a great man, in his position, would have foreseen and designed from the first, he, without designing it, has in the main executed, through the force of circumstances gradually shaping the conviction of a sincere and upright mind. He is an example [of] how far single[-]minded honesty will often go, in doing the work and supplying the place of talent.[69]

His point about the "force of circumstances" resonated with Marx's point about "the interplay of the forces of universal suffrage unaware of the great issues at stake." But for Mill the focus was on Lincoln the "honest" individual. For Marx it was on the circumstances that allowed someone like Lincoln to flower.

Mill's quotidian reality stood in dramatic contrast to that of Marx. His was clearly a more privileged world. Retired from the East India Company with a comfortable pension it allowed him comforts such as annual months-long vacations in his beloved France that weren't available to

Marx. A note from France in November 1861 to a friend in London is especially revealing:

> Life here is uneventful, and feels like a perpetual holiday. It is one of the great privileges of advanced civilization, that while keeping out of the turmoil and depressing wear of life, one can have brought to one's doors all that is agreeable or stimulating in the activities of the outward world, by newspapers, new books, periodicals, &c. It is, in truth, too self-indulgent a life for any one to allow himself whose duties lie among his fellow-beings, unless, as is fortunately the case with me, they are mostly such as can be better fulfilled at a distance from their society, than in the midst of it.[70]

In theory, the "distance from their society"—the last thing Marx desired—should have made it easier for him to "fulfill duties" to "his fellow-beings," in this case writing on behalf of the Union cause. And he certainly had more opportunities than Marx to get into print in Britain. But that wasn't the case. When he returned from his European trip he wrote what would be his last significant public piece on the American events.

"The Slave Power," published in the October 1862 issue of *Westminster Review*, was basically a review of Cairnes's book by the same name: *The Slave Power: Its Character, Career, and Probable Designs: Being an Attempt to Explain the Real Issues Involved in the American Contest*. About twenty pages in length it expertly distilled the book whose main thesis—the political economy of slavery required that it expand in order to survive, a political system to advance that end and, hence, the real reason for secession—he had already publicized in his "Contest in America" article nine months earlier.

For Mill it was another opportunity to challenge the pro-Confederacy stance of Britain's ruling elite. In so doing he sought to explain the reasons for their partisanship. But he cast the question not about the elite but about "England." As opposed to elsewhere in Europe, for example France, "Why is England an exception" in its pro-Confederacy leanings, "a sad aberration of English feeling at this momentous crisis"? If those who were assumed to be the most-informed segment of English society are so persuaded, then "what could be expected from the public?" So posed, the question betrayed Mill's own ruling elite/nationalist outlook—in telling contrast to that of Marx. England the nation was his starting point rather than the classes that composed England as a nation. Mill's shortsightedness allowed him to subordinate the largely working-class anti-interventionist movement from below that effectively stilled the hand of British imperialism's possible intervention in the War on behalf of the Confederacy, and that he certainly knew about, to his near obsession with the "England" of the ruling class—why he could feel "ashamed" and "grieved" about his country.[71]

Despite Mill's class blinders, Cairnes's book and his review were valuable ammunition in countering the duplicity of *The Economist* crowd. The problem is that by the time of their appearance in October 1862, the needs of the pro-Union cause in England had changed; a year or so earlier both texts would have been especially useful. But once Lincoln issued his Emancipation Proclamation on September 22, 1862, a central claim of the pro-Confederacy crowd was undermined, namely, that the War wasn't about the abolition of slavery. The Proclamation did more to win mass support to the Union cause than any erudite academic treatise and glowing review of it could ever have done. The task now was to understand the course of the War and probability of success for the Union—about which Mill had nothing to say publicly and only occasionally in private.

Stefan Collini, in his "Introduction" to the volume of the CWJSM in which "The Slave Power" article is reproduced, raises an interesting question about Mill's methodology vis-à-vis that of Marx:

> [I]t is worth noting that Cairnes himself recorded that his purpose had initially been of "a purely speculative kind—my object being to show that the course of history is largely determined by the action of economic causes." … But it is perhaps more surprising that [Mill] should let Cairnes' historical materialism pass without comment, since Mill was in general so concerned to insist that moral and intellectual rather than economic causes are the motor of history. He presumably felt that this was no time to be parading differences over the finer points of method; brothers-in-arms have more important things to do than criticizing the cut of each other's armour.[72]

I leave aside whether Cairnes employed a "historical materialism" perspective. My prior comment about Marx's and Engels's methodology—in relation to their year or more debate on the prospects for the Union—argues that it entailed much more than reading history as "largely determined by the action of economic causes." What Collini raises, however, allows for consideration of whether Marx and Mill were aware of each other's work.

Nothing I've found indicates that Mill knew anything about Marx other than his involvement—to be seen later—in what would be later called the First International. Marx, on the other hand, had read Mill's *Principles of Political Economy* years earlier and was evidently unimpressed. "On the level plain simple mounds," as he cuttingly put it about the book, "look like hills; and the imbecile flatness of the present bourgeoisie is to be measured by the altitude of its great intellects."[73] Later, he encouraged and assisted a working-class member of the Marx party, Johann Eccarius, to write in 1866, a critique of the latest edition of Mill's book. As intended, the critique was apparently well received in working-class circles.[74] Mill for Marx was sardonically "the Prophet Himself," and "the 8th sage of the world."[75] In that very moment, Marx was working untiringly—details to come shortly—to get the English working class to stop bowing to "their betters" and to look to itself for advancing its interests (see Appendix for more details).

Years later about his review of Cairnes's book Mill wrote:

> England is paying the penalty, in many uncomfortable ways, of the durable resentment which her ruling classes stirred up in the United States by their ostentatious wishes for the ruin of America as a nation; they have reason to be thankful that a few, if only a few known writers and speakers, standing firmly by the Americans in the time of their greatest difficulty, effected a partial diversion of these bitter feelings, and made Great Britain not altogether odious to the Americans.[76]

In Mill's vision only a "few known writers and speakers" saved his nation from shame. Working-class masses as protagonists of history and decisive in stilling British imperialism's hand in intervening on behalf of the slavocracy simply weren't on his radar. Whether he counted Marx among the illuminati of the "few" is unknown. Except for an occasional letter to be read at an event, this would be his last public writing on the War that still hung in the balance for another two years.[77]

THE FINAL YEARS OF THE WAR AND AFTERWARD

Without a journalistic venue to air and promote their views on the War, Marx and Engels seemed fated to only share their thoughts with each other and close contacts. Marx, however, found near the end of 1864 a singular way to break out of the public isolation which he seemed to have been confined to after the *Tribune* and *Die Presse* were no longer available to him. Mill, on the other hand, remained largely silent before the public. Only through his correspondence are his thoughts about the final years of the War and afterward known.

An advantage Marx and Engels had vis-à-vis Mill is that they had a party member actively engaged on the ground, literally, the battlefield. The occasional letters to the two of them from Weydemeyer, the ersatz head of the Marx party in the United States, were invaluable. As a Union colonel in the Missouri theater and close contact of one-time Republican presidential candidate John Frémont—a potential rival to Lincoln for his renomination in 1864—Weydemeyer supplied his two comrades with priceless intelligence about both the political and military progress of the War. Only by the summer of 1864, owing to Union victories, did Engels begin to come around to his partner's more optimistic assessment about Union prospects. Mill, too—based on his correspondence—remained optimistic about the eventual outcome.[78] The recruitment and deployment of black troops by Lincoln in the second half of 1863 was likely decisive in the turnaround. Both Marx and Mill had been in agreement for some time that Lincoln's "last card up his sleeve" option, as Marx put it, would improve Union fortunes.[79]

In March 1863, Marx attended an anti-interventionist meeting in London that in hindsight paved the way for his most public actions ever; Mill too was there and, unusually for him, was one of the speakers.[80] The meeting along with prior ones in Manchester and Lancashire registered the increasing degree to which English workers saw the need to have their own foreign policy. The class divide around the Civil War and other international issues was palpable. That's the sentiment that gave birth in September 1864 in London to the International Workingmen's Association (IWA) or, to be called later, the First International. Within weeks Marx emerged as its indefatigable de facto leader.[81] The press attention to the organization gave Marx media access he'd never had before and over time international renown for the first time. This is how Mill first came into contact with Marx.[82]

A couple of weeks prior to the IWA's foundation the American presidential election attracted attention. Marx and Engels sensed correctly that it would be arguably the most consequential election in U.S. history. "I consider the present moment, *entre nous*," Marx wrote to Engels on September 7, 1864, "to be extremely critical. If Grant suffers a major defeat, or Sherman wins a major victory, SO ALL RIGHT". … I fully agree with you that to date, Lincoln's re-election is pretty well assured. ... But election time in a country which is the archetype of democratic humbug is full of hazards that might unexpectedly defy the logic of events." One uncertainty was whether the Confederacy would try to sue for some kind of amnesty. The fact that they were now treating "Negro soldiers as 'prisoners of war'" gave that option credence. "[T]here is no mistaking the fact that during the next 8 weeks ... much will depend on military eventualities. This is undoubtedly the most critical moment since the beginning of the war. ... Should Lincoln succeed this time—as is highly probable—it will be on a far more radical PLATFORM and in completely CHANGED CIRCUMSTANCES. Then the old man will lawyer-fashion, find that more radical methods are compatible with his conscience."[83]

Because news of Sherman's capture of Atlanta on September 2 was now known in London, Mill had even more reason to feel optimistic a month later. "But everything," in a letter to Cairnes on October 7, "depends upon the reelection of Lincoln, or at all events upon the election of some one representing the same opinions and who will continue the same policy. It is impossible not to feel uneasy until the election is over."[84] He didn't elaborate as Marx had to Engels on the "hazards that might unexpectedly defy the logic of events."

News of Lincoln's reelection elated all pro-Union partisans in England. The IWA commissioned Marx to write a congratulatory message to him on its behalf. "We congratulate the American people upon your re-election by a large majority. If resistance to the Slave Power was the reserved watchword of your first election, the triumphant war cry of your re-election is, Death to Slavery."[85] In a letter that pedagogically distilled his historical materialist perspective for the American reality, Marx addressed Lincoln as "the single-minded son of the working class"; it was reprinted in both British and German newspapers.[86]

Lincoln's reply, delivered by the U.S. ambassador Charles Adams, elicited even more jubilation.[87] The organization to which Mill belonged, the London Emancipation Society, also sent a congratulatory message (it's not clear if Mill signed it) and also received a reply.[88] But unlike what Lincoln wrote to the latter his thank you reply to the IWA was distinctly less pro forma and more effusive, a difference recognized by the press.[89] As Marx later told Engels, the "difference between Lincoln's answer to us and to the bourgeoisie has created such a sensation here that the West End 'clubs' are shaking their heads at it. You can understand how gratifying that has been for our people."[90] Whether Lincoln recognized the name of one of the fifty-seven signatories to the IWA letter "*Karl Marx, Corresponding Secretary for Germany*" is uncertain. But as a long-time ardent reader of the *Tribune* it's very likely that publisher Horace Greeley at one time or another told him that the "occasional correspondent" in London was none other than Marx. More probable in having made the difference between the two replies Lincoln sent is Marx's last wartime dispatch to the *Tribune* in February 1862 that sung the praises of Britain's working classes—from which one of the epigrams that begins this article. Nothing Mill ever wrote about the War had achieved such distinction as Marx's congratulatory message to Lincoln on behalf of the IWA.

Marx's point to Engels on the eve of Lincoln's reelection about the need to "find … more radical methods" anticipated the post-War reality with particular regard to slavery and its legacy. Lincoln's history-making assassination in April 1865 provoked speculation on Marx's, Engels's and Mill's parts about whether the slavery question would be completely resolved. On behalf, once again, of the IWA Marx wrote a letter of condolence to the new president Andrew Johnson that was published in British and U.S. papers including the *Tribune*. As with his letter to Lincoln the one to Johnson had a clear political message:

> Yours … has become the task to uproot by the law what has been felled by the sword, to preside over the arduous task of political reconstruction and social regeneration. A profound sense of your great mission will save you from any compromise with stern duties … to initiate the new era of the emancipation of labour.[91]

Less tactfully, Marx explained to Engels a few days later what he was trying to get Johnson to understand about "stern duties": "Lincoln's ASSASSINATION was the most stupid act [the slave owners] could have committed. *Johnson* is STERN, INFLEXIBLE, REVENGEFUL and as a former POOR WHITE a deadly hatred or the oligarchy. He will make less fuss about these fellows, and because of the treachery, he will find the TEMPER of the North commensurate with his INTENTIONS."[92] Mill was invited evidently by one of the IWA leaders to add his name to the letter but declined saying "I should think that the initiative would be taken by friends of the cause who are in a position to act more effectually than I could."[93] One can only ponder what he meant by that response. Nevertheless, his reaction to the assassination was similar to that of Marx: "The glorious news from America is dreadfully dashed by the terrible report about Lincoln. The idea of its being true is scarcely endurable—but the cause will not suffer—may even benefit by it, now."[94] In other words, it would likely provoke even more demands in the North to be unforgiving with the rebels.

As early as January 1863 Mill began thinking about a post-slavery United States and the future for the former slaves. He was prescient in seeing the importance of an "enfranchised negro" proletariat in overcoming the baggage of slavery.[95] Cairnes was able to have published in the *Daily News* a letter Mill received from an American contact that was optimistic about such developments.[96] The hope and expectation of Marx, Engels and Mill that Johnson would be tough on the former slave owners was not to be fulfilled. In fact, he began to accommodate their interests. Mill expressed his concern within a month of Johnson's accession to the presidency in a letter to the editor of the New York *Evening Post*.[97] Marx did the same to Engels a month later: "Johnson's policy likes me not. ... The reaction has already set in in America and will soon be much fortified if the present lackadaisical attitude is not ended immediately."[98] Three weeks later, on July 15, Engels concurred: "Mr Johnson's policy is less and less to my liking, too. ... NIGGER-hatred is coming out more and more violently. ... Without COLOURED SUFFRAGE nothing can be done and Johnson is leaving it up to the defeated, the ex-slaveowners, to decide on that."[99]

The IWA decided to take action in September 1865. Its "Address to the People of the United States" was sent to all branches of the International in the United States and elsewhere. After congratulating the American people for their victory over the slavocracy, it asked to "add a word of counsel for the future":

> Injustice against a fraction of your people having been followed by such dire consequences put an end to it. Declare your fellow citizens from this day forth free and equal, without any reserve. If you refuse them citizens' rights while you exact from them citizens' duties, you will sooner or later face a new struggle which will once more drench your country in blood. The eyes of Europe and of the whole world are on your attempts at reconstruction, and foes are ever ready to sound the death-knell of republican institutions as soon as they see their opportunity. We therefore admonish you, as brothers in a common cause, to sunder all the chains of freedom, and your victory will be complete.[100]

It's not known if Marx wrote this but its message was consistent with what he and Engels had been saying in their correspondence and it is unlikely that it would have been sent, given his role in the IWA, without his approval.

Mill also wrote a letter that September to a former Union commander who too had progressive views on making former slaves full citizens. Georgios Varouxakis claims Mill knew it "was going to be published extensively in the United States." But there is no evidence that it was.[101] It's unfortunate it wasn't because his letter went into greater detail than the IWA "Address" about what it would take for "equal citizenship" for "negroes." Most significantly, Mill—yes Mill!—in anticipation of Radical Reconstruction, envisioned the need for "censorship" and a "military dictatorship" over the recalcitrant opponents of "freedom for the negroes" that might have to last for "two generations" in order that "the stain which the position of slave masters burns into the very souls of the privileged population can be expected to fade." What about the legality of such measures, he asked? "[S]cruples about legality" seem "wholly out of place. ... A state of civil war suspends all legal rights, and all social compacts, between the combatants."[102]

What Mill lacked, and what Marx had at his disposal, was an organization to publicize such radical views—by his standards certainly—to working-class masses. Mill's audience, once again, were elite opinion makers like intellectuals, newspaper editors and others who didn't always share with the masses such insider opinion—especially about the need for a "military dictatorship" to assure citizenship for the former slaves. And that is likely why his letter, contra Varouxakis, didn't get "published extensively in the United States" or elsewhere—or since then.

The one but most significant problem with Mill's much too ignored letter was his declaration that he had "too high an opinion of the intentions and feelings of the President [Johnson], and the practical good sense and determination of the American people, to believe that" the former slave power would be allowed to reimpose its rule. By November that illusion had been reinforced. An interview he had read with the President "revived my hopes; for it seems to shew that Mr. Johnson does not differ fundamentally from us; that he only hesitates on the question of time" for enfranchising blacks.[103] Mill could not have been more wrong. Johnson had made his peace with the former slave owners. In hindsight it would become clear that no individual did more to undermine America's first brief experiment in trying to realize racial equality than Johnson. Engels's point about him "leaving it up to the ... ex-slaveowners" goes a long way in explaining why Reconstruction eventually went down to bloody defeat. It would take another couple of decades for that to be clear—explaining perhaps why Marx, Engels and Mill had relatively little to say from then on about developments in America that had so occupied their attentions.

Marx could be excused from not having said more about Reconstruction. Unlike Mill he was deeply engaged in daily politics, the effective head of the IWA—empowering, in other words, the effective democrats. Also, he was putting the final touches on his magnum opus which finally appeared in 1867—the "scientific" ammunition "for the workers ... which was written only for them and for their sakes to be completed," as his wife Jenny put it shortly after its publication.[104] Only in 1869 did his financial situation improve. Engels retired from his family's business with a settlement that made it possible for the Marx household to have a degree of security it had never had before. His move to London from Manchester in 1870 allowed for even closer collaboration with his partner and his work in the IWA, especially needed when the organization would face its greatest challenge to date.

The U.S. Civil War was still on Marx's mind six years later when the proletariat of Paris took to the barricades once more. For the first time anywhere they seized state power—the Commune of Paris in 1871. They did, in other words, what their cohorts were unable to do in 1848. Marx correctly anticipated that a working-class uprising in Paris was a possibility in 1870–1871 but advised revolutionary restraint; the Parisian proletariat lacked the requisite leadership and necessary allies beyond the city to hold power. Despite a warning unheeded, Marx and Engels and their entire households immediately sprang into action in support of the Communards from London.[105] But increasingly isolated from the rest of France, the peasantry in particular, the Commune went down to bloody defeat after two and a half months in power. Estimates vary but at least 30,000 Parisian workers were executed by the counterrevolutionary forces—far more than any number of those who met the fate of the guillotine in the heady days of Paris circa 1793. The task then for communists was to draw a balance sheet on what had occurred in order for workers to be more successful in their next attempt at taking state power (lessons Lenin—in anticipation of the next chapter—absorbed to his very core). Marx's *Civil War in France* did just that—not unlike his *Eighteenth Brumaire* had done for the upheaval in France in 1848—and became the most popular of his writings in his lifetime; its title wasn't fortuitous. The only correction he and Engels ever made to the *Manifesto* was a product of the lessons he distilled about the Commune.

Just as Mill was at a loss for words when the French edition of the European Spring turned sour, its winter, he had little to say about the Commune, and all after the fact. Sincerely pained about the blood bath that unfolded, he replied when asked by the IWA to lend his name to the defense of Parisian political refugees in England from the long arm of the French government as follows: "I hardly know anything I would not do to support such a demonstration. But I have no hope of any such blessed results"—perhaps why he offered no more than condolences, in correspondence, to the martyrs of Paris.[106] The contrast with Marx, again, could hardly have been more different. Two years later he would be in his grave, a decade before Marx.

CONCLUSION

There are four main points to be made in comparing Marx and Engels to Mill in relation to the U.S. Civil War and its immediate aftermath.

First, if Tocqueville, as the prior chapter reveals, placed himself—literally—on the other side of the barricades from Marx and Engels in the European Spring of 1848–1849, his one-time English friend did just the opposite when another revolutionary moment erupted twelve years later. Mill, like Marx and Engels, was an unequivocal partisan of the Union cause. All three publicly declared their support for the overthrow of the slavocracy in the United States and, from the beginning, the Union cause led by Lincoln to end the secession. They did so, of course, at different times in the conflict and for different reasons. For Mill, slavery was an immoral abomination, an affront to human rights. For Marx and Engels it was more than that. As long as slavery was in place the working class, the efficacious democrats, could never realize its full potential and, hence, the obstruction of "human emancipation." Mill, as his history and practice demonstrated, would never have embraced Marx's and Engels's full agenda, that is, the working class in power. That option, unlike in France in 1848–1849, was never posed in the Civil War and, therefore, why all three could find themselves in 1861 on the same political page.

Second, Marx, Engels and Mill were in fundamental agreement about the cause of the Civil War, the political economy of slavery. All three arrived at that conclusion independently of one another—which gives credence to its validity. The economics of slavery required its extension to more fertile soils in order to be remunerative. That in turn required a political regime to allow the introduction of the "peculiar institution" into new U.S. territories. The election of Lincoln in 1860 threatened that arrangement. Thus, the decision of those states where slavery was most crucial to their economies to go, as Marx put it, "*va banque*," that is, secession.

Third, Marx, Engels and Mill all saw their analyses of the cause of the War not for their own sake but to impact politics and to advance victory for the Union. Mill left no doubt in his two major public interventions into the debate raging in Great Britain about which side to take in the War and why he wrote them. He could confidently tell himself that for the third time since his youthful writings in defense of 1789 and, later, the overthrow of Louis-Philippe in 1848, he was an engaged scholar. Urged on by Cairnes and his daughter Helen he wrote in order to impact politics. Marx and Engels did the same. By the time of the Civil War, they had been veterans in the class struggle and attuned to new revolutionary opportunities. After the decade-long lull following the demise of the European Spring they saw, especially Marx, the Civil War as an opportunity to pick up from where they had left off—just as the Marx party members and veterans of 1848–1849 who had migrated to the United States. Terming his writings as part of the "struggle in the press" left little doubt about their purpose.

But, therein, last of all, was the key difference. How to impact politics and how to advance the cause of the Union are what most differentiated Marx and Engels from Mill. For Mill it was about how to convince the enlightened English elite to support the Union. For Marx and Engels it was about winning and organizing the working class for the Union cause. And the most significant point about that difference was that Marx, especially, was willing to put in the requisite time and effort toward his goal. For reasons that can only be speculated on, Mill lacked the kind of energy and/or will—or maybe multitasking skills—Marx displayed to do what he sincerely thought needed to be done. But the evidence is convincing that the combination of working-class mobilizations in alliance with those few middle-class forces so inclined, liberal politician John Bright being exemplary, is what dissuaded the Palmerston government from intervening on the side of the Confederacy—a key moment in the fate of the Union cause.[107] The "single-minded son of the working class" is probably the best judge of the relative contributions of Marx and Mill to the Union victory. Lincoln's different replies to the two congratulatory messages about his reelection from their two organizations is evidence for his recognition that the milieu that Marx oriented to on behalf of the Union, the working class, had been of far greater value to its success than the world that Mill sought to influence. What he didn't know, summarized here, was Marx's level of activism in making that possible—including his last wartime dispatch to the *Tribune*.

It could be argued, as some do, that Mill did become political in the last decade or so of his life exactly because of the Civil War, specifically, his being "ashamed" and "grieved" at "England's" siding with the Confederacy.[108] But Mill's class position and politics placed limits on both the quantity and quality of his politicization. He entered politics as an intellectual, a very distinguished one at that, and remained so to the end. He agreed to be drafted to run for a parliamentary seat in 1865—a "sacrifice" for him but an opportunity to espouse his ideas—as long as he didn't have to campaign; others would do so on his behalf.[109] The increasingly heated debate about suffrage reform in England was the main reason he decided to run for the post. He'd written about and had a lot to say on the question. But once in parliament he blocked with those who weren't willing to give full suffrage rights to the working class—the fear of the "tyranny of the majority," a position he'd long held. On this issue he and the Marx party did find themselves on opposite sides of the barricades (an issue treated in the Appendix to this chapter).[110] His at best ambivalence about the working class in power explains his loss for words, once again, when the Parisian proletariat suffered another deadly blow as in 1871. Betraying his Enlightenment class politics, he was clearly more comfortable being an unequivocal advocate for chattel slaves and their struggle—and also women's rights—but not wage slaves.

In my 2000 *Marx and Engels* book, I argued that "no two people contributed more to the struggle for democracy in the [nineteenth] century than Marx and Engels."[111] The first chapter of this book makes, I think, a convincing case why Tocqueville, as I argued then, should not be an alternative candidate. I made a similar claim, based on limited research, I admit, about Mill and concluded that "if there were individuals who rivaled Marx and Engels's contribution to the democratic struggle, they're not likely to be found in the ranks of nineteenth-century liberalism."[112] The evidence unearthed for this chapter makes for a more compelling case for Marx's and Engels's democratic credentials being more deserved than those of Mill. It wasn't enough to be a partisan of liberal democracy as was undoubtedly the case with Mill. The democratic quest required theoretical acumen about which social forces to look to for its realization. But that too wasn't enough. It also required a willingness to put in the requisite time and energy to make it real—in other words, the realization of Marx's third and eleventh *Theses on Feuerbach* of 1845.[113]

The political Mill could have easily embraced, at least in principle, the more well-known 11th thesis: "the philosophers have only *interpreted* the world in various ways; the point is to *change* it." The third thesis, however, would have been indigestible. It addressed the age-old problem of the appropriate relationship between the illuminati or learned elite and the popular movements; how to avoid, specifically, the former becoming "superior to society." The solution the young Marx proposed is that the "educators" in the movement must engage in the same activities as the rank and file—*"revolutionary practice."* That's how, like the ranks, they too learned—exactly Marx's modus operandi in the worker's movement once he decided to burn bridges to the world he came from. That's how he successfully shrugged off class baiting given his social origins. It would take Engels, the primary sustainer of the Marx household, a couple of decades more to make the same break. Marx, an apparent "educator," had credibility in the worker's movement precisely because he was willing to instantiate the third thesis. He subordinated his life to its cause, or, in today's lingo, he was "24/7" for the movement.[114]

It is hard to imagine Mill being willing to subject himself to a similar regimen, especially at the age he decided to become, as he understood it, political. He epitomized exactly what the third thesis sought to counter— the well-meaning educated elite who decide to enlighten the masses with their wisdom when convenient. Though willing to enter into united fronts with figures like Mill—in support for the Union cause, for example—Marx was ever vigilant about him and the other "betters" not getting a foothold in the IWA. As he told Engels a month after the birth of the IWA in September 1864, "one has to be all the more careful the moment men of letters, members of the bourgeoisie or semi-literary people become involved in the movement."[115] The working class would never be able to exercise power as long as it thought it couldn't do so without the Mills of the world.[116] Lenin—in anticipation of the next chapter—drew the logical conclusion about a half-century later: "the role of the 'intelligentsia'," in the worker's movement, "is to make special leaders from among the intelligentsia unnecessary."

Marx's and Mill's very different class positions and understandings of what it meant to be political explain probably better than anything their very different responses to the most consequential moment in the democratic quest in their lifetimes.

APPENDIX: CLASS STRUGGLES IN ENGLAND—MARX CONTRA MILL

If the Civil War obligated Marx and Mill to be on the same political page, Britain's domestic class struggle, specifically, electoral reform, required that they go their separate ways—Marx being the most conscious about the need to do so.

As noted earlier, Mill, with due "respect," declined a request from the Chartists in 1842 to support their six-point program, which included universal male suffrage. It would mean "a legislature absolutely controlled by one class, even when that class numerically exceeds all others taken together," as he explained. The "tyranny of the majority," of the working class, in other words, was unacceptable. Marx and Engels, on the other hand, enthusiastically embraced the Chartist Program, foreshadowing what would again distinguish them from Mill two decades later.

Once settled in exile in London in 1849, Marx, owing to his politics and related research, had to learn about England's leading intellectual whereas the latter had no reason to know about the obscure German refugee from the European Spring. The seemingly strange claim about Marx by one of his exiled comrades in London in 1851 that he "leads a very retired life, his only friend[s] being John Stuart Mill," is telling in many ways.[117] It half-facetiously referred to the fact that Marx was intensely reading Mill's *Principles of Political Economy*, published in 1848, since the comrade added that "whenever one goes to see him one is welcomed with economic categories in lieu of greetings." Marx's *Capital*, published in 1867, revealed that he indeed had become acquainted with Mill, and not just his *Principles*. Not for naught did Marx subtitle his magnum opus *A Critique of Political Economy*. Mill came in for particular criticism.[118] For Marx, Mill's renown in England was a measure, in his opinion, of, again, the general mediocrity of intellectual life in his adopted country. Never did the German refugee think he couldn't best, at least at the level of ideas, England's leading light when the opportunity presented itself.

When Marx, as a representative of the German workers movement, became the effective head of the IWA shortly after its founding in September 1864, he quickly moved to limit the influence of "the betters" on the English working class. Informing his actions was the core lesson of the European Spring, the need for independent working-class political action. As he phrased it in the very first of the organization's Provisional Rules, "the emancipation of the working classes must be conquered by the working classes themselves." If the other members of its General Council

(GC), its leadership body, didn't fully understand what Marx meant, they would learn very soon. The 1848 revolutions taught that the proletariat should entertain no illusions about the petit-bourgeoisie, let alone the bourgeoisie. After more than a month of working with some of the petit-bourgeois forces on the GC, Marx told Engels—who was living in Manchester—that "one has to be all the more careful the moment men of letters, members of the bourgeoisie or semi-literary people become involved in the movement."[119] To address that concern, Marx initiated organizational rules that placed severe limits on middle-class qua middle-class participation in the leadership of the IWA. To head off requests such as that of Louis Blanc, the former head of the Provisional Government of the February Revolution of 1848, to become an "honorary member," Marx "got the BY-LAW accepted that no one (except workers' *SOCIETIES*) could be invited to join and that nobody at all could be an *honorary member*."[120] Blanc, also an exile in London, was a frequent dinner guest at the Mill home.

When Edmund Beales, a lawyer who campaigned for working-class representation in Parliament, sought a seat on the GC, Marx convinced other members to reject his request. As he explained to the French representative, "I believe him an honest and sincere man; at the same time, he is nothing and can be nothing save a Bourgeois politician." Precisely because Beales also aspired to a seat in Parliament in the upcoming general elections, "he ought to be excluded from entering our committee. We cannot become *le piedestal* for small parliamentary ambitions … [otherwise] others of his class will follow, and our efforts, till now successful at freeing the English working class movement from all middle class or aristocratic patronage, will have been in vain."[121] Marx was transparent about his agenda for the class struggle in England.

Marx, a "literary representative of the working class," as he and Engels occasionally described themselves, had license to be the effective leader of the IWA exactly because he had committed "class suicide" (as African revolutionary Amilcar Cabral might have put it) *and* subordinated his life to the working-class cause—duly acknowledged and appreciated by the working-class fighters with whom he collaborated.[122] He was able to render ineffective potential class baiting because of his willingness to take on the most menial tasks for the organization, the so called "s…t work." He complained, for example, to Engels on March 13, 1865, that "besides my work on the book [*Capital*], the [IWA] takes up an enormous amount of time, as I am IN FACT the HEAD of it. And what a waste of time!

(And it comes just now, with ... the election business...)." Neither Mill nor any of his cohorts was willing to make such a commitment and sacrifices—at least for the working class.

Regarding "the election business," it appears that the founding of the IWA revived after a two-decade lull in the Chartist campaign interest in suffrage for the working class, particularly amongst middle-class lawyers like Beales. Marx was understandably suspicious. One of them, John Bright, the famed industrialist who opposed his pro-Confederacy British cohorts, wanted, he charged, "to make use of the workers to beat the oligarchs!"[123] Whatever the reason, another leading bourgeois figure, Richard Cobden, Bright's Anti-Corn Law campaign colleague, invited the new organization to participate in a "MONSTER MEETING for MANHOOD SUFFRAGE" in London in February 1865—"the most remarkable thing of all" so far for the young organization, as Marx told Engels. To guard against Cobden's probable agenda, Marx moved that the GC take part provided that "MANHOOD SUFFRAGE," one of the six Chartist demands, be "proclaimed directly and publicly in the programme," and that "people *selected by us*," the GC, "are included on the *permanent* committee, so that they can keep an eye on those fellows and compromise them in the event of fresh treachery, which ... is *at any rate intended*."[124] The overture from one of the best of "their betters" and the joy it no doubt elicited from the grateful trade union heads on the GC tested Marx's leadership in the fledgling organization unlike ever before. "*Fortiter in re, suaviter in modo*" strong in deed, mild in manner, as he described his modus operandi, exemplified his response to the invitation.[125] The lessons, again, of 1848, weighed heavily on Marx's brain.

Born from the successful February 23, 1865, meeting was the Reform League, "to campaign for one man, one vote"—in hindsight, the first iteration of the famed nineteenth-century "Lib-Lab" coalition.[126] Marx enthusiastically, contrary to what his complaint to Engels might have suggested, endorsed the formation of the League. Six weeks later he bragged to his comrade: "The REFORM LEAGUE is OUR WORK. On the inner committee of 12 (6 MIDDLECLASSMEN and 6 WORKINGMEN), the WORKINGMEN are ALL MEMBERS OF OUR COUNCIL. ... WE HAVE BAFFLED all attempts by the middle class TO MISLEAD THE WORKING CLASS. ... If we succeed in re-electrifying the POLITICAL MOVEMENT of the ENGLISH WORKING class, our ASSOCIATION will already have done more for the European working class, WITHOUT MAKING ANY FUSS, than was possible IN ANY OTHER WAY. And there is every prospect for success."[127] Events a year later showed that Marx had been overly optimistic. Yet his enthusiasm registered the oft-ignored or unknown importance he gave to the electoral arena, with all its pitfalls, and revealed how independent working-class political action within it should be conducted—his first opportunity to do such work since the European Spring two decades earlier.

As the Reform League was getting off the ground, Mill, after urgings from some of his most ardent fans, decided to run for election to Parliament in the upcoming general elections as, what he dubbed, an "advanced liberal." The stances he took in defense of Lincoln and the Union had, apparently, whetted his appetite for being for the first time a public intellectual. But he set strict conditions for his candidacy: that he would not have to actually campaign for the London seat in Westminster; that he wouldn't have to, as was usually the case, employ his own funds for the campaign; and that he'd advocate for suffrage for women, more specifically, educated women—not unlike his position that only educated working-class men should be enfranchised, his long-held counter position to the Chartist demand for universal manhood suffrage. Both he and his supporters were surprised when he got enough votes, despite the conditions, to be elected to Parliament.

Worth mentioning is that Mill credited himself for initiating the women's suffrage movement in England.[128] That his endorsement of the vote for upper-class women in his well-publicized letter about a possible candidacy was evidently not an obstacle for election inspired women from that milieu to begin organizing such a movement. It isn't clear what proponents of universal male suffrage thought of the idea. There seems to have been no discussion about women's suffrage in either the Reform League or the GC of the IWA. The Chartist demand for universal manhood suffrage seems to have been unquestioned probably because it had yet to be realized.[129] Liberal opponents of the demand often counterpoised household suffrage as the alternative. But that meant that those who didn't belong to a "household," most likely men, had no chance for any kind of representation. What is certain is that if Mill thought that giving the suffrage to "educated" women was the way to advance women's rights, Marx had a different solution. Bringing women into the workers movement was exactly the alternative he promoted. From encouraging them to become members of the IWA, such as Engels's partner Lizzy Burns, to being on the GC, to bringing solidarity to the strikes of women workers, to getting the IWA to take programmatic positions on issues relevant to women workers Marx was the most conscious of all the GC members in putting women on the IWA's agenda.[130] As with the fight to overthrow the slavo-cracy, the women's question revealed the very different orientations of the two protagonists about which class to look to for advancing the demo-cratic quest.

At one of the three public meetings Mill deigned to participate in to inform his potential constituents about his views, one was noteworthy. A contingent of working-class attendees confronted Mill with a placard on which was something the candidate had written years earlier in his essay "Thoughts on Parliamentary Reform." In contrast to the "higher classes," Mill claimed, "the lower ... [are] mostly habitual liars." When asked if those were his words, he fessed up that they were indeed. Immediately, one of the attendees expressed his pleasure with Mill's honesty. The "working classes," he said, "wanted friends, not flatterers"—a response that garnered applause from the audience. The individual who came to Mill's rescue was George Odger, a trade union leader who happened, also, to be a member of the GC and one of its members of the Reform League's executive committee. Mill proudly recounted Odger's very opportune intervention on his behalf years later in his *Autobiography*. He had, there-fore, at least one fan on the IWA's executive body. Though Odger, no doubt, would have wanted the IWA to endorse Mill's candidacy, just as he did, there is no evidence that he ever sought it. Marx's success in blocking Beales's request, someone who had better pro-working-class credentials than Mill, had made that an impossibility. But neither is it likely that Mill would have expected IWA or Reform League support. Despite Odger's fawning over him, Mill claimed to never have hidden his opinion about the League: "I had always declined being a member of the League, on the avowed ground that I did not agree in its programme of manhood suf-frage. ... I could not consent to hoist the flag of manhood suffrage."[131] The key issue, then, that Marx insisted that the IWA members in the League defend is exactly what Mill opposed. Electoral reform in England exposed the irreconcilable politics of Marx and Mill, just as it did two decades earlier.

Mill's first speech in Parliament in favor of the Liberal government's electoral reform proposal on April 13, 1866, highly anticipated given his renowned pontifications on the topic, didn't disappoint. He distilled the argument in his 1861 book *Considerations on Representative Government* that granting the suffrage to "educated artisans" was a way to have working-class opinions represented in Parliament's deliberations—"this class is not represented"—and to avoid the "hatred" of the working class for the ruling class, as was so often the case elsewhere. The bill was "moderate indeed … more moderate than is desired by the majority of reformers." It was "not a democratic measure … there is no question at present about making the working classes predominant." In making the case that the working class was educable, contrary apparently to the opinion of his peers, Mill referred to Odger's intervention on his behalf at the public meeting a year earlier: "there is no class which so well bears to be told its own faults—to be told them even in harsh terms, if they believe that the person so speaking to them says what he thinks and has no ends of his own to serve by saying so." The remarks evoked loud "cheers" from fellow MPs.[132]

Worth noting is Mill's point about the "hatred" of the working class for its "betters." Granting them the suffrage, even if not fully, would be a way to avoid their wrath. Tocqueville, too, to be recalled, admitted that the right to work clause in the draft constitution that issued from the February Revolution of 1848 that he and others went along with was due to "fear of outside events and the excitement of the moment."[133] Two of the leading liberals of the nineteenth century admitted, therefore, that liberal reforms were likely to be conceded to the working class by ruling elites because of violence or the threat of violence—an all-important lesson that's been verified by subsequent research.[134]

Ten months after the founding of the League, Marx was having his doubts about its course and the toll it was taking on the International's other priorities: why it failed to hold a congress the first year. But, Marx told Engels, in December 1865, "if I resigned tomorrow, the bourgeois element, which looks at us with displeasure in the wings (FOREIGN INFIDELS), would have the upper hand" in the League.[135] Like Marx, the middle-class reformist forces in the League were evidently aware that they too were in a contest with him about its direction.

About ten days before Mill's speech, Marx wrote to Engels: "the accursed traditional nature of all English movements is manifesting itself again in the REFORM-MOVEMENT. The same 'INSTALMENTS' which but a few weeks ago were rejected with the utmost indignation by the people's party—they had even refused Bright's ultimatum of HOUSEHOLD SUFFRAGE—are now treated as a prize worthy to be fought for. And why? Because the Tories are screaming blue murder. These fellows lack the mettle of the old Chartists."[136] The "fellows" were Odger and William Cremer, another trade union head on the GC who was also on the executive committee of the League. Under increasing pressure from Bright and other bourgeois and middle-class reformists, they gave up the demand for universal manhood suffrage and supported in its place household suffrage in the bill the Liberal government submitted to the Commons on March 12. It was the watered-down proposal that Mill spoke in favor of.

Four months later, therefore, the "bourgeois element" had gotten, contrary to Marx, "the upper hand" in the League. As he admitted months later to a German comrade, "Cremer and Odger have both *betrayed* us in the Reform League, where they came to a *compromise with the bourgeoisie* against our wishes."[137] Though Marx had expected liberal betrayal—the lessons of 1848—he seemed surprised by the cowardice of the labor aristocracy, a new phenomenon in the history of the workers movement. That it first manifested itself in England was probably not surprising—the country that had been in the vanguard of the proletarian political cause, the Chartists. The "betrayal" of Odger and Cremer registered that Chartism was a spent force. Almost a quarter century would pass before a new militant labor movement came into existence in Britain.

Despite the positive reception for Mill's speech on its behalf, at least within Parliament, the 1866 Liberal Reform Bill couldn't garner enough votes for enactment. It died in the Parliamentary minefield in June 1866 along with the Liberal government. With nothing to lose, the Reform League now found courage to tack left—to resurrect the universal manhood suffrage demand. Tory and right-wing Liberal opposition to the watered-down bill, blatantly dripping with contempt for the working classes—Mill had only been patronizing—so angered London's proletariat that tens of thousands of them took to the streets in support of the League's apparent rebirth.

Beginning in July, a series of demonstrations that the League called for became increasingly militant, culminating in a scenario at the end of the month in which, as Marx put it, the "government has almost caused a mutiny here. Your Englishman first needs a revolutionary education."[138] Contrary to Marx's hopes, that didn't happen. No one did more to make sure than Mill. At a crucial moment in an unprecedented confrontation in Hyde Park on July 25, he took leadership in a way he'd never done—a moment he proudly recounted in his *Autobiography*. Essentially, he challenged the reformist leaders of the demonstration with the reality of their actions: were they prepared for a potentially revolutionary situation? They realized—what he already knew—that they weren't. They backed down.[139]

Almost a half-century later Prime Minister Lloyd George would do something strikingly similar with other trade union leaders, with the same outcome.[140] Mill prided himself for having diffused the situation. It may have been his most consequential contribution to his class. Anything but "a revolutionary education," Marx's hope, is what Mill wanted English workers to have.

The July protests carried on into the next year, enabling the enactment by a Tory government headed by Benjamin Disraeli of the 1867 Reform Act. It actually went beyond the Liberal proposal in granting more voting rights for workers, the more privileged layers. Yet, Disraeli could confidently and assuredly say about the bill: "'We do not live—and I trust it will never be the fate of this country to live—under a democracy'."[141] Mill came close to saying something similar about the 1866 Liberal proposal. Marx, who could have rightly been cynical about the Reform League's efforts in all of this and, thus, dismissive, seems to have been hopeful that something would finally happen. But there is no evidence that he actively got on board or encouraged as before the IWA to do so. Building the organization with all of its international obligations was now the priority—empowering, again, the effective democrats. As for the League, as he explained to a German correspondent in October 1866, "I have always kept behind the scenes and have not further concerned myself with the matter since it has been under way."[142] It would take the bloodletting of the Great War a half-century later before universal manhood and then universal suffrage could become a reality in Britain for the first time.

If it can be said that Mill got the best of Marx because of the capitulation of the Reform League in 1866, Marx, being Marx, was not about to declare defeat. He sought another way to go after Mill. From late 1866 to about March 1867, he worked closely with Johann Eccarius, a self-taught German tailor and GC member, to write and publish a series of articles entitled "A Working Man's Refutation of Some Points of Political Economy endorsed and advocated by John Stuart Mill."[143] The title said it all. Almost three decades later, the young Lenin argued, again, that the "role of the 'intelligentsia'" in the workers movement, "is to make the special leaders from among the intelligentsia unnecessary."[144] In aiding Eccarius, that's precisely what Marx was doing. To Engels he happily reported in June 1867 that Eccarius's "critique of Mill has impressed them [a group of English intellectual/activists] hugely, they having previously been believers in Mill"—what Marx had hoped.[145] Published in a working-class venue, Eccarius's fourteen articles were for that apparent reason never on Mill's radar.

Marx, in effect, carried out from late 1864 to 1867 both a frontal and guerrilla campaign to limit Mill's influence among the English working class. In the Marx–Engels correspondence Mill was derisively and sardonically known as "the Prophet," "the Prophet Himself" or the "8th sage of the world." Nothing suggests that Mill was even faintly aware of what Marx was doing. Though there is no evidence Mill ever sought either IWA or Reform League support for his candidacy, his biggest working-class fan occupied key posts in both organizations. George Odger, no doubt, would have gladly acceded to such a request. But Marx, the IWA's effective head, was the obstacle to any possibility it might have been granted. Odger eventually parted company with the IWA, exactly because of what Marx was promoting—independent working-class political action. Whether the English section of the IWA could have made a difference in Mill's second and unsuccessful bid to be returned to Parliament in 1868 is pure speculation. Mill was unapologetically a person who felt most at home, as he admitted in 1831, the most revolutionary moment in England in his lifetime, in the realm of ideas. Real-world politics was not, unlike for Marx, his natural home. Again, what makes Marx so unique—effectively at home in both worlds—which real-time politics reveals.

Not only, then, is it accurate to say that Marx had better democratic credentials than Mill when it came to overthrowing the slavocracy in America; it's also true for the struggle for electoral reform in England. More reason to claim that no two individuals did more to contribute to the democratic quest in the nineteenth century than Marx and Engels.

NOTES

1. The two most recent biographers provide ample evidence: Richard Reeves, *John Stuart Mill: Victorian Firebrand* (London: Atlantic Books, 2007), and Nicholas Capaldi, *John Stuart Mill: A Biography* (New York: Cambridge University Press, 2004); the latter purports to be an intellectual biography.
2. Collected Works of John Stuart Mill, vol. 1, p. 66 (hereafter *CWJSM, 1*, p. 66). For the difference, see Hal Draper, *Karl Marx's Theory of Revolution: Volume III* (New York: Monthly Review Press, 1986), pp. 365–66.

3. Capaldi, p. 84. Capaldi acknowledges that Mill would later break philosophically with the Saint Simonians though keeping a lifelong connection with one of their chief lieutenants, Gustave Eichthal.

4. Reeves, p. 187.

5. For details, see Antonia Fraser, *Perilous Question: Reform or Revolution? Britain on the Brink, 1832* (New York: Public Affairs, 2013), especially, chapter 10.

6. *CWJSM*, vol. 12, p. 79.

7. Mill's lack of enthusiasm for the masses in the streets in 1832 in England probably explains a puzzling lacuna in his work; no sustained discussion on the English Civil War of 1642–1649. A likely answer is supplied by James Kloppenberg in his richly informed work, *Toward Democracy: The Struggle for Self-Rule in European and American Thought* (New York: Oxford University Press, 2016). Due to the counterrevolution that unfolded after the Civil War, "[d]octrines associated with the Levellers, the New Model Army, James Harrington and John Milton were now anathema" (p. 139). Rather than take a position on the radical democracy of these forces, Mill thought best, evidently, to simply ignore them.

8. As possible evidence, see Engels's juvenile verse *Florida* in solidarity with American Indian resistance to European encroachment and composed when he was 17; *Marx-Engels Collected Works*, vol. 2, pp. 407–09 (hereafter, *MECW*, 2, pp. 407–09).

9. Reeves, p. 5.

10. See my *Marx, Tocqueville*, chapter 1, for details.

11. *CWJSM, 13*, p. 533.

12. It's true that he thought Tocqueville needed to be more specific about "the tyranny of the majority" but he didn't object in principle to the point (see *CWJSM, 18*), pp. 175–78. For a discussion on how Marx drew, like Mill, on Tocqueville and other European narratives on the American experience for conclusions about democracy, see my *Marx, Tocqueville and Race in America* (Lanham, MD: Lexington Books, 2003), chapter 1.

13. John Cairns, in his introductory essay, "Mill and the Revolution of 1848," in vol. 20 of the *CWJSM*, is a bit too harsh on Mill for not having foreseen the upheaval. Others closer to the scene also missed it. While it's true, as we'll see, that Marx and Engels had more foresight, they were the exception to the rule. The criticism, hence, smacks of hindsight.

14. *CWJSM, 13*, p. 732. Whether Mill knew what Engels had been doing in Paris on behalf of "Communism" is unknown.

15. *CWJSM, 25*, p. 1111.

16. *CWJSM, 14*, p. 76.

17. *CWJSM, 15*, p. 32.

18. Engels, before returning to Germany, happened to be in Paris when the Revolution exploded. His three extant letters are, not surprisingly, far richer than the two of Mill writing from afar. But they are also more pre-scient about the course of the provisional government owing to his differ-ent political framework, his and his partner's historical materialist perspective. See *MECW*, *38*, pp. 165, 166, 167–69.
19. *CWJSM*, *25*, p. 1102. Engels mistakenly thought that the Chartists might actually take power: ibid., p. 171.
20. *CWJSM*, *1*, p. 266.
21. *CWJSM*, *21*, p. 95.
22. Ibid., p. 87.
23. There is no reason to believe that Mill had read their *Manifesto*. Only toward the end of 1850 was it published in English for the first time, in a Chartist organ; for details, see Hal Draper, *The Adventures of the Communist Manifesto* (Berkeley, CA: Center for Socialist History, 1994), pp. 28–30.
24. For details, see my *Marx, Tocqueville*, chapter 2.
25. Ibid., p. 61.
26. Only afterward: *CWJSM*, *1*, p. 266 and *21*, 133n.
27. My *Marx, Tocqueville*, chapter 2, pp. 71–75.
28. See Harold Holzer's talk, "Lincoln and Immigration," https://www.c-span.org/video/?418240-2/abraham-lincoln-immigration.
29. *MECW*, *41*, p. 242. In the *MECW* upper case text indicates the original in English.
30. *CWJSM*, *15*, p. 720.
31. *MECW*, *41*, p. 277.
32. See, for example, Joseph Glatthaar's, "Black Glory: The African American Role in Union Victory," in Gabor Boritt, ed., *Why the Confederacy Lost* (New York: Oxford University Press, 1993).
33. *MECW*, *41*, p. 278.
34. Details can be found in my *Marx, Tocqueville*, chapter 3. Thankfully, a new edition of Marx's and Engels's *The Civil War in the United States* (New York: International Publishers, 2016) is available.
35. *CWJSM*, *15*, p. 208.
36. *CWJSM*, *1*, p. 267.
37. *MECW*, *41*, pp. 294–96.
38. Marx argued, contra *The Economist* et al., that Southern efforts to have slavery formally legalized had been unsuccessful. He was right about the so-called Crittenden plan. But evidently he didn't know about the pas-sage by Congress in March 1861 of a proposed amendment to give constitutional protection to slavery—the Corwin amendment—and duly submitted by the just inaugurated Lincoln to the states for ratification.

39. *MECW, 41*, pp. 7–16.
40. *MECW, 19*, p. 42.
41. Ibid., pp. 49–50.
42. Ibid., p. 91.
43. Ibid., p. 99.
44. Ibid., pp. 137–38.
45. Dan Doyle, *The Cause of All Nations: An International History of the American Civil War* (New York: Basic Books, 2015), pp. 154–55. When he lamented to Engels that he was no longer receiving the *Tribune* since March 1862, he called it "a rotten trick of Greeley's and McElrath's," a co-publisher of the paper; *MECW, 41*, p. 362. For a useful overview of Greeley's politics in relation to Marx, see Adam-Max Tuchinsky, "'The Bourgeoisie Will Fall and Fall Forever': the 'New-York Tribune', the 1848 French Revolution and American Social Democratic Discourse," *Journal of American History*, vol. 92, no. 2 (September 2005).
46. See his complaint to Engels about his unpublished articles, *MECW, 41*, p. 338.
47. See *MECW, 41*, Letters, 1860–1864.
48. *CWJSM, 15*, p. 750.
49. *CWJSM, 1*, pp. 267–68.
50. *CWJSM, 15*, p. 767.
51. *CWJSM, 15*, p. 774.
52. *CWJSM, 21*, p. 19.
53. *CWJSM, 21*, pp. 125–42.
54. *CWJSM, 1*, p. 268. On the attacks, see Georgios Varouxakis, "'Negrophilist' Crusader: John Stuart Mill on the American Civil War and Reconstruction," *History of European Ideas*, 39:5 (2013), pp. 736–37.
55. Ibid., p. 733.
56. *MECW, 19*, pp. 153–56.
57. Doyle, pp. 145–50. For more on the scholarship, see my *Marx, Tocqueville*, p. 134n73.
58. For a distillation of how Marx and Engels read the War, see my *Marx, Tocqueville* book, chapter 3. For the primary data, see the recently reissued Marx and Engels, *The Civil War in the United States* (New York: International Publishers, 2016).
59. *MECW, 19*, p. 178.
60. Ibid., p. 203
61. Ibid., p. 204.
62. His response in 1877 to a Russian critic who suggested otherwise; *MECW, 24*, p. 201.
63. *MECW, 41*, p. 416.

64. In less politically correct language for today, certainly, Marx in more than one letter to Engels employed the "N-word." For example, "One single NIGGER REGIMENT would have a remarkable effect on Southern nerves" (*MECW, 41*, p. 400). I leave aside only for space considerations the validity of the comment which I think was accurate. Again, for the *MECW*, the editors put in small capitalization words originally in English in German text. Only in correspondence does the N-word appear in their writings. I, an African American, caution against any rush to judgments on this issue. See my footnote in my *Marx, Tocqueville*, p. 131n35.

65. *MECW, 19*, pp. 227–28.

66. Ibid., p. 250.

67. *MECW, 41*, p. 380.

68. *CWJSM, 15*, p. 801.

69. *CWJSM, 15*, pp. 911–12.

70. *CWJSM, 15*, p. 747.

71. As an example of his awareness of working-class opinion about the War, see his letters to Cairnes on December 16, 1862, and February 7, 1863, or to an unidentified correspondent on February 21, 1863, *CWJSM, 15*, p. 810, pp. 835–36 and 842. His letter of February 15, *CWJSM, 15*, p. 589, is particularly interesting because of Mill's advice that the English working class should not combine it's pro-Union work with its demand for the suffrage—a stance Marx would have certainly disagreed with.

72. *CWJSM, 21*, p. 19.

73. Marx, *Capital*, vol. 1 (New York: International Publishers, 1972), p. 518.

74. J. G. Eccarius, "A Working Man's Refutation of some Points of Political Economy endorsed and advocated by John Stuart Mill," *The Commonwealth*, nos. 192–95, 198, 200, 203, 204, 206–11, November 1866–March 1867. There is no evidence that Mill was aware of the critique. *MECW, 42*, p. 394.

75. Ibid. and p. 269.

76. *CWJSM, 1*, p. 268.

77. See, for example, *CWJSM, 15*, p. 842fn2.

78. See, for example, his letters in *CWJSM, 15*, of May 17, 1863, p. 860; August 24, 1863, p. 877; September 24, 1863, p. 886.

79. For Mill's correspondence on this, see Varouxakis, p. 741.

80. *MECW, 41*, p. 468; *CWJSM, 15*, p. 851. Capaldi, p. 307. Paul Foot, *The Vote: How It Was Won and How It Was Undermined* (New York: Viking, 2005), pp. 125–26. The fact that John Bright would be the key note speaker probably explains Mill's decision to be present. He'd been the most prominent bourgeois figure to side with the Union.

81. For details, see my *Marx and Engels*, chapters 7, 8, and 9.

82. *CWJSM, 32*, p. 220. About the First Address of the IWA on the Franco Prussian War in 1870 that Marx wrote, Mill said: "highly pleased with the address. There's not one word in it that ought not to be there; it could not have been done with fewer words." Given that Marx's name was listed as one of the 33 signers, Mill may not have known its author.

83. *MECW, 41*, pp. 561–62.

84. *CWJSM, 15*, pp. 957–58.

85. Cairnes's *The Slave Power* informed Marx's letter and, thus, no coincidence the same term is employed.

86. My "Marx and Engels on the US Civil War," *Historical Materialism* 19.4 (2011) provides details. See also *MECW, 20*, p. 453n16. For Marx's letter and Lincoln's reply, see https://www.marxists.org/archive/marx/iwma/documents/1864/lincoln-letter.htm.

87. That Adams's son, Charles, was a commander of an all-black Union unit is probably of import. Through his eyes, the ambassador likely sympathized with the most militant supporters of the Union cause like the IWA. See, for example, the son's praise of Lincoln's Second Inaugural Address, the president's most revolutionary statement on the slavery question: http://ap.gilderlehrman.org/essays/lincoln%C3%A2%E2%82%AC%E2%84%A2s-interpretation-civil-war.

88. There is no evidence, such as in his correspondence, that Mill was active in the organization—Varouxakis's claim about his "activism" for "the 'cause'" notwithstanding (p. 749). For useful details on the London Emancipation Society, see Doyle, p. 246.

89. *MECW, 20*, p. 604n112.

90. Ibid., *42*, p. 86.

91. Ibid., *20*, p. 99.

92. Ibid.

93. *CWJSM, 16*, p. 1043.

94. Ibid., pp. 1038–39.

95. Ibid., XV, p. 890.

96. Varouxakis, p. 742, writes that "he made sure [it] was published in the *Daily News*." More accurately, he told Cairnes to whom he sent it: "Perhaps after reading it, you may think [it] useful to send it, or part of it, to the *Daily News*." This suggests that Varouxakis is a bit overzealous in promoting Mill's "Negrohilist" credentials. I suspect it's because he knows—as some of his footnotes indicate—that Marx's record is clearly superior.

97. *CWJSM, 16*, pp. 1051–52. Varouxakis suggests that the letter was published in the paper but there's no evidence of that because it's not included in the CWJSM, specifically, *25*, Newspaper Writings, 1847–1873. Overzealous Varouxakis?

98. *MECW*, *42*, p. 163.
99. *MECW*, *42*, p. 167.
100. *Marx, Tocqueville*, pp. 142, 188n8.
101. Varouxakis, p. 744. But oddly, he doesn't cite such publications and neither does the CWJSM, specifically, *25*, Newspaper Writings, 1847–1873. Overzealous Varouxakis again?
102. *CWJSM*, *21*, pp. 1098–101. Varouxakis, except for the last, tellingly ignores these passages from the letter.
103. *CWJSM*, *16*, pp. 1117–18.
104. *MECW*, *42*, p. 579.
105. For details, see my *Marx and Engels*, pp. 214–15.
106. *CWJSM*, *16*, pp. 1821, 1865. The editors of the *CWJSM* put the executions as high as 80,000; p. 1821.
107. Most recently, see Doyle, Part II. Duncan Andrew Campbell, *English Public Opinion and the American Civil War* (London: Royal Historical Society, 2003), argues—unconvincingly in my view because for him "the chief cause of the war was not in fact slavery" (p. 240)—that Marx's praise of the pro-Union sentiment of much of the working class was unwarranted.
108. Reeve, pp. 333–37.
109. Ibid., pp. 353–57.
110. Nimtz, *Marx and Engels*, pp. 236–37. See his *Autobiography, CWJSM, 1*, pp. 278–79, for his rationale. Also, see how he applauded himself for defusing what could have been a significant revolutionary working-class moment in London in 1866. For Marx's reaction, see *MECW*, *42*, p. 300.
111. Nimtz, *Marx and Engels*, p. 294.
112. Ibid., p. 300.
113. *MECW*, *5*, pp. 3–5.
114. For evidence in support of this claim, see my *Marx and Engels*, pp. 182–88.
115. *MECW*, *42*, pp. 54–55. See how Marx convinced other IWA leaders to keep at bay Louis Blanc, one-time political ally, one-time member of the provisional government that issued from the Paris revolt in 1848 and frequent dinner guest at the Mill household; ibid.
116. For what Mill might have thought about "Marxism," see Reeve, pp. 463–65.
117. *MECW*, *38*, pp. 269–70.
118. *Capital*, pp. 125, 371, 506, 516–18, 610.
119. *MECW*, *42*, pp. 54–55.
120. Ibid.
121. Ibid., pp. 92–93. For more details, see Marx's letter to Engels, *42*, pp. 109–10.

122. For details, see chapters 7, 8 and 9 in my *Marx and Engels*.
123. Ibid., p. 71.
124. Ibid., p. 74.
125. See, specifically, chapter 8 in my *Marx and Engels*.
126. Paul Foot, *The Vote: How It Was Won and How It Was Undermined* (New York: Viking Press, 2005) chapter 4, "The Leap into the Dark," provides the most current overview of the events. It stands on the shoulders of Royden Harrison's breakthrough *Before the Socialists: Studies in Labour and Politics, 1861–1881* (London: Routledge & Kegan Paul, 1965).
127. *MECW, 42*, p. 150.
128. Mill, *Autobiography, CWJSM, 1*, p. 275. To his credit, he acknowledged that his late wife Harriet Taylor was the real source of his enlightenment on the issue.
129. Foot, p. 173.
130. For details, see my *Marx and Engels*, pp. 199–202.
131. *CWJSM, 1*, p. 278.
132. *CWJSM, 28*, pp. 60–66.
133. Chapter 1, p. 37.
134. See Daron Acemoglu and James Robinson, "Democratization or repression?," *European Economic Review*, vol. 44, nos. 4–6 (May 2000); also, my "Violence and/or Nonviolence in the Success of the Civil Rights Movement," *New Political Science*, vol. 38, no. 1 (2016).
135. *MECW, 42*, p. 207.
136. Ibid., p. 253.
137. Ibid., p. 314.
138. Ibid., p. 300.
139. *CWJSM, 1*, pp. 278–79. See also, Capaldi, pp. 326–27.
140. Foot, pp. 247–48.
141. Ibid., p. 152.
142. *MECW, 42*, p. 327.
143. Ibid., p. 726.
144. *Lenin's Collected Works*, vol. 1 (Moscow: Progress Publishers, 1976), p. 298.
145. Ibid., p. 394.

CHAPTER 4

Two Takes on the Russian Revolution
of 1905: Lenin versus Weber

[As] a bourgeois scholar … I am a member of the bourgeois classes.
I feel myself to be a bourgeois, and I have been brought up
to share their views and ideals.
Weber, 1895

this piece of professorial wisdom of the cowardly bourgeoisie … is
a subterfuge … which sees in the proletariat its most dangerous
class enemy.
Lenin, 1917

After the Bolshevik-led Russian Revolution of October 1917, Vladimir
Lenin and Leon Trotsky, its leading protagonists, would often say that the
Revolution of 1905 served as a "dress rehearsal." On the twelfth anniversary of the beginning of the latter, January 9 (22), 1917, the original
"Bloody Sunday," Lenin addressed a meeting of young workers in Zurich,
Switzerland, to commemorate that momentous event.[1] He had no idea as
he spoke that within weeks Russia's toilers would be making history again.
His focus was on the lessons of 1905, to ensure that his audience was
politically equipped for whatever lay ahead. Toward the end of the talk, he
mentioned another balance sheet on the upheaval. "The bourgeoisie likes
to describe the Moscow uprising [December 1905] as something artificial,
and to treat it with ridicule. For instance, in German so-called scientific
literature, Herr Professor Max Weber, in his lengthy survey of Russia's
political development, refers to the Moscow uprising as a 'putsch.' 'The

© The Author(s) 2019
A. H. Nimtz, *Marxism versus Liberalism*, Marx, Engels,
and Marxisms, https://doi.org/10.1007/978-3-030-24946-5_4

Lenin Group,' says this 'highly learned' Herr Professor, 'and a section of the Socialist-Revolutionaries had long prepared for this *senseless* uprising'."

If there is one figure Western intellectuals and academics regard as an alternative to Marx—at least for most of the twentieth century—it is likely to be Max Weber; he continues to exercise considerable influence in that milieu. His "lengthy survey" of the 1905 Revolution proved to be the most detailed political analysis ever published by the distinguished doyen of the German academy but mostly unknown by his admirers. Lenin, however, wasn't impressed. He offered data to dispute Weber's reading. The archival record challenges, as well, Weber's "putschist" portrait of "the Lenin group." Implicit in Lenin's 1917 critique of Weber was his own real-time reading—and part authorship, not insignificantly—of the events of 1905. Weber's more than 600-page account was also written in real-time and, also, from afar. Thus, two of the most influential figures in the twentieth century read in real-time—Weber was 41 and Lenin 35 at the time—from polar opposite class perspectives one of the most consequential events in modern history, the Russian Revolution of 1905.[2]

Because Weber focused almost exclusively on the prospects for Russian liberalism, the comparison of their texts permits a real-time answer to a question that has arguably been at the center of politics since 1917: why wasn't there a liberal alternative to the Bolsheviks? Or, why couldn't Russian liberals "get their act together" with all that implied for subsequent history?

That both Lenin and Weber were aware to varying degrees that the two of them were reading the same events, and that Lenin knew that Weber was reading him, makes for a rare opportunity in the history of ideas—certainly different from the two prior cases. The archival record, therefore, permits another opportunity to evaluate the relative merits of competing theoretical perspectives for doing real-time political analysis. Given the richness of both sets of texts, relative to the first two cases, this comparison, however, can only highlight the key contrasts between Lenin and Weber. An appendix that distills their all so different responses to the upheaval that came with the October 1917 revolution enriches the comparison with another needed coda.

PRELUDE TO 1905: WEBER'S AND LENIN'S POLITICS

When Russia's 300-year-old Romanov dynasty faced rebellion in 1905, the uprising immediately took world center political stage. The last absolute monarchy in Europe's largest country had been the staunchest dike against the unceasing tide of liberal democracy. Modern Europe hadn't seen an explosion of such proportions since at least the Revolutions of 1848–1849. Russia's ruling class had seemed, until then, immune to such upheavals. Given that Germany's edition of the European Spring had been aborted and, thus, why liberal democracy had yet to be instituted there, it is understandable why what was unfolding to its east would be of interest to its modernizing intelligentsia. This fundamentally is what attracted the attention of Germany's leading social science scholar, Max Weber (1864–1920), to the unprecedented threat to the Romanovs in St. Petersburg. Not only could there be lessons for their Hohenzollern relatives in Berlin and Potsdam but, more importantly, for Weber, "the German nation." So determined to understand what was taking place he—not unlike another German, Marx, who did the same three decades earlier—decided to suspend his other research projects in order to learn Russian to be able to read original sources. The result was the most detailed political analysis in the Weber oeuvre.

Some background to Weber's writings is in order. Unlike Lenin, Weber was first and foremost an academic-intellectual. His most formal induction into that role took place in May 1895, when he gave his "Inaugural" address as the newly appointed chair of economics at Freiburg University. His prior research on agriculture and labor in Prussia had called into question received wisdom and, thus, the raison d'être for the promotion. Nothing best captured Weber than his all too often ignored self-descriptions in the lecture: "we economic nationalists," and "a bourgeois (*bürgerlich*) scholar like myself … a member of the bourgeois (*bürgerlich*) classes. I feel myself to be a bourgeois, and I have been brought up to share their views and ideals."[3] His honesty facilitates the comparison with Lenin, whose class characterization of him in 1917—the "cowardly bourgeoisie"—was, therefore, not necessarily gratuitous.[4] The lecture's central message was about the need to defend the German "nation" and "race"—terms he used interchangeably—against those with a "habitually low physical and intellectual standard of living," or "less developed types of human beings" such as the "starving Slavs," specifically, the Poles who were migrating increasingly to Prussia. The economic imperatives of capitalism for German agriculture had provoked the situation which called for, he argued, a nation-state response; it couldn't be left to the market to solve.

Weber also attacked the "vulgar materialists," that is, the Marxists. Thus his conscious counterpoising of race, culture, nationality and their corresponding ideas and ideologies to class analysis—at least the class anal-

ysis practiced by the German Social Democratic Party.[5] Because the party
was the largest in the country, it understandably exercised a degree of
intellectual influence. The increasing proletarianization of rural labor
posed the threat of even more growth for the Social Democrats. This
explains Weber's pushback against any idea that German workers should
become the country's ruling class. He made no pretense of being a politically neutral observer of socio-political reality. Rather he sought to influence the political direction of "the fatherland." At stake in his opinion was
the future of the German race/nation/culture. "Our successors will hold
us answerable to history not primarily for the kind of economic organization we hand down to them, but for the amount of elbow-room in the
world which we conquer and bequeath to them."[6] His complaint was that
Germany's "bourgeois classes seem to be wilting as bearers of the *power-
interests of the nation, while there is still no sign that the workers are
beginning to become mature enough to take their place."[7] Whether he, a
"bourgeois scholar," would have really welcomed a working-class solution
is doubtful. Whatever the case, Weber's lecture was intended to be a wake-
up call and one for action. In hindsight his call for "elbow-room" was
prescient—in anticipation of the call for lebensraum of German National
Socialism only a few decades later.[8]

Again, Weber made no pretense of being a dispassionate non-partisan
observer of socio-political reality. His anti-Polish sentiments on display in
the address, for example, persisted until the end and are well-documented.[9]
At least four times in the speech he spoke of the desirability of "vocation,"
that is, purpose or task, and specifically, the "political vocation" of the
social scientist—to advance the interests of the German nation. The Junker
class, once headed by Bismarck, was now a has-been. Yet, Germany's
bourgeoisie had yet to display an ability to take its place. And as a "bourgeois scholar" Weber dismissed the idea that the German working class
could play such a role. What Weber could be certain in saying is that his
task, the vocation of the social scientist, was to contribute to "the *political*
education of our nation."

While Weber would later be known by modern social science as a vigor-
ous defender of the "fact/value" distinction, seldom recognized is the
political context in which he did so. As a self-described "bourgeois scholar"
and "economic nationalist," Weber, again, was an active opponent of
German Social Democracy and all that he understood it to be for. The
"vulgar materialists" defended their project in the name of science, "scientific socialism," and, thus, their justification for the values they espoused.

I argue that is was against that claim, that from science could values be deduced, that Weber's insistence that there was no necessary link between facts and values must be understood. Germany's national interests and the values associated with it had an ontological existence independent of social science.

Weber promised his audience that he would carry out research to sustain his claims. But that would take about a decade to materialize because from shortly about two years later in 1897 after the speech to about 1903 he suffered from a severe bout of depression brought on apparently by the death of his father (not unlike, to be remembered, what happened to John Stuart Mill).[10] The affliction severely limited his intellectual output. Before the onset of the depression he helped to found in 1896, the National Social Union that Andrew Zimmerman describes as "one of the many new 'social' parties offering a patriotic and religious alternative to the Social Democrats."[11] A trip to the U.S. in 1904, which allowed him to learn about the proletarianization of African American toilers in the former Confederacy, helped rejuvenate his intellectual instincts, including the consideration for the first time of cross-country comparative analysis.[12]

Before and immediately after his American trip Weber completed his most famous work, *The Protestant Ethic and the Spirit of Capitalism*. As a later introduction to the book explained, its central research question was to locate "the origin of the Western bourgeois class" and to make sense "of its peculiarities."[13] Except for a few pages in one of the book's five chapters, the proletariat, the other essential class in the capitalist mode of production, is virtually absent in Weber's inquiry. The "entrepreneur," the "employer," the "capitalist" was rather his priority. For Weber, therefore, the bourgeoisie was the class to look to for advancing humanity. What he prioritized and neglected in the *Protestant Ethic* anticipated his portrait of Russia's first revolution. Both the book and his earlier lectures and writings are the necessary background for understanding his interpretation of the Russian upheavals a year later.

At almost the same time that Weber was studying the penetration of capitalist relations of production into Prussia's countryside, Lenin, six years his junior (1870–1924), was doing exactly the same for Russia's rural scene; he had picked up from where Marx had left off.[14] "New Economic Developments in Peasant Life," his first extant writing, was written in the spring of 1893. Unlike Weber, who saw capitalism as a threat to the "fatherland," Lenin, like Marx and Engels, viewed the proletarianization of the Russian countryside as an advance for the class struggle—more gravediggers for capitalism. A year later, and a year ahead of Weber, Lenin published what could be called his "inaugural address." *What the "Friends of the People" Are and How They Fight the Social-Democrats* was Lenin's 200-page opening salvo into the debates that racked Russia's revolutionary circles.

Three main themes informed Lenin's writings and actions for the decade leading up to 1905; the indispensability of, first, the democratic revolution for the socialist revolution; second, a proletariat-led alliance with peasants to realize the democratic revolution; and, third, the proletariat having its own political party—the guarantee for the socialist revolution.[15]

Following Marx's and Engels's lead in their *Communist Manifesto* and other pronouncements, Lenin argued that on the political agenda for Russia was a bourgeois democratic revolution and not a socialist revolution. Feudal and semi-feudal relations, especially in the countryside, still prevailed under the rule of the Romanovs. Until all of that baggage of the past had been consigned to the proverbial dustbin of history, Russia's still small proletariat could never carry out and consolidate a socialist revolution.

Lenin's position that a bourgeois democratic revolution rather than a socialist revolution was on Russia's agenda would have resonated with Weber, had he known about it. But there was a crucial difference between their views. The lessons of the 1848 Revolution that Marx and Engels distilled (see Chap. 1) and that Lenin absorbed to his core, taught that the bourgeoisie could not be counted on to carry out such a transformation. They had gotten cold feet in moving in such a direction. The distant sound of the feet of the newly emerging proletariat caused them to think twice about such an upheaval. They would rather settle for a strong man to maintain stability, in the person of a Louis Napoleon Bonaparte or an Otto Bismarck—that is, a Bonapartist outcome. Only the proletariat in alliance with the peasantry could be counted on for instituting bourgeois democracy. For Weber, that was the exclusive task of the bourgeoisie.

Russian communists in Lenin's view, given the conclusions Marx and Engels had distilled about how to realize bourgeois democracy and to which he wholeheartedly subscribed, were, therefore, obligated to bloc with whatever social forces prepared to fight for the end of feudal survivals. Thus, the quite limited democratic concessions the Romanovs were forced to grant to Russia's toilers due to their mid-nineteenth-century insurgencies—and against the backdrop of bourgeois democratic advances in the West—were to be tested to see if they could be deepened. Chief amongst them were the newly established organs of local rural government, the Romanov's first dalliance with representative government. The *zemstvo*, as it was called, would be a key point of entry for Weber's inquiry into Russian developments in 1905.

By the time Weber discovered the *zemstvo* in 1905 Lenin had already devoted considerable attention to them, that is, to the possibility of a liberal democratic alternative to tsarist Russia—and ignored by virtually all of his critics. In a polemic in 1899 with "social democrats" who mistakenly subordinated the political to the economic struggle, the "economists," Lenin spelled out the requisites for instituting democracy in Russia. "What is meant by the overthrow of the autocracy?"

> It implies the tsar's renunciation of absolute power; the granting to the people of the right to elect their own representatives for legislation, for supervision over the actions of the government officials, for supervision over the collection and disbursement of state revenues. This type of government in which the people participate in legislation and administration is called the constitutional form of government (constitution law on the participation of people's representatives in legislation and the administration of the state). Thus, the overthrow of the autocracy means the replacement of the autocratic form of government by the constitutional form of government ... [It means the convening of] a Zemsky Sobor [a national *zemstvo*] of representatives of the people for the elaboration of a constitution ("to win a democratic constitution") [people's constitution, drawn up in the interests of the people], as it is put in the draft programme of the Russian Social-Democrats published in 1885.[16]

Here, Lenin stated for the first time in very clear language what he meant by "constitutional government," in essence, the content for Russia's democratic revolution, the sine qua non for the socialist revolution. It would require the institution of genuine representative governance in Russia, a parliament—what Russian Social Democrats should look forward to participating in just like their sister parties in Western Europe.

In his 1901 pamphlet *The Persecutors of the Zemstvo and the Hannibals of Liberalism*, Lenin argued that the "question of the relation of the Zemstvo to political freedom is a particular case of the general question of the relation of reforms to revolution." The oft-made claim of liberals "that the 'principle of progress is that the better things are, the better'... is as untrue as its reverse that the worst things are the better."

Revolutionaries, of course, will never reject the struggle for reforms, the struggle to capture even minor and unimportant enemy positions, *if* these will serve to strengthen the attack and help to achieve full victory. But they will never forget that sometimes the enemy himself surrenders a certain position in order to disunite the attacking party and thus to defeat it more easily. They will never forget that only by constantly having the "ultimate aim" in view, only by appraising every step of the "movement" and every reform from the point of view of the general revolutionary struggle, is it possible to guard the movement against false steps and shameful mistakes.[17]

Lenin spilled a lot of ink on the *zemstvo*, ignored by friend and foe alike. I'll return to the topic because Weber too had a lot to say about them and the comparison will be instructive. Suffice it to say here that in general Lenin argued for the need of Social-Democrats to fight side by side with liberals in defense of the organs, if they were prepared to fight; but be harbored no illusions that they would actually do so.

The challenge, Lenin felt, for democratic forces at the end of 1904 was to "to guard … against false steps," in this instance the wink and nod from the regime that it might grant the long-held hope of liberals for convening a national *zemstvo*, or Zemsky Sobor—what some erroneously thought would be Russia's États-Généraux. The context was the Russo-Japanese War that had commenced in January and not going well for Tsar Nicholas's forces. It was in a similar situation, the monarchy's defeat in the Crimean War (1853–1856), that the regime made democratic concessions—the *zemstvo*—in an attempt to shore up domestic support. Liberal forces were hoping for something similar and were heartened when Nicholas's liberal-inclined interior minister made such a proposal. Lenin had more foresight. In November he wrote: "the game ["the tsarist government"] has started with the Zemstsvo constitutionalists is bound to get it into a tangle; whether it makes some paltry concessions or whether it makes no concessions at all, discontent and exasperation will inevitably spread wider."[18] When Nicholas rejected the proposal on December 12, Lenin concluded: "the tsar intends to preserve and uphold the autocratic regime. The tsar does not want to change the form of government and has no intention of granting a constitution."[19] Within a month his forecast about "discontent and exasperation" would be realized.

Lenin, to be noted, wrote all of this from afar, in exile since 1900. Weber, perhaps because of his trip to the U.S. in 1904, did not appear, at least from his correspondence, to know about the increasingly precarious situation Nicholas faced owing to his missteps in the war with his Japanese feudal counterpart.[20] When the Russian commander at Port Arthur surrendered to Japanese forces on January 2, 1905, Lenin wrote: "The capitulation of Port Arthur is the prologue to the capitulation of tsarism ....Yes, the autocracy is weakened. The most skeptical of the skeptics are beginning to believe in revolution. General belief in revolution is already the beginning of revolution."[21] Never would Lenin be so prescient about the timing of a revolution.

1905: YEAR ONE OF THE REVOLUTION

"Bloody Sunday" was no exaggeration. Though there is no certain figure, hundreds of if not a thousand unarmed workers were slain by tsarist military forces when tens of thousands of them peacefully marched upon his palace in St. Petersburg on January 9 (22) to present a petition asking for relief from both the harsh economic and political situation they were facing.[22] Lenin's immediate response is instructive:

> The working class has received a momentous lesson in civil war; the revolutionary education of the proletariat made more progress in one day than it could have made in months and years of drab, humdrum, wretched existence .... The revolution is spreading ... The demand of the insurgent St. Petersburg workers—the immediate convocation of a Constituent Assembly on the basis of universal, direct, and equal suffrage by secret ballot—must become the demand of all the striking workers .... The arming of the people is becoming an immediate task of the revolutionary moment .... We Social-Democrats can and must act independently of the bourgeois-democratic revolutionaries and guard the class independence of the proletariat. But we must go hand in hand with them during the uprising .... The overthrow of tsarism in Russia, so valiantly begun by our working class, will be a turning point in the history of all countries.[23]

Though it would take thirteen years to verify, Lenin's forecast proved to be, again, extraordinarily accurate.

When word spread to other cities about the slaughter and the belief that tens of hundreds, if not more, had been slain, it set into motion an unprecedented rebellion in Russia that lasted with ebbs and flows until December. The regime sought to put a lid on the upheaval in the way it had before—both the carrot and the stick. In February it floated the idea that it might grant a Zemsky Sobor for the first time. Among the demands of the Bloody Sunday petitioners were, as Lenin reported, "the immediate convocation of a Constituent Assembly on the basis of universal, direct, and equal suffrage by secret ballot."[24] Though Lenin had advised at the end of 1904 against buying into "false steps," the expected bait and switch operation around the promise of a constitutional assembly, he wasn't obdurate about the latest offer. He initiated a discussion within the Bolshevik faction of the party about how to respond.

In anticipation of what would later be known as the Bulygin Duma proposal, Lenin gave his first public stance on how the Bolsheviks should respond. As he told the delegates at the Bolshevik gathering of the RSDLP, "it is impossible to reply categorically whether it is advisable to participate in the Zemsky Sobor. Everything will depend on the political situation, on the electoral system, and on other specific factors which cannot be estimated in advance. Some say that the Zemsky Sobor is a fraud. That is true. But there are times when we must take part in elections to expose a fraud." Yes, the regime was offering only "sham concessions," but the RSDLP, as he put it in the relevant resolutions, "should *take advantage of them* in order, on the one hand, to *consolidate* for the people every improvement in the economic conditions and every extension of liberties with a view to intensifying the struggle, and on the other, steadily to expose before the proletariat the reactionary aims of the government ... [The Party has] to make use of each and every case of open political action on the part of the educated spheres and the people ... all legal and semi-legal channels." And to be clear, "while maintaining and developing their underground machinery" party units should take the necessary steps to prepare for "open Social-Democratic activity, even to the point of clashes with the armed forces of the government."[25]

To participate or not in the electoral process could not, Lenin argued, be answered in the abstract. Participation depended on the political context and, most importantly, on whether it offered opportunities to advance the revolutionary process, including material improvements and the extension of liberties for the masses. Also evident is that Lenin did not make virtue out of underground work; it was necessary only when the opportunity for "open political action" was not available.

The mass mobilizations, unprecedented in modern history, only deepened over the summer, forcing Tsar Nicholas to play the carrot card—to concretize the representative government proposal he floated in February. On August 6 his government issued an Imperial Manifesto that set the conditions and timetable for its institution. Named after the minister who drew up the guidelines, the Bulygin parliament or Duma would be elected by indirect vote based on a very limited suffrage. The electors of the deputies were to be elected in the curiae or electoral colleges of four categories of the population: landowners (which included the clergy), urban property owners, peasants on communal land, and lastly, city residents. High property qualifications existed for all the categories.[26] Russia's small but increasingly vocal working class was not included. It didn't take Lenin long to condemn the proposal: "a consultative assembly of representatives of the landlords and the big bourgeoisie, elected under the supervision and with the assistance of the autocratic government's servants on the basis of an electoral system so indirect, so blatantly based on property and social-estate qualifications, that it is sheer mockery of the idea of popular representation."[27] Especially reprehensible was that the *entire urban working class, all the village poor, agricultural labourers, and peasants who are not householders, take no part whatever in any elections.*"[28]

The proposal was so patently antidemocratic that even many liberals denounced it, calling for a boycott of the Duma that Lenin endorsed. But,

> we must exert every effort to make the boycott of real use in extending and intensifying agitation, so that it shall not be reduced to mere passive abstention from voting. If we are not mistaken this idea is already fairly widespread among the comrades working in Russia, who express it in the words: an *active* boycott. As distinct from passive abstention, an active boycott should imply increasing agitation tenfold, organizing meetings everywhere, taking advantage of election meetings, even if we have to force our way into them, holding demonstrations, political strikes, and so on and so forth.

Just how active? By

> advocating an insurrection and calling for the immediate organization of combat squads and contingents of a revolutionary army for the overthrow of the autocracy and the establishment of a provisional revolutionary government; spreading and popularizing the fundamental and absolutely obligatory program of this provisional revolutionary government, a program which is to serve as the banner of the uprising and as a model for all future repetitions of the Odessa events.[29]

For the first time, in August, Lenin publicly called for an insurrection to overthrow the regime and replace it with a provisional government. 1905, as he and other revolutionary veterans of that era would later remark, was the "dress rehearsal" for 1917.

Not every oppositional current was on board with the insurrectionary road. As bourgeois liberal forces began maneuvering for partaking in the Duma, Mensheviks saw an opening. Perhaps real change could come via the parliamentary route in an alliance with such forces. Lenin rebuked them and drew on Marx and Engels to support his argument. To entertain such a possibility means "playing at parliamentarism when no parliament whatever exists. It has been well said: we have no parliament as yet, but we have parliamentary cretinism galore."[30] Rather than cozying up to the liberals, Lenin—to let the reader know he had been thoroughly schooled in the lessons his mentors drew about 1848–1849—wrote, "we must expose the venal soul of a 'Frankfurt Parliament windbag' in every [Russian liberal] adherent who shuns this slogan of insurrection."[31] Not for the last time Lenin would invoke the lessons Marx and Engels's drew on the 1848–1849 revolutions to criticize those who viewed the parliamentary arena as the engine of real politics as opposed to what was actually taking place in Russia—the masses in the streets and a lesson worth revisiting.

Lenin's strategy regarding the Duma was based on the assumption that insurrection was still on the agenda; as long as that was true, all energy should be devoted to its realization. "Only an uprising holds out the possibility that the Duma farce will not be the end of the Russian bourgeois revolution, but the beginning of a complete democratic upheaval, which will kindle the fire of proletarian revolutions all over the world." To begin maneuvering for the parliamentary road, as the Mensheviks were now doing, would undercut that effort. Yet, he was sober about the situation. The proletariat could be "defeated" and, therefore, "a new era will be inaugurated ... European history will repeat itself, parliamentarism will for a time become the touchstone of all politics." But until that happens "prepare for insurrection, preach it, and organize it."[32] As he explained to the Bolshevik leader Anatoli Lunacharsky in St. Petersburg in early October, "there is no parliament as yet .... We must fight in a revolutionary way *for* a parliament, but not in a parliamentary way for a revolution."[33] For a "*detailed* analysis of the relation of 'parliamentarism' to revolution," Lenin recommended that he read "Marx on the class struggles in France in 1848."

In criticizing the Mensheviks, Lenin made clear that he was not opposed in principle to making deals with liberals. It all depended on context, as he explained in an article toward the end of October. "Under a parliamentary system it is often necessary to support a more liberal party against a less liberal one. But during a revolutionary struggle for a parliamentary system it is treachery to support liberal turncoats [the Cadets] who are 'reconciling' Trepov [a Czarist official] with the revolution."[34]

As prescient as Lenin had been for much of 1905, a development took place that he had not anticipated—the soviets or councils, an alternative form of representative democracy. More will be said about the soviets when Weber discovered them. Suffice it to say here that Leon Trotsky, who had managed to sneak his way back into Russia as early as February, became the effective head of its most important, the St. Petersburg Council of Workers Deputies. In hindsight, its three-month existence proved to be the political high watermark of the 1905 revolution.

Buffeted by a near nation-wide revolt, the regime relented once again. On October 17, the tsar issued a new Manifesto. In Lenin's words, it "promises a regular constitution; the Duma is invested with legislative powers; no law can come into force prior to approval by the people's representatives, ministerial responsibility has been granted; civil liberties have been granted—inviolability of the person, freedom of conscience, speech, assembly and association." Whereas the Bulygin Duma would have been only a consultative assembly, the new one being proposed would actually have "legislative powers." The earlier proposal was effectively rendered null and void—vindication for Lenin of the policy of "active boycott." The newly granted "concessions" were for Lenin profound confirmation of Marx and Engels's basic political premise—unlike what "parliamentary cretins" believed—that what takes place in the streets is decisive in explaining the fate of the parliamentary process, a point he would forever make.

Lenin, of course, was under no illusion about Nicholas's Manifesto. The regime was simply buying time. "*Only*," he responded, "by a victorious rising of the people, *only* by the complete domination of the armed proletariat and the peasantry [Lenin's 'democratic dictatorship of the proletariat and peasantry']," could "real liberty," "genuine popular representation," and a real "*constituent* assembly with the power to set up a new order in Russia" be realized.[35] And crucial in that fight was the need to "pay special attention to the army ... [W]e must attract the soldiers to workers' meetings, intensify our agitation in the barracks, extend our liaisons to officers, creating, alongside of the revolutionary army of workers, cadres of class conscious revolutionaries among the troops as well."[36] This was no abstract proposal. The regime struck back using the terrorism of the Black Hundreds, incipient fascist-like forces, particularly targeting Jews. "There were 690 documented pogroms—with over 3000 reported murders—during the two weeks following the declaration of the October

Manifesto .... The worst pogrom took place in Odessa, where 800 Jews were murdered, 5000 wounded and more than 100,000 made homeless."[37] If ever there was a need to win the ranks of the army to the fight for "real liberty," the time was now.

Despite the state-sponsored terrorism, Lenin and other émigrés eventually returned to Russia. Sensing that with a mobilized working class and civil liberties at least on paper there was now sufficient space to do open political work. His immediate task was to reorient the Bolsheviks and to urge them out of their semi-sectarian existence with regard to the mass movement, particularly the St. Petersburg soviet. He was willing, also, unlike a number of other Bolshevik leaders, to work with Trotsky, the effective head of the St. Petersburg soviet but an opponent since the Second Congress in 1903—in anticipation of 1917. In addition to broadening the party, Lenin said "the elective principle" could now be implemented (or, as he put it a few months later, "should be applied from top to bottom"[38]); that is, the party could now elect its leadership; more evidence that he never made virtue out of underground work.

WEBER TAKES NOTICE

Sometime in the summer of 1905 Weber began to pay attention to the cataclysmic developments unfolding to the east. In Heidelberg, where he was living, he had access to Russian publications and was soon able to read them to try to make sense of what was under way. *Zur Lage der bürgerlichen Demokratie in Rußland* or, *Bourgeois Democracy in Russia* (hereafter, BDR), a 200-page essay—chockfull with notes—was the first product of his intense reading of the situation.[39] In the first of Weber's copious footnotes, he begged off from having "expert knowledge" about the developments and described what he wrote as "a piece of 'journalism' (note the inverted commas)" and was at best "a temporary substitute for the serious socio-political report which I hope will at some future date come from a Russian pen." Then, "for reasons of space," Weber noted that he would make "no attempt ... to go into the earlier history of the movement, with the exception of a few indications .... A 'history' of this memorable period will only be possible if those in Russia *now* make it their business immediately to start *collecting* all the reports, resolutions, circulars, press bulletins etc. concerning the individual events, especially *all* official statements of the associations, which are simply not accessible abroad."[40] According to Wolfgang Mommsen, Weber originally intended to publish a daily account of the Russian Revolution and not an essay the length of *Zur Lage*.[41]

Weber's introductory caveats are instructive when compared to Lenin, who too, like Weber, was then living abroad, in Switzerland. The distinction between "journalism" and a "serious socio-political report" was one Lenin had earlier rejected despite a similar practice common in German Social Democratic party circles—the theoretical venue versus the daily party organ. Weber's two major writings on the Russian Revolution of 1905 were published in the semi-annual *Archiv für Sozialwissenschaft und Sozialpolitik*, one of Germany's most prestigious intellectual venues. The comparison here is limited to his *Zur Lage der bürgerlichen Demokratie* or, *Bourgeois Democracy in Russia*, the essay that makes for the most instructive contrasts with Lenin.

Lenin, unlike Weber, thought it important to weave theoretical issues into quotidian reporting, a way to narrow the all too frequent divide between the world of the intelligentsia and the class-conscious worker activist. Thus, Lenin's theoretical views on the unfolding developments in 1905 are not to be found in a theoretical venue but in his "journalism"— in publications that were illegal in tsarist Russia and, thus, had to be smuggled from abroad—with all the uncertainty that entailed—into the hands of its workers. Unlike Weber, Lenin the daily activist couldn't afford to wait for the moment when a "serious socio-political report" could be written. Therein already is a key difference between the two; not unlike the Marx/Mill difference in this regard (see Chap. 2). Being political for a Marxist, in other words, required making daily judgments—only what a newspaper and not a magazine, journal or similar venue permitted. Weber, at the same time, was emphatic that his essays were not "academic," making, therefore, for a fairer comparison with Lenin's writings.

Beyond the preliminaries in his introductory footnote, it becomes immediately clear that Weber's focus in his BDR was narrow. Anyone new to what was under way in Russia would never have learned from his account about the details of Bloody Sunday or anything of substance about the chief dynamic in the upheavals, the massive strikes. For Weber, rather, his concern was for the prospects of the liberal movement as an alternative to not only the monarchy but the Bolsheviks as well.[42] He began with a brief history of the "Zemstvo Movement," one of the two milieus that birthed the liberals of 1905, specifically, the Constitutional Democrats or Cadet Party. The *zemstvo*, again, were the organs of local government that the monarchy instituted in 1864, a concession to the democratic yearnings from below but without any real power. Along with their officials were the civil servant professionals they employed such as teachers, doctors, statisticians, the so-called Third Element (discussed later).

The other milieu from which the liberals of 1905 originated was the intelligentsia. They grouped, in Weber's account, around the bimonthly publication of Peter Struve, *Osvobozhdenie* (Liberation), beginning in 1902. Tsarist censorship required publication abroad and for its supporters, the Union of Liberation, to resort to "necessarily 'conspiratorial' organization." Struve, Weber added, "is well known to readers of this journal, with his profound and expert knowledge of capitalism, originally influenced by Marx." His most important contribution was to declare "in favour of—in the broadest sense of the word—'bourgeois democracy', especially for driving 'populist' romanticism out of the heads of the social reformers." Weber no doubt was referring to the Marxist critique of the populist Narodnaya Volya Party, or, the Narodniks. And in that connection he made his first reference to Lenin who too had briefly collaborated with Struve in this campaign.[43] Weber noted, but without comment, that when the Union was formed in 1903 "only official Social Democracy had excluded itself"—that is, before the split into the Bolshevik and Menshevik wings.

But Weber's main purpose in his essay was to render a judgment on the democratic content of the constitutional proposals of the Cadets. Before examining his assessments, a look at what Lenin also wrote about the liberal movement prior to 1905 is in order—which can only be at best a distillation since it was at least twenty-fold greater than all that Weber wrote.

Lenin, as Weber's point about Russian Social Democracy suggests, had long followed and commented on the "Zemstvo Movement" to also determine its potential for contributing to Russia's bourgeois democratic revolution—a fact, again, ignored by friend and foe alike.[44] His fifty-page aforementioned 1901 pamphlet, *Persecutors of the Zemstvo and the Hannibals of Liberalism*, registered how informed he was about its history, the first of his in-depth writings about the institution and its accompanying political current that Weber only discovered in 1905.

On the eve of Bloody Sunday Lenin explained in a twenty-page pamphlet that there were two stages in his writings on the *zemstvo* current—judgments prior to and *after* the formation of the already mentioned Union of Liberation in 1903. For the first stage, he viewed them as possible allies to advance the much-needed bourgeois democratic revolution in Russia, "possible" being the operative word. But his pamphlet disputed Struve's claim that they might be "the embryo of a constitution." Yet, Lenin encouraged liberals to fight for "political liberties" because their acquisition was in the interest of the proletariat who "must have freedom in order to develop the struggle for socialism to the utmost."[45]

Ever in search of any political openings, Lenin followed the *zemstvo* movement closely. About a secret congress some of them held in 1901 he implored that they show some courage as one of the delegates had demanded:

> We are in complete agreement with the outcry of this liberal who is prepared to challenge the bureaucratic autocracy to open struggle. If the best Zemstvo men do not today take energetic measures, if they do not get rid of their usual [servile] attitude, their trivial questions of secondary importance—"tinkering", as one venerable Zemstvo man put it—the Zemstvos will lose their adherents and turn into the usual "government offices". Such an inglorious death is inevitable; for one cannot with impunity for whole decades do nothing but show cowardice, offer thanks, and humbly petition; one must threaten, demand, stop wasting time on trifles, and settle down to the real work.[46]

Lenin clearly was prepared to fight side by side with the *zemstvo* liberals—if they were prepared to fight. They were not, as events would show; hence, as he accurately foresaw, "their inglorious death." In his 1902 classic *What is to be Done?*, for example, he wrote "that the workers cannot look on indifferently while the government is waging a struggle against the Zemstvo, and the Zemstvos are called upon to stop making mild speeches and to speak firmly and resolutely when revolutionary Social Democracy confronts the government in all its strengths."

There was one component of the *zemstvo* that both Lenin and Weber were positive about, the previously mentioned "Third Element." These were, again, the professionals hired by them such as doctors, teachers, agronomists and statisticians.[47] For Weber the "evident idealism and willingness to make sacrifices shown by these men, the only category of civil servants who really live 'among and with the people', is one of the most ethically pleasing and estimable things that today's Russia has to offer."[48] Four years earlier in 1901 Lenin came to their defense against tsarist detractors who feared that the hired professionals had interests independent of the land-owning elites. In so doing, Lenin came also to the defense of "parliamentarism" against its tsarist detractors, that is, those who claimed that a political system based on the interests of the landed elite, an autocracy, was somehow politically and morally superior to parliamentary governance.[49] Not the first or last time would he counterpoise the advantages of parliamentarism against the backwardness of tsarism.

Once Struve's Union of Liberation was formed in 1903 Lenin took a more critical stance—but not on principle. Rather, it was the actual conduct of the liberals that earned his ire. Their tendency to prevaricate and be irresolute when it came to actually fighting for bourgeois democracy was the reason.

Never was Lenin as clear about needed sobriety about Russian liberalism than on the eve of the 1905 Revolution. Two months before the social earthquake he urged Russian Social Democrats to recognize that the *zemstvo* movement, its redeeming features notwithstanding, was being bypassed by history—an admonishment to the Menshevik wing of Russian Social Democracy.

> At this of all times, the political activity of the proletariat must be focused on organising powerful pressure on the government, not on the liberal opposition. Particularly now, agreements between the workers and the Zemstvo-ists about peaceful demonstrations—agreements which would inevitably boil down to the staging of musical-comedy effects—are utterly out of place; what is needed is to rally the advanced, revolutionary elements of the proletariat in preparation for a decisive struggle for freedom .... Particularly now, it is vital to build up in the revolutionary proletariat the firm conviction that the present "emancipation movement in society" will necessarily and inevitably prove a bubble like all the others before it unless the force of the worker masses, capable of and ready for an uprising, intervenes .... The way for the workers to give serious support to the Zemstvo petitions is not by concluding agreements about the conditions on which the Zemstvo-ists would have a right to speak in the name of the people, but by striking a blow at the people's enemies .... And the workers will rise still more fearlessly, in still greater numbers, to finish off the bear, to win by force *for themselves* what is promised as charity to the liberal bourgeois gentry—freedom of assembly, freedom of the workers' press, full political freedom for a broad and open struggle for the complete victory of socialism.[50]

In clear and unequivocal language, quintessential Lenin, he explained how workers in that moment should respond to the *zemstvo* campaign and to liberal initiatives in general. Unlike those of the liberals, its demands had to be for full political democracy—needed for the socialist revolution. Of crucial significance for real-time politics, Lenin penned these lines about a month and a half before Bloody Sunday. It is hard to find anything in the Lenin arsenal before 1905 that is so exemplary of the spirit of his 1902 polemic, *What is to be Done?*—how to prepare for a revolution.

When Weber, therefore, discovered the *zemstvo* movement sometime in mid-1905 with the hope that it could be the agent of Russia's bourgeois democratic movement, Lenin had concluded at least a half year earlier that it was Russia's still developing working class that would actually be the protagonist for the country's democratic revolution. Nothing in Weber's political make-up would had made him open to that alternative. If he dismissed Germany's working class in playing such a role, as he argued in his Inaugural Address, why would he have thought any better of Russian workers?

Lenin, on the other hand, was open, at least for five years, to the possibility that Russian liberals could "get their act together," to actually lead a democratic revolution—just as Marx and Engels had once thought about their German counterparts. They never did. And therein lies the essential answer to the age-old question that opens this chapter: why wasn't there a liberal alternative to the Bolsheviks in the Russian Revolution? In the years and months leading up to 1905, Russian liberals had an opportunity to duplicate what their counterparts in the West had done. But once the blood-letting of January 9 (22) had taken place, the Russian working class was forced onto the center stage of history to become the leading protagonist, ensuring, therefore, that Russia's democratic revolution would not be limited to meeting the class interests of its bourgeoisie. Liberals, again, had missed their moment in the sun; they had prevaricated far too long. And even then, two days after learning about Bloody Sunday, Lenin wrote: "Liberalism, of whatever kind, merits support by the Social-Democrats only to the extent that it actually opposes the autocracy."[51] Actions, as always, and not words were decisive for Lenin.

There is no reason to believe that had Weber paid attention to Russia before that fateful Sunday he would have looked beyond its liberal layers for realizing its bourgeois democratic revolution. His political blinders and prejudices about the working class prevented him from seeing what Lenin could. It stamped, to be seen, ineluctably what so distinguished his reading of the Russian events from Lenin's.

COMPARING LENIN AND WEBER IN REAL-TIME 1905

Most evident about Weber's backstory to 1905 is the absence of any sustained discussion about its essential dynamo from the very beginning in January—the unruly crowds in the streets. It gets at best cursory treatment. Bloody Sunday merits only one mention, "the slaughter of 9/22

January." Lenin, on the other hand, argued that it was precisely the mass mobilizations throughout the year that made it possible for there to be even any consideration of a liberal option like a national *zemstvo*, a Zemsky Sobor, a constitutional monarchy or better, a republic. Hence, his retort in October to those who thought like Weber: "We must fight in a revolutionary way *for* a parliament, but not in a parliamentary way for a revolution." And by "revolution," he meant, again, a bourgeois democratic revolution. The near-exclusive attention to the writing of the constitution, the focus of Weber's BDR, was for Lenin putting the proverbial cart before the horse.

There is one telling point Weber made about the constitutional drafters that Lenin would probably have agreed with: "the economic clash of interests and the class character of the proletariat is a stab in the back for the specifically bourgeois reformers; that is the fate of their work here as everywhere."[52] This reveals that Weber was not only conversant with but in apparent agreement with some of the basic premises of the historical materialist fount that informed Lenin. Liberal reformers and workers—at this stage in history—had fundamentally different and conflictual class interests. Hence, as Lenin had increasingly recognized, that is why liberals would not lead Russia's democratic breakthrough; their visceral fear that it would aid and abet working class hegemony, "a stab in the back." Weber, a "*bürgerlich* scholar," could easily recognize and identify with that fear and, hence, I argue his reading of 1905.

Nowhere in his essay were Weber's politics on better display than in his treatment of "The Socialist Parties." His description of Russian Social Democracy and the Bolshevik/Menshevik split that emerged after the 1903 party congress is accurate for the most part. But his characterization of Lenin and the Bolsheviks as "putschists" is problematic—maybe the origins of this time-worn charge about Lenin. Though Weber didn't define "putschism," it generally meant then and now a political orientation that advocates for the overthrowing of a government by a small group of fighters—exactly why Lenin took umbrage. In 1916, a half year before he criticized Weber's charge, Lenin offered a definition. "The term 'putsch', in its scientific sense, may be employed only when the attempt at insurrection has revealed nothing but a circle of conspirators or stupid maniacs, and has aroused no sympathy among the masses."[53] As already documented, nothing in his calls for an "insurrection" in 1905 ever suggested such a strategy. When he first did in August that year, after the mass uprising in Odessa, it was always about the "overthrow of the autocracy" rather than just a government. And it could be realized "*only* by a victorious rising of the people, *only* by the complete domination of the armed proletariat and the peasantry"—a mass mobilization in other words. It is just why Lenin criticized, long before 1905, terrorists; they, always a courageous but tiny minority, relegated the masses to being spectators rather than protagonists. That the Odessa uprising coincided with the famed sailors mutiny on the battleship *Potemkin*—"for the first time," Lenin wrote, "an important unit of the armed forces of tsarism, a battle ship, has openly gone over to the side of the revolution"—gave him good reason to think a mass-based insurrection was a possibility. "Social-Democracy never stooped to playing at military conspiracies; it never gave prominence to military questions until the actual conditions of civil war had arisen."[54] Odessa and its significance is virtually absent in Weber's account.

Weber may have been right that there were indeed Bolsheviks who believed that an insurrection to overthrow the autocracy could be done by a small group of armed men. Not Lenin. In a stinging rebuke to such thinking in the most intense moment in 1905, September–October, during the broadest strike wave in the country, when insurrection was a real possibility, he declared that unless the Bolshevik "Combat Committee" in St. Petersburg makes "contact with … a minimum of 200 or 300 groups… then it is a dead Combat Committee. It will have to be buried." Its task was to "train hundreds of experienced fighters, who tomorrow will be leading hundreds of thousands." It was a plea to the Bolsheviks to broaden their ties to the mass movement—"do not refuse to contact any group"— and to take initiatives—"do not wait for our help."[55] Writing from afar, Weber might be excused for not knowing about the real Lenin given the audience his letter was directed to. Nevertheless, those are the facts and it behooves like-minded Lenin detractors to produce the putschist smoking gun; it simply does not exist, at least when Weber's otherwise observant eyes paid attention to the Russian events.

Weber's characterization "of the sect-like character of Social Democracy with its close ties to strictly precise dogmas" is instructive.

> Like the thoroughgoing Jesuit, the devout Marxist is imbued by his dogma with a blithely superiority and the self-assurance of the somnambulist. Disdaining to strive for lasting political success, and confident of being above reproach, he accepts with equanimity and a mocking laugh the collapse of all hopes—his own included—of overcoming the mortal foe he shares with other groups; is always exclusively concerned with the preserva-

tion of the pure faith and—if possible—the increase of his own sect by a few souls; and seeks the 'unmasking' of 'those who are also catholics' here of 'traitors to the people' there, in neighbouring groups.[56]

Clearly on display were Weber's anti-Catholic biases—related to his lifelong anti-Polish tendencies—in opining about the Bolsheviks.

Here is an excerpt from the article "Social Democracy's Attitude Toward the Peasant Movement" (discussed later) Lenin wrote to fellow Bolsheviks at about the same time when Weber was disparaging them.

> The urban and industrial proletariat will inevitably be the nucleus of our Social-Democratic Labour Party, but we must attract to it, enlighten, and organise all who labour and are exploited as stated in our programme—all without exception: handicraftsmen, paupers, beggars, servants, tramps, prostitutes—of course, subject to the necessary and obligatory condition that they join the Social-Democratic movement and not that the Social-Democratic movement join them, that they adopt the standpoint of the proletariat, and not that the proletariat adopt theirs.[57]

If Lenin was creating a "sect," as Weber charged, it was a remarkably inclusive one.

When the monarchy issued its Manifesto on October 17 (30), its first real flirtation with representative democracy, Lenin saw it as vindication for Bolshevik support to the mass insurrectionary movement that the uprising in Odessa in July spearheaded.[58] Long familiar with Russia's liberal bourgeoisie and its lack of resolve for the democratic struggle, Lenin, as always, sought to make it a teachable moment: "No, gentlemen of the bourgeoisie, the workers will never forget the enforced nature of the tsar's capitulation! The workers will never forget that it was only by force, by the force of their organization, their unanimity and their mass heroism, that they wrested from tsarism a recognition of liberty in a paper manifesto; and only in this way will they win real liberty for themselves."[59] It was also vindication, he declared, for those like the Bolsheviks who called for an "active boycott" of the aforementioned Bulygin Duma proposal in August, the regime's moribund attempt to pretend to be granting representative democracy.

The most that Weber had to initially say in BDR about why the Manifesto was granted is "that it appeared to be due to the effect of the strike"—without any elaboration—and done "so quickly … that it made the structural weakness of the old regime seem considerably greater than it was."[60] "No," wrote Lenin, "tsarism is still far from having surrendered.

The autocracy has by no means fallen as yet." And most prophetically, "many great battles will still have to be fought by the revolutionary proletariat, and the first victory will help it to rally its forces and enlist new allies in the struggle."[61] Barely able to utter "strike" to explain the tsar's concessions, Weber could have been one of those "bourgeois gentlemen" Lenin was needling.

As previously noted, the soviets or councils were an unexpected development for Lenin. Again, they began simply as organs for factory workers to coordinate the general strike in the summer/fall. Weber described the most important of the approximately fifty throughout mainly western Russia, the Council of Workers Deputies in St. Petersburg: "it consists of deputies of each factory with at least 400 workers, and is thus a representation of the specifically workers' elite of big industry on a local basis, not on the basis of specific industries." Though "most prominent" among the "workers' organizations ... of a socialist character," they "were not created by the party."[62] Further comments suggest that he followed as close as he could from afar the deliberations of the St. Petersburg soviet including the regime's arrest of its Menshevik president on November 26, portending its eventual fate.

But what Weber accurately described was only the beginning of wisdom for Lenin. In his first substantive comments on the soviets he began almost apologetically in begging to differ with the Bolsheviks on the scene. He was writing as "an *onlooker*" from the "accursed 'afar.'" Nevertheless, he disagreed with those who had a narrower or, perhaps, more sectarian attitude toward the soviets, specifically, the main one in St. Petersburg.

> I think it would be inadvisable for the Soviet to adhere wholly to any one party .... The Soviet of Workers' Deputies came into being through the general strike, in connection with the strike, and for its aims. Who led the strike and brought it to a victorious close? The *whole* proletariat, which includes non-Social-Democrats—fortunately a minority. What were the aims of the strike? They were both economic and political. The economic aims concerned the *whole* proletariat, all workers and partly even all working people, not the wage-workers alone. The political aims concerned all the people, or rather all the peoples, of Russia. Those aims were to free all the peoples of Russia from the yoke of the autocracy, survivals of serfdom, a rightless status, and police tyranny .... It seems to me that the Soviet ... as an organization representing all occupations, should *strive* to include deputies from *all* industrial, professional and office workers, domestic servants, farm labourers, etc., from *all* who want and are able to fight in common for a better life for the whole working people.[63]

Again, if Lenin was seeking to create a sect as Weber charged, he was remarkably ecumenical in his approach. His inclusivity, to the contrary, was consistent with his long-held views. Obviously, as his letter suggests, there were Bolsheviks who deserved Weber's criticism. But not Lenin.[64]

There was another side to the St. Petersburg soviet of even greater import for Lenin that had to do with its inclusive or potentially inclusive character for which he advocated. The fact that there were fighters active in it from other political parties, particularly, the Socialist-Revolutionaries "was an advantage, not a disadvantage." As long as they were "revolutionary bourgeois democrats" willing to fight was all that mattered. That they "believe in God," or "defend mysticism" was of no import. Decisive is that they possess "vitality."[65] "The Soviet," in fact, he declared:

> must proclaim itself the provisional revolutionary government, or form such a government, and must by all means enlist to this end the participation of new deputies not only from the workers, but, first of all, from the sailors and soldiers, who are everywhere seeking freedom; secondly, from the revolutionary peasantry, and thirdly, from the revolutionary bourgeois intelligentsia.[66]

Thus, for the first time Lenin sketched out soviet representative democracy as an alternative to parliamentary representative democracy. In hindsight, Lenin's 1905 letter from that "accursed 'afar'" anticipated, almost uncannily, his more famous "Letters from Afar" in March 1917, that outlined his course for that momentous year.

Weber may be forgiven for not knowing Lenin's actual views since his letter wasn't published until 1940.[67] Nevertheless, again, those are the facts about the real Lenin—far from the sectarian portrait he painted. For Lenin's critics since then, their calumnies about Lenin the ogre, certainly for this period, are inexcusable.

There is clearly one sentence in Weber's narrative that Lenin would have readily embraced. It introduces the lengthiest section in BDR, "The Agrarian Question." "The crucial question which will determine the future not only of the Constitutional Democratic movement but, more importantly, of its fundamental programme, and beyond that the chances of a liberal 'development' in the Western European sense, concerns the *peasants*."[68] Lenin, about the same time, in his previously cited article about the significance of the Manifesto of October 17 and in "what-is-to-be-done" mode, wrote:

The revolutionary proletariat has brought about the first great victory of the urban revolution. It must now broaden and deepen the foundations of the revolution by extending it to the countryside. To raise the peasantry to the level of conscious defence of the cause of liberty, to demand that serious measures be taken in the interests of the peasantry, and to prepare in the countryside a movement which, in conjunction with the advanced urban proletariat, will deal the final blow at the autocracy and win complete and genuine liberty—such is Russian Social-Democracy's next task.[69]

Both he and Weber were, therefore, at least on the same page about the weighty role of the peasantry in Russia's future.

After a detailed account of how the mainstream parties, especially the Cadets, addressed the all-important issue of agrarian reform, Weber concluded: "the party that aims to carry through the reform by *legal* means has an unenviable task."[70] The reality of the autocracy, in other words, made real agrarian reform unlikely. And that's exactly why Lenin argued that all efforts to carry out a real agrarian reform depended on the overthrow of the autocracy. Thus, while Weber was examining what parties like the Cadets had written about the peasantry, Lenin was trying to figure out how to link the urban struggle with the yet fully emergent rural struggle—"the advance guard" with "the rear guard" as he put it. Two weeks after the tsar's October Manifesto, Lenin wrote: "Events have begun to provide telling confirmation of a truth we long ago proclaimed to our readers, and shall repeat over and over again, namely, that until tsarism's actual power is overthrown, all its concessions, and even a constituent assembly, are a phantom, a mirage, a piece of deception."[71]

While in agreement with Lenin about the import of the peasant question, Weber thought it inconceivable, unlike Lenin, that Russia's peasants could be won to "the cause of liberty"—let alone in an alliance "with the advanced urban proletariat" headed by "the Lenin group": "the work to be done on the formidable and fundamental agrarian problem cannot possibly be undertaken with the intellectual tools of Marxism."[72] To be successful "it seems vital that liberalism continues to see its vocation as fighting against both [state] bureaucratic and Jacobin *centralism*." Opposing all that Lenin represented, as he understood, was Weber's recommendation to Russian liberals. Never did he examine Lenin's proposals for agrarian reform—an issue the Bolshevik leader had given extensive attention to from the very beginning of his political career. No formulation epitomized more the weight he gave to it than his slogan "the

Revolutionary Democratic Dictatorship of the Proletariat and the
Peasantry" elaborated on in his 100-page book in 1905, *Two Tactics of
Social-Democracy in the Democratic Revolution*. In the context of an insurgency still unfolding, the task was figuring out how to realize that slogan.
Only if the proletarian/peasant majority imposed its will, "complete
domination"—a dictatorship in other words—could the "agrarian problem" Weber correctly diagnosed be solved.

Weber's contempt for the Bolsheviks explains his portrait of the Moscow
uprising which was in progress when he ended his essay. In fact, he provided hardly any details other than to say in one of his many notes that
"the Leninist group ... and a section of the Socialist Revolutionaries, have
been *planning* the foolish revolt for a long time."[73] Weber did elaborate
on what he thought of the "Lenin group."

> "Correct" Social Democracy drills the masses in the intellectual parade-ground step and ... refers them to a paradise in this world, making of it a
> kind of inoculation against change for those with an interest in preserving
> the status quo. It accustoms its charges to the unquestioning acceptance of
> dogmas, submissiveness towards party authorities, to ostentatious mass
> strikes which achieve nothing, and to the passive consumption of the tiresome invective of their journalists, which ... provides its authors with a comfortable living; it accustoms them, in other words, to a "hysterical indulgence
> in emotion", which takes the place of economic and political thought and
> action. On this barren ground, once the "eschatological" age of the movement has passed and generation after generation has clenched its fists in its
> pockets in vain or bared its teeth heavenwards only intellectual torpor
> can grow.[74]

Weber was clearly no friend of the Bolsheviks. His characterization of what
came to be called "Leninism" may be the first of its kind. It anticipated
many of the usual subsequent charges about "Leninism-cum-Stalinism."
But it wasn't the reality Lenin knew about the Bolsheviks. Even if he had
wanted to—and there is nothing to suggest that he did—Lenin was in no
position to impose his will. The fact that he couldn't get his comrades to
publish his article calling for a non-sectarian stance toward the soviets
speaks volumes about the "Lenin group" in 1905.

Once Lenin was back in Russia in early November, his paper trail—
unfortunately for posterity—was much thinner; only in March next year
would he have regular access to a newspaper. Thus, it is not clear to what
extent he knew beforehand, as Weber suggests, about the Moscow upris-

ing in early December—the last gasp of the 1905 Revolution. Local Bolsheviks were certainly involved. It erupted while he and other Bolshevik leaders were meeting in Tammerfors, Finland, which they ended early in order to get to the scene. What is known is that Lenin, like Trotsky, thought that Russia's urban proletariat, particularly in St. Petersburg, was by November "exhausted" after months of continuous mobilizing. In a letter to St. Petersburg comrade Maria Essen on October 26 he recommended the "time for the uprising" along with details about how to prepare it. "I repeat, I would *willingly postpone* until the spring."[75] It would give the "rear guard," the peasantry, time to catch up with the "advance guard," the urban proletariat. A month before the uprising he wrote: "the revolutionary people have still to solve many important military problems before they will be able to carry the revolution to real and final victory."[76] Lastly, his actions at the Tammerfors meeting suggests that he thought the revolutionary wave had already ebbed before the Moscow uprising and, therefore, would have been an unlikely advocate for it.[77]

In January 1917, as noted at the outset of this chapter, Lenin excoriated "Herr Professor Max Weber" for characterizing the Moscow uprising as a "putsch" and a "*senseless* uprising" that had been "long-prepared" by "the Lenin group and a section of Socialist Revolutionaries."[78] Lenin countered with a list of figures to show that the revolt was in fact a mass action accompanied by a general strike that lasted for more than a week. What he didn't say, understandably, is that it failed owing to poor planning and was probably premature, contravening, in other words, Lenin's advice.[79] Whether he knew or was involved in the plans, he also didn't say. But there is no evidence that he did—and why it likely failed.

In the last weeks of 1905, if not before, Weber became pessimistic about the chances for a liberal outcome in Russia. The defeat of the Moscow rebels heralded, he accurately saw, a new era—"pseudo-constitutionalism." He could envision by then only one ending for the Romanovs: "Only in the tragic event of a *European* war would the autocracy finally be destroyed."[80] Here was Weber at his prophetic best for indeed that is exactly how the 300-year-old dynasty came to its ignominious end, in February 1917. The problem is that Weber could not envision any party other than the liberals being the beneficiaries of such a conflagration. Certainly not Lenin's Bolsheviks. "For the time being," Weber concluded, Russia's liberals "may have to be content for this brilliant movement of zemstvo liberalism, of which Russia has as much reason to be proud as we Germans have to be proud of the Frankfurt Parliament, to be 'consigned to history', at least in its present form."[81]

Lenin, as already noted, had a quite different opinion about the Frankfurt Parliament of 1848. In fact, he drew on its example—by way of Marx and Engels—to rebuke Russian liberals and those like the Mensheviks who had any hopes in them. The context, to repeat, was the monarchy's August 6 Bulygin Duma proposal, the moribund faux parliament, to which he counterposed an "active boycott," that is, insurrection. Going along with the tsar's bait and switch trick, he charged, meant "playing at parliamentarism when no parliament whatever exists. It has been well said: we have no parliament as yet, but we have parliamentary cretinism galore." Coined by Engels and often employed by Lenin, "parliamentary cretinism" referred to the mistaken belief of the Frankfurt parliamentarians— disproportionately academics—that their deliberations, including the writing of the ideal liberal constitution, were the beginning and end of politics. Prussian King Frederick IV sent them packing without a fight a year later in 1849. "[W]e must expose," Lenin demanded, "the venal soul of a 'Frankfurt Parliament windbag' in every [Russian liberal] adherent who shuns the slogan of insurrection."[82] Humanity paid dearly for the failure; two world wars were required to plant liberal democracy in German soil for the first time. Lenin's lines are worth repeating because nothing in their texts better reveals the core differences between him and Weber than their attitudes about the Frankfurt Parliament.

It was when the Moscow revolt was being suppressed that Weber revisited his explanation for the tsar's October 17 Manifesto. "Without the warning from foreign financiers—not in so many words but by implication—the Manifesto of 17 October would perhaps never have been issued or at least it would soon have been revoked. Fear of the rage of the masses and of the mutiny of the troops, and the weakening of the authoritarian regime by defeat in the east [the Russo-Japanese War], would have been ineffective had not the autocracy been at the mercy of the cool, hard hand of the banks and stock exchanges."[83] A few months later he added: "It is quite correct to say (as the reactionaries maintain) that the 'Jews' forced through, brought about by stealth or at least helped to construct the Russian Constitution [i.e. the Manifesto] … [those] in high finance in Berlin and Paris, who are entrusted with the control of the prices of Russian government stocks."[84] Thus, for the first time the reader of BDR sees what is so sorely missing in Weber's account of 1905—but only for the purpose of rendering them at best a secondary factor. Weber was politically incapable of thinking that the crowds in the streets are decisive in history.

Lenin too acknowledged the role finance capital, both foreign and domestic, played in the drama of 1905 (and without reference to the ethnicity of any of its members). Hence, his explanation for the regime's ill-fated August Bulygin Duma proposal: "It was impossible to govern the country, to obtain money, or to continue existing without coming to terms with the Right wing of the bourgeoisie ... the autocratic government is ... the government of a capitalist country, linked with Europe, with international markets and international capital by thousands of inseverable ties."[85] As for Nicholas's October Manifesto, Lenin noted: "the European bourgeoisie is sighing with relief .... The stock exchange is hastening to express fuller confidence in Russia's finances. Russian securities, which have been falling for the last few days, are now going up. The foreign bankers who fled from revolutionary St. Petersburg are promising to return within a fortnight. In the constitution [what the Manifesto promised on paper] the European bourgeoisie sees a pledge of 'peaceful' minor concessions, which will wholly satisfy the propertied classes without at the same time allowing the revolutionary proletariat to acquire 'too much' freedom."[86] Lenin's comments came after a round up, in highly distilled form, of the many revolts throughout the empire leading up to the issuance of the October Manifesto. For him it was the "cool, hard" facts on the ground, literally, in the streets, which were decisive in explaining the regime's decision to appear to be making concessions and not, contrary to Weber, the all-powerful hand of finance capital.[87] If anyone sounded like one of the "vulgar materialists" he often criticized, it was Weber himself and not Lenin.[88]

The issue of European finance capital allowed Weber at the very end of BDR to drop all pretenses of just writing "a piece of journalism." His real "vocation" called. Though confined to the last of his many corpulent notes, he issued his own warning, to German finance capital—Weber's "what-is-to-be-done" moment. If it was hoping for a liberal outcome in Russia, it should refrain from enabling the Russian autocracy. "Let the German 'bourgeois', who is expected to invest capital in Russian government stocks, take careful note of that. The list of arrest warrants and bans on assembly is *infinitely more important* for his business interests than the financial reports 'embellished' with the aid of Russia's foreign credits."[89] As Germany's foremost social scientist, it was the best advice a "*bürgerlich* scholar" could offer to his class—to think about their long-term rather than short-term interests. Whether they could is another matter.

CONCLUSION

Weber's 400-page essay *Rußlands Übergang zum Scheinkconstitutionalismus* or, *Russia's Transition to Pseudo-constitutionalism*, was his last pronouncement on the 1905 Revolution. It details the failure of Russia's first semblance of parliamentary democracy. Revolutionary forces were unable to overcome Nicholas's intransigence to ending his absolutist rule. Lenin spilled as much if not more ink documenting the same outcome but under more trying circumstances, the regime's ever-present censorial machine. Their texts make for fascinating reading but not as rewarding for comparative purposes as the period when the revolution was on the ascent.[90] As political space by the end of 1907 was increasingly contracting, Lenin made his escape into exile once again, almost losing his life in the process.

Weber explained at the end of his second book-length essay why "we must break off this chronicle." It was shortly after Tsar Nicholas sent packing the country's first parliament, or Duma, on July 8, 1906—not unlike, again, what his distant relative had done to the Frankfurt Parliament in 1849. "The dissolution of the Duma," Lenin wrote within a few days, "has most strikingly and clearly confirmed the views of those who warned against being obsessed with the external 'constitutional' aspect of the Duma and ... the constitutional surface of Russian politics during the second quarter of 1906."[91] It was as if Lenin was speaking directly to Weber about his 400-page doorstopper.

The reasons Weber gave for the "break" in his "chronicle" were that the "Russian freedom struggle reveals few of the features of 'greatness'" and has a "lack on both sides of really 'great leaders' on whom the emotional interest of observers could focus." About the opposition to the regime: "the tiny percentage of the population represented by the industrial proletariat can have little significance at the moment, while the ideals of the peasant ["peasant communism"] lie, in spite of everything, in an unreal world."[92]

Though Weber continued his interest in Russia, it clearly took a back seat to other priorities. Other than a talk in 1908 and a letter to a Russian newspaper in 1909, he had little to say about developments there.[93] The question that attracted him in the first place—and the one that introduces this chapter—was answered by the tsar's proroguing of the Cadet-led First Duma. Russian liberalism's moment in the sun was now history. And because Weber couldn't fathom any alternative to Russian liberals, especially an alliance of a "tiny" urban proletariat and peasants that Lenin campaigned for, his attention turned to other topics. Not unlike Tocqueville in the wake of another liberal failure, Weber found history more interesting than contemporary politics.

Weber returned to the Russian story in 1917 in two short essays that amount to about twenty pages (treated in the accompanying Appendix).[94] It was unavoidable given the Revolution's origins in World War I and his nationalist core. What he had once forecast, a Romanov ending due to "the tragic event of a *European war*," was now a reality. By not following, however, the Russian theater in the way he once had, Weber was unprepared to understand what ensued eleven years later. His last pronouncements in 1906, particularly about the "lack of really great leaders" on either side, and the unlikelihood that Russia's "tiny industrial proletariat" would be of any "significance," were especially disabling.

Lenin and Trotsky would later say after the Bolshevik Revolution of October 1917 that 1905, to repeat, was a "dress rehearsal" for 1917. Weber's more limited writings in 1917 and afterward are, however, almost devoid of any reference to his rich 1905/1906 essays except for the repeated claim that finance capital was still determinant in Russian developments. Perhaps the reason is due to his above-quoted forecasts that proved to be all-so wrong. But he could have justifiably claimed to have been right about Russia's liberal bourgeoisie—their failure to lead the democratic revolution. It's just that the class who did was simply not on his radar, or better, to his political liking. It is undeniable that the laboring masses who led the February Revolution produced what Lenin could rightly call "the freest country in the world"—certainly more so than Weber's homeland. But by 1917, in the middle of World War I, Weber's nationalist proclivities were on full display. And Weber never claimed that his values were informed by objective reality—his fact/value distinction. It's not that he couldn't see what had happened in Russia; it's that he disagreed with it in a most fundamental political way. He was, after all, a "*bürgerlich*" scholar.

One claim in the 1905–1906 essays would have been especially difficult to reconcile with reality after the October Revolution of 1917. If the "Lenin group" of Social Democracy was truly a "sect … disdaining to strive for lasting political success," then Weber had a problem in explaining the outcome of October. The best he could come up with was that rather than the Bolsheviks he once wrote about, it was a "military dictatorship, not, it is true, of generals, but of corporals" that was actually in power.[95] Here, tellingly, Weber's politics trumped his scholarship. As astute an observer of social reality as Weber was, especially with regard to the peasant question, he missed what Lenin had long understood about the military; its ranks were peopled by, as he put it in early 1917, "peasants in uniform."[96] Hence, his insistence on realizing what would be his winning formula for the October Revolution, and first declared in 1905, the "revolutionary democratic dictatorship of the proletariat and peasants"— the alliance Weber thought inconceivable. So, yes, Lenin might have said to Weber: there indeed was a "military dictatorship" in power after October—but of both peasants and workers.

In his still highly regarded—within academic and mainstream circles— *A People's Tragedy: A History of the Russian Revolution*, Orlando Figes made a pregnant comment about the Cadet's fall from grace—their failure to offer any meaningful resistance to Nicholas's dismissal of the First Duma in July 1906 that they led and their subsequent rightward trajectory. "Never again would the Kadets place their trust in the support of 'the people'. Nor would they claim to represent them. From this point on, they would consciously become what in fact they had been all along: the natural party of the bourgeoisie. Liberalism and the people went their separate ways."[97] But that is hindsight wisdom. In real-time Lenin and Weber thought the Cadets could actually lead the democratic revolution and both acted—most important for politics—especially, Lenin, on that assumption. It took Weber about a year longer than Lenin to realize the nullity of Russian liberalism. But he was politically incapable of seeing the only effective alternative to the Cadets—Russia's "tiny" industrial proletariat in alliance with the peasantry.

The richness of Weber's and Lenin's texts does not allow in a book this length and with other comparisons anything more detailed. Presented here are the most significant contrasts. I admit that "significant" is informed by hindsight, that is, the subsequent course of the Bolshevik project. Thus, one topic that I could be faulted for not taking up since it would presumably, as some might argue, put Weber in better light, in terms of prescience, is that of bureaucracy. Lenin's final judgment in 1922 on his life-long project, a "bureaucratically deformed worker's state," might be reason enough. Yet, as the record would show, Lenin was not derelict in treating the topic of bureaucracy, as his last characterization of the Soviet Union suggests. It is likely, in fact, that he addressed it, despite being six years his junior, even before Weber. There is no evidence I contend, should the reader inquire, that Weber was more insightful than Lenin on the topic, at least for Russia. If anything, the Soviet Union case reveals that bureaucracy, as Lenin argued, can't be fully understood separate and apart from fundamental socio-economic-political reality, as Weber was prone to believe.

This comparison of Lenin and Weber, two of the most influential figures of the twentieth century, is not just of historical significance. Their core differences, about how best to institute and defend democracy, are at the very heart of politics today—through the electoral/parliamentary arena or through the crowds in the streets.

Lastly, it could be argued that comparing Weber to Lenin isn't fair; he simply wasn't the activist Lenin was. Subsequent events, however, challenge the all too often disengaged scholar image of Weber. As is true for the Marxological enterprise that has long depoliticized Marx, Weber's fans, an almost exclusively academic lot, have too virtually expunged his political activism. Maybe because it was only in his final years did Weber make a "painful confession ... I was born for the pen and for the speaker's platform, not for the lectern."[98] The "pen" referred to political journalism and not his more famous academic writings; "the speaker's platform" to his renowned public talks designed to shape German public opinion when World War I erupted. Like Lenin, who too was at home with "the pen" and "speaker's platform," Weber was willing to plunge himself into the political fray but only as he understood how to do so and, not the least important, from the other side of the class divide.

Appendix: From August 1914 to March 1919—Lenin versus Weber

With the coming of the October Revolution in 1917, Lenin's and Weber's political differences were no longer confined to texts as was the case for 1905–1906. They were now vividly and consequentially on display on different sides of the barricades, almost literally, Lenin the proletarian internationalist and Weber the self-denominated German bourgeois nationalist scholar. The overarching context for understanding their differences was the Great War. This appendix purports only to distill the key contrasts from the commencement of the conflagration to its end, moments when Lenin and Weber both sought at the same time to shape outcomes—a precis for a future, possibly, comparative real-time political analysis project.

Lenin's and Weber's responses to the Guns of August of 1914 were, not surprisingly, diametrically opposed. "*Whatever* the outcome, *this war is great and wonderful,*" emphasized the *bürgerlich* scholar in a letter when it commenced.[99] To the bitter end, Weber's patriotism was unwavering. Salvaging the "honor" of his beloved nation was the axis around which all his actions in the next five years orbited. His main concern was to make sure Berlin conducted the war in a way to ensure Germany's long-term imperial ambitions. "We have to be a world power, and in order to have a say in the future of the world we had to risk the war."[100] Lenin, conversely, was incensed to learn that German socialists had succumbed to the patriotic fervor that Weber proudly displayed. "I am extremely anxious & angry with the position of the European socialists in the present war. My conviction is that all—& the German socialists first and all & chief of all— got 'chauvinists.'"[101] He responded by organizing anti-war activities in Russia and planting the seeds for a new communist international, one that would seek to end the conflagration through socialist revolutions in the countries now at war.[102] The war's capitalist perpetrators, Britain, France and Russia on one side and Germany, Austria and Italy on the other, would have to pay a price for the bloodletting.

Weber's ardor for the war began to cool as it became increasingly clear that the policy makers in Berlin were increasingly toying with the idea of territorial acquisitions as the goal of the war. Needless annexations in Europe, in his opinion, would make for diplomatic obstacles for Germany becoming "a world power." The need for "elbow room" for Germany—in anticipation of National Socialism's *lebensraum*—that he had spoken about in his 1895 Inaugural Address continued to be at the center of his patriotism but by now on a global scale. The political right and the war profiteers were now, he feared, driving war policy and, thus, jeopardizing Germany's long-term imperial interests. The solution to their undue influence, he proposed, was "parliamentarization" of the Reich and an accompanying necessary suffrage reform. In other words, a political system that was more representative of German public opinion, especially those in uniform who actually had to prosecute the war.

Most instructive about Weber's campaign for suffrage reform is that it went into high gear in 1917 after the February/March Revolution in Russia that deposed Czar Nicholas. Along with a new provisional government, Russia's Duma, its version of a parliament, was revived. But it was rivaled by another representative institution which also reappeared, the Petrograd Soviet of Workers and Soldiers. Which of the two bodies was the legitimate authority was at the heart of the drama of the Russian Revolution and only resolved in October with Bolshevik ascent. Nicholas's deposal instituted universal suffrage for the first time in Russia, making it, as Lenin put, the "freest of all the belligerent countries in the world."[103] Though elections to both the Duma and the Soviet were based on universal suffrage, the latter proved to be much more representative, as its name suggests, of working class and soldier opinions. As the war's bloody toll ratcheted up, the main reason for the czar's fall, anti-war sentiment expressed itself more in the Soviet than in the Duma. The Bolshevik election campaign slogan, "peace, land, and bread," was, hence, more popular in the latter than in the former. Lenin, not surprisingly, called for "all power to the soviets," his strategy for Russia's exit from the conflagration—what essentially happened in October. Socialist revolution, in other words, was, as he had promised, Lenin's road to peace.

Weber too sought to have German public opinion better represented in the policies Berlin was making, especially the voice of its soldiers. Through speeches, letters and newspaper/magazine articles, he pushed for electoral reform. But all so tellingly different from Lenin, Weber's quest for more democracy in Germany, particularly the suffrage for soldiers, was intended to *strengthen* the war effort—not unlike what the ruling class in Britain had just done in making universal male suffrage a reality for the first time in its domain. Weber's strategy, again, was to ensure that Germany emerged from the war in a better position to advance its global "elbow room."

Shoring up the war effort in Germany explains why Weber now feared what had taken place in Russia; it could be contagious. Two newspaper articles in April 1917, "Russia's Transition to Pseudo-Democracy" and "The Russian Revolution and the Peace," consciously sought to dissuade German Social Democrats from taking seriously the significance of Czar Nicholas's deposition. What now existed in Russia, he claimed, was "pseudo-democracy" and the provisional government was as imperialist as was Nicholas's regime: "given the present composition of the Russian governing powers there can be *no question* of the majority of the politically prominent men in Russia having sincerely peaceful intentions, let alone being well-disposed towards the German people." Germany, therefore, was compelled to continue the war. To make his case, Weber also played the race card. The colonial subjects of the forces of the Entente Powers with whom the provisional government was still allied meant that there was "an army of negroes, ghurkas and all the barbarian rabble in the world standing at our borders, half crazed with rage ... for vengeance, and craving to devastate our country." Hence, it was "absolutely necessary for the

German workers to *know* that at the moment there can be no question of any genuine 'democracy' in Russia, and why this is so."[104] And for German workers to emulate in any way the revolutionary actions of their cohorts in Russia would be "to stab the army which is protecting our country from the savage nations in the back"—a charge German National Socialism would later employ to come to power. Weber ended with a challenge to the Russians: "There is *only one* reliable *test* of a genuinely democratic and non-imperialist attitude. Does the politician in question restrict himself to cleaning up in his own backyard, i.e. to creating democracy within his own country *or not*?"[105] As Germany's leading authority on Russia owing to his detailed analysis of the 1905 Revolution, Weber's opinion had weight.

Weber's critique of the provisional government's war course was strikingly similar to what Lenin was also arguing. A few weeks later on June 17, 1917, at the first All-Russian Congress of Soviets of Workers and Soldiers, Lenin charged, like Weber, the provisional government with being beholden to Russia's capitalists, especially the war profiteers and, thus, why they didn't want peace. He implored the soviets to take power because they constituted a "more democratic type of state" than what the provisional government represented—"revolutionary democracy." "The war," he continued, "can only be ended by taking the revolution further …. If you were to take power into your hands, if power were to pass to the revolutionary organizations to be used for combating the Russian capitalists, then the working people of some countries would believe you and you could propose peace …. Power transferred to the revolutionary proletariat, supported by the poor peasants, means a transition to revolutionary struggle for peace in the surest and most painless forms ever known to mankind."[106] No "working people of some countries" were as important for Lenin as those in Germany—the way to end the bloodbath. When he declared that the Bolsheviks were prepared to lead such a transformation—evoking both derision and applause amongst the delegates—it was as if he was responding directly to Weber's challenge. There was indeed, in other words, "a politician" in Russia who not only wanted to but was capable of leading Russia via the soviets in a more thoroughgoing democratic fashion in order to end the war. But just as Weber dismissed the Bolshevik alternative in 1905–1906, he did the same in 1917, to his peril. He was politically incapable of conceiving a revolutionary workers party leading a worker/peasant alliance to power; his values would not allow for such a scenario—giving new meaning to his fact/value distinction. He intentionally misrepresented what was under way in Russia.[107]

When a majority of parties in the Reichstag including the Social Democrats took the initiative to put forward a peace proposal in July 1917, Weber was alarmed. He feared that they were being naively seduced by developments in Russia—Lenin's siren call. Though publicly on record in support of the parliamentarization of the German Reich, when the Reichstag actually began to assert itself with a proposal Weber objected; it would be interpreted by Germany's enemies as a sign of weakness. His public endorsement of parliamentarization and suffrage reform in Germany was, as he would have labeled it, purely instrumental—to advance the war effort. Lenin might have understood Weber's calculus. He too was being instrumental. His call for "all power to the soviets" was intended to deepen representative democracy in Russia—the route to peace. If Lenin wanted more democracy to end the slaughter, Weber wanted it to continue the war more effectively. When it appeared that more democracy via Reichstag assertion would threaten the war effort in his view, because it appeared to be granted under duress, Weber, with all of the obvious contradictions, grew lukewarm if not hostile to the fledgling efforts toward democratization in Germany.

Just as Lenin had promised at the Congress of Soviets in June, the Bolsheviks immediately took steps to end the war after leading the worker–peasant alliance to power in October/November 1917. Bolshevik ascent allowed Weber to tact to the left; Russia was no longer an imminent threat to his beloved country, specifically because of the peace decrees issued by Moscow. He became an active advocate of suffrage reform and parliamentarization of the Reich. He headlined, along with a Social Democratic speaker, a mass rally in Munich in November 1917, in favor of a negotiated peace—his most public intervention yet. The radical democratic opening in Russia that the Bolsheviks led ironically made it possible for Weber to be at his progressive best.

Weber and the Bolsheviks were initially on the same political page about the peace negotiations under way in the Polish town of Brest-Litovsk in December and January. A peace without annexations of the territories of other nationalities, the Bolshevik proposal, was to his liking. Unnecessary territorial acquisitions he felt would be a diplomatic obstacle to Germany becoming a real "master nation." When the German negotiators began demanding exactly that, it distressed him. The culprits were the revanchist right-wing Pan-German movement in combination with the Supreme Command. But his anger was confined to private communications; defending "the honor" of the nation prevented him from saying so publicly. The harsh German demands prompted Leon Trotsky, who headed up the Russian delegation to walk out of the negotiations on January 28, 1918, and to declare "no war, no peace."[108]

Rather than fault the German party to Brest-Litovsk, Weber blamed the Bolsheviks, Trotsky in particular, for his country's intransigence at the talks. Trotsky's revolutionary appeals to the German working class showed that he "was not content to carry out this ["proletarian dictatorship"] experiment in his own house and to place his hopes on the fact that, if it succeeded, it would result in unrivalled propaganda for socialism throughout the whole world .... One cannot make peace with people who are fighting for their faith. One can only render them harmless, and that was the meaning of the ultimatum and the enforced peace at Brest."[109] Weber admitted in a letter that his portrait of the Bolsheviks at Brest-Litovsk was tendentious: "I have only given one side of the picture in describing the Bolsheviks (which I addressed to the Social Democrats!) The other pacifistic current is also there." Indeed, it was the "pacifistic current" in the Bolshevik party led by Lenin that rejected Trotsky's "no war, no peace" ultimatum. Two months earlier, he was able to convince a majority of the party to sign the very onerous Brest-Litovsk Treaty that involved the ceding to Germany of major portions of what had once been the Russian empire. Peace was needed, Lenin passionately argued, in order to consolidate the revolution, contrary to what Weber claimed. Germany's foremost social scientist consciously misrepresented, again, the Bolsheviks and in the process became an apologist for his nation's territorial aggrandizement, against his better judgment. Germany, Weber knew, would pay dearly for its rapaciousness at Brest-Litovsk, eighteen months later at Versailles.[110] Again, "never the twain shall meet" when it came to facts and values for Weber.

The context for Weber's disparagement of the Bolsheviks is instructive. It's from his famous lecture, "Socialism," given in June 1918 in Vienna to non-commissioned officers and rank and file in Austria's military. At the most critical juncture in the war he wanted to ensure Austria's loyalty to Berlin. Countering the Bolshevik alternative was priority number one in the lecture—thus his attack on them at Brest-Litovsk. About the talk's purported theme, "I would like to begin by drawing your attention to the fact that there are 'socialists' of the most diverse kinds." Yet, all "*parties* of a purely socialist character are *democratic* parties nowadays." But "Democracy can mean an infinite variety of things." After showing the democratic limitations of "old-style Swiss democracy," he then proceeded to take down what was widely seen as the paragon of modern democracy. "This American democracy … rests on" the "rotation" of parties in an out of office—known in the U.S. as the infamous "spoils system"—in which "at some point everyone had a turn of putting their hands in the pork barrel." Workers, he claimed he spoke with during his visit in 1904, were aware that they were "governed by these corrupt people who are notorious for robbing you of hundreds of millions." As well as being dominated by monied interests, US politics were also influenced by warmongers, based on, he claimed, what his 1904 visit revealed: "it was the American universities and the strata educated by them, not the military contractors who exist in every country, who were the originators of the war."[111] America like Russia, in other words, Weber's subtext, was neither to be looked to as an alternative to the then extant governing arrangements in Austria and Germany. Important to point out is that Weber, like Tocqueville, was a defender of constitutional monarchy; only after the November Revolution, to be seen shortly, did he become a convert to republican government.

Lenin, too, also instructively, pronounced on US politics—especially the contrast. Like Weber, he was aware of how money dominated its outcomes. But Lenin objected when a pro-czarist organ "wrote about the 'power of money'" in the 1912 presidential election, "relating with malicious joy the facts about the monstrous venality of Taft, Roosevelt, Wilson and, indeed, *all* Presidential candidates put up by the bourgeois parties. Here is a free, democratic republic for you, hissed the venal Russian newspaper." Unlike what Weber implied in his "Socialism" lecture regarding the political reality in Austria and Germany, Lenin disputed the newspaper's suggestion that the political system in the U.S. was no better than what existed in Russia. "The class-conscious workers will reply to this calmly and proudly: we have no illusions about the significance of broad democracy. No democracy in the world can eliminate the class struggle and the omnipotence of money. It is not this that makes democracy important and useful. The importance of democracy is that it makes the class struggle broad, open and conscious. And this is not a conjecture or a wish, but a fact."[112] Superior, in other words, about the U.S. reality, Lenin countered, was that it offered more political space for the working class— needed space in order to take political power.

No doubt influential in explaining Weber's legerdemain about the Bolsheviks was the outbreak of strikes in Berlin and Vienna in late January 1918. For Weber they constituted his long-dreaded fear of the Russian contagion and about which he was not alone. "The Supreme Command and the government saw the January strike as evidence that revolution *à la russe* was a real possibility in Germany."[113] Weber intended his tendentious reading of the Bolshevik call for a negotiated peace to persuade German and Austrian workers to stay the course of the war. Soviet power, led by the Bolsheviks, he contended, would be no less imperialist or belligerent than the provisional government it overthrew or the czarist regime the latter replaced. Trotsky was a favorite target of all who smelled a Bolshevik mole. About the Berlin strike, a government official charged in the Reichstag, "Trotsky had tried to make a revolution in Germany."[114]

What Lenin and Trotsky had been banking on since Bolshevik ascent finally occurred a year later. The long-awaited revolt of German workers on November 9, 1918, ended the reign of Wilhelm II, Europe's last major monarch and ushered in Germany's first republic. The news was greeted with multitudinous rapture by Russia's toilers. Lenin wasn't unprepared. A month earlier, he alerted other Bolshevik leaders: "Things have so 'accelerated' in Germany that we must not fall behind …. We are ready to die to help the German workers advance the revolution which has begun in Germany."[115] Ever since the October Revolution the Bolsheviks did all they could through propaganda efforts to stimulate something similar on German soil. Their embassy in Berlin was the headquarters for the covert operations.[116] They strove mightily, for example, to get into the hands of German soldiers President Woodrow Wilson's famous Fourteen Points speech of January 8, 1918, in which he praised the peace initiatives of the Bolsheviks at Brest-Litovsk (details in the next chapter).

Weber, too, anticipated the upheaval. But unlike Lenin, he greeted Wilhelm's demise with dread. He had tried unsuccessfully to persuade him to abdicate to make way for a constitutional monarchy rather than a republic—not his preference. Instead, he got, to his horror, a government of the Council of the People's Representatives, a version of soviet governance but without the Bolsheviks at its head. Even with the moderate Social Democrats in the leadership, he "raged against this 'bloody carnival' that does not deserve the honorable name of a revolution."[117] He continued to defend Eric Ludendorff, Quartermaster General of the German Army and Field Marshall General Paul von Hindenburg at the head of the Supreme Command although he knew their overreach on the battlefield is what led to, in his opinion, the fiasco. To have criticized them in that moment would have meant, again, a "stab in the back" of Germany's military. Through personal contacts in Munich, he tried unsuccessfully to prevent a revolution there.[118]

Forced to deal with the new reality in Germany, Weber did all he could to moderate the revolution. To that end, he was willing to collaborate with the moderate Social Democrats—for good reason. The new Social Democratic chancellor Friedrich Ebert, in his first public utterance, pleaded with the revolutionary masses in Berlin on the day of the revolt: "Fellow citizens! I urgently appeal to you: leave the streets! Maintain law and order!"[119] The Ebert government offered the best guarantee against an outcome even more horrible in Weber's view—a government headed by the Spartacist League whose leaders were Karl Liebknecht and Rosa Luxemburg, in other words, a Bolshevik-like outcome. He didn't mince words about his opinion of the two as he told an audience in Karlsruhe: "Liebknecht belongs in the madhouse and Rosa Luxemburg in the zoo."[120]

Weber's fears weren't unfounded. The German revolt bore many similarities to the Russian overturn. Councils of workers and soldiers, as in the February Revolution, spontaneously appeared in various cities in Germany. In Berlin on November 9 workers marched under their banner, "Peace, freedom, and bread," unmistakably similar to the slogan that lifted the Bolsheviks to power, "Peace, land, and bread." Moscow's propaganda campaign for almost a year appeared to have paid off. So profound had the overturn been that even Weber served briefly on the Heidelberg workers' and soldiers' council.[121]

But for all the similarities, missing in Germany was a battle-tested party like the one Lenin had forged for such a moment. Beginning in 1904, Luxemburg disputed Lenin's claim that a party was needed to organize and lead a revolutionary outbreak, Lenin's oft-disparaged "vanguard party"; the moment itself, Luxemburg claimed, would spontaneously organize such a party. Lenin vehemently disagreed but that was now water under the bridge. From afar and with state power, he did all he could to aid and abet the fledgling party, first the Spartacist League, and then, the German Communist Party, when founded on December 30, 1918. Weber, on the other hand, as previously noted, was no admirer of Liebknecht and Luxemburg. He continued to disparage the two and their organization even after their assassination on January 15, 1919, probably on orders of the Ebert Social Democratic government with which he had once collaborated. Though he denounced their murders, he came close to blaming them for their own deaths in his famous lecture, "The Profession and Vocation of Politics," in Munich shortly afterward. "Have we not seen that the Bolshevik and Spartacist ideologues, precisely because they use this political instrument ["power, backed up by the use of violence"], bring about exactly the same results as any militarist dictator?"[122] In other words, with a quote from the bible, "All they that take the sword shall perish with the sword." As well, he now felt emboldened to discredit the new governing institution that emerged in the November Revolution: "What, apart from the identity of the holders of power (and their amateurism) distinguishes the rule of the Workers' and Soldiers' Councils from the rule of any wielder of power under the old regime?" What the Bolsheviks had instituted, in other words, was no different from previous regimes. For Lenin, however, the deaths of Liebknecht and Luxemburg was a blow, "the most dramatic and tragic event in the revolution beginning in Germany."[123] In hindsight, their loss spelled the end of the November Revolution.

Weber eventually came to support a republican Germany; revolutionary Germany made him a convert—not unlike Tocqueville in 1848.[124] Republican Germany was preferable to a Soviet Germany. In so doing, he entered active party politics, helping to found in 1919 the German Democratic Party, a "bourgeois party." He was simply acting on his long-held conviction that Germany's future rested on its capitalist class. His political career was, however, short lived. Germany's most eminent scholar could never find it in himself to master the art of being "a politician." The revolutionary situation in Germany made Weber less influential. Wolfgang Mommsen argues persuasively that he was best suited for the Germany Bismarck helped put in place.[125] His premature death in 1920 due to tuberculosis saved him from being seen so out of place in the cataclysmic developments that then ensued.

From the collapse of the Brest-Litovsk talks at the end of January 1918 to the end of the November Revolution in March 1919, Lenin and Weber actively opposed one another from different sides of the barricades, almost literally. The assassinations of Liebknecht and Luxemburg at the end of January 1919 effectively meant that they had fought to a standstill. Weber was certainly aware of his opponent's actions. Whether Lenin knew about Weber's efforts is uncertain. But he would not have been surprised. Two years earlier Lenin characterized Weber's portrait of the Bolsheviks in the "dress rehearsal" of 1905 as a "piece of professorial wisdom of the cowardly bourgeoisie." Weber's dismissal of the Bolsheviks, not only in 1905 but in 1917 as well, handicapped his ability to spar effectively with his formidable class enemy.

In Adam Tooze's otherwise informative account about these years, Weber makes only one appearance. The "great sociologist ... one of the most penetrating political commentators of the day" is applauded for having understood "the lasting damage done to Germany's political culture by Bismarck."[126] The point is in reference to the inordinate role the military Supreme Command had come to play in the Reich. But it's telling that Tooze has nothing more to say about "one of the most penetrating commentators of the day." It's because he knows all too well the counter-revolutionary and most problematic—to put it charitably—role Weber played in the drama between August 1914 and the Treaty of Versailles in 1919.[127] To reveal that story might suggest that in comparison to Weber, Lenin had better democratic credentials—the last thing Tooze would ever want to do (more on Tooze in the next chapter).

NOTES

1. As is the practice in the *Collected Works* of Lenin, hereafter, *LCW*, I employ both the Julian—in use at the time—and Gregorian dates, respectively, January 9 and January 22 and hence from now, for example, January 9 (22).
2. Richard Pipes, "Max Weber and Russia," *World Politics*, 7 (3), April 1955, is probably the first critical assessment of Weber's Russia writings, certainly in English, based on actual political outcomes. Lenin, unfortunately, receives only cursory treatment.
3. Max Weber, *Political Writings*, eds. Peter Lassman and Ronald Speirs (New York: Cambridge University Press, 1994), pp. 20–23.
4. Gordon C. Wells and Peter Baehr, in their introduction to *Max Weber: The Russian Revolutions* (Ithaca, NY: Cornell University Press, 1995), p. 24, implies that it was. Hereafter the Wells and Baehr translation of Weber's writings on the Russian Revolution will be designated as MWRR.
5. Whether the party was faithful to Marx's and Engels's understanding of class analysis has been the subject of much debate. I argue that the two became increasingly critical of much that was being claimed for "Marxism," including the German party. See my *Marx and Engels*, pp. 254–72; and *Lenin's Electoral Strategy*, vol. 1, chapter 1, particularly, "Bernstein and Kautsky."
6. Ibid., p. 16.
7. Ibid., p. 26.
8. Conservative German scholar and expert on fascism Ernst Nolte wrote about the address that "it abounds in phrases which, in meaning and sometimes in formulation [that] could have appeared in *Mein Kampf*" (*Three Faces of Fascism: Action Française, Italian Fascism, National Socialism*, trans. Leila Vennewitz [1963; New York: Holt, Rinehart and Winston, 1966], p. 446), and brought to my attention by Andrew Zimmerman (see next note).

9. Andrew Zimmerman is the first scholar to make a convincing case. See his *Alabama in Africa: Booker T. Washington, the German Empire, and the Globalization of the New South* (Princeton, NJ: Princeton University Press, 2010), p. 101, and especially, p. 286n149.

10. J. M. Barbalet, "Weber's Inaugural Lecture and Its Place in his Sociology," *Journal of Classical Sociology* 1:2 (2001), makes a convincing case that Weber's better-known writings, especially, *The Protestant Ethic and the Spirit of Capitalism*, were anticipated in the inaugural address. Rita Aldenhoff-Hübinger, "Max Weber's Inaugural Address of 1895 in the Context of the Contemporary Debates in Political Economy," *Max Weber Studies* 4:2 (2004), argues that a number of its themes had been pre-viewed in Weber's earlier work.

11. Zimmerman, p. 101.

12. For details about the US trip and its significance, see Zimmerman, pp. 207–12. John Patrick Diggins, *Marx Weber: Politics and the Spirit of Tragedy* (New York: Basic Books, 1996), makes a persuasive case that the American trip was determinant in Weber's subsequent intellectual trajectory.

13. https://ebookcentral.proquest.com/lib/umn/reader.action?docID=242182&ppg=8, p. xxxvii.

14. One of Marx's last research projects focused on the Russian peasantry and why he learned to read Russian. See my *Marx and Engels: Their Contribution to the Democratic Breakthrough* (Albany, NY: SUNY Press, 2000), pp. 245–48 for details.

15. What follows is a distillation of chapter 2 in my *Lenin's Electoral Strategy*, vol. 1.

16. Lenin, *Collected Works*, vol. 4, p. 265; hereafter *LCW*, 4, p. 265.

17. *LCW*, 5, p. 74. So much, then, for the oft-alleged "Leninist approach of 'the worse the better.'"

18. *LCW*, 7, p. 514. Marx made a strikingly similar prediction about czarist "constitutional tomfoolery" but in the context of the Russo-Turkish War in 1877; Marx and Engels, *Collected Works*, vol. 45, p. 278; hereafter *MECW*, 45, p. 278.

19. *LCW*, 8, pp. 21–22.

20. See *Max Weber Gesamtausgabe* Bd. II/4, Briefe, 1903–1905. Wolfgang J. Mommsen, "Max Weber and the Regeneration of Russia," *Journal of Modern History*, vol. 69 (1) March 1997, p. 1 suggests, however, that Weber was indeed aware during his travels abroad of the significance of the Russo-Japanese War.

21. *LCW*, 8, pp. 53–55.

22. Lenin, in his above-quoted 1917 commemoration speech said "over one thousand were killed and over two thousand wounded on that day

according to police reports." Abraham Ascher, without citation, says "the
official figures, possibly on the low side, indicate ... 130 killed and 299
seriously wounded" (Ascher, *The Revolution of 1905: Russia in Disarray*
[Stanford, CA: Stanford University Press, 1988], pp. 89–90).

23. *LCW, 8*, pp. 97–100.
24. Ibid.
25. *LCW, 8*, pp. 375–78.
26. See Alfred Levin, *The Second Duma: A Study of the Social-Democratic
    Party and the Russian Constitutional Experiment* (New Haven: Yale
    University Press, 1940), pp. 7–10, for details.
27. *LCW, 9*, p. 179.
28. Ibid., p. 193.
29. Ibid., pp. 182–84.
30. Ibid., p. 258.
31. Ibid., p. 273.
32. Ibid., pp. 258–61.
33. *LCW, 4*, p. 353.
34. *LCW, 9*, pp. 383–84. Lenin's contextual approach to politics indeed
    informed his response once the revolutionary upsurge had exhausted
    itself and the First Duma became a reality; see my *Lenin's Electoral
    Strategy*, vol. 1, chapter 2.
35. Ibid., p. 461.
36. Ibid., pp. 431–32.
37. Figes, p. 197.
38. *LCW, 10*, p. 163.
39. For this comparison with Lenin I employ Max Weber, *The Russian
    Revolutions*, translated and edited by Gordon Wells and Peter Baehr
    (Ithaca, NY: Cornell University Press, 1995), hereafter, MWRR. Their
    "Editor's Introduction," provides valuable details about the origins of
    Weber's writings on the Russian events and their place in his oeuvre.
    Their translation and rendering of Weber's essay and the others on the
    Russian Revolution is an abridgement of the originals in the *Max Weber
    Gesamtausgabe*, I/10 (Tübingen: J.C.B. Mohr, 1989). A perusal of the
    originals reveals that nothing essential has been left out for a meaningful
    comparison with Lenin. The comparison is limited to Weber's first essay
    "Bourgeois Democracy in Russia," hereafter, BDR.
40. MWRR, p. 113.
41. Mommsen, p. 2.
42. Mommsen, pp. 2–5, provides useful background for Weber's interest in
    the Russian scenario. But his exposition of *Zur Lage* implies that Weber
    foresaw that the liberal alternative would fail. That, I argue, is a hindsight
    reading of the essay. Weber was open to the possibility of liberal success
    and only reconsidered that view as events actually unfolded.

43. Ibid., pp. 42 and 115, n10.
44. See, for example, Terence Emmons and Wayne Vucinich, eds. *The Zemstvo in Russia: An Experiment in Local Self-Government* (London: Cambridge University Press, 1982). In this otherwise rich collection, the reader would never know the detailed attention Lenin gave to the *zemstvo* beginning at least with his 1901 pamphlet.
45. *LCW, 5,* pp. 73–4, 78–9.
46. *LCW, 5,* p. 102.
47. Statisticians had a special place in Lenin's world; one of them made him a life-long aficionado of psephology.
48. MWRR, p. 45.
49. *LCW, 5,* pp. 281–89.
50. *LCW, 7,* pp. 513–15.
51. *LCW, 8,* p. 79.
52. MWRR, p. 49.
53. *LCW, 22,* p. 355.
54. *LCW, 8,* pp. 561–65.
55. *LCW, 9,* pp. 344–46.
56. MWRR, p. 69.
57. *LCW, 9,* p. 238.
58. For modern scholarship on 1905, the general strike, its significance and so on, see Abraham Ascher, *The Revolution of 1905: Russia in Disarray* (Stanford, CA: Stanford University Press, 1988).
59. Ibid., p. 431.
60. MWRR, p. 71.
61. *LCW, 9,* p. 430.
62. MWRR, p. 69.
63. *LCW, 10,* pp. 19–20.
64. About those Bolsheviks who did, see Robert Service, *Lenin: A Political Life, Vol. 1* (Bloomington: Indiana University Press, 1985), pp. 142–43.
65. Once back in Russia and able to attend the soviet Lenin uncharacteristically "'sat and kept silent.'" Service thinks it is because he was "possibly under Central Committee pressure" to do so—clearly in the minority in his enthusiasm for the soviet (Service, p. 143).
66. *LCW, 10,* p. 23.
67. Ibid., p. 17. One can only speculate why Stalin allowed the letter to then be published, so at odds with Stalinist authoritarianism. It was in the context of World War II and his campaign to curry favor with Roosevelt and Churchill, his popular front policy. Lenin's letter could be useful in trying to reinvent his image and, thus, the USSR, in the eyes of his class enemies.
68. MWRR, p. 74.

69. *LCW, 9*, p. 433.
70. MWRR, p. 101.
71. *LCW, 9*, p. 448.
72. Ibid., p. 108.
73. MWRR, p. 143n211.
74. Ibid., p. 110.
75. *LCW, 34*, p. 361.
76. *LCW, 9*, p. 427.
77. See my *Lenin's Electoral Strategy*, vol. 1, pp. 96–97.
78. *LCW, 23*, pp. 250–51.
79. Modern scholarship supports Lenin's claims; see Ascher, chapter 11.
80. MWRR, p. 142n200.
81. Ibid., p. 107.
82. *LCW, 9*, p. 273.
83. MWRR, p. 102.
84. Ibid., p. 151.
85. *LCW, 9*, p. 399.
86. Ibid., p. 430.
87. A leading voice for capital said as much in 2018: "Global financial markets … are … the most powerful force on earth, more so even than nuclear weapons" (Roger Altman, "The Markets Will Stop a Trade War," *Wall Street Journal*, July 26, 2018).
88. For a recent and similar critique of "vulgar materialists," see an op-ed that describes them as "those who posit ["the human person"] as but a physical combination of matter and energy" (*Wall Street Journal*, July 31, 2018), p. 15.
89. MWRR, p. 147n232.
90. For example, their detailed analyses of the elections for the First Duma find them in more agreement than disagreement as is generally the case for Weber's second essay—unlike for the first.
91. *LCW, 11*, p. 111.
92. MWRR, pp. 231–32.
93. Mommsen, pp. 9–10.
94. MWRR, pp. 241–66.
95. Max Weber, *Political Writings*, eds. Peter Lassman and Ronald Speirs (New York: Cambridge U.P., 1994), p. 299.
96. Recent scholarship confirms the indispensable role of the "peasants in uniform" in the success of Bolshevik ascendancy; see Olga Porshneva, "World War I Russian Soldiers and the 1917 Revolution," https://www.c-span.org/search/?searchtype=All&query=Olga+Porshneva.
97. Orlando Figes, *A People's Tragedy: A History of the Russian Revolution* (New York: Viking, 1996), p. 221.

98. Mommsen, p. 282.

99. Mommsen, p. 191. Regarding Weber, this appendix is informed almost exclusively by Wolfgang Mommsen's book, *Max Weber and German Politics, 1890–1920* (Chicago: University of Chicago Press, 1984), and article, "Max Weber and the Regeneration of Russia," *The Journal of Modern History* (vol. 69, no. 1, 1997), still the most authoritative accounts about his politics.

100. Ibid., p. 192.

101. *LCW, 42*, p. 432.

102. See next chapter for details.

103. Nimtz, *Lenin's Electoral Strategy, 1917*, p. 119.

104. Wells and Baehr, pp. 241, 255.

105. Ibid., p. 263.

106. *LCW, 25*, pp. 26–28.

107. Mommsen, p. 254, characterizes the first of the two articles as "an outspokenly tendentious tract." I'd also include the second one.

108. On the details and drama of the Brest-Litovsk negotiations for the Bolsheviks, the differences between Lenin and Trotsky, see Alexander Rabinowitch, *The Bolsheviks in Power: The First Year of Soviet Rule in Petrograd* (Bloomington, IN: Indiana University Press, 2007), chapters 5 and 6.

109. Lassman and Speirs, pp. 299–300. To his wife Marianne he wrote: "I think Trotsky is smarter than our people." Marianne Weber, Max Weber: A Biography (New Brunswick, NJ: Transaction Books, 1988), p. 619.

110. Weber was prophetic about what was needed for Germany to become a "master nation"—a powerful military. Thus his objections to the revanchist posture of its negotiators at the Brest-Litovsk talks. It would unnecessarily provoke, he felt, its European rivals to want to put a bridle on the German military. That is exactly what happened with the outcome to the two imperialist wars. Though Germany is an economic powerhouse today, it can't claim "master nation" status, Weber's hope. Germany continues to lack the kind of military machine to make that possible—what the victors of the two imperialist wars ensured and what Weber feared.

111. Lassman and Spiers, pp. 277–78.

112. *LCW, 18*, p. 335.

113. Stephen Bailey, "The Berlin Strike of January 1918," *Central European History*, vol. 13, no. 2 (June 1980).

114. Ibid., p. 171.

115. John Riddell, ed. *The German Revolution and the Debate on Soviet Power: Documents: 1918–1919* (New York: Pathfinder Press, 1986), p. 26.

116. For details see the articles of John Reed, "How Soviet Russia Conquered Imperial Germany," US journalist and Bolshevik sympathizer, who was deeply involved in the efforts (https://www.marxists.org/archive/reed/1919/conquered/conq1.htm).
117. Mommsen, p. 296.
118. Ibid., p. 295.
119. Riddell, p. 41.
120. Mommsen, p. 305.
121. Ibid., p. 297.
122. Lassman and Spiers, p. 357.
123. *LCW*, *28*, p. 413.
124. On the reality of Weber's conversion, see Jan Rehmann's *Max Weber, Modernisation as Passive Revolution: A Gramscian Analysis* (Chicago: Haymarket Books, 2015), pp. 105–18.
125. Mommsen, pp. 329–30.
126. Adam Tooze, *The Deluge: The Great War, America and the Remaking of the Global Order, 1916–1931* (New York: Viking, 2014), p. 58.
127. See Diggins, pp. 223–33, for a more nuanced account of Weber and his many contradictions during the November Revolution, especially the Munich events.

CHAPTER 5

The October Revolution and End
of the "Great War": Lenin versus Wilson

Wilson represents a bourgeoisie which has made billions out of the war ...
Lenin, January 1917

Here is the ever-recurring question. How shall we deal with the Bolsheviki?
Wilson, January 1918

Max Weber was prescient when he wrote in 1905 about the prospects for the 300-year-old Romanov dynasty in Russia: "Only in the tragic event of a *European* war would the autocracy finally be destroyed."[1] Weber wasn't the first to speculate on how a war of such magnitude and developments in Russia could be interrelated. Frederick Engels raised that possibility in 1888: "revolution in Russia at this moment would save Europe from the horrors of a general war and would usher in universal social revolution."[2] He returned to the issue three years later:

> if war is to break out ... one thing is certain. This war, in which fifteen to twenty million armed men would slaughter one another and devastate Europe as it has never been devastated before—this war would either lead to the immediate triumph of socialism, or it would lead to such an upheaval in the old order of things, it would leave behind it everywhere such a heap of ruins, that the old capitalist society would become more impossible than ever, and the social revolution, set back by ten or fifteen years, would only be all the more radical and more rapidly implemented.[3]

© The Author(s) 2019
A. H. Nimtz, *Marxism versus Liberalism*, Marx, Engels,
and Marxisms, https://doi.org/10.1007/978-3-030-24946-5_5

Engels, as events would show, proved to be more foresighted than Weber.

The "Great War," or World War I, inaugurated an era that continues to resonate a century later. The most consequential of its products was doubtless the Russian Revolution of 1917—first, the February/March edition and second, the Bolshevik-led revolution in October/November.[4] The fate of the war, how long it would last after two and a half years of futile carnage, became inextricably linked to those two momentous outcomes. No one was as conscious of that fact and did more to *act* on it than Vladimir Lenin.

The world's most powerful actor also came to recognize that developments in Russia would be determinant for World War I, more specifically, its duration. When President Woodrow Wilson of the U.S. eventually decided, after more than two years of official neutrality toward the war, that US ruling class interests were better served by siding with the Entente coalition—Britain, France and Russia—against the Central Powers—Germany, Austria-Hungary and Italy—he faced a problem. As long as the Romanovs were a key member of the alliance, it was difficult to sell the Entente to the U.S. public. Once overthrown, however, in February/March 1917, Wilson's task became easier. "Making the world safe for democracy" was more credible without Europe's last absolutist dynasty in tow. But what about the Bolsheviks when they came to power later in October/November, led arguably by Marx's and Engels's ablest student? Would Wilson continue to be enthusiastic about the Russian Revolution as he had when it began in February/March 1917? Would Lenin and the Bolsheviks aid and abet his project to make America the beacon of liberal internationalism? Thus began a fascinating and underappreciated drama that lasted for almost three years that is the focus of this chapter.

Unlike in the three prior cases, the two protagonists compared in this chapter, Lenin and Wilson, not only read the same events in real-time but knew, as well, how each other was responding to them—including, most importantly, the actions of each other. At stake were consequences of world-historical significance. Both were engaged in a high wire act—Lenin especially—and understood to varying degrees that their pas de deux entailed dangers that could be fatal. This makes for a truly unique moment in the history of ideas and real-time political analysis.[5] That the archival record is more definitive, certainly in Wilson's case, makes for a comparison more robust than the three other cases.[6] Thus, another opportunity to compare and contrast a Marxist and liberal world view to determine which had a more accurate reading of arguably the most consequential set of events of the last century.

Prelude to the February Revolution: Lenin

By the time Tsar Nicholas was overthrown on February 27/March 12, 1917, Russia had been at war for more than two and a half years. The estimated dead and wounded were in the millions. Russia's masses were generally supportive when Nicholas declared war on Austria and Germany on July 19/August 2, 1914, in response to German Emperor Wilhelm II's declaration a day earlier—the opening of the "Guns of August," "the Great War" or World War I. The Bolsheviks were virtually alone in waging an active but futile anti-war effort—at least for the first two years of the conflagration. They were acting as they saw it in conformity with the lessons Marx and Engels had bequeathed. "The working men have no country," one of the most memorable lines in the *Manifesto of the Communist Party* that Marx and Engels wrote for the Communist League in 1848 was accompanied at the very end with probably the document's most quoted sentence: "Working Men of All Countries, Unite!" Two decades would pass before those two lines, the essence of what would come to be called "proletarian internationalism," gained currency.

The Franco-Prussian War of 1870 required Marx and Engels to put proletarian internationalism to the test for the first time, to see if workers could be recruited to an anti-war course when their ruling classes embarked on wars that didn't advance the interests of the proletariat. The U.S. revealed that some wars, specifically, for national self-determination and the overthrow of pre-capitalist social systems like chattel slavery, could actually do just that, distinguishing Marxists from pacifists, and thus the need for theoretical and political clarity. Written on behalf of the International Working Men's Association, the First International, that he effectively headed, Marx's *First* and *Second Addresses* on the war called for, first, a working-class anti-war response to the war drive in France and Germany and, second, opposition, particularly for German workers, to any territorial aggrandizement on the part of Bismarck, specifically, Alsace-Lorraine. Mass distribution of the two pronouncements not only in the belligerent countries but beyond was a distinctive and unprecedented feature of the anti-war campaign. Along with that effort, the use of the parliamentary podium by working-class parties, particularly in Germany, to denounce the war and lead the opposition to it—a model Lenin emulated in revolutionary Russia. Most prophetically, Marx wrote that the annexation of Alsace-Lorraine by Germany could provoke Russian intervention on behalf of France, and a German-Russian war would then "act as the midwife for the inevitable social revolution in Russia."[7] If the arithmetic was wanting in terms of timing, the algebra was nonetheless elegant— exactly what happened five decades later.

With Marx's death in 1883, it fell largely to Engels to lead on the war question for the worker's movement. He foresaw and criticized, as quoted in the introduction to this chapter, the increasing militarization drive on the part of the major European powers and warned about the expected carnage. War, again, was not inevitable; revolutionary action on the part of Europe's working classes could prevent such a slaughter.

Five years after Engels's death in 1895, leaders of various working-class parties inspired by him and his partner's project launched what would become the Socialist or Second International. At their annual meetings, delegates of party affiliates took up the question of "militarism"—how to counter it with a working class rather than liberal pacifist response, as was often the case with rival formations. The gathering in Basle, Switzerland, two years prior to the Guns of August proved to have been the most portent. The now famous Basle Manifesto of 1912, which passed unanimously, and in the context of the Balkan War of 1912–1913, appealed to fraternal parties and members to

> raise your protest in the parliaments with all your force; unite in great mass demonstrations; use every means that the organization and the strength of the proletariat place at your disposal! See to it that the governments are constantly kept aware of the vigilance and passionate will for peace on the part of the proletariat! To the capitalist world of exploitation and mass murder, oppose in this way the proletarian world of peace and fraternity of peoples![8]

"Raise your protest in the parliaments," most noteworthy, asked party affiliates who had members in such bodies, to do just that should war break out. At the heart of the manifesto was a threat: make war bourgeois gentlemen, and your working classes will make revolution. "War against war," as the threat became known. The opening sentences of the document were unambiguous, as made clear by the emboldened clauses in the original:

> in case war should break out anyway it is their duty **to intervene in favor of its speedy termination** and with all their powers to utilize **the economic and political crisis created by the war to arouse the people and thereby to hasten the downfall of capitalist class rule.**

Threats, as always, are only effective if they appear to be realizable. Only one of the signatories to the Basle Manifesto made good on the threat.

The Bolshevik faction of the Russian Social Democratic Labor Party led by Vladimir Lenin (1870–1924) had a long record going back to the Revolution of 1905 of trying to convert dynastic predatory wars—the 1904–1905 Russo-Japanese War specifically—into a "civil war," that is, the overthrow of their own regime. The 1912–1913 Balkan War gave them another opportunity to try again. But increasingly irritated by Bolshevik efforts to thwart Tsar Nicholas's pan-Slavic war agenda in the mountainous tinderbox, the regime squashed in early summer 1914 the publication of their daily, *Pravda*. The clamp down, in hindsight, was a prelude to Nicholas's most fateful decision—declaration of war on Austria-Hungary and Germany on July 19/August 2, 1914.

Of the parties that signed the 1912 Basle Manifesto, the parliamentary deputies of only two Socialist International affiliates carried out what the signatories had pledged: the eleven in Russia's Duma, or parliament—five Bolsheviks and six Mensheviks—and the two Serbian Social Democrats in their parliament. Rather than go along with voting for war credits to finance the slaughter about to take place, they refused and walked out. The parliamentary deputies of the vast majority of the signatories, on the other hand, with the German party in the lead, voted for war credits. Lenin would forever insist that those parties betrayed the Basle declaration and, hence, proletarian internationalism.[9]

As the Basle Manifesto had required, the five Bolshevik deputies, with Lenin in the lead but in exile—with all the logistical challenges that entailed for coordinating the work—used their parliamentary immunity to campaign against the war. They spoke publicly, when possible, against the war and distributed anti-war propaganda—in a cat-and-mouse game with the regime's police. Lenin wrote a set of "theses" for them to campaign on. All were consistent with the *Manifesto* and Marxist fundamentals. One, however, number six, seemed exceptional. "From the viewpoint of the working class and the toiling masses of all the people of Russia, the defeat of the tsarist monarchy and its army [which oppresses the many nationalities in the Russian empire and fosters ethnic hatred to serve the divide and rule strategy of the regime] would be the lesser evil by far."[10]

Lenin, in other words, took proletarian internationalism so seriously that he was willing to risk patriotic opprobrium by calling for the defeat of the tsarist forces. Bolsheviks, he argued, should wage a campaign, includ-ing amongst Russian troops, for what came to be called "revolutionary defeatism." For the proletariat of the aggressor nation to be convincing in calling on the proletariat of the aggrieved nations to practice proletarian internationalism, it had to make clear, in no uncertain terms, its disinterest in defending "the fatherland," what some Marxists called "revolutionary defensism." Not surprisingly, Lenin's call was not popular even amongst many Bolsheviks; he was clearly in the minority on this. But it was a strategy that began to pay off as the body count on the battlefield mounted inexorably.

"Revolutionary defeatism" was the unpardonable sin of the Bolsheviks in the eyes of Nicholas's regime—treason. It now had a smoking gun for the arrest of the five Bolsheviks deputies in 1915. Their trial, however, Lenin wrote, had unintended consequences for the regime.

> Thanks to the trial, the words cited in the indictment: "The guns should be directed, not against our brothers, the wage slaves of other countries, but against the reactionary and bourgeois governments and parties of all countries"—these words will spread—and have already done so—all over Russia as a call for proletarian internationalism, for the proletarian revolution. Thanks to the trial, the class slogan of the vanguard of the workers of Russia has reached the masses of the workers.[11]

The trial and its coverage in the press did more to publicize the anti-war/proletarian internationalist stance of the Bolsheviks than anything prior to then—enabling what they would do two years later.

With the Bolshevik deputies now imprisoned and, thus, no longer able to do open anti-war work inside Russia, Lenin turned his attention to the international scene. If the majority of parties in the Socialist International had betrayed proletarian internationalism, then it was time to build a new international. Taking its name from the Swiss town where it first met in 1915, the Zimmerwald movement soon found enough like-minded forces including in the German party and one-time foes of Lenin like Leon Trotsky and Rosa Luxemburg. The axis around which they united was the call to workers in the belligerent countries to turn the war into a civil war, that is, against their own bourgeois governments—just as the Basle Manifesto had demanded. It was in this context, in April 1916, that Lenin first pointed to the anti-war sentiment inside the U.S.

> even there, in a neutral country, two irreconcilably hostile trends in the Socialist Party have become revealed: on the one hand, the adherents of the so-called "preparedness", i.e., war, militarism, and navalism, and on the

other, socialists like Eugene Debs, former presidential candidate from the Socialist Party, who openly preaches civil war for socialism, precisely in connection with the coming war.[12]

The significance of Lenin's point, a "civil war for socialism" in the U.S., would become clear two years later.

Lenin's anti-war campaign required a theoretical explanation for World War I. Thus, his 1916 classic *Imperialism: the Highest Stage of Capitalism.* "The war," he argued, "was imperialist (that is, an annexationist, predatory, war of plunder) on the part of both sides; it was a war for the division of the world, for the partition and repartition of colonies and spheres of influence of finance capital, etc." Such wars, he added, were "absolutely inevitable under *such* an economic system, as long as private property in the means of production exists," that is, the capitalist mode of production.[13] To be noted is that these lines were penned for a later introduction to the book, written in July 1920, that is, after the war. He stressed, however, that his claim about the origins of the war wasn't hindsight: "with an eye to the tsarist censorship" he had to couch his argument in language—"I had to speak in a 'slavish' tongue"—seemingly non-threatening to the censors. But a close reading of *Imperialism* leaves no doubt that for Lenin the logic of the capitalist mode of production ushered in an epoch of unprecedented warfare, global conflagrations. If the interests of workers could be served by wars of liberation for oppressed nationalities or of republican against monarchial regimes, imperialist wars had nothing to offer the proletariat; they were to be opposed to the hilt. That claim, more than any other, informed his actions not only for the next two years—the focus of this chapter—but also for the rest of his life.

Adam Tooze argues that the "logic" of Lenin's *Imperialism* meant that "Washington must sooner or later declare war on Germany."[14] But nowhere did Lenin say that. Economics for Lenin was always mediated by politics, specifically, the class struggle. The example of Debs showed that there was working-class opposition in the U.S. to Washington sending troops to Europe. Therefore, it wasn't inevitable that President Woodrow Wilson would intervene; trying to dissuade him by widening and deepening that anti-war sentiment through the proletarian internationalist campaign of the Zimmerwald movement was the real Lenin. This was arguably Lenin's first effort to influence Wilson's actions.

Sensing that war weariness was setting in on both sides, Lenin warned fellow socialists in early January 1917, to be wary of "pious phrases about peace" from any "bourgeois governments." Buying in to such talk could lead to "socialist pacifism" in alliance with "bourgeois pacifism." Lenin was referring to Wilson's December 18, 1916, "Peace Note," an offer to begin possible mediation as a "neutral nation," between the two warring alliances.[15] But, Lenin countered,

> Wilson's pronouncement is a downright lie and sheer hypocrisy because Wilson represents a bourgeoisie which has made billions out of the war, because he is the head of a government that has frantically armed the United States obviously in preparation for a *second* great imperialist war.[16]

This was Lenin's first extended comment about Wilson in relation to the war. The article in which he wrote these lines, originally intended for a Russian exile publication in New York, was not published until 1924, after the death of both of them. Thus, Wilson probably never knew what Lenin really thought of him—possibly to Lenin's advantage, as events would show. Lenin's bottom line, again, was that only if the war became a "civil war," with workers "turning their weapons against *their own* bourgeoisie" and taking power, could there be any chance for a "democratic peace." If not, the outcome would be an "imperialist peace" ensuring, then, "a *second* great imperialist war." Lenin didn't live long enough to learn how tragically prescient he had been.

A few weeks before the February/March Revolution, Lenin told an audience of revolutionary workers in Zurich, Switzerland, in a talk on the twelfth anniversary of the beginning of the 1905 Russian Revolution that

> the history of the Russian revolution, like the history of the Paris Commune of 1871, teaches us the incontrovertible lesson that militarism can never and under no circumstances be defeated and destroyed, except by a victorious struggle of one section of the national army against the other section. It is not sufficient simply to denounce, revile and 'repudiate' militarism ... it is foolish peacefully to refuse to perform military service. The task is to keep the revolutionary consciousness of the proletariat tense and train its best elements, not only in a general way, but concretely, so that when popular ferment reaches the highest pitch, they will put themselves at the head of the revolutionary army.[17]

Regarding the "Russian revolution," Lenin no doubt had in mind a crucial moment in the 1905 upheaval when, as he then wrote, "an important unit of the armed forces of tsarism [battleship *Potemkin*] ... has openly gone over to the side of the revolution."[18] Revolutionary civil war, in other words, was what he was advocating—exactly the course he charted for the next nine months. He had no idea as he spoke how soon he would have the opportunity to realize that goal—with a single-mindedness informed by all of the preceding.

PRELUDE TO THE FEBRUARY REVOLUTION: WILSON

As head of the most powerful state on the planet, Woodrow Wilson (1856–1924) would too—as Lenin's critique of his December 18, 1916, "Peace Note," suggests—become a protagonist in the destiny of "the Great War," in fact, the leading one. Wilson, unlike Weber or John Stuart Mill, was the rare intellectual/academic—at least from that era—who subordinated his life to politics. Underappreciated, however, is that he chose an academic career *in order* to become a political figure—not unlike Tocqueville—making, therefore, for a fairer comparison with Lenin.[19] Once the Guns of August exploded in 1914, Wilson's actions, however, were uninformed by as rich a tradition as the one Lenin—fourteen years his junior—drew on to both make sense of and to respond to the war. From the other side of the class divide, he would have to innovate with consequences that reverberate until today.

Wilson was the first and, until now, only US president to be doctored, from Johns Hopkins, in history and political science. He taught at three prestigious colleges, including Princeton, and published ten books, one of which was a popular biography of George Washington, and a five-volume history of the U.S. From 1902 to 1910 he served as Princeton's president. His academic renown earned him the presidency of the American Political Science Association from 1909–1910. The American politics sub-field of the just emerging discipline of political science traces its origins to Wilson. No president before or since Wilson has had such sterling academic and intellectual credentials. Noteworthy, however, is that his scholarship was strikingly bereft, especially for a political scientist, of any sustained attention to international politics (let alone international political economy), the subject for which his presidency would be most remembered. The academy was a steppingstone, unusual in US politics, to Wilson's first publicly elected post as the Governor of New Jersey from 1911 to 1913, from where he captured national attention.

Key to understanding how Wilson would respond to the Great War is that his family was on the losing side of the most sanguinary but consequential conflict in the nineteenth century. He was nine years old living in prostrated Georgia when Lee surrendered to Grant at Appomattox, Virginia, in April 1865. His father had been a Presbyterian chaplain for the defeated Confederate army and his mother had attended to its wounded soldiers. The U.S. Civil War, always to be remembered, claimed more American lives than all the wars the U.S. has since fought in. The fact that it was a bloody revolutionary war would forever, Adam Tooze argues, mark Wilson—not unlike how the French Revolution marked Alexis de Tocqueville.[20] If Marx, Engels, and Lenin regarded the Civil War as an advance for world humanity, Wilson emphatically did not. An essay by Edmund Burke, the eminent British conservative critic of the French Revolution, offered intellectual ammunition for Wilson to hone his arguments about the ills of revolutions in an 1893 essay.[21] If Tocqueville was responsible for the sanitization of the First American Revolution, his preferred alternative to the bloodletting in his native France, Wilson, given his intellectual-cum-political stature, was probably most responsible for the defanging of the Second, the Civil War and Reconstruction, of its revolutionary content. Bloody revolutions were, in the tradition of Burke and Tocqueville, un-American.[22] Marx and Engels—Lenin too to be seen shortly—thought otherwise.

The Spanish-American War, 1898–1901, instantiated for Lenin his thesis about the new epoch in the capitalist mode of production, imperialism. The war's outcome is what first got Wilson's attention about US foreign policy. With no apparent interest in why and how it was done—"almost accidental"[23]—the U.S. now possessed former Spanish territories including the Philippines and Puerto Rico. While he, "not an imperialist of expansionism,"[24] would have preferred that the U.S. not become a colonial power, "my personal wish"[25] was better that it get the Philippines than Germany or Russia, "our greatest rivals … inasmuch as hers was the light of day, while theirs was the light of darkness."[26] "Practicality" rather than "theory" demanded that the U.S. government face up to its responsibilities and try to be an enlightened colonial authority. But that didn't mean "savages"[27] could adopt institutions that came with the colonial project because, as Burke had advised, they weren't part of their traditions. Be especially wary, he warned, of freedom for the "undisciplined Filipinos,"[28] particularly, the "Filipino rebels."[29] Governing colonial subjects required compliance, "law and order," the incessant mantra of more seasoned colonial powers. After all, "they are children and we are men in these deep matters of government and justice."[30]

After three years of US occupation of the Philippines, Wilson was less the idealist and more the realist, as an address in late November of 1903 reveals: "It may be that politicians in Washington had their own selfish interests to serve in bringing us to blows with Spain and in sweeping the foreign dominions of the Spanish Crown under our own rule; but the consciences of the vast majority of us are void of offense in that great matter."[31] And for the first time he suggested how he personally felt about the war. "We know that our pulses beat high in that war because we truly believed ourselves to be defending peoples who are trodden upon and degraded by corrupt and selfish governors." If the Civil War may have once made Wilson squeamish about war, the booty America acquired in besting "corrupt and selfish" Spain seems to have convinced him that war could actually have noble ends.

His new realism about the U.S. as a colonial power was clearly on display in a presentation at the end of January 1904. With the Philippines as the new western "frontier" of the U.S., it could serve as prior frontiers had done, a place "to turn loose the colts of the race." Then, an instructive next sentence: "Because of our Americanism we had no patience with anti-imperialist weepings and wailings that came out of Boston ... we knew that the time had come for men to look out of dry eyes and see the world as it is." And in justifying a more robust American colonial project, he concluded: "We are a sort of pure air blowing in world politics, destroying illusions and cleaning places of morbid miasmatic gases."[32] No sentiment anticipated more his response to the Great War a decade later.

Finally, when the secretary of the New York Anti-Imperialist League asked Wilson to sign on to a letter calling for independence for the Philippines, he respectfully declined: "I do not think the movement in favor of Philippine independence either wise or opportune."[33] The rejection anticipated policies Wilson would pursue a decade later as US president.

Like the rest of the world, Washington too was shaken when the Guns of August of 1914 exploded four days into that fateful month and year. The eighteen-month-old Wilson administration wasn't totally unprepared since its fabled adviser, Colonel Edward House, had visited the capitals of the belligerents prior to then to see if armed conflict could be avoided. Unlike Lenin, Wilson seems never to have had a thought-out explanation for the war. At the most it was "a 'quarrel to settle economic rivalries between Germany and England,'" superficially akin to Lenin's *Imperialism* thesis.[34] When House told him four years later that he "thought the two great causes of war were territorial and commercial greed," he apparently agreed or "made no argument against."[35] Whatever the case, Wilson issued on August 19 a declaration of neutrality because "the people of the United States are drawn from many nations ... now at war." To take sides would be divisive and, hence, "fatal to our peace of mind." It would also make it hard for Washington to play the "part of impartial mediation" to end the war. Neutrality no doubt suited Wilson's personal preferences owing to his basic belief that the belligerents, the Entente on one side, Britain, France, Russia and Italy, and the Central Powers on the other, Germany, Austria, Turkey and Bulgaria, constituted the "morbid miasmatic gases" of the past—a plague, hence, on both their houses. He hoped to prove that America could be the alternative to old world realities, again, "a sort of pure air blowing in world politics."

To make clear that the American alternative wasn't starry eyed idealism, Wilson intervened with US troops in Mexico's 1913–1916 civil war, in the name of protecting "American lives." He threatened to occupy northern Mexico to the consternation of pacifists who tried unsuccessfully to get Wilson to reconsider his actions, including the future defender of the Bolshevik Revolution, John Reed.[36] As Wilson had stated in 1903, he would have no truck with "anti-imperialist weepings and wailings." Only because the victorious side in the civil war was willing to concede to his demands did he not carry out his threat. Similarly, he operated in an admittedly "high-handed" way in imposing with "our marines" a treaty on "the dusky little republic" of Haiti in 1915. The pretext was another intra-ruling class conflict on the island. To not intervene would leave "the best and most responsible Haitians ... prey to the most sordid chaos." The treaty, to be in place for at least a decade, would "give us practically complete control of the finances of the Haitian government."[37] The island's major creditor, City National Bank in New York, would be the main financial beneficiary of the "stability" Washington imposed.

Despite official neutrality, Wilson embarked on a campaign that came to be called "preparedness," mentioned above in Lenin's comment about Eugene V. Debs. Launched in New York on November 4, 1915, he stated that "the "great war" in Europe had raised the question "how far we are prepared to maintain ourselves against any interference with our national action or development ... to be prepared ... not for war, but only for defense."[38] A month later in his State of the Union address to Congress he spelled out his "defense" proposals. US interventions in the Philippines, Hawaii, Mexico, Puerto Rico and Haiti taught that "the regular army" of

108,008 needed to be increased to 141,843 plus increases in various support units. And in order to be ready to "assert some part of its real power promptly and upon a larger scale, should occasion arise," Wilson proposed "supplementing the army by a force of four hundred thousand disciplined citizens, raised in increments of one hundred and thirty-three thousand a year throughout a period of three years .... At least so much by way of preparation for defense seems to me to be absolutely imperative now. We cannot do less."

The navy too, "our first and chief line of defense," Wilson argued, needed major upgrading. He proposed the "construction within five years of ten battleships, six battle cruisers, ten scout cruisers, fifty destroyers, fifteen fleet submarines, eighty-five coast submarines, four gunboats, one hospital ship, two ammunition ships, tow fuel oil ships, one repair ship." But, Wilson pointedly noted, "armies and instruments of war are only part of what has to be considered if we are to consider the supreme matter of national self-sufficiency and security in all its aspects." Trade and commerce were crucially important. US economic independence required its own merchant marine fleet. And while "private capital must undertake and achieve" that goal, "the government" must "assume the initial financial risks ... it should take the first steps, and should take them at once."[39] Thus, at the very moment Lenin was researching and writing his *Imperialism: Highest Stage of Capitalism*, Wilson was launching an unprecedented campaign to advance the global reach of US capital.

Ideological preparedness was also required. Wilson lambasted those "professing to be the voices of Americans which were not indeed and in truth American, but which spoke alien sympathies, which came from men who loved other countries better than they loved America, men who were partisans of other causes than that of America and had forgotten that their chief and only allegiance was to the great government under which they live."[40] Wilson was vague about who were these "citizens of the United States ... born under other flags ... [who] have formed plots to destroy property, they have entered into conspiracies against the neutrality of the Government." He was probably, as a subsequent speech revealed, referring to radical pro-German nuclei in the U.S. To Congress he said, "we are without adequate federal laws to deal with it. I urge you to enact such laws at the earliest possible moment."[41] Wilson's call in hindsight initiated the nation's first xenophobic dragnet, in anticipation of the Red Scare. Whether he was consciously preparing for US intervention into the Great War—with his call for an unprecedented increase in the nation's military capabilities and the enactment of legislation that would be used to stifle domestic opposition to an intervention—will probably never be known; but objectively that's exactly what he was doing. Wilson's public and private utterances suggest someone who could be self-deceiving—telling not only others, but himself what he wanted to hear.

To carry out his military buildup Wilson had to overcome widespread anti-war, anti-interventionist, anti-militarism and pacifist sentiment—what Lenin's above-mentioned comment about Debs and the debates in the Socialist Party about the war alluded to. Wilson's secretary of state, William Jennings Bryan, not only a well-known Democrat but probably the country's leading pacifist, resigned his post, in fact, in June 1915, when he thought Wilson was veering too far away from neutrality in favor of the Entente powers. To win public support for his "preparedness" program, Wilson embarked on an eight-state speaking tour in January and February 1916 with particular focus on the Midwest where opposition to his proposals was strongest. Pro-"preparedness" rallies were organized in other cities, especially in the West and were often greeted with protests by anti-war activists, sometimes leading to violence.

Anti-militarist activists responded quickly to his proposals with mass meetings, some of the biggest in the Twin Cities, Minnesota, obliging Wilson to invite their leaders to the White House for a "colloquy" on May 8, 1916, to "clarify the discussion."[42] An unidentified participant at the very end of the encounter suggested to Wilson that his proposals would only embolden "our economic organizations" that "are more active, more powerful, in reaching out and grasping for the world's trade." That, s/he continued, "would lead to an aggressive nationalism in trade which would," when Wilson interrupted: "It might, very easily, unless some check was placed upon it by some international arrangement which we hope for." To which another unidentified voice added, "if they get the educational thing with it." "I quite see your point," the professorial Wilson concluded the session with according to the transcript.[43] Thus, for the problem someone might have posed who had read the manuscript Lenin soon published, *Imperialism*, that is, how to curb the innately predatory character of capital and the global war drive it generates, Wilson's solution was some kind of "international arrangement"—in anticipation not only of his beloved League of Nations but other post-World War I and World War II "arrangements."

For his reelection campaign in the summer and fall of 1916, Wilson ran on the slogan, "He kept us out of war"—despite the fact that US troops were battling revolutionary forces in Mexico at the same time. With the active support of pacifists like Bryan and the American Federation of Labor leader Samuel Gompers, he was able to win by a slim margin over his more pro-"preparedness" Republican and officially anti-intervention Socialist Party rivals. Though his electoral college vote was much smaller than what it had been in his 1912 victory, Wilson's popular vote totals suggest that a majority of the electorate favored his official neutrality stance. The more revolutionary forces in the working-class movement like Debs, however, thought—like Lenin—that Wilson had been duplicitous about his real aims.[44] More evidence for their suspicions was his formation during the campaign of a Council of National Defense because a "country is best prepared for war which is best prepared for peace." Consisting of leading figures in the private sector, including Gompers, its charge was to "render possible in time of need the immediate concentration and utilization of the resources of the Nation."[45]

With the electoral victory safely under his belt Wilson launched a new peace initiative, his previously mentioned "Peace Note" of December 18, 1916. Again, he offered to serve as a possible mediator for the belligerents but with the understanding that a long-term solution was needed, "a league of nations to insure peace and justice throughout the world." The U.S., he pointed out, had a stake in the end of the conflagration; "the situation of neutral nations [is] now exceedingly hard to endure."[46] Wilson was "satisfied" with the response of the Entente powers to his initiative except for one of them. "President and advisors," according to Britain's ambassador in Washington, "are particularly anxious about the Russian situation, fearing that power has gone back into the hand of the reactionaries."[47]

Wilson informed Congress on January 22, 1917, about his initiative. The responses of the belligerents indicated that "we are ... much nearer a definite discussion of peace" to end the war and "a discussion of the international concert which ... will make it virtually impossible that any such catastrophe should ever overwhelm us again." And famously, "it must be a peace without victory ... a peace between equals." In conclusion, "speaking for liberals and friends of humanity in every nation and of every programme of liberty ... I am proposing ... that no nation should seek to extend its polity over any other nation or people, but that every people should be left free to determine its own polity ... I am proposing government by the consent of the governed."[48]

On that very same day Lenin lambasted "social-pacifists" for being "foolish to expect a 'democratic' peace from bourgeois governments that are waging an imperialist predatory war." He did so in the same aforementioned talk he gave in Zurich, Switzerland, in which he argued that the only counter to "militarism" is the "victorious struggle of one section of the national army against the other section"—exactly why he so vehemently opposed pacifism of any variety. He ended with a forecast: "we must not be deceived by the present grave-like stillness in Europe. Europe is pregnant with revolution. The monstrous horrors of the imperialist war, the suffering caused by the high cost of living everywhere engender a revolutionary mood; and the ruling classes, the bourgeoisie, and its servitors, the governments, are more and more moving into a blind alley from which they can never extricate themselves without tremendous upheavals." Lenin clearly didn't realize the imminence of his forecast to his mostly youthful audience when he said, "we of the older generation may not live to see the decisive battles of this coming revolution."[49]

FROM FEBRUARY TO NOVEMBER 1917

When Germany announced on February 1, 1917, that its submarines would fire on all ships in the war zone, Wilson decided to break off diplomatic relations with Berlin. The discovery of a secret diplomatic telegram that Berlin was considering a maneuver with Mexico at the expense of the U.S. was also portentous. And when three US merchant marine ships were sunk on March 18, he came under increasing pressure to abandon official US neutrality and to declare war on Germany. Three days earlier a development took place that would weigh heavily in the momentous decision he was about to make. Wilson's fear "that power has gone back into the hand of the reactionaries" in Russia proved to be unwarranted. It was in fact just the opposite.

Until March 2/15, Tsar Nicholas's regime had been Exhibit A for the "morbid miasmatic gases" of the past that had once been Wilson's characterization of Europe. The sclerotic 300-year-old dynasty came to an ignominious end that day when Russia's long-suffering subjects became its protagonists. Both Lenin and Wilson were ecstatic with Nicholas's disposal after more than a week of mass protests but for quite different reasons. To a cabinet meeting on March 23, Wilson hoped that the "Russian revolution was permanent. 'It ought to be good' said Wilson with a smile, 'because it has a professor at the head.'" He was especially pleased "that

America ["that pure air blowing in world politics" as he once counter-poised to Europe] was the first nation to recognize the new Russian government."[50]

About two weeks later, Lenin, about to make his way back to Russia, wrote a farewell letter to Swiss workers on behalf of the Bolshevik central committee in exile. "The objective circumstances of the imperialist war make it certain that the revolution will not be limited to the *first* stage of the Russian revolution, that the revolution will *not* be limited to Russia. *The German proletariat is the most trustworthy, the most reliable ally of the Russian and the world proletarian revolution.*"[51] No two lines foretold as much as these Lenin's course for the next two to three years. Like Wilson, he too wanted a "permanent" Russian revolution, but in a profoundly different way.

At the heart of Lenin and Wilson's differences, as first revealed in that moment—and in anticipation of their fraught pas de deux the next two years or more—is that while both saw the February/March Revolution as a bourgeois revolution, for Lenin, unlike Wilson, it was, while necessary, only the means to an end, the socialist revolution. For Wilson the bourgeois democratic revolution was the end. Their differences had a rich genealogy going back to the 1848–1849 revolutions. Liberals, as epitomized by Tocqueville, wanted to limit the revolution while Marxists, as the *Communist Manifesto* put it, wanted to ensure that the "bourgeois revolution be but the prelude to an immediately following proletarian revolution," and with all that implied internationally. What the Marxist project was unable to do in 1848–1849 it could seven decades later in the hands of its most able student.

In his speech to a joint session of Congress on April 2, in which he asked for its approval for declaring war on Germany, Wilson sought to explain why the long-avoided outcome had come to be. "A steadfast concert for peace can never be maintained except by a partnership of democratic nations. No autocratic government could be trusted to keep faith within it or observe its covenants." The reign of autocracy in Germany, in other words, is what forced, he claimed, the U.S. out of it position of neutrality. Only democratic governments could be counted on for maintaining the peace—the first application of the thesis of the democratic peace in a major policy statement.[52]

From a solemn tone Wilson then struck for the first time in the speech an optimistic note. "Does not every American feel that assurance has been added to our hope for the future peace of the world by the wonderful and heartening things that have been happening within the last few weeks in Russia?" Unlike in Germany, the "Russian people" had just discarded the "autocracy that crowned the summit of her political structure." They had now "been added in all their naïve majesty and might to the forces that are fighting for freedom in the world, for justice, and for peace. Here is a partner for a League of Honour."[53]

The Russian revolution initiated in February/March 1917 was for Wilson the ray of hope in the sea of despair that had engulfed much of Europe. About the developments then unfolding, "I have great sympathy with them."[54] In considering the composition of a US delegation to the new Russia, Wilson required that they "should be all genuinely enthusiastic for the success of the Russian revolution."[55] It is difficult to say how determinant the history-making events in Russia were in Wilson's calculus for going to war with Germany. Colonel House is reported to have said "that but for the Russian Revolution and [the] famous German telegram to Mexico [the] President would have found it very difficult to take [the] decisive step."[56] The disposal of the last absolute monarch in Europe, Nicholas II, certainly made it easier for him to sell it to the U.S. public.[57] Wall Street, the financier J. P. Morgan in particular, on the other hand, would have had no need for a democratic cover. Wilson's promise that Washington would facilitate "the extension to [the Entente] governments of the most liberal financial credits" was all that it needed to hear.[58] One can only imagine what Lenin thought of Wilson's declaration. Nothing, unfortunately, is available in the published record, probably because in that moment he was forced, mainly by the Entente governments, to take an unusually circuitous route back to Russia.[59] Wilson's declaration, to be noted, came a month after his second inauguration, made possible by an election campaign on the slogan, "He kept us out of war." Not the last time a Democratic Party "anti-war candidate" would lead the nation to war.

Once back in Russia on April 5/18, Lenin quickly picked up from where he had left off in 1914, using the newly conquered political space to propagate the Bolshevik program in the electoral/parliamentary arena in order, as Marx and Engels taught him, "to count their forces" to determine the best time to launch the armed struggle.[60] Not only were the local municipal councils, the dumas, back in operation but as well, and more importantly, the councils of workers, soldiers and peasants, the soviets. They appeared spontaneously with the overthrow of the tsar just as they had, momentarily, in the 1905 revolution and why Lenin often referred to that upheaval as the "dress rehearsal" for 1917 (see Chap. 3). He had a very able partner to assist him. Leon Trotsky, the leader of the fabled St. Petersburg Soviet of Workers and Soldiers in 1905 as well as bitter opponent of Lenin for more than a decade, returned from exile—most recently in New York—in early May. He immediately joined Lenin to lead the Bolsheviks eventually to power in October—arguably the most consequential political reconciliation in history.

In print and public speeches Lenin prioritized the pressing question—how to end the war. Beware of those, he advised in *The Tasks of the Proletariat in Our Revolution*, a pamphlet intended to arm the Bolsheviks politically—his so-called *April Theses*—who promoted "revolutionary defencism," the claim that the war now had a progressive character with the tsar's deposition. "The bourgeoisie deceives the people by working on their noble pride in the revolution and by pretending that the *social and political* character of the war, as far as Russia is concerned, underwent a change because of this stage of the revolution, because of the substitution of the near republic … for the tsarist monarchy." Written on April 10 /23, it was effectively Lenin's response to Wilson's April 2 speech to Congress, specifically, his newfound admiration for "the Russian people," in all "their naïve majesty … that are fighting for freedom in the world, for justice, and for peace." To make his point Lenin continued most pedagogically.

> What is required of us is the *ability* to explain to the masses that the social and political character of the war is determined not by the "good will" of individuals or groups, or even of nations, but by the position of the *class* which conducts the war, by the class *policy* of which the war is a continuation, by the *ties* of capital, which is the dominant economic force in modern society, by the *imperialist character* of international capital, by Russia's dependence in finance, banking and diplomacy upon Britain, France, and so on. To explain this skilfully in a way the people would understand *is not easy*, none of us would be able to do it at once without committing errors.[61]

It is doubtful that Lenin had read Wilson's speech—he would have referenced it—but his thesis on "revolutionary defencism" spoke directly to his siren call to the Russian people to maintain the course. And to be as transparent as possible he concluded:

> It is *impossible* to slip out of the imperialist war and achieve a democratic, non-coercive peace without overthrowing the power of capital and transferring state power to *another* class, the proletariat.

The Russian revolution of February-March 1917 was the beginning of the transformation of the imperialist war into a civil war. This revolution took the *first* step towards ending the war; but it requires a *second* step, namely, the transfer of state power to the proletariat, to make the end of the war a *certainty*. This will be the beginning of a "break-through" on a world-wide scale, a break-through in the front of capitalist interests; and only by breaking through *this* front *can* the proletariat save mankind from the horrors of war and endow it with the blessings of peace.[62]

Published in the Bolshevik's daily, *Soldatskaya Pravda*, or *Soldier's Truth* (the name of the organ is instructive), Washington had no excuse now for not knowing Lenin's agenda.

The "professor" that Wilson placed his hopes in, Pavel Miliukov—who he had met as an academic in the U.S. some years earlier—an eminent Russian historian and leader of the Constitutional Democrats or Cadets, the leading liberal party in Russia, quickly, pardon the pun, became history. The government he had served in as minister of foreign affairs was brought down in early May by mass protests owing to its insistence that Russia stay in the war to fulfill its treaty commitments to the other Entente powers. In the first of only two direct messages Wilson ever sent to the provisional government, on May 22, he urged that Russia, now "a great democracy," continue "the persecution of the war against the German autocracy … whatever the cost in life and treasure … to bring victory to the cause of democracy and human liberty."[63] And to back up its request Washington provided major financial and material aid to the new government. To the very end, the provisional government assured Wilson that it would stay in the war—to its peril.

In calling on Russians to persecute the war, "whatever the cost in life and treasure," Wilson's message could be evidence for war-weary Russians for Lenin's claim that he'd been making in print and in speeches as in this concluding comment to a group of soldiers on April 10/23:

Our government, a government of the capitalists, is continuing the war in the interests of the capitalists. Like the German capitalists, headed by their crowned brigand Wilhelm, the capitalists of *all* the other countries are carrying on the war only for a division of capitalist profits, for domination over the world. Hundreds of millions of people, almost all the countries in the world, have been dragged into this criminal war. Hundreds of billions of capital have been invested in "profitable" undertakings, bringing death, hunger, ruin, and barbarism to the peoples and staggering, scandalously high profits to the capitalists. There is only one way to get out of this frightful war and conclude a truly democratic peace not imposed by force, and that is by transferring all the state power to the Soviets of Workers' and Soldiers' Deputies. The workers and poor peasants, who are not interested in preserving the profits of the capitalists and robbing the weaker nations, will be able to do effectively what the capitalists only promise, namely, end the war by concluding a lasting peace that will assure liberty to all peoples without exception.[64]

Maybe if Lenin's pamphlet and speeches had been available to Wilson, he might have been more aware of the actual sentiment of the "naïve" Russian people. By 1917, if not before, they were less interested in bringing autocratic Germany to heel and exacting capital's pound of flesh than simply ending the bloodletting. Wilson would soon regret his myopia; he and the class interests he represented would pay a high price for the blinders they wore.[65]

The war issue was all so determinant in the course of the Russian revolution because of the carnage, increasingly exhausting the Russian people and their patience. And inextricably linked to the war was the fundamental question of democratic representation, as Lenin constantly underscored; how best to ensure the desires and interests of the masses in the governing process?[66] Key in understanding the dynamic from February to November was the contestation between two radically different forms of representative democracy. On the one hand, Western European style parliamentary democracy, what the provisional government represented—or, at least potentially once it convened a constituent assembly (more about later)—and on the other, a uniquely Russian invention, soviet democracy. Washington's ambassador in Petrograd alerted his superiors on May 11 that the soviets gave voice to the overwhelming sentiment in Russia to pull its troops out of the war, even, alarmingly in his opinion, using for justification Wilson's pledge in his January 22 address, "peace without victory."[67] No protagonist was as single-minded in promoting soviet governance as Lenin. For the first time, on May 15/June 2, he called publicly, in *Pravda*, for "*All power to the Soviets of Workers' and Soldiers' Deputies! No confidence in the government of the capitalists.*" The context makes clear that he did so for propaganda purposes and not for agitation or to incite—at least then.[68]

The Bolshevik leader first appeared on Wilson's radar by mistake, but the reason is instructive. He had been erroneously identified as leading a march on the U.S. embassy in Petrograd to protest the impending execution of the radical labor leader Tom Mooney in California. As noted earlier, some violent anti-"preparedness" demonstrations took place in the U.S. West the previous year. Mooney was convicted of having been responsible for one in San Francisco and was sentenced to death. Wilson asked the governor of California to commute the sentence because it would "greatly relieve some critical situations outside the United States," which he did.[69] What the incident revealed is that Wilson was by now sensitive to the impact of the Russian revolution elsewhere, especially in the U.S.; he now had a name to help make the connection.

By early August 1917, Wilson learned that he should have known that "the opposition to the war on the part of the extremists" in Russia had "been so strong" and met "with such popular response."[70] The "extremists" were, of course, Lenin's Bolsheviks. In an effort to shore up the sagging morale of the provisional government, headed now by Alexander Kerensky of the peasant-based Socialist Revolutionary Party, Wilson sent a message of solidarity on August 24 to the "Democratic Conference" called by moderate and reformist forces looking for an alternative to revolution. He assured them that the "people of the United States" were confident in "the ultimate triumph of ideals of democracy and self-government against all enemies within and without" and prepared to provide "every material and moral assistance they can extend to the government of Russia in the promotion of the common cause," to defeat autocratic Germany.[71] His goal, again, to convince the provisional government to stay the course—in the war. The Bolsheviks attended the Conference but were critical of its deliberations. For Lenin it was a diversion, to sidetrack the real movement, the masses in the streets.

Almost exactly two months later, October 25/November 7, the Bolsheviks led Russia's war weary workers, soldiers and peasants to power by overthrowing the provisional government in order to have for the first time a government that represented their interests, especially on the war question. The prominent journalist and one-time illuminati of the Socialist Party Charles Edward Russell tried to explain to Wilson the mood in Russia while, unbeknownst to him, the overthrow was under way on November 7. The problem for those who wanted Russia to stay the course was that the "average Russian sees nothing in that war that appeals to the soul in him. The war was made by the Czar; that mere fact prejudices the average Russian against it … The typical Russian … only acknowledges the duty of a democrat to fight for democracy." The task was then to convince

Russians through an "education campaign ['film pictures and printed appeals'] ... addressed to the Russian passion for democracy, and if it shows him that his beloved Revolution is in peril, he will be ready to fight with all his strength, and there is no better fighter in the world."[72] "I deeply appreciate your letter," responded Wilson on November 10, when he would have known by then about the overthrow. "It runs along the lines of my own thought, only you speak from knowledge and I have thought by inference." He said that he'd do his "best to act along the lines" Russell suggested but admitted that it would be "extremely difficult because no one channel connects with any other, apparently." Washington, in other words, now lacked the kinds of connections it once had to the provisional government.

Thus, Wilson, at least in that moment, the first few days of the Bolshevik October/November revolution, implicitly acknowledged that the "extremists" came to power on a popular wave of mass opposition to the provisional government owing to its failure to extricate Russia from the bloodletting that the war had become.[73] In real-time, in other words, Wilson viewed the Bolshevik Revolution as a popularly supported overturn—in stark contrast to the Cold War portrait painted by subsequent US presidents. The popularity of the revolt was registered in the fact that in Petrograd, the main scene of the action, only "a total of five people had been killed and several more wounded, most from stray bullets."[74] That must have impressed Wilson who had had an aversion to revolutions owing to their usually bloody character. The challenge he now faced with the Bolsheviks in power was how to convince Russia to stay in the war in the name of "making the world safe for democracy" and to show the Russian people that Washington was not a threat to their "beloved Revolution" when the Bolsheviks refused to go along with his agenda. Those increasingly incompatible goals engendered increasingly contradictory actions on his part. Wilson, as events would show, was at a disadvantage. Lenin knew more about him than Wilson did about his new adversary.

THE BOLSHEVIKS IN POWER

"Peace, land, and bread," had been the Bolsheviks months-long campaign slogan for taking power. Enabling their success had been their almost decade-long usage of the electoral/parliamentary process, the soviets and the dumas, to determine when best to carry out an armed struggle.[75] Most significant about that work is that it was also, as already noted, carried out in the soviets amongst the armed forces. Soldiers and sailors were for Lenin "peasants in uniform," crucial in the realization of "the democratic dictatorship of the proletariat and the peasantry"—the imposition or domination of majority rule.[76] Lenin, to be remembered, had long argued that only if the working-class masses were in power could imperialist wars be prevented. By September 1917 the tactic of using the electoral/parliamentary venue for revolutionary action began to pay off when the Bolsheviks emerged as the leading party in the elections to the soviets, campaigning, again, on the "peace, land, and bread" slogan. That's when Lenin was able to convince the rest of Bolshevik leadership that the time for an armed taking of power via the authority of the soviets had arrived. Trotsky's assistance was invaluable without which it's unlikely Lenin would have prevailed. With Lenin as head of the new Soviet government and Trotsky as its minister of foreign affairs, the Wilson administration now had a formidable adversary.

The very first decrees of the new Soviet government, drafted by Lenin and ratified by the Second Congress of the Soviets of Workers' and Soldiers' Deputies on October 25–26/November 7–8, were about, not unexpectedly, the war and land issues. The first called on the belligerent powers to immediately end hostilities and to commit to a peace "without annexations (i.e., without the seizure of foreign lands, without the forcible incorporation of foreign lands," that is, for the self-determination of nationalities, "and without indemnities." It appealed to workers in those countries to support the Soviet government's proposals and to demand that their respective governments enter into peace negotiations on those terms. Most consequential,

> The government abolishes secret diplomacy, and for its part, announces its firm intention to conduct all negotiations quite openly in the full view of the whole people. It will proceed immediately with the full publication of the secret treaties endorsed or concluded by the government of land-owners and capitalists from February to October 25 [November 7], 1917. The government proclaims the unconditional and immediate annulment of everything contained in these secret treaties insofar as it is aimed, as in mostly the case, at securing advantages and privileges for the Russian landowners and capitalists and at the retention, or extension, of the annexations made by the Great Russians.[77]

What soon ensued was the first equivalent of a mass WikiLeaks dump on the part of the Bolshevik-led government, including the infamous Sykes-Picot agreement, much to the anger of the Entente governments of Britain and France. In the debate on the peace decree, Lenin said that he would "vigorously oppose lending our demand for peace the form of an ultimatum. An ultimatum may prove fatal to our cause" because it could give the "imperialist governments" the excuse for not entering into negotiations—what he clearly wanted to get under way as soon as possible. His point carried.

The land decree proclaimed that "private ownership of land shall be abolished forever" so that land could "become the property of the whole people, and shall pass into the use of those who cultivate it." It recognized in effect what had already been in progress throughout rural Russia and crucial in winning the support of the peasantry to the revolution—decisive in the outcome of the soon to be launched civil war that Washington participated in to overthrow the revolution. The implementation of both decrees meant, implicitly and explicitly, that Russia was now being governed by the soviets or "Soviet Power" as Lenin put it, effectively resolving, in other words, the eight-month old contest about which form of representative democracy would prevail in Russia.

In his diary entry for November 27, Wilson's secretary of the navy Josephus Daniels wrote about a cabinet meeting that day:

> The President read speech & message of Trotsky, who said America entered war at behest of Wall Street and men whose prosperity came through making munitions. [Secretary of State Robert] Lansing thought T—misguided but honest. Once he worked at $12 a week on N Y Socialist paper & stopped writing for it because he thought paper was unfair to President. No answer now unless in message to Congress, for any answer would imply recognition WW said action of Lenine & Trotsky sounded like opera bouffe, talking of armistice with Germany when a child would know Germany would control & dominate & destroy any chance for the democracy they desire.[78]

Trotsky gave the speech, translated and summarized by the U.S. ambassador David Francis, on November 21, but it's not clear to whom. Its tone and content were similar to many things Lenin had said about the imperialist character of the war. New was Trotsky's explanation for the U.S. involvement, what most attracted Wilson's attention; he seemed unusually informed about the U.S. and, thus, the comment about his having lived briefly in New York City. Specifically, according to the translated version:

When in January Germany announced unlimited submarine warfare all railway stations and docks in United States were crammed with products of war industry. To remove them was impossible. Transportation was disorganized and New York experienced hunger riots such as we have not seen here. At that time financial capital presented Wilson an ultimatum: the sale of products of industry must be guaranteed which Wilson obeyed hence the preparation for war and later the war itself. America is not aiming at territorial acquisition. America can patiently receive the fact of Soviet Government as she is sufficiently satisfied by exhaustion of Allied countries and of Germany, in addition America is interested in investing her capital in Russia.[79]

For the first time, then, the Wilson administration learned why the Bolshevik leadership thought Washington intervened in the war and what it hoped to reap. Lenin's charge in January that "Wilson represents a bourgeoisie which has made billions out of the war" suggests he and Trotsky were on the same page; Wilson no doubt thought so. That both Bolshevik leaders, apparently, in Wilson's view, assumed that Washington could "patiently receive the fact of Soviet Government" must have figured into his calculations about how to respond to their revolution.

Trotsky, about the same time, gave a talk to the central executive committee of the Soviet regarding its peace initiative. He mentioned: "Judson appeared at the Smolny Institute and declared, in the name of America, that the protest to the Dukhonin staff against the new power was a misunderstanding and that America had no desire to interfere in the internal affairs of Russia and, consequently, the American question is disposed of." Brig. Gen. William Judson, the U.S. Military Attaché, "made a well-publicized visit to" Trotsky on December 1, at his office to let him know that the "misunderstanding" with the new government about the military staff that served under the provisional government, "the Dukhonin staff," had been resolved. While Judson "had repeatedly urged the necessity of working at least informally with" the new government, Trotsky didn't know that others in the embassy and in Washington held a quite different opinion.[80] The "American question" was far from being "disposed of."

Also noteworthy about the November 27 cabinet meeting is Wilson's comment that "action of Lenine & Trotsky sounded like opera bouffe, talking of armistice with Germany when a child would know Germany would control & dominate & destroy any chance for the democracy they desire." Wilson's read of the Bolsheviks, desirous of "democracy"—at least in his understanding—is, again, in striking contrast to portraits of them by Cold War era US presidents. Yet, his still patronizing attitude. The Russian people "in all their naïve majesty," as he put it in his April 7 message, didn't realize they were being duped by the German autocracy. About a week later and with no knowledge of the cabinet meeting discussion, Lenin would offer a rebuttal.

Should Wilson respond to Trotsky's charge in his "message to Congress"? That's exactly what he did, not only to Trotsky but to Lenin also. His speech to a joint session of Congress on December 4 was the first of two speeches to the body in which the Bolshevik leaders would figure significantly as one of the intended audiences. Because "the American people," Wilson claimed, "desire peace by the defeat once for all of the sinister forces" of German autocracy, they are "deeply and indignantly impatient with those who desire peace by any sort of compromise." Acknowledging the anti-war sentiment inside the U.S., "they'll be equally impatient with us if we do not make it plain to them what our objectives are and what we are planning for in seeking to make conquest of peace by arms." The "any sort of compromise" sentiment, Wilson opined, was being "expressed in the formula 'No annexations, no contributions, no punitive indemnities'"—that is, the peace decree of the Soviet government that Lenin drafted. "Just because this crude formula expresses the instinctive judgment as to right of plain men everywhere it" was misguided. It "has been made diligent use of by the masters of the German intrigue to lead the people of Russia astray—and the people of every other country their agents could reach, in order that a premature peace might be brought about before autocracy has been taught its final and convincing lesson"—before it has been "crushed."

Wilson expressed regret that he had not made his intentions plain before then.

> I cannot help thinking that if they had been made plain at the very outset the sympathy and enthusiasm of the Russian people might have been once for all enlisted on the side of the Allies, suspicion and distrust swept away, and a real and lasting union of purpose effected. Had they believed these things at the very moment of their revolution and had they been confirmed in that belief since, the sad reverses which have recently marked the progress of their affairs towards an ordered and stable government of freemen might have been avoided. The Russian people have been poisoned by the very same falsehoods that have kept the German people in the dark, and the poison has been administered by the very same hands. The only possible antidote is the truth.

He then elaborated on the need for more legislation to crack down on the activities of "alien enemies," that is, those dissenting against the war. "For us," he concluded in a ringing defense, it's "a war of high, disinterested purpose … just and holy … for nothing less noble or less worthy of our traditions."[81] Trotsky, in other words, was sorely wrong for believing otherwise.

Wilson's December 4, 1917, speech to Congress, too often ignored, is an implicit admission that his switch from "peace without victory" to "peace with victory" over the German autocracy aided and abetted Bolshevik ascent—"the sad reverses which have recently marked the progress of [Russian] affairs." But rather than fault himself he blamed the Germans for spreading "falsehoods," particularly to Russia, about his "noble" intentions. And the Russian people "in all their naïve majesty" believed it. The Bolshevik's uncompromising anti-imperialist war stance in combination with Wilson's insistence, backed by enormous political and material resources, that Russia stay in the war, and the Russian liberal/ moderate buy-in to his agenda is, in other words, what made Bolshevik hegemony possible. Unintended consequences take many forms. Lansing, his secretary of state, now wanted Wilson to play hardball with the two Bolshevik leaders.[82] Their "class despotism"—the "dictatorship of the workers and peasants"—had to be opposed; he began drawing up plans for an armed counterrevolution.

A day later Lenin gave a talk to the new Soviet government's navy personnel. Though there is no suggestion he knew what Wilson had said to the Congress hours earlier, some of his comments offered a rebuttal. To the charge that the Bolsheviks were naïve about reaching an agreement with the Germans, made explicit at the November 27 cabinet meeting and a subtext in his speech to Congress, Lenin said: "Now the struggle for peace is on. It is a difficult struggle. It is highly naïve to think that peace can be easily attained, and that the bourgeoisie will hand it to us on a platter as soon as we mention it. Those who ascribed this view to the Bolsheviks are cheating. The capitalists are embroiled in a life and death struggle over the share-out of the booty. One thing is clear: to kill a war is to defeat capital, and Soviet power has started the struggle to that end." The publication of the secret treaties, the original WikiLeaks dump, was done to show "the workers of all countries … that the rulers of all countries are brigands. This is not propaganda by word but by deed." When Lenin told Swiss workers in his farewell letter in March that the "German proletariat is the most trustworthy, the most reliable ally of the Russian and the world proletarian revolution" it anticipated, again, his future course. Revealing the secret treaties could help drive a wedge between German workers and their ruling class. A recent "open mutiny in the navy even in Germany" was encouraging. Nothing in Wilson's nationalist-constituted DNA would have made him understand Lenin's strategy; hence, it had to be "naïve." Lenin was enough of a realist to know, however, that German workers might not be won over to his overtures and could end up "siding with their government of imperialist plunderers and confronting us with the need to continue the war ... But we put our trust in the international solidarity of the working masses, who will surmount every obstacle and barrier in the struggle for socialism."

Lenin also addressed the major objection of the Entente powers to Russia's pulling out of the war and concluding a separate peace treaty with Germany—that it would free up the armed forces of the latter to better fight those of France and Britain to the west. He noted that "when the Germans gave an evasive reply to our demand not to transfer any troops to the Western and Italian fronts, we broke off the talks and shall resume them in a little while. And when we do tell this to the world, no German worker will remain ignorant of the fact that the peace talks had been broke off through no fault of ours."[83] Lenin's faith in the German working class was fulfilled but later than he had hoped, thus, making the negotiations with Berlin an even more "difficult struggle."

Talks with the Germans and their allies, Austria-Hungary, Bulgaria and Turkey, began on December 22, 1917, in the small Polish town of Brest-Litovsk. During a ten-day recess at the beginning of January, Trotsky, who headed Moscow's team of negotiators, issued a public call to London, Paris, Rome and Washington to join the Russians. He began with a distillation of the basic negotiating position of the two sides. The Russian program has "for its object the creation of such conditions, first, that every nationality, independently of its strength and the level of its general evolution, should have complete freedom for its national progress, and, secondly, that all the people should be united in economical and cultural cooperation." The German side was willing to forego "the forcible annexation of territories occupied during the war" such as Belgium. Historical conquests, however, such as Alsace-Lorraine, of dear interest to Paris, were not on the table for negotiation. Unknown, he pointedly noted, was the position of London, Paris, Rome and Washington. Would they be willing to recognize the right of "self-determination" for the peoples of Egypt, India, Ireland, Indo-China, Madagascar and elsewhere "just as under the Russian Revolution this right has been given to the peoples of

Finland, Ukrainia, White Russia, and other districts?" The peace process could be advanced, Trotsky proclaimed,

> if the Governments of the Allied countries would express their readiness, together with the Russian Government, to found a peace upon the complete and unconditional recognition of the principle of self-determination for all peoples in all States, if they would begin by the giving of this right to the oppressed peoples of their own States, this would create such international conditions that when the inherently contradictory programmes, of Germany, and especially Austro-Hungary, were shown in all their weakness objection would be overcome by the pressure of all the interested peoples. But up to the present, the Allied Governments have in no way shown, and, in view of their class character, they could not show, their readiness to accept a really democratic peace.[84]

The clock was ticking, Trotsky then noted. "Ten days were given for the continuation of the peace negotiations. Russia is not depending in these negotiations upon having the agreement of the Allied Governments. If these continue to be opposed to a general peace, the Russian delegation will nevertheless continue the peace negotiations." Transparent like Lenin, he made clear the premise that informed the Russian position in the deliberations. "The success of our programme will depend upon the degree in which the will of the Imperialistic classes will be paralysed by the work of the Revolutionary proletariat in every country." The class struggle in the belligerent countries, in other words, would determine how much the new Soviet government would have to pay at Brest-Litovsk—a sobering but accurate forecast.

"The Allied Governments," to repeat, "have in no way shown, and, in view of their class character, they could not show, their readiness to accept a really democratic peace." Not the first time that Trotsky challenged the bona fides of Washington. Until the October Revolution Wilson could claim to be the sole occupant of the moral high ground in the Great War, the political voice for humanity's alternative to the "miasmatic gases" that had too long emanated from old Europe. The Bolshevik challenge to that space necessitated a response.

Despite secretary of state Lansing's lobbying for a counterrevolutionary response to the Bolshevik-led revolution, Wilson continued to believe that Trotsky and Lenin represented an understandable if not "misguided" alternative to old world business as usual. Wilson decided to pick up the gauntlet that Trotsky had thrown in his direction. His "Fourteen Points" speech to Congress a few days later on January 8, his most memorable, was an attempt to retake the moral high ground.

Wilson's very first paragraph acknowledged that his speech was indeed a response to Trotsky's challenge that Washington and its Entente allies take a stance on the negotiations in Brest-Litovsk, now in recess. "The Russian representatives," in his view, had been "sincere and earnest. They cannot entertain such proposals of conquest and domination" being demanded by Berlin. They "have insisted, very justly, very wisely, and in the true spirit of modern democracy"—the only time the word appears in the speech[85]—"that the conferences they have been holding with the Teutonic and Turkish statesmen should be held within open, not closed doors, and all the world has been audience, as was desired ... It will be our wish," Wilson added, "and purpose that the processes of peace, when they are begun, shall be absolutely open and that they shall involve and permit henceforth no secret understandings of any kind." As for Trotsky's call that Washington and its allies be transparent about their aims, he said: "whether their present leaders believe it or not, it is our ['the people of the United States'] heartfelt desire and hope that some way may be opened whereby we may be privileged to assist the people of Russia to attain their utmost hope of liberty and ordered peace."[86] Wilson made "open" diplomacy the first of his fourteen points he then listed to serve as the basis for peace talks. A year earlier in his speech to Congress in which he proposed that the U.S. take the lead in ending the war—three months before he declared war on Germany—he stated that "it makes a great deal of difference in what way and upon what terms it [the war] is ended." But there was no mention or even hint in that speech of the kind of "open diplomacy" he proposed a year later. The Bolshevik example, in other words, explains Wilson's embrace of a new way to conduct diplomacy.[87]

After the first point about "open diplomacy," Wilson's next four points dealt with the need for open seas, the casus belli for his war declaration against Germany, free trade, arms reduction and a nod toward the possibility of self-determination for colonized peoples. Wilson had to be careful on the last point since his Entente allies were vulnerable to the Bolshevik charge of being colonial masters. Wilson, too, as he probably recognized, was skating on thin ice on this issue, specifically with regard to Puerto Rico. The last seven points dealt with the territorial conquests of the war and Wilson's solution, the most famous of the fourteen, for ensuring that such a war would never be repeated, the League of Nations.

But it was point number six that was truly original and crucial for the real-time political analysis of this chapter.

> The evacuation of all Russian territory and such a settlement of all questions affecting Russia as will secure the best and freest cooperation of the other nations of the world in obtaining for her an unhampered and unembarrassed opportunity for the independent determination of her own political development and national policy and assure her of a sincere welcome into the society of free nations under institutions of her own choosing; and, more than a welcome, assistance also of every kind that she may need and may herself desire. The treatment accorded Russia by her sister nations in the months to come will be the acid test of their good will, of their comprehension of her needs as distinguished from their own interests, and of their intelligent and unselfish sympathy.

Wilson, in essence, was taking, in a most public way, the side of the Soviet government in its negotiations with Berlin at Brest-Litovsk. And he did so in a manner that constitutes his most significant public utterance about Bolshevik-led Russia.[88] "Under institutions of her own choosing" effectively granted a seal of approval from the leader of the world's foremost liberal democratic government to the new and unique mode of governance that was in place in the new Russia. Wilson was willing to at least appear to be open to soviet representative democracy—at least as he understood it.[89] With the onset of the Cold War it's no wonder that the sixth point in Wilson's Fourteen Point speech was virtually forgotten.

Lenin had been on a well-earned vacation in Finland when Wilson gave his speech to Congress. Once back at work he immediately recognized its significance. As Arno Mayer details, he had a quickly translated copy sent to Trotsky at Brest-Litovsk and then made sure that it was widely disseminated to the Russian people—what Wilson had intended. "All in all, in its different handbill, poster, and pamphlet forms, the printed issues of the speech totaled 3,463,000 copies issued from Petrograd and Moscow presses, and this sum took no account of the millions of distributions through the *Izvestiya* and other newspapers, nor of the handbills printed" in the country's major cities. Of particular significance, given Lenin's hope in *"the German proletariat,"* "about one million of these 'copies' were disseminated to German soldiers who were in the Eastern trenches or were prisoners inside Russia."[90]

Ten days after Wilson gave his historic speech to Congress, a development took place in Russia that could have made him rethink his public endorsement of the Soviet government. As already noted, the core issue in Russia from the February/March revolution to the October/November overturn was which form of representative governance would prevail: western-style parliamentary democracy or soviet democracy? And underlying that debate was the more fundamental question: which class coalition would rule Russia, the bourgeoisie/liberal left or the worker/peasant alliance? Lenin's basic argument was that parliamentary governance favored the former while soviet governance favored the latter. The issue was formally settled on January 6/19.

When the western-style Constituent Assembly—the elections to which were held on November 12/25, that is, under Bolshevik rule—finally convened on January 5/18, Lenin's motion that it concede sovereignty to the Soviet government was defeated. The Bolsheviks and their allies, the Left Socialist Revolutionaries, who together had won about 37 percent of the seats in the elections, withdrew. They returned to the site of the Soviet government and voted to dissolve the Constituent Assembly, unceremoniously ending its two-day existence. The virtual absence of any effective resistance to the Bolshevik initiative revealed that for the vast majority of the Russian population the effective executive in Russia was the Soviet government that had been in place since October 26/November 7. Nothing was more determinant in understanding the failure of the forces for a pro-western-style parliamentary governance to rally support to their side than the war question. They had been the official governors of Russia from February/March to October/November in the Provisional Government. In that seven-month period they refused not only to break with the Entente and Wilson to withdraw Russia from the carnage but to convene a constituent assembly. They lacked, in other words, credibility. Two months of Bolshevik-led governance had at least produced a road map to peace, just as they had promised—and, to boot, the long-awaited Constituent Assembly elections. The "Russian people's fundamental indifference to the fate of the Constituent Assembly" explains its very brief moment in the sun.[91] Russian liberalism, not for the first time, missed the revolutionary train and for the same reasons (see Chap. 3).

When Wilson learned what happened to the Constituent Assembly he expressed dismay and bemoaned to House: "Here is the ever-recurring question. How to deal with the Bolsheviki?"—one of the epigrams that open this chapter.[92] But there is no record of a public rebuke of the

Bolsheviks. In fact, two months later, March 11, he sent a letter of encouragement to the Congress of Soviets that was to debate the Bolshevik proposal to accept the onerous conditions Berlin had imposed at Brest-Litovsk. The delay in the German working class doing what their cohorts in Russia had done, to make a revolution, forced the taking of that bitter pill. "May I not," Wilson began,

> take advantage of the meeting of the Congress of the Soviet to express the sincere sympathy which the people of the United States feel for the Russian people at this moment when the German power has been thrust in to interrupt and turn back the whole (process of revolution) (great) *struggle for freedom* and substitute the wishes of Germany for the purposes of the people of Russia. Although the Government of the United States is unhappily not now in a position to render the direct and effective aid it would wish to render, I beg to assure the people of Russia through their Congress that it will avail itself of every opportunity that may offer to secure for Russia once more complete sovereignty and independence in her own affairs and full restoration to her great role in the life of Europe and the modern world. The whole heart of the people of the United States is with the people of Russia in the attempt to free themselves forever from autocratic government and become the masters of their own life.[93]

Unlike his Fourteen Points speech, Wilson's message was directed to "the Russian people"; this time there was no mention of "their present leaders." But as long as he thought their "beloved revolution" was still a fact he couldn't risk alienating them with any hint of an overt attack on Lenin and Trotsky. Also noteworthy is that he implicitly accepted, despite the proroguing of the Constituent Assembly, the mode of governance of "their beloved revolution," that is, "their Congress" of soviets.

Wilson's message required Lenin to be at his diplomatic best in responding to the apparently friendly gesture. Following Wilson's lead, he addressed his message of March 14—endorsed by the delegates to the gathering—to "the American people."

> The Congress expresses its gratitude to the American people, and primarily to the working and exploited classes of the United States of America, in connection with President Wilson's expression of his sympathy for the Russian people through the Congress of Soviets at a time when the Soviet Socialist Republic of Russia is passing through severe trials.

The Russian Soviet Republic, having become a neutral country, takes advantage of the message received from President Wilson to express to all peoples that are perishing and suffering from the horrors of the imperialist war its profound sympathy and firm conviction that the happy time is not far away when the working people of all bourgeois countries will throw off the yoke of capital and establish the socialist system of society, the only system able to ensure a durable and just peace and also culture and well-being for all working people.[94]

If Wilson could "take advantage" of the moment, so too could Lenin—to encourage not only the toilers in the U.S. but elsewhere to consider civil war against their own exploiters. He gave, in doing so, new meaning to what the Bolsheviks meant by "open diplomacy." Exposing secret treaties and having public diplomatic negotiations was for driving a wedge between the toilers and their rulers. Wilson wasn't clueless. "Russian trust of America was held by a very slender thread," he told the British ambassador a few days later. "Trotsky and Lenin evidently had a notion that the American Administration existed for the benefit of the capitalists."[95] The Bolsheviks continued to needle Wilson's liberal self-image. Lenin's March 14 message to "the American people" was the first of three, signaling the pas de deux he now engaged in with Wilson.

FROM THE COUNTERREVOLUTION TO VERSAILLES

Wilson increasingly came under pressure from Prime Minister Lloyd George of Britain and President Georges Clemenceau of France to give military support to the counterrevolutionary forces in Russia that were grouping to overthrow Bolshevik rule. He eventually relented to the entreaties but in his own unique way. He could only justify to himself the decision on July 6, 1918, to send US troops to Russia on the grounds he was providing humanitarian aid to prevent a German takeover of the embattled country. "I have been sweating blood," he wrote on July 8, "over the question what is right and feasible (*possible*) to do in Russia … I hope I see and can report some progress presently doing the double line of economic assistance and aid to the Czecho-Slovaks."[96] On August 7: "I have felt no confidence in my personal judgement about the complicated situation in Russia."[97] The "Czecho-Slovaks" issue referred to about 70,000 combatants from the Austro-Hungarian Empire recruited by the Provisional Government to fight against the Central Powers. After the Bolshevik ascent and Brest-Litovsk they were no longer needed and, thus, essentially stranded in Russia. Whereas the British saw them as potential cadre for both the counterrevolution and continuing war against Germany—interrelated goals in their view—Wilson's stated priority was to evacuate them out of Russia. Sending US troops to do so, he insisted, was neither to "interfere with internal affairs in Russia"[98] nor to be "a military intervention." The latter, as explained in the aide-memoire to General William Graves who headed up the Siberian intervention, would only "add to the present sad confusion in Russia rather than cure it, injure her rather than help her, and that it would be of no advantage whatever in the prosecution of our main design, to win the war against Germany."[99] Graves, to be seen, faithfully obeyed what was on paper—with all the consequences. As for the offer of "economic assistance" to the new Soviet government, Wilson assumed that it would be seen as a display of good will on his part.

Lenin, however, refused to be seduced. Six weeks later he denounced the "predatory expedition against [Russia] on the plea that they want to 'protect' Russia from the Germans!" The "they" were the governments of America, France and Britain that were beholden to the "handful of multi-millionaires"—the "American multimillionaires were, perhaps, richest of all"—who had reaped untold profits from the "ocean of blood that had been shed by the ten million killed and twenty million maimed in the great, noble, liberating and holy war."[100] Yet Lenin's famous 5000-word "Letter to American Workers" of August 20, 1918, was a measured response to Wilson's decision to send US troops to Russia for the first time. It seemed to have sensed Wilson's all too familiar liberal hand wringing and replied accordingly.[101] Lenin, however, couldn't resist at least one poke to Wilson's liberal underbelly. It had to do with the jailing of socialist leader Eugene V. Debs for his anti-US intervention stance into the War. "I am not surprised that Wilson"—the only direct reference to him—"the head of the American multimillionaires and servant of the capitalist sharks, has thrown Debs into prison."

More importantly, Lenin's letter was a direct appeal to the U.S. proletariat—in response, apparently, to a letter of solidarity with the Bolsheviks from workers in Seattle[102]—pedagogically written to explain the raison d'etre of the Russian revolution in order to counter the "lies and slanders" about it in the "American bourgeois newspapers." He drew parallels between US revolutionary history, especially, the Civil War, and developments under way in Russia. He reminded readers why the revolution had to make painful decisions, such as the onerous concessions to Germany at Brest-Litovsk, and to take harsh measures, such as the "Red terror" against opponents:

It is this imperialist war that is the cause of all these misfortunes. The revolution engendered by the war cannot avoid the terrible difficulties and suffering bequeathed it by the prolonged, ruinous, reactionary slaughter of the nations. To blame us for the "destruction" of industry, or for the "terror", is either hypocrisy or dull-witted pedantry; it reveals an inability to understand the basic conditions of the fierce class struggle, raised to the highest degree of intensity that is called revolution.[103]

Lenin readily admitted to the "hundred mistakes we commit" such as the overnight abolition of "private ownership of land" or the nationalization of "almost all the biggest factories and plants" with a workforce lacking the skills to manage them. "We know," toward the end, "that circumstances brought *our* Russian detachment of the socialist proletariat to the fore not because of our merits, but because of the exceptional backwardness of Russia, and that *before* the world revolution breaks out a number of separate revolutions may be defeated."[104] Events within a few months would justify Lenin's sobriety. His letter, published in *Pravda*, was, with some difficulty, given the Allied/Central Powers blockade of Russia, republished in numerous socialist venues in the U.S. Though there's no mention of it in *The Papers of Woodrow Wilson*, it's unlikely he didn't read or know about Lenin's most conscious intervention yet into US politics.

The "Red terror," in response to the assassination on July 5 of the German ambassador to Russia by Left Socialist Revolutionaries—their attempt to restart the war with Germany because of the harsh conditions of Brest-Litovsk—and near assassination of Lenin shortly afterward, and his defense of the bloody crackdown were no doubt deeply unsettling to Wilson. Because Lenin reminded his readers about the time when "terror was just and legitimate ... the terror ... of the French bourgeoisie ... in 1793," the "Letter" may have triggered Wilson's anti-French Revolution sensibilities. To an interviewer a few months later, he said: "The present state of Russia is very much the same as that of France during the revolution. The acts of violence which are taking place in Russia now are as much to be deplored as were those which took place in France then."[105] And for Lenin to call "for the other detachments of the world socialist revolution to come to our relief" was probably the beginning of Wilson's rethinking his so far hands-off stance toward the Bolsheviks.

The suggestion that Lenin's "Letter" was a measured response to Wilson's decision to send US troops to Siberia is reinforced by a report a few weeks later of the new Commissar of Foreign Affairs, Georgy Chicherin

(Trotsky now headed up the Red Army to defeat the White counterrevolutionary armies). "'Although the government of the United States has been obliged to consent to intervention,' he told the executive committee of the Soviet government on September 2, 'this consent is merely formal'. The committee agreed with Chicherin's policy."[106]

A month later Chicherin sent a 3600-word "Note" to Wilson for which Lenin provided the outline and tone. It began by reminding Wilson about point six in his Fourteen Points speech, his pledge to respect Russia's self-determination, and message of solidarity in March to the Congress of Soviets. Landing US troops not only in Siberia but in northern Russia, under British command, and support to the stranded Czech-Slovak troops contradicted, Chicherin argued, Wilson's stated claims of neutrality about Russia's course. Despite Washington's actions, he continued, "we are ready, Mr. President, to conclude an armistice on these conditions ["the evacuation of occupied territories"] and we ask you to notify us when you, Mr. President, and your Allies intend to remove your troops from Murmansk, Archangel [in northern Russia] and Siberia."[107]

Then the "Note" went on the offensive, to make the case for the legitimacy of the October/November Revolution. Soviet governance, it argued, represented "at least eighty per cent of the Russian people. This cannot, Mr. President, be said about your Government." That probably stuck in Wilson's craw. He knew that unlike in Russia, women in America had yet to gain the right to vote. He also knew that America's darker-hued denizens were in an even more precarious position given his own administration's policies toward them. If "Red terror" was to his liberal distaste, "white terror" in the face of the Ku Klux Klan was somehow digestible for this son of the Confederacy. For the Bolsheviks to hint at such hypocrisy must also have been galling. To add insult to injury Chicherin advised Wilson how to construct a "League of Nations which you propose as the crowning work of peace … You know as well as we, Mr. President, that this War is the outcome of the policies of all capitalistic nations … We propose, therefore, Mr. President, that the League of Nations be based on the expropriation of the capitalists of all countries."

The message dripped with sarcasm. About Wilson's "demand" for "independence" for various "peoples" in Europe: "strangely enough we do not find among your demands the liberation of Ireland, Egypt or India, nor even the liberation of the Philippines, and we would be very sorry if these peoples should be denied the opportunity to participate together with us, through their freely elected representatives, in the organization of the League of Nations." If the Bolsheviks pioneered "open diplomacy" with their exposure of the secret treaties and public negotiations with Berlin, Chicherin's "Note" initiated what might be called "cheeky diplomacy." Lenin advised Chicherin about how to compose it: "Write it in detail, politely, but caustically, saying: in any case we consider it our duty to propose peace—even to governments of capitalists and multimillionaires—in order to try to stop the bloodshed and to open the eyes of the people ... Do the capitalists want some of the forests in the north, part of Siberia, interest on 17 thousand millions [of the tsar's loans]? Regarding the Brest peace—Germany will agree to withdraw her troops. What's the matter then? Do you want to replace the German troops with *your own* troops? And so on."[108] Not surprisingly, Wilson chose to ignore the "Note" as his Secretary of State Lansing advised. Having long wanted to do away with the Bolsheviks since their ascent in October/November 1917, he urged his boss to see the message as a "definite turning point in our relations with the Bolsheviki."[109] But most objectionable about the Bolsheviks for Lansing wasn't their insolence or even "the Red terror." Rather, it was their "giving special recognition to a particular class of society as if it possessed exceptional rights,"[110] that is, as he put it a year earlier, "the despotism of a class"—what the Bolsheviks called the dictatorship of the proletariat.

On November 2, William Bullitt, the State Department's point man on Russia submitted an informative report to Lansing, "The Bolshevist Movement in Europe ... indicating increase of Bolshevism" and "methods of combating Bolshevism." [111] Three days later at a Cabinet meeting the "President spoke of the Bolsheviki having decided upon a revolution in Germany, Hungary, and Switzerland, and that they had ten million dollars ready in Switzerland, besides more money in Swedish banks held by the Jews from Russia, ready for the campaign of propaganda."[112] Wilson must have felt vindicated about his warning when he received the next day the following cable: "Outbreak of revolution in Germany begun by sailors on the dreadnought *Kaiser*, later spread to rest of the fleet in harbor, finally spreading through the entire province of Schleswig. The sailors mounted the red flag and took possession of the town after seizing ships."[113] In Lenin's view, the peace decrees of the new soviet government in October/November 1917, the publication of the secret treaties of the Entente powers, the onerous concessions made at Brest-Litovsk had finally paid off. The "German soldiers have been infected by Bolshevism."[114]

Though the uprising in Germany put an end to the carnage of World War I—what the armistice of November 11 agreed to—as well as Germany's last monarch, Wilson and his allies greeted it with dread. It threatened to be a replay of what the Bolsheviks had done a year earlier. Revolutionary Germany, more than anything, convinced Wilson to see the Bolsheviks now as a "poison," the term he most often employed in referring to them from then on. It's as if he was reading Lenin. On board the *George Washington* on his way to Paris for the negotiations to end the Great War, Wilson gave a press conference on December 9 about his agenda for the deliberations. Bullitt's diary entry is revealing: "The President did not mention Russia directly but said: 'The only way I can explain susceptibility of the people of Europe to the poison of bolshevism, is that the Governments have been run for wrong purposes, and I am convinced that if this peace is not made on the highest principles of justice it will be swept away by the peoples of the world in less than a generation.'"[115] Wilson didn't live long enough to learn how prophetic his warning had been.

Lenin accurately recognized Wilson's new anti-Bolshevik posture. Four days earlier he advised a workers meeting in Moscow to beware of "Wilson's agents … crushing the revolution in Austria … playing the gendarme [and] issuing an ultimatum to Switzerland: 'You'll get no bread from us if you don't join the fight against the Bolshevik Government'… Theirs is a simple weapon—the noose of famine. That is what they are using to strangle the peoples."[116] "Bread" referred to Wilson's answer to the Bolsheviks as he put it so plainly a month later on January 10, 1919, to Lansing and his secretary Joseph Tumulty: "The real thing with which to stop Bolshevism is food … Bolshevism is steadily advancing westward, has overwhelmed Poland, and is poisoning Germany. It cannot be stopped by force but it can be stopped by food … to our real friends in Poland and to the people of the liberated units of the Austrian-Hungarian empire and to our associates in the Balkans."[117] A future US president would manage for Wilson this new modern "weapon," Herbert Hoover. "Our job now," Lenin told the Moscow gathering, "is to wage a desperate struggle against British and American imperialism. Just because it feels that Bolshevism has become a world force, it is trying to throttle us as fast as possible in the hope of dealing with the Russian Bolsheviks, and then, with its own."[118] Lenin's reference to "its own" anticipated Wilson's domestic version of the Red Terror, the anti-Bolshevik campaign his administration launched in the summer of 1919 known as the "Red Scare." The successes of the

Red Terror in combination with the German revolution meant, Lenin argued, that the Bolsheviks were now in a stronger position than when they made the harsh concessions at Brest-Litovsk. "No wonder Wilson declared: 'Our enemy now is world Bolshevism.' That is what the bourgeoisie all over the world are saying. The fact that they are preparing to attack us means they realize that the Bolshevik government is not only a Russian but a world phenomenon."[119]

Wilson, indeed, by the end of 1918 was almost obsessed with "checking the advance of Bolshevism to the Westward" and the need for an Allied "general policy as to how to meet the social danger of Bolshevism."[120] And to that end he needed intelligence: "I am … keenly interested in … finding the interior of their minds."[121] While Wilson's Allied partners may have wanted "to attack" the Bolsheviks he called rather for negotiations as he argued at the Paris deliberations on January 21, 1919:

> One of the things that was clear in the Russian situation was that by opposing Bolshevism with arms they were in reality serving the cause of Bolshevism. The Allies were making it possible for Bolsheviks to argue that Imperialistic and Capitalistic Governments were endeavoring to exploit the country and to give the land back to the landlords, and so bring about a reaction. If it could be shown that this was not true and that the Allies were prepared to deal with the rulers of Russia, much of the moral force of this argument would disappear. The allegation that the Allies were against the people and wanted to control their affairs provided the argument which enabled them to raise armies. If, on the other hand, the Allies could swallow their pride and the natural repulsion which they felt for the Bolsheviks, and see the representatives of all organized groups in one place, he thought it would bring about a marked reaction against Bolshevism.[122]

As Lenin and Trotsky had recognized for more than a year, Wilson's image of himself and his nation—morally superior to Old Europe with its imperialist history—could be to their advantage. His advice to negotiate with the Bolsheviks rather than "attack" them was consistent with his aide memoire to General Graves who headed-up the U.S. intervention in Siberia—it was *not* to be "a military intervention." Hence, why the Bolsheviks were willing to engage in a diplomatic dance with Wilson—Lenin for sure.[123] About a month earlier, on December 23, they sent a peace offer to the Allies, one no doubt that Lenin had a hand in composing.[124] While he had to be on guard for the worst—"they are preparing to attack us"—he couldn't afford to be an inevitablist. Though rejected, the offer forced Wilson et al. to come up with an alternative, a conference of all the Russian belligerents to be held on the Turkish island of Prinkipo near Constantinople. Wilson's recommendation that his allies "swallow their pride" was a plea that they invite the Bolsheviks to partake in the talks. Because the counterrevolutionary White Army leaders refused to attend at the urgings of the French, it never happened. That didn't deter the Bolsheviks from taking other diplomatic initiatives that they thought might be attractive to Wilson since he held most of the cards in the Allied coalition.

Wilson's liberal contradictions about Russia were on full display in his closed-door remarks to members of the Democratic Party National Committee on February 28, 1919, following a couple of sobering months of negotiations with his Allied partners. In words that resonate all so well a century later, "the present danger in this world is that peoples of world do not believe in their own governments. They believe these governments to be made up of the kind of men who have always run them, and who did not know how to keep them out of this war, did not know how to prepare them for war, and did not know how to settle international controversies in the past without making all sorts of compromising concessions." While "we" in the U.S., he continued, are not "ideal people … we are infinitely better than the others." With, again, such a low opinion of Old Europe, Wilson could then say what he did about the Russian question.

> The only thing that that ugly, poisonous thing called Bolshevism feeds on is the doubt of the man on the street of the essential integrity of the people he is depending on to do his governing. That is what it feeds on. No man in his senses would think that a lot of local Soviets could really run a government, but some of them are in a temper to have anything rather than the kind of thing they have been having; and they say to themselves: "Well, this may be bad, but it is at least better and more immediately in touch with us than the other, and we will try it and see whether we cannot work something out of it" … [But] it is not our business to dictate what kind of government Russia shall have. The only thing to do is to see if we can help them by [the Prinkipo] conference and suggestion and recognition of the right elements to get together and not leave the country in a state of chaos.[125]

In other words, the Bolshevik appeal, despite they being "the most consummate sneaks in the world," was understandable. Wilson took serious enough the new mode of soviet governance in order to dismiss it. He was still peeved about Trotsky's dig about his morally superior homeland, that "the United States is in the hands of capitalists and does not serve anybody else's interests but the capitalists.' And the worst of it, I think he honestly believes it." For this son of a pre-capitalist world, the confederacy, Trotsky's charge was incredulous. Not surprising again, Lenin was willing to engage Wilson in all his contradictions, liberal and pre-liberal. A Cold War reading of the Soviet Union may see Wilson's opinion of Lenin's Russia as, at best, naïve, or worst, unpardonable. But that's hindsight about the Bolshevik revolution.

Wilson's assessment of developments in Russia is almost a class mirror image of that of Lenin, from the other side of the barricades. Just a few days later Lenin told the opening session of the first congress of the Communist International—his answer to Wilson's League of Nations— the "bourgeoisie are terror-stricken at the growing workers' revolutionary movement. This is understandable if we take into account that the development of events since the imperialist war inevitably favors the workers' revolutionary movement, and that the world revolution is beginning and growing in intensity everywhere." [126] A month later to the Moscow soviet he opined, "the imperialists of Britain, France and America are making their last attempt to bring us to our knees, but they will fail." [127] He was heartened by reports about the squabbling amongst the Allied powers at Paris: "the Committee of Ten has now been reduced, and there are now only four—Wilson, Lloyd, Clemenceau and [Italian Prime Minister Vittorio] Orlando. These are the leaders of the four nations, but even they cannot reach an agreement ... Our enemies cannot agree among themselves. Five months have passed since they won their victory [the armistice of November 11, 1918], but they have not concluded peace." [128] And a week later to another Moscow gathering: "We might say that Messrs. Wilson and Clemenceau have set out to help us. The cables which every day bring us news about their quarrels, about their desire to slam the door in each other's faces, show that these gentlemen are at each other's throats." [129] It's as if Lenin knew why Wilson's candid report to Democratic Party National Committee members on the Paris negotiations had to be, as Wilson put it, "in the confidence of this company." [130]

As for what Lenin thought of Wilson's "poison" charge about the Bolsheviks: "The imperialists of the Entente countries are blockading Russia in an effort to cut off the Soviet Republic, as a seat of infection, from the capitalist world ... Just think of it, the advanced, most civilized and 'democratic' countries, armed to the teeth and enjoying undivided military sway over the whole world, are mortally afraid of the *ideological* infection coming from a ruined, starving, backward, and even, they assert, semi-savage country."[131] At that very moment the Senate Judiciary committee was conducting hearings in Washington on "Bolshevik propaganda activities in the United States." Washington had reason to be concerned. A week-long general strike in Seattle in February 1919, the first of its kind in the U.S., had been inspired in part by soviet power and Lenin's writings.[132] His "Letter to American Workers," to be remembered, was a response to a worker's solidarity message from Seattle. Regarding Wilson's anti-interventionist declarations, Lenin told another Moscow gathering a few weeks later: "No matter how much the Lloyd Georges, Wilsons and Clemenceaus may assure us that they have abandoned the idea of intervention, we know they are lying."[133] Events in Seattle and elsewhere in the world convinced Lenin that his enemies had every reason to fear the Bolsheviks.

Lenin's remark in his "Letter to American Workers" that "*before* the world revolution breaks out a number of separate revolutions may be defeated" was instantiated when the two most Bolshevik-like leaders in the German revolution were assassinated in January 1919, Rosa Luxemburg and Karl Liebknecht. Though Lenin recognized that "the brutal and treacherous murder … is … the most dramatic and tragic event in the revolution beginning in Germany,"[134] only in retrospect would the costly consequences of their loss become clear—the failure of Germany's working class to duplicate what their Russian cohorts had done.

If Lenin understood the significance of the assassinations of Luxemburg and Liebknecht, Wilson didn't. As far as he could see, the German revolution was alive and well and just as foreboding. His reaction to the news Travers Grayson, his doctor and close confidant, gave him on March 10, 1919, on board the *U.S.S. George Washington* on his way back to the Paris negotiations is all so telling. According to Grayson's diary entry, the article reported that the settlement of a general strike in Berlin included recognition by the government of "soldiers and workers councils."

> After reading this article the President said that this looked bad; that if the present government of Germany is recognizing the soldiers and workers councils, it is delivering itself into the hands of the bolshevists. He said the American negro returning from abroad would be our greatest medium in conveying bolshevism to America. For example, a friend recently related the experience of a lady friend wanting to employ a negro laundress offering to pay the usual wage in that community. The negress demands that she be

given more money than was offered for the reason that "money is as much mine as it is yours." Furthermore, he called attention to the fact that the French people have placed the negro soldier in France on an equality with the white man, and "it has gone to their heads."[135]

For this son of the confederacy for whom Radical Reconstruction had been a nightmare, the specter of Black Americans being a spearhead for Bolshevism in the U.S. must have been deeply troubling. Lenin had, again, every reason to prepare for the worst from Wilson.

Yet, Wilson's liberal handwringing may have proved in the end to be determinant. As much as he disliked the Bolsheviks, he could never bring himself to do what would have been necessary to overthrow them—a full-scale US military intervention. His declarations about support for Russia's national self-determination—point six in his Fourteen Points speech—wrapped him in a bundle of contradictions. Grayson's diary entry continued in capturing that fact: "Discussing bolshevism, the President referred to the fact that its theory had some advantages but the trouble was that an attempt was being made to accomplish it in the wrong way." Lenin seemed to have sensed Wilson's liberal ambivalence about the Bolshevik project and, thus, treated him accordingly.[136]

Lenin pursued two other initiatives to end the war with the Allied powers, the Bullitt and Nansen missions. Responding to overtures from Moscow, Wilson sent Bullitt in March to hold secret negotiations with Lenin and Chicherin to explore the possibilities of ending the Allied war against their government and for diplomatic recognition. Lenin pledged to make major concessions to end the aggression but once the anti-Bolshevik press in Britain and the U.S. learned about what was agreed to, Wilson disowned the proposals Bullitt had carefully crafted with a wall of silence. Disillusioned, Bullitt parted ways with Wilson.[137] His thirteen-page March 25, 1919, report on the mission only became public when he testified before a Senate committee later in September.[138]

A month later the well-known Norwegian explorer Fridtjof Nansen proposed a solution to the food crisis the Russian people were facing owing to the Allied blockade. Made in agreement with future US president Herbert Hoover, who headed-up food relief programs for the Allied powers, the proposal came with conditions designed to undermine Bolshevik hegemony. Though a non-starter for him, Lenin advised Chicherin and Litvinov to respond diplomatically and politically to the offer. "My advice is: use it *for propaganda,* for clearly it can serve *no other* useful purpose. Be extremely polite to Nansen, *extremely insolent* to Wilson, Lloyd George and Clemenceau. This is very useful, the *only way* to speak to them, the right tone."

After reading Chicherin and Litvinov's draft response, Lenin made suggestions. The failed Bullitt mission a month earlier was certainly on his mind in recommending that a clear distinction be made in the reply between Nansen's "humanitarian aims" and Hoover's all-too apparent Allied "politics" in the proposal. As for the former, "all thanks and compliments to Nansen *personally*." As for "politics," that is, *"for peace,"* tell them "you are perfectly aware that we are for it. We agreed *(even!)* to the Princess [Prinkipo] Islands. We confirmed this to Bullitt who, unfortunately, proved, like the whole of *American policy*, to be a *captive* of Clemenceau and Lloyd George, for what Bullitt promised us, assuring us that America would make Clemenceau and Lloyd George come to heel, remained *unfulfilled* (it would be useful to 'taunt' Wilson about it." And in a footnote, Lenin added: "it is extremely useful *in practice* to set Wilson at variance with them by declaring that Wilson is a *pawn* in the hands of Clemenceau and Lloyd George, in submitting to these *two*, to this 'majority.'"[139] If the archival record has until now only suggested why Lenin was ready to engage Wilson in what I call a diplomatic pas de deux, these notes to Chicherin and Litvinov in early May 1919, leave little doubt. Lenin thought Wilson's liberal contradictions made him "tauntable" in a way that Old Europe diplomats were not. He could be "set at variance with them." After receiving Chicherin's letter, which delivered the political blows that Lenin recommended, Hoover told Nansen that the Allied powers "consider it extremely inadvisable to arrange any meetings with Bolshevik representatives."[140]

Lenin's strategy to try to divide Wilson from George and Clemenceau, again, may have been ultimately successful. The most Wilson was willing to do to aid and abet their quest to end Bolshevik rule was to provide material and financial aid to the White army of Alexander Kolchak in the Siberian theater, the only viable counterrevolutionary force left by the summer of 1919. But as long as General Graves was committed to following to the letter Wilson's July 6, 1918, directive about the Siberian expedition, not to be a "military intervention," British and French imperial interests could never be realized.

Despite candid on-the-scene reports about Kolchak's utterly reactionary project and, thus, its increasing alienation of Russia's peasants, Wilson continued to back him with funds and arms.[141] His distaste for the

Bolsheviks seems to have been the sole motivating factor. Never were those sentiments on display so publicly than when Wilson embarked on a national tour to promote the recently signed, June 28, Treaty of Versailles with its League of Nations provisions. The tour coincided with his Department of Justice's offensive against Bolshevik sympathizers in the U.S. The anti-interventionist and pro-Bolshevik declarations of Debs had recently earned him a ten-year prison sentence. And the founding convention of what would become the Communist Party of the U.S., inspired by the Bolshevik Revolution, was about to take place in September. That all proved to be fodder for Wilson's leitmotif in the tour that the League would be the best means to halt the poison of Bolshevism. In the end, Wilson was unable to convince the U.S. public to partake in his prized project. That both his secretary of state Lansing and Bullitt came out against the treaty in testimony before a Senate committee certainly didn't help the cause. There's evidence, also, that the xenophobic character of the Red Scare campaign, the mass arrests and deportation of foreign-born Bolshevik sympathizers, awakened isolationist tendencies in the public against Wilson's globalist aspirations, further derailing his hopes for the League.[142]

To challenge Wilson's anti-Bolshevik offensive, Lenin agreed in July to answer five questions submitted by a United Press reporter "on condition of the fulfilment of the written promise that my answers will be printed in full in over a hundred newspapers in the United States of America."[143] The first four questions dealt mainly with the Soviet government's economic and foreign policy, especially in regard to the U.S., and the prospects for peace with the Allied powers and the White Armies. He emphasized Moscow's willingness to reach an accord and the concessions it would grant to do so. But it was the fifth question that was the priority for Lenin: "what else would you care to bring to the notice of American public opinion?" He seized the opportunity to make an accessible and pedagogical defense of the revolution that was clearly, like his "Letter" a year earlier, intended for the American working class—a transparent effort to counter the anti-Bolshevik campaign Wilson was leading. The news agency, however, didn't include Lenin's fifth answer when it distributed the interview. *The Liberator*, the popular socialist monthly, did publish it in its October 1919 issue under the title "A Statement and a Challenge" with a note saying the UP "suppressed [Lenin's] *statement* as 'unadulterated Bolshevist propaganda.'"[144]

As Wilson was fighting an uphill and eventually losing battle for Senate ratification of the Treaty of Versailles and US participation in the League of Nations, he suffered another setback. Kolchak, who he had placed his money on, literally, lost his capital to the Red Army in November 1919, two years after Bolshevik ascendancy, and was eventually captured, tried and executed. Whether determinant or not is uncertain but a month earlier unionized dockworkers in Seattle refused, in solidarity with the Bolsheviks, to load a ship with a massive amount of arms they discovered that were meant to aid Kolchak.[145] And on top of all of this Wilson's health deteriorated precipitously, making it impossible for him to run for a third term.

The last US troops, never having seen combat, departed from the Soviet Union on April 1, 1920. Eight months later, Wilson's Democratic Party lost badly in the elections that ushered in his Republican Party successor, Warren G. Harding. The same week, the Bolsheviks celebrated the third year of their revolution. By July 1921, they declared victory over the last remaining counterrevolutionary armies, thus, ending Russia's civil war and Wilson's hope for their demise. From his jail cell in Atlanta came Debs' harsh but understandable schadenfreude: "No man in public life in American history ever retired so thoroughly discredited, so scathingly rebuked, so overwhelmingly impeached and repudiated as Woodrow Wilson."[146]

CONCLUSION

As these lines are being written, events are under way in Europe to commemorate the centenary of the end of "The Great War," the armistice of November 11, 1918. The conflagration was truly—despite its overuse—a turning point in world history. Never before had our species suffered on a global scale such human made carnage. It was a catastrophe, however, unlike natural phenomena (at least to that point), not unforeseen. A quarter century before its commencement Engels, again, anticipated such a war. But it wasn't inevitable. A "revolution in Russia would save Europe from the horrors of a general war and would usher in universal social revolution." Three years later he opined that owing to the increasing lethality of modern arms "fifteen to twenty million armed men would slaughter one another"—a remarkably accurate and tragic forecast. And even more prescient, the resulting devastation "would either lead to the immediate" or later "triumph of socialism."

Engels's later prediction, as history would reveal, was more accurate. Rather than a Russian revolution saving Europe from a "general war," it was "the Great War" that brought into being the world's first socialist revolution beginning with the February/March overthrow of the Romanov dynasty. The failure of the provisional government to extricate Russia from the carnage owing to Entente/Allied power pressure to stay in the war is what made Bolshevik ascendancy possible. But perhaps Engels was right in his earlier forecast, at least partially. Once in power the Bolsheviks acted on their promise to do what the provisional government had not—to end Russia's involvement in the war. First, the immediate peace decrees in October/November and, then, a proposal for talks with Berlin at Brest-Litovsk—initiatives that Wilson labeled "naïve" and "misguided." But the Bolsheviks challenged Wilson and the Allied powers to join them in the peace talks. Not wishing to appear less interested in ending the slaughter than the Bolsheviks, it provoked Wilson to issue his Fourteen Points proposals. With Russia no longer a threat to Germany owing to the onerous concessions made at Brest-Litovsk, and the continuing campaign of the Bolsheviks to fraternize with German soldiers, it became increasingly difficult for the German regime to convince its workers in uniform that they had a class interest in defending the fatherland. Thus the revolution in the first week in November 1918, the deposition of the Kaiser, and, the armistice. Eight months later the belligerents signed the Treaty of Versailles. The Bolsheviks, in other words, were responsible for setting into motion the process to end the slaughter that may have carried on much longer. If socialist revolution was unable to prevent the Great War, it played a key if not decisive role in its termination.[147]

Nothing was inevitable about Bolshevik ascent and survival. Historical contingency is a better explanation. As Lenin put it in his "Letter" to the American proletariat, "we know that circumstances brought *our* Russian detachment of the socialist proletariat to the fore not because of our merits." He clearly had an agenda and was single-minded in its realization: lead the toilers to state power in order to end the carnage. Wilson was less informed and less focused—explaining perhaps the unintended consequences of his actions. In enticing and pressuring the provisional government that issued from the February/March revolution to stay the course, he unwittingly aided and abetted Lenin's project. He misread, unlike Lenin, the depths of the anti-war sentiment amongst Russia's masses. Never have unintended consequences been so consequential in modern history. Wilson came close to admitting his mistake—a rare and maybe singular admission in his career.

The survival of the Bolshevik project precariously hung in the balance for almost three years after the October/November 1917 triumph. The real-time record reveals that the Bolsheviks, especially Lenin, astutely took advantage of Wilson's liberal contradictions to avoid its Red Army having to engage in combat with US troops—or, to keep it to a minimum as in the northern Archangel-Murmansk operation[148]—the only effective force that could have spelled their demise. Wilson's conundrum began with what posterity knows as his "peace without victory" speech to Congress in January 1917, in which he declared "that every people should be left to determine its own polity." A year later and two months after Bolshevik ascendancy, he was most specific in point six in his more famous Fourteen Points speech. Russia, he stated, should know that it would have "an unhampered and unembarrassed opportunity for the independent determination of her own political development and national policy ... under institutions of her own choosing." That the Bolsheviks did all they could to advertise, with Wilson's blessing, the speech for which he was most proud and remembered was to be expected. If ever the "useful idiot" metaphor had currency—often but erroneously attributed to Lenin— those three years might have been the most appropriate moment. But Wilson's seal of approval wasn't a gratuity. The Bolsheviks earned it due to their principled conduct from October/November, beginning with the world's first WikiLeaks dump, the secret treaties, and then to the Brest-Litovsk talks. The numerous peace proposals they proposed or agreed to were also designed to keep Wilson from being an implacable foe. Lenin, thus, engaged in a high wire act with Wilson and without a safety net. And not the least of the liberal contradictions that entangled Wilson was his awareness that Bolshevik rule was popular—the most popular of all the warring parties in the civil war.

Lenin unlikely knew of Engels's forecast about the interconnectivity between social revolution in Russia and a generalized conflagration in Europe. Otherwise, he, arguably Marx and Engels's most faithful and capable student, would have cited it in *Imperialism*, his key text to explain the Guns of August. In the 1920 introduction to the 1916 book, he offered some hindsight.

The Treaty of Brest-Litovsk dictated by monarchist Germany, and the subsequent much more brutal and despicable Treaty of Versailles dictated by the "democratic" republics of America and France and also by "free"

Britain, have rendered a most useful service to humanity by exposing both imperialism's hired coolies of the pen and petty-bourgeois reactionaries who, although they call themselves pacifists and socialists, sang praises to "Wilsonism," and insisted that peace and reforms were possible under imperialism.

The tens of millions of dead and maimed left by the war—a war to decide whether the British or German group of financial plunderers is to receive the most booty—and those two "peace treaties," are with unprecedented rapidity opening the eyes of the millions and tens of millions of people who are downtrodden, oppressed, deceived and duped by the bourgeoisie. Thus, out of the universal ruin caused by the war a worldwide revolutionary crisis is arising which, however prolonged and arduous its stages may be, cannot end otherwise than in a proletarian revolution and in its victory.[149] The claim of "universal ruin caused by the war" and its consequences for "proletarian revolution" uncannily echoed and confirmed what Engels uttered a quarter of a century earlier. Unlike Wilson, Lenin, fourteen years his junior, had benefited from a head-start program that the more academically credentialed Wilson had no inkling of its existence. For Wilson's generation in the American academy, the writings *and* practice—Lenin's priority—of Marx and Engels were simply unavailable. And that Lenin, without a foot in the formal academy, could offer what was probably the first critical take on what would later be called "Wilsonianism" is even more noteworthy.

Lenin's critique of the Treaty of Versailles anticipated the far more informed assessment of the economist John Maynard Keynes who participated in the talks on the side of the British. Keynes's stinging rebuke of the treaty, *The Economic Consequences of the Peace,* was invaluable ammunition for Lenin. To the delegates at the Second Congress of the Communist International in July 1920, he declared: "I do not think any communist manifesto, or one that is revolutionary in general, could compare in forcefulness with those pages in Keynes's book which depict Wilson and 'Wilsonism' in action ... The masses of the workers now see more clearly than ever, from their own experience ... that the 'roots' of Wilson's policy lay in sanctimonious piffle, petit-bourgeois phrase-mongering, and an utter inability to understand the class struggle."[150] Both he and Trotsky heartily recommended that communists, as they now called themselves, read Keynes's book.

Four months before his last and ultimately fatal stroke, Lenin was wrapping up his balance sheet on the October/November Revolution, now in its fifth year, for delegates to the Fourth Congress of the Communist International, December 1922. "Undoubtedly, we have done, and will still do, a host of foolish things. No one can judge and see this better than I … but I must also say a word or two in this respect about our enemies." Their "foolish things," he continued, are worst. "Take, for example, the agreement concluded by the U.S.A, Great Britain, France and Japan with Kolchak. I ask you, are there any more enlightened and more powerful countries in the world? But what happened? They promised to help Kolchak without calculation, without reflection, and without circumspection. It ended in a fiasco, which, it seems to me, is difficult for the human intellect to grasp." But more consequential of their "foolish things" was the Treaty of Versailles. "I ask you, what have the 'great' powers which have 'covered themselves with glory' done? How will they find a way out of this chaos and confusion?"[151] It is hard to imagine Wilson going before a public audience, especially an international one, to offer any kind of remorse about his actions. As for Lenin not seeing the "foolish things" that might explain the Stalinist outcome of the revolution, that, I argue, is hindsight and not real-time analysis—a point I'll revisit in the concluding chapter.

Unlike Lenin, unable to speak and completely paralyzed from March 10, 1923, to his death on January 21, 1924, Wilson continued to be active. His last substantive publication, a 1000-word essay in the August 1923 issue of *Atlantic Monthly* magazine, reveals that he was still, since January, 1918, grappling with "the ever-recurring question. How shall we deal with the Bolsheviki?" They were still on his brain five years later due to "these doubtful and anxious days, when all the world is at unrest." "The Road Away from Revolution," the title of the essay, sought an explanation for and an alternative to "the Russian Revolution, the outstanding event of its kind in our age." The overturn was "the product of a whole social system … it was against 'capitalism' that the Russian leaders directed their attack… and it is against capitalism under one name or another that the discontented classes everywhere draw their indictment." And might not there be just cause for those grievances? "Is it not … too true that capitalists have often seemed to regard the men whom they used as mere instruments of profit, whose physical and mental powers it was legitimate to exploit with as slight cost to themselves as possible, either of money or of sympathy?" Wilson affirmed that it was. "These offenses against high morality and true citizenship have been frequently observable."

With great irony, Wilson and Lenin agreed, apparently, at the end of the lives about the cause for generalized discontent—capitalism. No wonder, again, Lenin had seen the need to take advantage of his contradictions. But most unlike Lenin, the antidote to the sins of capitalism, that is, the ones who "regard the men whom they used as mere instruments of profit," wasn't what the Bolsheviks offered but rather, Wilson argued, Christianity. "Only thus can discontent be driven out and all the shadows lifted from the road ahead. Here is the final challenge to our churches, to our political organizations, and to our capitalists—to everyone who fears God or loves his country. Shall we not all earnestly cooperate to bring in the new day?"[152] Wilson thought, therefore, there were capitalists who had better angels.[153] Despite such illusions, as Lenin would have contended, Wilson's too oft-ignored essay registers the profound impact the Bolshevik Revolution had on ruling elites in real-time.[154] The triumphalism that greeted the collapse of the Soviet Union in 1991 gave the false impression that Wilson's class heirs were always confident they would prevail over what the Bolsheviks had initiated. His essay clearly says otherwise.[155]

Wilson and Lenin died within a couple of weeks of one another in 1924. The images of their funerals stand in stark contrast. To understand consider a couple of vignettes of Lenin from Bullitt's March 1919 report that Wilson disowned. The food situation in Moscow and Petrograd was dire. Lenin and the other leaders of the revolution were on rations, "the same as that of a soldier in the army or of a workman at hard labor … Breakfast: a quarter to a half pound of black bread, which must last all day, and tea without sugar. Dinner: a good soup, a small piece of fish, for which occasionally a diminutive piece of meat is substituted, a vegetable, either a potato or a bit of cabbage, more tea without sugar. Supper: what remains of the morning ration of bread and more tea without sugar." The second vignette was when Bullitt first met Lenin at the Kremlin: "I had to wait a few minutes until a delegation of peasants left his room. They had heard in their village that Comrade Lenin was hungry. And they had come hundreds of miles carrying 800 [pounds] of bread as the gift of the village to Lenin. Just before them was another delegation of peasants to whom the report had come that Comrade Lenin was working in an unheated room. They came bearing a stove and enough firewood to heat it for three months. Lenin is the only leader who receives such gifts. And he turns them into the common fund."[156] That Bullitt came away from the visit with a more sympathetic opinion of the Bolshevik leader is not surprising—for which the anti-Bolshevik press roundly criticized him.[157]

Their funerals were held in the dead of winter in Washington, D.C. and Moscow, in fact, thirty-five below Celsius in the latter. Images of the public response to both were captured on film.[158] But it's not hard to imagine, given Bullitt's report, where the greatest outpourings of grief took place— at least a thousand-fold greater.[159] The volumes speak volumes about how their own citizens regarded both leaders—in real-time.

NOTES

1. Max Weber, *The Russian Revolutions*, trans./eds. Gordon C. Wells and Peter Baehr (Ithaca, NY: Cornell U.P. 1994), p. 142.
2. *Marx-Engels Collected Works*, vol. 48, pp. 134–5 (hereafter *MECW*, *48*, pp. 134–5).
3. Ibid. *27*, p. 245.
4. Until February 1918 the Gregorian calendar, 13 days behind the Julian calendar, was in use in Russia. I employ both calendars until the narrative reaches that point.
5. As this chapter was being conceived, Arthur Herman's *1917: Lenin, Wilson, and the Birth of the New World Disorder* (New York: Harper, 2017) appeared. He too argues that the actions of the two protagonists in that moment had global consequences far beyond—the origins, he argues, for the Cold War. Herman is less concerned, however, with comparing the real-time decision making of the two—the focus here.
6. I'm unaware of anything that exists for Wilson that's not in his *Papers of Woodrow Wilson* (69 volumes); hereafter *PWW*. For Lenin, I can't say the same. It's known that his archives from exile in Krakow have never been made available to the public (Robert Service, *Lenin: A Political Life*, vol. 2 [Bloomington, Indiana: Indiana University Press, 1991] p. 353n32). But that's prior to his return to Russia in 1917. Richard Pipes suggests that there is a lot that's not available to the public; what he translated was no doubt intended to cast aspersions on Lenin; so I can't say for certain if anything relevant to this comparison isn't in the *Lenin Collected Works*, 45 volumes (Moscow: Progress Publishers, 1977), hereafter, *LCW*.
7. *MECW*, *44*, p. 57.
8. https://www.marxists.org/history/international/social-democracy/1912/basel-manifesto.htm.
9. Michael W. Doyle, *Ways of War and Peace* (New York: W.W. Norton, 1997) claims that Lenin's position and actions "was not Marxism" (p. 316). For a real-time Bolshevik defense of their reading of Marx and

Engels, see Gregory Zinoviev's 1916 article, "Wars: Defensive and Aggressive," in *3 Study Guides on Lenin's Writings* (New York: Pathfinder Press, 2017). Hal Draper provides copious evidence that disputes Doyle: Draper, *Karl Marx's Theory of Revolution, Vol 5: War and Revolution* (N.Y.: Monthly Review, 2005).

10. *LCW, 21*, p. 18.
11. Ibid., p. 176.
12. *LCW, 22*, p. 179.
13. Ibid., pp. 189–90.
14. Adam Tooze, *The Deluge: The Great War, America and the Remaking of the Global Order, 1916–1931* (New York: Viking, 2014), p. 50.
15. https://wwi.lib.byu.edu/index.php/President_Wilson%27s_Peace_Note,_December_18,_1916.
16. *LCW, 23*, p. 190.
17. *LCW, 23*, p. 246.
18. *LCW, 8*, pp. 561–5.
19. See John Milton Cooper, "Woodrow Wilson: The Academic Man," https://www.vqronline.org/essay/woodrow-wilson-academic-man.
20. Tooze, pp. 43–4.
21. Tooze, p. 61. *PWW, 5*, pp. 341–2; also, *12*, pp. 217–8.
22. For a recent version of the myth see David Brooks' op-ed, "Understanding student mobbists," *New York Times*, March 9, 2018. On the actual scale of the violence in the War for Independence, see Allan Kulikoff, "Revolutionary Violence and the Origins of American Democracy," *The Journal of the Historical Society*, vol. II, no. 2 (Spring 2002).
23. *PWW, 12*, p. 11.
24. Ibid., *11*, p. 94.
25. Ibid., p. 298.
26. Ibid., p. 66.
27. Ibid. p. 299.
28. *PWW, 12*, p. 44.
29. Ibid., p. 218.
30. Ibid., p. 223. Wilson distinguished between Puerto Rico and the Philippines. The inhabitants of the former, he surmised, were content with their new overlord unlike those in the latter who had rebelled. As for Cuba, he took at face value official US policy that unlike the Philippines and Puerto Rico its inhabitants would actually exercise self-rule.
31. *PWW, 15*, p. 41.
32. Ibid., p. 143.
33. Ibid., p. 175.
34. Tooze, p. 45.
35. *PWW, 45*, p. 551.

36. *PWW, 30*, pp. 231–8.
37. Wilson was at his candid best in a letter to his wife Edith Bolling Galt and closest confidant: *PWW, 34*, pp. 208–9.
38. *PWW, 35*, p. 168–9.
39. Ibid., pp. 298–302.
40. Ibid., p. 172.
41. Ibid., pp. 306–7.
42. *PWW, 36*, pp. 633–48.
43. Ibid., p. 648.
44. For details on the debates in the worker's movement about Wilson, see Farrell Dobbs, *Revolutionary Continuity: The Early Years—1848–1917* (New York: Monad Press, 1980), chapter 6.
45. *PWW, 38*, p. 272.
46. *PWW, 40*, pp. 273–6.
47. Ibid., p. 504.
48. Ibid., pp. 534–9.
49. *LCW, 23*, pp. 237–53.
50. *PWW, 41*, p. 461. About the "professor," see below.
51. *LCW, 23*, p. 373.
52. I thank my colleague Raymond Duvall for suggesting this formulation.
53. *PWW, 41*, p. 524.
54. *PWW, 42*, p. 237.
55. *PWW, 42*, p. 44.
56. Ibid., p. 141.
57. A one-time leading opponent of intervention told Wilson he changed his mind "when the Russian Revolution came" (*PWW, 43*, p. 278). Intervention did cause many of the illuminati in the American Socialist Party to leave when the majority opposed Wilson's move. Wilson regarded the stance of the anti-war majority as "almost treasonable" (Ibid., p. 274).
58. *PWW, 42*, p. 522.
59. Much ink has been spilt, mostly needlessly, about the journey. For a recent example, see Sean Memeekin's "Was Lenin a German Agent?," *New York Times,* June 19, 2017. After reading this chapter readers should have an informed opinion about the question.
60. For a distillation of Lenin's strategy, see my "'The Bolsheviks Come to Power': A New Interpretation," *Science & Society,* vol. 81, no. 4 (October, 2017).
61. *LCW, 24*, p. 65.
62. Ibid., p. 67.
63. *PWW, 42*, p. 368.
64. *LCW, 24*, pp. 108–9.

65. A central argument in Tooze's *The Deluge* is that twentieth-century history would have been profoundly different had Wilson responded differently to the Russian Revolution in its "first step" as Lenin put it; see his chapter 3.
66. My two-volume, *Lenin's Electoral Strategy* (New York: Palgrave Macmillan, 2014), provides details on Lenin's deserved but long-ignored democratic credentials.
67. *PWW, 42*, p. 319.
68. For an example of the kind of propaganda literature the Bolsheviks employed amongst the armed forces, see Lenin's article, "Bolshevism and the 'Demoralization' of the Army," *LCW, 24*, pp. 570–2.
69. *PWW, 42*, pp. 270–3.
70. *PWW, 43*, p. 408.
71. *PWW, 44*, p. 38.
72. Ibid., p. 558.
73. Lenin would have concurred. A year later he told an audience in Moscow that in addition to Russia being a "backward country," there was the "other reason behind the Russian revolution: Russia had no alternative. The war had caused such destruction and starvation everywhere, made the people and the soldiers so weary, they realized they had been tricked for so long, and that the only way out for Russia was revolution" (*LCW, 28*, p. 358.).
74. Herman, p. 281. Tooze's claim that the Bolsheviks "had violently usurped the right to represent" (p. 121) the Russian people echoes the standard Cold War account of Bolshevik ascendancy.
75. See again, my "The Bolsheviks Come to Power" for an overview of that experience.
76. For recent research on how influential the Bolsheviks had been amongst the armed forces, see Olga Porshneva, https://www.c-span.org/video/?436435-5/world-war-russian-soldiers-1917-revolution.
77. *LCW, 26*, pp. 250–1. Lenin's call for an end to "secret diplomacy" and the "full publication of the secret treaties" reiterated the same in his aforementioned *April Theses* (*LCW, 24*, p. 59).
78. *PWW, 45*, p. 147.
79. Ibid., p. 119. For details on the "hunger riots" see: https://newyorkhistoryblog.org/2018/10/1917-food-riots-led-by-immigrant-women-swept-u-s-cities/
80. *PWW, 46*, p. 22n1.
81. *PWW, 45*, pp. 195–202.
82. See his December 4 memo to Wilson, intended to influence his speech to Congress regarding the Russian question; Ibid., pp. 205–7.
83. *LCW, 26*, pp. 345–6.

84. https://www.marxists.org/archive/trotsky/1918/01/international-appeal.htm.
85. Tooze misspeaks, then, when he says "democracy" doesn't "appear in the text" (p. 119).
86. *PWW*, *45*, pp. 534–9. In almost all standard copies of Wilson's speech, the opening paragraphs about Russia are missing; one can only speculate on the reason for that.
87. Arno Mayer was the first western scholar to recognize the Bolshevik precedent. See his *Political Origins of the New Diplomacy, 1917–1918* (New Haven, Connecticut: Yale University Press, 1959) for the rich details. For a more recent account that mainly supports Mayer's reading, see Erez Manela, *The Wilsonian Moment: Self-Determination and the International Origins of Anti-Colonial Nationalism* (New York: Oxford U.P., 2007), pp. 40–3.
88. House, who helped Wilson write the speech, says this in his diary about the Russian passages: "As to Russia, I urged him to be at his best. I read him a sentence that I had prepared regarding Russia, which I had submitted to the Russian Ambassador who thoroughly approved. I told the President that it did not make any difference how much we resented Russia's action, the part of wisdom was to segregate her, as far as we were able, from Germany, and that it could only be done by the broadest and friendliest expressions of sympathy and a promise of more substantial help. There was no argument about this because our minds ran parallel, and what he wrote about Russia is I think, in some respects, the most eloquent part of his message" (*PWW*, *45*, p. 553). "Resented Russia's action" no doubt refers to their objection to Soviet agreement to negotiate with Germany to end its participation in the war.
89. On the impact that Wilson's speech had on European politics and the negotiations in Paris to end the war, see Mayer, pp. 368–93.
90. Mayer, pp. 372–73. Mayer's note p. 373n12 is useful about Bolshevik circumspection regarding Wilson's speech.
91. Alexander Rabinowitch, *The Bolsheviks in Power: The First Year of Soviet Rule in Petrograd* (Bloomington, Indiana: Indiana University Press, 2007), p. 127. This reading of the fate of the Constituent Assembly stands in sharp contrast to Tooze's characterization, "its violent suppression" at the hands of the Bolsheviks (p. 128).
92. *PWW*, *46*, p. 45.
93. *PWW*, *46*, p. 598. See p. 597 on House's role and intent for the note.
94. *LCW*, *27*, p. 171.
95. *PWW*, *47*, p. 79.
96. *PWW*, *48*, p. 550.
97. *PWW*, *49*, p. 203.

98. *PWW*, *48*, p. 543.

99. Ibid., pp. 627–8. Tooze, chapter 8, "Intervention," argues that Lenin's diplomatic maneuverings with Berlin caused Wilson to intervene. London and Paris may indeed have been so motivated but there is nothing in the record in regard to Wilson to sustain such a claim. It is what Wilson thought that proved to be decisive. See David S. Foglesong, *America's Secret War Against Bolshevism: U.S. Intervention in the Russian Civil War, 1917–1920* (Chapel Hill, NC: U of North Carolina Press, 1995) chapter 6, that also challenges Tooze's explanation.

100. *LCW*, *28*, pp. 62–3.

101. Lenin apparently sent a message—unfortunately lost—directly to Wilson "containing the demand to stop the intervention" (*LCW*, *28*, p. 499n27. Supposedly, it also "called for peaceful and friendly relations. (Wilson never revealed the contents of this letter.)"; see James H. Williams, "From Russia with Love: Lenin's Letter to American Workers," *New Politics*, August 23, 1917.

102. R.B. Spence, "The Voyage of the *Shilka*: The Bolshevik Revolution Comes to Seattle, 1917," *American Communist History*, 2017, vol. 16, nos. 1–2, p. 100.

103. *LCW*, *28*, p. 68.

104. As for the "detachment" that Lenin had long banked on, the Germans, Lenin a month earlier made to a Russian audience one of his most trenchant observations about the revolutionary process: "It was easier for us to start the revolution, but it is extremely difficult to continue it and consummate it. It is terribly difficult to make a revolution in such a highly developed country as Germany, with its splendidly organized bourgeoisie, but all the easier will it be to triumphantly consummate the socialist revolution once it flares up and spreads in the advanced capitalist countries in Europe" (*LCW*, *27*, p. 547).

105. *PWW*, *53*, p. 575.

106. Richards, p. 178.

107. https://www.marxists.org/history/etol/newspape/fi/vol03/no04/ chichtowilson.htm. Another translation of the document is in *PWW*, *51*, pp. 508–10, 555–61.

108. *LCW*, *44*, pp. 152–3.

109. *PWW*, *53*, p. 152.

110. *PWW*, *53*, p. 6.

111. *PWW*, *51*, pp. 563–8.

112. Ibid., p. 604.

113. *PWW*, *51*, p. 607.

114. *LCW*, *28*, p. 358.

115. *PWW*, *53*, p. 352.

116. *LCW, 28,* p. 209.
117. *PWW, 53,* p. 709.
118. *LCW, 28,* p. 216. It's not clear if Lenin was referring to a specific declaration of Wilson or not.
119. Ibid., p. 218.
120. *PWW, 54,* p. 8.
121. *PWW, 53,* p. 709.
122. Ibid., p. 183.
123. Bullitt, who later conducted secret negotiations with Lenin and Chicherin to end the Allied intervention, claimed that Trotsky was less open to engaging Wilson; see his report, "The Bullitt Mission to Moscow" https://www.masterandmargarita.eu/estore/pdf/eren004_bullitt.pdf.
124. *LCW, 30,* p. 191; Richard, p. 101.
125. *PWW, 55,* p. 314–20.
126. *LCW, 28,* p. 455. As well as Germany, Hungary and Britain were beset with, respectively, revolutionary and near revolutionary working-class upsurges.
127. *LCW, 29,* p. 267.
128. Ibid., p. 269.
129. Ibid., p. 285.
130. *PWW, 55,* p. 314.
131. *LCW, 29,* p. 305
132. For details, see Harvey O'Connor, *Revolution in Seattle* (Chicago: Haymarket Books, 2009), pp. 119–45.
133. Ibid., p. 341.
134. *LCW, 28,* p. 413.
135. *PWW, 55,* p. 471.
136. For details on Lloyd George's own liberal contradictions, particularly when "an explosion of Bolshevism in England" was a possibility in his opinion, see *PWW, 56,* p. 320.
137. Richard, pp. 112–21. Regarding speculation whether Wilson read the report, see *PWW, 56,* pp. 512–13n1.
138. https://www.masterandmargarita.eu/estore/pdf/eren004_bullitt.pdf.
139. *LCW, 44,* pp. 224–5.
140. Richard, p. 125.
141. See Richard, pp. 125–33, for details.
142. Ibid., p. 133.
143. *LCW, 29,* pp. 515–9. For a slightly different translation, see *The Liberator,* October, 1919, p. 3.
144. Ibid.
145. O'Connor, pp. 158–9.

146. Herman, p. 410.
147. For a rare and recent recognition in the mainstream literature of the indispensable Bolshevik role, see Alexander Anievas, *Capital, the State, and War* (Ann Arbor: University of Michigan Press, 2014), chapter 4.
148. For a summary of the current scholarship about that operation, see Michael M. Phillips, "An American Tragedy in Russia" (https://www.wsj.com/articles/the-one-time-american-troops-fought-russians-was-at-the-end-of-world-war-iand-they-lost-1541772001). Also, Eric Trickey, "The Forgotten Story of the American Troops Who Got Caught Up in the Russian Civil War," *Smithsonian.Com*, February, 2019 (https://www.smithsonianmag.com/history/forgotten-doughboys-who-died-fighting-russian-civil-war-180971470/).
149. *LCW, 22*, p. 191.
150. *LCW, 31*, p. 223.
151. *LCW, 33*, pp. 429–30.
152. *PWW, 68*, pp. 393–5.
153. I thank Alex Anievas for pointing out the distinction Wilson made between "good" and "bad" capitalists.
154. Wilson's most current authoritative biographer, John Milton Cooper, Jr., says "the essay sounds like some of Wilson's immature writings during and just after college" (*Woodrow Wilson* [New York: Alfred Knopf, 2009], p. 584). But that ignores his May 1919 State of the Union message to Congress, his so-called labor and capital speech, that anticipated in many ways the essay.
155. The second volume of James Bryce's classic *Modern Democracies* was also published in 1923. The final chapters, "Democracy and the Communist State," and "The Future of Democracy" register the same liberal anxiety as that in Wilson's essay.
156. Richard, pp. 113, 116.
157. According to another interviewer of Lenin in December 1919, Lenin had favorable impressions of Bullitt; "if Bullitt were president of the United States peace would soon me made" (*Guardian*, December 4, 1919). So much, then, for the widely held claim that Lenin viewed him as a "useful idiot." (https://www.nytimes.com/1987/04/12/magazine/on-language.htmlthe 1987).
158. https://www.youtube.com/watch?v=96AWrpSOdOY; https://www.youtube.com/watch?v=t6ud1IPamaM.
159. Another telling vignette about Lenin is his penultimate published letter to a family member, his sister Anna, sometime at the end of 1922. He was embarrassed by the fact that "an exception" had been made for him to take a book out of the party's library that he hadn't returned: "my fault." He begged her to do so. *LCW, 37*, p. 549.

CHAPTER 6

Conclusion

What, to repeat, are the broad and key conclusions to be drawn from the four real-time politics comparisons? How do the claims, again, that Marx, Engels and Lenin made about the historical moments under examination, the French edition of the European Spring, the American Civil War, the Russian Revolution of 1905, and the Bolshevik Revolution of 1917 and end to World War I, compare and contrast to those of Tocqueville, Mill, Weber and Wilson? What about the events with which I've supplemented the Marx-Mill and Lenin-Weber comparisons, respectively electoral reform in Britain and the consequences of the October 1917 Revolution for Germany? To what extent are the readings of the protagonists of the events in agreement and disagreement? Which of them had a more accurate reading and made better forecasts? How did their theoretical/political views influence their responses? How do the four comparisons reveal key differences between Marxist and different varieties of liberal real-time politics? Most important, to what extent did their actions advance the democratic quest that was posed in all four moments? Can, lastly, a case be made for a superior theoretical purchase of either perspective for doing real-time politics? These are the questions to interrogate the four comparisons.

Attention then turns to subsequent historical developments; first, how fascism *and* Stalinism enabled World War II and, second, a Cold War scenario that continues to resonate—Washington versus Havana. Can comparative real-time political analysis for both cases as is done for the four in

© The Author(s) 2019   245
A. H. Nimtz, *Marxism versus Liberalism*, Marx, Engels,
and Marxisms, https://doi.org/10.1007/978-3-030-24946-5_6

this inquiry, namely, Marxist versus liberal readings and actions, bring new clarity to them? Lastly, and in the spirit of real-time politics, are there lessons from the four comparisons for contemporary politics in all their complexity and unprecedented character?

FOUR COMPARISONS

Marx and Engels versus Tocqueville

The European Spring, the French edition certainly, was no surprise for Marx, Engels and Tocqueville. They all saw it coming, if not the timing. They also agreed that the class interests of the bourgeoisie, the class actually in power during Louis-Philippe's regime, would come under threat. For the first time, unlike the 1789 Revolution, social rights, like the right to work, and not just political rights, like the right to vote, were on the agenda. For Tocqueville it would be the "Haves" versus the "Have Nots," whereas for Marx and Engels, as they announced in their just published *Manifesto of the Communist Party*, the modern proletariat versus the bourgeoisie. And two months earlier Engels predicted—accurately in a metaphorical if not literal sense—that liberal reformers like Tocqueville would "hide themselves in the darkest corner of their houses, or be scattered like dead leaves before the popular thunderstorm."

Tocqueville would not have disagreed with Marx's and Engels's framing the coming revolt in terms of the proletariat against the bourgeoisie. But if he thought it was "strange doctrines ... spreading among" the French proletariat that explained the February Revolution, that is, "socialist ideas," Marx had a more accurate read. Working-class starvation, due to the first transnational capitalist crisis, was the more proximate cause of the revolt; socialist consciousness amongst the Parisian proletariat was still a work in progress. He therefore differed sharply with Tocqueville on what the February overthrow of Louis-Philippe had ushered in. February for Marx was "to complete the rule of the bourgeoisie" whereas for Tocqueville "socialism will always remain the most essential feature of the February Revolution." The differences are instructive and most relevant for contemporary debates about socialism.

A "republic surrounded by social institutions," due to the social demands of the Parisian proletariat who were decisive in Louis-Philippe's deposition, is how Marx described the provisional government. Instituted in Paris, in other words, was, in today's lingo, a liberal welfare state or, perhaps, the first social democratic government in history. A genuine socialist revolution as Engels explained before the February Revolution would "destroy not only the political, but the social power of capital that will guarantee their [the proletariat] social welfare, along with their political strength." The "social power" of the bourgeoisie, as the *Manifesto* explained, rested on private property—still very much in place after February. The overthrow could not, therefore, have been, contra Tocqueville, a socialist revolution. Only in June would that possibility be posed.

Despite Tocqueville's misreading of the social content of February, he did grasp something of profound importance that Marx and Engels would have agreed with. He was smart enough to see that "the social power of capital" was still in place, before and after February, that is, private property, "the foundation of social order" as he put it. Being still in place, private property created understandable, but not acceptable—betraying Tocqueville's class orientation—resentment amongst the working classes. The Revolution of 1789 has stripped private property of its ancient aristocratic entitlements and trappings. Yet it continued to exercise its "social power" in a world in which those at the bottom of society could now vote or expect to do so, the result of 1789. Along with increased prosperity owing to the new mode of production, capitalism, the new political/economic scenario bred frustration—relative deprivation as modern social science calls it—amongst the historically excluded layers of society. And that frustration was being fed by "dangerous ideas" amongst which was that the "unalterable laws that constitute society—resting upon "the foundation of social order," that is, private property, and "providence"—could be repealed. Increasing working-class awareness that this new social arrangement was "the main obstacle to equality among men" was inherently destabilizing for bourgeois hegemony. Marx and Engels would have concurred with Tocqueville's keen insight, for them one of the redeeming features of the capitalist mode of production. As the opening pages of the Manifesto explained: "the modern bourgeois society that has sprouted from the ruins of feudal society has not done away with class antagonisms ... it has simplified class antagonism." That Tocqueville could consider that the "unalterable laws" of class society, private property, were not set in stone and, thus, be repealed would also have resonated with Marx and Engels. Though he confessed to having been "tempted" to consider the socialist alternative—unsettling for some of his modern-day admirers—his class allegiances wouldn't allow him to go there.

The June Revolution put a definitive end to any possible convergence of political perspectives of Marx and Engels, and Tocqueville. In the run up to the upheaval, Marx and Tocqueville often agreed about the ineptness of the provisional government, particularly regarding the peasantry, though from different sides of the class divide. Once the revolt began, however, it required both of them to take sides, to vote with their feet. Can there be any doubt that the democratic credentials of Marx were more deserved than those of Tocqueville? That moment more than any other defined the political Tocqueville, about which there is still a deafening silence amongst his admirers. If he had once been a prevaricating liberal, in June he found his voice. While Marx and Engels were doing everything they could at the same moment to advance the democratic revolution in Germany, Tocqueville made sure it would be crushed in France. Perhaps, to be charitable, he couldn't see that the bloodbath he helped to lead would undermine France's second attempt to institute liberal democracy. Marx, on the other hand, accurately foresaw that the slaughter spelled the beginning of the end of the Second Republic. Eliminating the working class from the picture, specifically the Parisian component, meant that republican governance had lost its most ardent and capable defender. Only the working class, he and Engels had concluded in 1844, had the interest and capability in advancing the democratic quest—what Tocqueville could never imagine. If ever there were a moment in history when two competing political perspectives were so starkly counterpoised, the June Revolution must certainly qualify as a leading candidate.

The best that Tocqueville defenders might say about his actions in June is that the road to hell is oftentimes paved with good intentions. But from then on he actively campaigned to limit political space in France, all in the name of trying to save the Republic and to be led by a small group of like-minded moderate liberals. There was a remarkable and instructive coincidence of opinion between Marx and Tocqueville about the right to work provision in the draft constitution before and after the June Revolution, that the latter played a major role in writing. Though Marx thought the provision to be "in the bourgeois sense, an absurdity, a miserable pious wish," Tocqueville confirmed one of the essential lessons in the Marx-Engels arsenal. He admitted that the only reason it was included in the pre-June draft, the first time ever anywhere, was due to "fear of outside events and the excitement of the moment," and "pressure of revolutionary ideas." In Germany, Marx and Engels had argued against reform liberals like Tocqueville who believed that what takes place within the parliamentary arena is the "ultima Thule" of politics, what they ridiculed as "parliamentary cretinism." Those afflicted with "the incurable malady," as Engels sarcastically put it, think that "all and everything going on outside the walls of their house—wars, revolutions … and whatever else … is nothing compared to the incommensurable events hinging upon the important question, whatever it may be, just at that moment occupying the attention of their honorable House."[1] Tocqueville's invaluable admission would have been welcomed ammunition for them in their debates with the liberals—including current varieties (discussed later).

What about Marx's explanation for the defeat of the Parisian proletariat, the lack of leadership and organization? Was that hindsight? Both he and Engels had argued at least four years earlier that the working class needed to prepare itself for its revolutionary tasks in order to be successful; the raison d'être for their *Manifesto*. Engels reported approvingly three months before the revolt that the French proletariat was engaged in study and smartly avoiding being prematurely provoked into combat. Though fragmentary, their real-time accounts indicate that they recognized that the preparatory process in France was still a work in progress in the lead-up to June. In Germany, at the very same moment, they were doing all they could to provide leadership, program and organization to its proletariat facing a similar situation. The hindsight accusation, if made, is therefore unwarranted. Assuming, however, as they did that socialist revolution was on the agenda in 1848–1849 is a valid accusation. Their subsequent balance sheets, their own second-guessing, admitted to that mistaken assumption.[2]

The defeat of the Parisian proletariat emboldened Tocqueville to not only strike the right to work provision from the draft constitution but to go after other democratic rights won in the February Revolution—to endorse the imposition of what he unabashedly termed a "parliamentary dictatorship." From then on, the most outstanding difference between Tocqueville and the Marx-Engels team was the former's belief that he and his coterie could save the republic by appeasing the most conservative elements in the National Assembly and Louis-Bonaparte himself. Far earlier than Tocqueville, Marx recognized that it was only a matter of time, given the routing of the Parisian proletariat, that Napoleon's nephew would seek to emulate his uncle.

Louis-Bonaparte's election in December 1848, the first presidential election in Europe based on universal male suffrage, the product of

February, had raised, Tocqueville recognized and feared, working-class expectations. Both he and Marx recognized the dilemma the bourgeoisie had created for itself. For Marx, however, there was a deeper problem for Tocqueville and the class he sought to represent. The granting of universal male suffrage in company with a constitution that guaranteed, at least on paper, private property—"the social power" of the bourgeoisie—made for an inherently tense-fraught political reality. Not for naught did those with property resist for so many centuries the granting of the vote to those without property; their fear that the latter would use the vote to infringe on their property. The tension was resolved in May 1850 when the Assembly abolished universal male suffrage, the "coup d'état of the bourgeoisie" as Marx called it.

From then on, in Marx's opinion, it wasn't a question if but only when Louis-Bonaparte would rid himself of the "irksome" republic. Tocqueville and his faction either enabled or acquiesced in developments that paved the way for his fateful decision. "If ever," Marx later wrote, "an event has, well in advance of its coming, cast its shadow before it, it was Bonaparte's coup d'état." Tocqueville wasn't clueless about what was in the making. It's just that his core political being would not allow him to do what would have been necessary to prevent the coup. Though written after the fact, Marx's forecast that mobilizing the masses was the last thing Tocqueville and faction would do to resist the overthrow was consistent with all he had said in his real-time reading of them as they operated in alliance with the Party of Order. For Tocqueville to have admitted as much in the lead-up to the coup—and unavailable to Marx—is one of those rare moments in the annals of real-time politics of near perfect complementarity of opposing views.

At the very core of the differences between Marx and Engels, on one hand, and Tocqueville, on the other, was which class to look to for advancing the democratic quest. Tocqueville thought that like-minded liberals like himself could do the job. But when it became clear that wasn't possible, he decided, rather than "appeal to revolutionary passions," to hold his nose and stomach "the grotesque mediocrity," Marx's indelible label for Louis-Bonaparte. Liberal betrayal, in Marx's and Engels's opinion, was the chief lesson of the European Spring. Only if the working class, as well, organized itself independently of them could "true democracy" and "human emancipation" become a reality. No one, as the third and fourth cases in this book reveal, took those lessons to heart as much as Lenin. What Marx and Engels distilled from the European Spring would be, therefore, enormously consequential. Tocqueville, then, beginning with what his *Democracy in America* taught the young Marx, and then later what the lessons of the liberal handwringing of his cohorts in 1848–1851 taught Lenin, aided and abetted, inadvertently, the communist project—one of the great ironies of modernity.[3]

Marx versus Mill

The overthrow of the American slavocracy was the decisive political event of the nineteenth century. It advanced the democratic quest unlike any other development since the 1789 French Revolution. It was *the* test for anyone's democratic credentials, including those of John Stuart Mill and Karl Marx.

Marx and Mill, unlike Marx/Engels and Tocqueville regarding the French events in 1848–1851, both observed and responded to the American conflagration from afar, the same city, London, and a few miles from one another—making thus for a fairer comparison. They both relied, for the most part, on the same sources for making their claims. Tocqueville's *Democracy*, also, played a major role in their understanding of the country, though in different ways—informing their different motives for supporting the Union cause. For Marx, the communist, the end of chattel slavery would advance the class struggle and, thus, the fight for "true democracy." For Mill, the liberal, it was mainly a moral cause.

How Marx and Mill read and responded to the French edition of the European Spring anticipated their reaction to the Civil War. Mill, for the most part, took a more progressive stance on the Revolution than his erstwhile friend Tocqueville. Unlike the latter, he supported the provisional government, though skeptical about its endorsement of the right to work demands of the proletariat. There is no evidence that he sanctioned the bloodbath in June 1848 that Tocqueville enabled. Problematic was Mill's denial of the slaughter: "not one person has been shot, not one life taken, by the authority of government in consequence of the insurrection." His embrace of the world's first social democratic government made him effectively an apologist for its sanguinary actions. From afar like Mill, Marx reported more accurately the brutality meted out to the Parisian proletariat.

What most distinguished Marx from Mill regarding the European Spring was his willingness, under very difficult personal circumstances, to find the time, energy and resources to draw a balance sheet on what had taken place in France, his *Class Struggles* and *Eighteenth Brumaire*.[4] Mill, on the other hand, after having written a detailed article-length defense of the February Revolution, began to lose interest in developments in France as the revolution increasingly degenerated. Living in far more comfortable circumstances a few miles from Marx, he wrote virtually nothing about what was taking place in France after 1849, including anything about Louis-Bonaparte's coup d'état. Like Tocqueville at the same time, he found it easier to turn his attention away from real world politics and retire to his passion, intellectual activities.

Regarding the Civil War, what most stands out in comparing Marx's and Mill's reading of and response to the conflagration? Neither one of them, first, foresaw the Civil War, specifically, its timing in April 1861. Both followed closely in different ways, owing to their different political perspectives, the developments that led to the war. Marx and Engels, always tuned to real-time politics, had a premonition owing to the John Brown raid in 1859, which didn't seem to register on Mill's radar. Most instructive about the differences between the Marx-Engels team and Mill is that the former had an ersatz party in the U.S.—most of whom were veterans of the German edition of the European Spring—who began working to ensure that Abraham Lincoln would be the Republican Party candidate and winner in the fateful presidential election in November 1860. Lincoln, they thought, was the best practical hope for ending chattel slavery. Mill, though it's not clear, may have thought the same about Lincoln; but he lacked forces in the U.S. to try to make that hope a reality. Revolutionary practice, in other words, immediately distinguished Marx from Mill in the lead-up to war; it anticipated their key differences during its four-year long course. The conclusions that Marx and Engels had reached in 1844 regarding the proletariat and "revolutionary practice," the commencement of their partnership, explain why.

Once the war began, Marx prioritized it above his other activities, including his research and writing for *Capital*; why his entire magnum opus never saw the light of day in his lifetime. That decision stood in stark contrast to Mill and spoke volumes about the essential differences between the two. Mill, also a supporter of the Union, was never willing to subordinate his other interests to its defense. Marx, on the other hand, quickly concluded that the immediate task was to defend Lincoln and the Union against its detractors in the overwhelming majority pro-Confederacy British press; their class interests were on naked display—unimpeded access to the slavocracy's cotton.

After about six months of intense reading on American history on the decades prior to the Civil War, Marx wrote what would be eighteen published articles in defense of the Union cause. The political economy of slavery explained why the slavocracy seceded, to defend their "peculiar institution"—what the pro-Confederacy British press tried to deny. The survival of chattel slavery depended on its expansion into the free territories, what the platform upon which Lincoln ran for the election prohibited. Most significant is that many of the articles appeared in America's leading newspaper, the *New York Daily Tribune* that counted amongst its readers Abraham Lincoln. Even more remarkable, he accurately predicted a full year in advance that despite Lincoln's protestation that the Union only sought to end the secession and not to abolish slavery, the president would indeed have to do just that to end the slave owners' rebellion. Marx's "materialist conception of history" informed his foresight. And when it looked like British rulers had found a pretext to intervene in the war on behalf of the slavocracy, the *Trent* affair, Marx used his access to the *Tribune* to ensure that would not happen. Whether his articles were influential in any way can only be the basis for speculation; he acted as if they could.

By the time Marx's last article in the *Tribune* appeared, February 1862, which praised the British working class for opposing the interventionist stance of its ruling class, Mill's first writing on the war appeared. In one of England's foremost journals, he countered the claim of the pro-Confederacy British press that the war had nothing to do with slavery. The institution, to the contrary, and its internal logic was the raison d'être for the secession—not unlike what Marx had argued six months earlier. Mill and Marx were on the same page about the origins of the war—explaining their pro-Union sympathies. Their correspondence with others revealed also a mutual appreciation of Lincoln.

What most distinguished them was to whom to look to in England to support the anti-slavery cause and, second, how much time and energy to devote to that end. Their different responses to the *Trent* affair in the fall of 1861 was especially telling. When Mill could have played a crucial role in stilling the hand of his government's intervention into the war on behalf of the slavocracy, what could have been decisive in its outcome, he remained silent. His nationalist sentiment and unwillingness, as he admitted, or maybe lack of courage, to challenge British ruling-class opinion caused him to have writer's block. Marx the proletarian internationalist, on the other hand, did all he could with more limited resources to prevent

London from coming to the aid of the Confederacy. To claim, as I do, that Marx's democratic credentials are more deserved than those of Mill is no exaggeration.

When Mill did finally find his voice, he directed it "to persons of talent, the more known and respected the better," as he explained. Only the enlightened elite like himself could save his beloved country from the shame of kowtowing to the slavocracy solely for pecuniary interests. The conclusions he and Engels has drawn in 1844 explains why Marx, rather, prioritized the English working class in defending the Union cause. Lincoln, it appears, agreed with Marx. His thank you note to the International Workingmen's Association for their congratulatory message on his reelection, written by Marx, contrasted in warmth with the perfunctory one he sent to the middle-class crowd with which Mill was associated. Lincoln, "the singled-minded son of the working class," as Marx put it the message, had, like him a more favorable opinion of England's workers than "the betters."

Whether Mill was right in prioritizing like-minded liberals to effectively challenge the pro-Confederacy proclivities of the British ruling class—an unanswerable question—the fact is that he wasn't willing to do what Marx did, to put in the requisite time and energy to achieve that goal. Though rich in content, he could only muster the time and energy to write two articles, both in prestigious journals. The amount of his literary output pales in comparison to what Marx wrote on the war. And Marx would have written more had he had the kind of access to venues that Mill clearly had. In this regard, it's instructive to note another key difference between Marx and Mill. Real-time politics requires access to a newspaper or something akin; the means for making real-time judgments in order to know how to act. Almost from the beginning of coming of age politically, Marx figured that out; it was never on Mill's radar. Though the venture failed after a year, Tocqueville also saw the necessity of having an organ for real-time politics. For Lenin, to be seen, it was indispensable.

When the opportunity arose to support the Union by other means, the birth of the IWA in September 1864, Marx didn't hesitate for a moment to get on board—again, while trying to complete *Capital*. There is, in fact, some evidence that Engels was leery of his partner taking on the organizational/programmatic responsibilities that he did in the organization's founding; it might come at the expense of the completion of the long-awaited book. If which class to look to advance the democratic quest was the first essential difference between Marx and Mill, the second had to do with "what is to be done?" A liberal, at least one like Mill, could be either a theorist/educator or an activist, or perhaps both. A communist, for Marx and Engels, had to be both. The 1845 *Theses on Feuerbach*, specifically the third one, argued that "the educator" learns from "revolutionary practice"—the laboratory of the class struggle. For Mill, being a theoretician took priority over being an activist—what his self-admission in 1833 had accurately anticipated.

It's true that the theoretical conclusions that the Marx-Engels partnership drew in 1844 informed what I argue were more foresighted conclusions about the war and its outcome, particularly, that it would have to be turned into a war to abolish slavery for the Union to be victorious. But that claim shouldn't suggest that Marx operated with an "all-purpose formula of a general historico-philosophical theory" as he later critiqued such an interpretation of their method. The only documented political disagreement between Marx and Engels had to do with the Civil War, lasting for maybe two to three years. Not long after the war began, and with Confederate battlefield victories, Engels grew increasingly pessimistic about Union victory. Marx, on the other hand, continued to believe as he argued at the outset that in "the long-run" the North would win. Not only did the North have the material means for doing so but it also could play "the last card up its sleeve"—the arming of blacks. Marx chided his partner for focusing too much "on the military side of things." His more holistic approach proved to be more accurate about the war's outcome. The dispute reveals, again, that Marx's and Engels's "materialist conception of history" was more of a theoretical approach than a template. Their discussions/debates on the Civil War offer, I argue, the most instructive example of how they employed their method in doing real-time political analysis—an unexpected benefit of the Marx-Mill comparison.[5]

Had Mill been willing to being the activist Marx was, some of his insights about the war and its outcome could have been valuable for the democratic quest in America. Prior to the end of the conflict and afterward he opined in correspondence about the prospects for the former slaves, some of it quite prescient. He correctly foresaw, for example, in a letter to a former Union commander, the need for "censorship" and a "military dictatorship" over the unrepentant former slave owners who did all they could to obstruct "freedom for the negroes." Unfortunately, again, Mill failed to publicize such solely needed views—unlike what the IWA had done in its September 1865 "Address to the People of the United States." Mill's actions or lack thereof betrayed what so distinguished him from Marx—the assumption that liberal elites like himself would be sufficient in making democracy real for the first time in the U.S. and that it could be done without the commitment of an inordinate amount of time and energy.

Never were Marx's and Mill's democratic qualifications so strikingly and tellingly on display and in contrast than during the campaign for electoral reform in Britain between 1866 and 1868. If Mill's sincere but relatively lackluster defense of the Union cause suggests that he was simply incapable of being politically active, that campaign demonstrated otherwise. He could exert energy when he thought it counted, especially on home turf. His election to Parliament enabled the subversion of the struggle for universal manhood suffrage—what Marx supported—in favor of the less democratic household suffrage. His opposition to the former testified to one of his core political beliefs, the fear of the "tyranny of the majority." How to explain? Like Tocqueville, who too feared "the mob," class and class orientation were determinant. The tyranny of the minority was preferable to the unruly masses. Mill, unlikely aware, got the best of Marx politically. Not only did he help to derail the fight for universal manhood suffrage, but he stifled what could have been a revolutionary moment for the English working class, the Hyde Park confrontation on July 25, 1866. What Marx sought to do in England, the institution of independent working-class political action—the means, he argued, for making liberal democracy in England a reality for the first time—would only be realized a decade after his death, the founding of the Independent Labour Party in 1893. In hindsight, he was only able to plant the seeds.

At the end of my *Marx and Engels*, I wrote, "if there were individuals who rivalled Marx and Engels's contribution to the democratic struggle, they're not likely to be found in the ranks of nineteenth-century liberalism."[6] Like Tocqueville, Mill too, I suggested, came up short when compared to the democratic credentials of the two communists but without providing corroborating evidence. The reader can decide if I've now made a convincing case about the limitations of both liberal icons.

Lenin versus Weber

Though less well known than the two prior historical moments, the 1905 Russian Revolution was of major significance because it proved to be the precursor to maybe the most influential event in the twentieth century, the Bolshevik Revolution of October 1917. Two of the key protagonists in both dramas, Vladimir Lenin and Leon Trotsky, often referred to the 1905 upheaval as the "dress rehearsal" for the better-known revolt. That 1905 attracted the detailed attention of Max Weber, the western academy's leading alternative to Marx—at least for most of the twentieth century—the upheaval allows for an opportunity in comparative real-time politics too important not to be taken advantage of. Though Weber's focus was narrow, the possibility of a liberal alternative to the sclerotic 300-year-old Romanov dynasty, Lenin also devoted considerable attention to the issue. The Lenin-Weber comparison permits, therefore, an answer to one of the more intriguing questions of the twentieth century: why wasn't there a liberal alternative to the Bolshevik outcome to the Russian Revolution?

Unlike Weber, Lenin accurately foresaw the 1905 Revolution. He anticipated the cataclysmic events that became Bloody Sunday, January 9, 1905, almost a week in advance. Though also abroad, in Geneva, he had the advantage of being closer to the scene. Weber, on the other hand, spent most of 1904 traveling and speaking in the U.S. But he certainly knew about the Russo-Japanese War, the proximate cause of the revolution, which had been under way for more than a year. Lenin had been preparing for the upheaval for at least five years; thus, why he could respond so rapidly to developments in Russia while it took Weber about six months, including mastery of Russian to read original sources, to get up to speed. The conclusion Lenin reached in 1901 that if revolutionaries did not have a party in place when the proverbial "s—t hits the fan," it would be too late to try to construct one in the midst of the maelstrom. But it's to Weber's credit that he was willing to drop everything to get up to speed—like Marx had to do when the Confederacy attacked Fort Sumter, but so unlike Mill.

The head start advantage Lenin had no doubt explains why he was savvier about the Constitutional Democrats, or Cadets, the liberal party that Weber had been in contact with and placed his hopes on. Though Lenin had concluded at least six months before Weber that the liberal Cadet party would unlikely lead a real fight to institute constitutional democracy in Russia for the first time, his willingness to appeal to them to do just that reveals a crucially important aspect of his method and practice. While theory, inherited from Marx and Engels, specifically, the lessons of 1848–1849, including those of Tocqueville's actions, suggested that little could be expected of liberals for advancing the democratic quest, that claim could only be verified in practice in the actual world. That Lenin called on the

Cadets to get their act together as late as in the immediate aftermath of Bloody Sunday, January 1905, meant that he didn't regard the claim as proven until actually proven. Only the laboratory of the class struggle could settle such matters.

By the end of 1905, Lenin and Weber were both on the same page about the Cadets; they were increasingly looking like a spent force. Though they did better than expected in the elections to the First Duma in early 1906 and had the largest bloc of seats in it, they proved unable to step up to the plate when necessary—to challenge the monarchy. Weber's second book-length essay on the 1905–1906 events—not included for this comparison—documents their demise and largely coincides with Lenin's assessment of the Cadets. In many ways, Weber agreed with Lenin about the Cadets' failure of nerve. To have successfully confronted Tsar Nicholas's regime would have meant a renewal of the revolutionary wave that was ebbing by spring 1906; what the Cadets had no class interest in promoting. The answer, then, to one of the more puzzling questions about the October Revolution on 1917, why were the liberals unable to effectively rival the Bolsheviks, was essentially revealed in that moment. The Cadets had missed the revolutionary train. They would from then on be by-passed by history. Weber, unlike Lenin, however, was unwilling to consider any other alternative to the Cadets and, thus, failed to see what laid ahead.

What most distinguished Lenin from Weber regarding the Cadets and the liberal alternative was his insistence that determinant in their fate were the developments outside the parliamentary arena, specifically, the strikes, the mass mobilizations in the streets. Lenin's admonition to a fellow Bolshevik in fall 1905, at the height of the strike wave, "we must fight in a revolutionary way for a parliament, but not in a parliamentary way for a revolution," could easily have been directed at Weber. Weber's account was confined to the writing of the ideal liberal constitution and the deliberations within the parliamentary arena—the essence of politics for him and so unlike Lenin. Lenin, not surprisingly, subscribed to Marx's and Engels's critique of irresolute and myopic liberals in the Frankfurt Assembly in 1848–1849 for being afflicted with "parliamentary cretinism," as discussed in the Marx-Engels/Tocqueville comparison. Fascinating is it to learn that Weber applauded those same liberals. Lenin denounced them as precursors for the Cadets; another rare moment in the complementarity of opposing sides in real-time political analysis.

Weber's account, in terms of scholarship, is in general beyond reproach; why he has so long been a model for modern social science research. For the most part he got the facts right. The problem was his egregiously selective reading of the facts. To have virtually ignored the key dynamic of 1905, what was crucial in opening up political space for a liberal alternative is unpardonable. The strike movement, a term that Weber could barely utter, was as Lenin correctly argued what made it possible for a meaningful liberal opening to take place in Romanov Russia for the first time. It's ebbing, as Lenin also correctly understood, was the fundamental reason, and not simply the ineptness of the Cadets or historical destiny as Weber believed, for the end of Russian liberalism's brief moment in the sun.

The most consequential disagreement between Lenin and Weber had to do, not surprisingly, with the Bolshevik question—what provoked Lenin's ire in January 1917. Despite Weber's detailed attention to Russian developments, informed by a reading knowledge of Russian, the bottom line is that the *bürgerlich* scholar missed the most significant political event in his lifetime—the Bolshevik Revolution. The Western academy's paragon of social science research for much of the twentieth century, and maybe since, not only failed to anticipate Bolshevik ascent but as well its staying power, a reality he continued to deny until the end when he died in 1920. To put it more derisively as Lenin might have justifiably done, the best of bourgeois scholarship flunked the test of real-world politics when it came to the October Revolution. Ironically, Weber's insistence on erecting the proverbial Chinese Wall between facts and values was the most likely culprit. He was seemingly incapable of allowing the facts about the Bolsheviks, especially the mass support they had, to inform and, thus, challenge his value-laden opinions about them. Lenin's party, contrary to the facts, could only have been for him an ineffective "putschist sect"—a charge that's been repeated ever since by the class opponents of the Bolsheviks. Those of us who were force-fed Weber's fact/value distinction in our graduate school training and were skeptical about it had good reason to be leery. Only now is it possible to understand why. Others have recognized Weber's blinders about the Bolsheviks.[7] What I claim to do is to lay bare for the first time the significance of Weber's failure and offer an explanation. The values of the self-proclaimed *bürgerlich* scholar prevented him from seeing the actuality of the Bolsheviks—a cautionary tale to be revisited when looking at contemporary developments.

Just as domestic politics revealed Mill's democratic limitations, the same was true for Weber. Like Tocqueville, he supported a constitutional monarchy rather than a republic. As the Great War began to go badly for Germany, he called for parliamentarization of the Reich, thinking that more democracy would strengthen the war effort. Lenin also fought for more democracy in Russia once Czar Nicholas was deposed in the February Revolution in 1917—but something more radical than the parliamentary form that replaced monarchial rule. Soviet democracy, he argued, was more representative of working-class and peasant opinion—that is, those in uniform—and, thus, the route to extricating Russia from the increasingly hated bloodletting. Weber began to lose enthusiasm for democratizing Germany when he thought it would undermine morale amongst its troops—exactly what Lenin was promoting amongst Russian troops. Recent research confirms that anti-war sentiment was greatest amongst the ranks of Russia's soldiers and sailors and what enabled Bolshevik ascent in the October Revolution—Lenin's strategy. The Bolshevik propaganda campaign to encourage German soldiers to emulate their Russian cohorts alarmed Weber and put him directly at loggerheads with Lenin. A year later, Germany's working class did just what Weber feared—the November 1918 Revolution, instituting republican government in the country for the first time. It confirmed Lenin's dictum, just as it had in Russia, that only through revolutionary means could parliamentary democracy be instituted and not, as was Weber's position, through parliamentary means. Only with the deposition of Germany's monarch, Wilhelm II, did Weber become a supporter of republican government, mainly as a way to moderate the upheaval. Ironically, it was what the Bolsheviks unleashed that compelled Weber to move toward a more democratic posture—further evidence for my claim that Lenin's democratic qualifications were more deserved than those of Weber.

Lenin versus Wilson

If Weber was in denial about the Bolsheviks, Woodrow Wilson was certainly not. His problem, rather, was an inability to make sense of them as they both irritated and perplexed him. Wilson's dilemma revealed perhaps better than anything from the other side of the class divide the actuality of the Bolsheviks—what real-time political analysis can divulge.

Both Lenin and Wilson anticipated, to varying degrees, the Great War, the event that more than any other birthed the Russian Revolution. Lenin, owing to the rich legacy he inherited from Marx and Engels—again, fourteen years Wilson's junior—was better prepared theoretically and programmatically to make sense of and to respond to the conflagration. Little if anything in Wilson's academic/political background could do the same for him. Within months of the Guns of August 1914, Lenin began to do the research and writing to add to that rich legacy. His *Imperialism* offered an explanation for the war with corresponding policy implications. Advanced capitalism had evolved into imperialism, leading to rivalries amongst its bearers and, hence, the tendency toward warfare. Only if the working class overthrew their capitalist lords could war be avoided. Wilson, though also a prolific writer, never produced anything comparable. His solution to predatory capitalism, as he told a "colloquy" at the White House in May 1916, was "some check ... upon it by some international arrangements"—in anticipation of his League of Nations proposal.

As for program, Lenin inherited in addition to the Marx-Engels arsenal the agenda of the Socialist or Second International, especially, the Basle Manifesto of 1912 that the Bolsheviks had endorsed. It directed all SI affiliates to turn an imperialist war into a civil war, that is, to organize the proletariat of the belligerent governments to overthrow their own ruling classes. Nothing informed Lenin's actions from August 1914 to the end of the war in 1919 and afterward as much as that directive. Wilson, on the other hand, without a strategic program of his own, had to improvise—reacting to events with all the potential pitfalls therein.

Better prepared than Wilson, Lenin long knew about the U.S. president before the latter knew about the Bolshevik leader. Not only was his dismissal of Wilson's "Peace Note" in December 1916 instructive—"Wilson represents a bourgeoisie which has made billions out of the war"—but apparently prescient: "he is the head of a government that has frantically armed the United States obviously in preparation for a *second* great imperialist war." Was Lenin predicting World War II? Driving his comment was the logic of his *Imperialism*. But as with his claim about Russian liberalism, a general tendency was not the same as a particular outcome. Whether there would be another "imperialist war" depended on the class struggle, on whether the working class would be able to organize itself and take power out of the hands of its capitalist rulers. Engels had said as much in 1891. For Wilson the solution was the League of Nations. Lenin, too, believed in international organizing but done by and in the interest of the working class, a tradition going back to the International Working Men's Association or First International that Marx led. He had been active at least since 1907 in the SI in advocating for its anti-militarist and anti-colonial stances. Wilson, on the other hand, had never participated in an international body, let alone one advocating for peace. He, in fact, had displayed contempt for American anti-interventionists around US actions in Mexico and the Philippines.

Once the Great War began, the key issues that divided Lenin and Wilson were, first, how to end the war and, second, how to insure a democratic peace. Is there evidence that supports the effectiveness of either perspective?

The failure of the German Social Democrats, the flagship party of the Socialist International, to carry out the Basle Manifesto played a key if not decisive role in enabling the Guns of August. The Bolshevik deputies in the Duma under Lenin's direction not only voted against funding the war but used their parliamentary immunity to organize against it once the hostilities began—one of only two SI affiliates to have done so. The "betrayal" of the German party as he labelled it propelled Lenin to begin organizing a new international beginning with the Zimmerwald movement in 1915 that eventually became the Third or Communist International in 1919. Thus, by the time the League of Nations came into being in 1920, Lenin had had more than a decade of international anti-war work under his belt. Did that head start pay off?

Equipped with a program and international organization in the making, Lenin, from at least 1915, was single-minded in realizing the Basle Manifesto. He sought not only to lead Russia's working classes to power in a civil war against their capitalist overlords to end the carnage they were enduring but to leverage the victory to inspire Germany's cohorts to do the same—the key to bringing the entire bloodbath to an end. Under Lenin's leadership, in collaboration with Trotsky, Russian workers and peasants took power in October/November 1917. Within days and weeks, Russia withdrew from the war as the Bolsheviks had promised. Aiding and abetting their ascent was the Wilson administration's campaign to keep the Provisional government in the increasingly unpopular war. The longer Kerensky's government went along with Washington and its Entente allies, the more popular became the message of the Bolsheviks, "Peace, land and bread." Lenin's strategy, peace through working-class ascent, was therefore validated, at least for Russia's participation in the war. Wilson's December 4, 1917, speech to Congress recognized, implicitly at least, the all so unintended consequences of his inducements to the Provisional government.[8] His effort to keep Russia in the war failed spectacularly; Lenin outmaneuvered him.

What about Lenin's expectation that Russian working-class ascent and its call for peace would inspire Germany's toilers to do the same? Here the story became complicated, as is often the case in the real world of politics.

Lenin's claim, even before the February/March Revolution, that the overthrow of capitalism in Russia would end the Great War was credible. The Bolshevik decrees upon taking power in October/November initiated the peace process beginning first with Brest-Litovsk. Lenin's strategy was basically to play for time in the hope that the German workers and peasants in uniform would do as their counterparts in Russia had done— embark on a civil war against their own ruling classes. Missing, however, as Lenin knew all so well, was the equivalent of a Bolshevik party, the necessary ingredient in a successful working-class revolution. Yet, as always, Lenin knew the answer to whether Germany's toilers could successfully emulate their Russian cohorts could not be determined in advance but only in the real world of politics. For brief moments, November 1917 and January 1918, revolts of German sailors and soldiers gave heart to the Bolsheviks; perhaps Germany's version of Russia's February/March Revolution. The Brest-Litovsk talks in the meantime spurred Wilson's Fourteen Points speech, his framework for the eventual peace. The immediate withdrawal of Russia from the war gave Germany's workers and peasants in uniform less reason to either obey or actively comply with the orders of their officer corp. Combined with an active Bolshevik policy of Russian soldiers fraternizing with their German counterparts, German forces proved increasingly incapable of contesting Allied forces now reinforced with US troops.[9] Demoralization began to set in leading to a revolt of German soldiers and sailors in November 1918, the departure of Germany's last monarch and the armistice. Weber, to be noted, was glad to see the Kaiser go, but not the monarchy itself; it was needed to legitimize the Reich.[10] Six months later the Treaty of Versailles formally ended the war. Without the Bolsheviks coming to power eighteen months earlier, the bloodletting would have likely continued. Incontrovertible is that Bolshevik ascent ended the carnage for the country with the highest casualties in a war with no redeeming features; thus, the popularity of the Bolsheviks and why they were able to win the civil war.

Lenin's long-game strategy hinged on the German proletariat making a revolution. That never happened. Was it a pipe dream for him to think that was ever a possibility? That he, like other Bolshevik leaders, found incredulous the vote of the Reichstag Social Democrats to fund the Great War when it began in August 1914 suggests that they were out of touch with the reality in Germany. So, taken aback, Lenin sought an answer but not from his mentors, Marx and Engels, but their mentor, Hegel; his philosophical notebooks in 1914–1916 were the product of that intense reading. If the charge is that Lenin mistakenly thought that socialist revolution was on the immediate agenda in Germany, that, I argue, is hindsight. Bolshevik ascent in October/November 1917 immediately evoked an echo from Germany's workers in uniform, in December and January, when Moscow made public its peace proposals. Fertile ground for a revolution clearly existed in Germany, in other words. Whether it could result in a revolutionary outcome, however, could not be foreordained. Only the laboratory of the class struggle would reveal the answer. Lenin indeed knew that the German proletariat lacked the kind of vanguard party it had taken him over a decade to forge. But his reading of history revealed that what might take place over years, as he often said, could be compressed in months and days in a revolutionary moment. His task, as a real-time politician, was to do all he could to advance that agenda—from afar to be remembered. That, I argue, is the criteria to employ to judge his readings and actions. Could he have done more or been more effective, for example, in trying to stimulate a revolution in Germany? Those are the appropriate questions but the imponderables of politics for which only the confident Monday morning quarterback has an answer. Wilson certainly thought and feared, beginning in November 1918, that Germany's toilers was vulnerable to the Bolshevik appeal, elsewhere also.

What about Wilson's "peace with victory" policy? Was it the decisive factor in ending the war? It is true that the presence of a million US troops in the war by the end of the summer of 1918 was of utmost importance. But their contribution, even in combination with the Allied troops, never led to the defeat of the German forces. Rather they helped to exhaust the enemy. That fact more than any other explains why Berlin reached out to Wilson for an armistice in October. In so doing, they hoped he would give them the best deal. They agreed to negotiations on the basis of his Fourteen Points. Wilson's concurrence meant effectively "peace without victory," his original peace proposal in January 1917. When it looked like Berlin might back out of the armistice deal—because it required the Kaiser's departure (not unlike what his cousin Nicholas had to do in February/March 1917)—the revolt of German sailors and soldiers in the first week of November 1918, leading some of them to establish "soviets" to press their demands, guaranteed the German government's signature to the agreement on November 8. General Pershing, who headed US forces, felt that the armistice deprived him of a military victory over the Germans.[11] In the end, then, rather than Wilson's "peace with victory" strategy that ended the most sanguinary war in history, it was a combination of US troops, Wilson's Fourteen Points and German "soviets"—belatedly fulfilling Lenin's hopes—that made it possible for Wilson to claim authorship for the end of the Great War. Of these three factors, two of them were the product of what the Bolsheviks had done a year before.

What about Wilson's long-term strategy for peace—the League of Nations? And Lenin's alternative, proletarian internationalism, that is, the Communist International, founded in 1919, a year ahead of the League? This isn't the place to address the success of either; the next section does. What can be said here is that Lenin was highly critical of Wilson's solution. As long as capitalism was in place, inter-imperialist rivalries would be in place making, therefore, warfare probable—a point made to Wilson in a letter he helped to craft. There is no evidence about what Wilson thought of Lenin's solution. It can be assumed, however, that he didn't view the CI's founding favorably for reasons to be discussed shortly.

The other major divide between Lenin and Wilson was the Bolshevik Revolution itself. By winter 1918 it was clear that for Wilson "Bolshevism" was a "poison" that required an "antidote." He had reason to be concerned. Not only did the November revolt in Germany look like a repeat of what took place exactly a year earlier in Russia but in April 1919 the short-lived Bavarian Soviet Republic was founded. A similar development took place in Hungary. Even in staid England, a massive strike wave there threatened to become revolutionary. That all of this coincided with the founding in March 1919 in Moscow of the CI was no doubt for Wilson further proof of the lethality of the poison. Lenin's response to these developments was, of course, quite different—more reason for the defense of the Bolshevik project, an inspiration for workers elsewhere. Both protagonists acted on those assumptions. Which of them was more successful?

Once the Bolsheviks withdrew from the war and sued for peace, the Wilson administration thought it might be able to entice the Bolsheviks to stay the course—what its lack of knowledge about them sorely betrayed. Thus began what I call the pas de deux between Moscow and Washington for about two years. Both sides, even before Brest-Litovsk, tried to play one another for their own purposes. Complicating the picture for Wilson were his liberal contradictions, particularly his professed support for Russia's "independent determination of her own political development" in his Fourteen Points speech—words that Lenin was all too happy to recall to him. When Wilson, for example, first sent US troops to intervene in Russia's civil war, he convinced himself that he wasn't taking sides. His directive to General Graves said as much. Lenin thought otherwise but cautiously responded in order that Wilson not make a full-scale US military commitment on the side of the counterrevolutionary White Army forces. Lenin made at least five peace overtures to Washington. Wilson responded with both the carrot and stick. But his liberal handwringing and irresoluteness redounded eventually to the advantage of the Bolsheviks and ensured their survival. It's not clear if Wilson fully understood his failure in the way that Lenin did. His last publication in 1924 suggests that he was still clueless.

Perhaps at the heart of Wilson's dilemma was his mistaken assumption that the October Revolution was simply a deepening of the liberal democratic revolution that opened with the deposal of Czar Nicholas. Nothing in his academic/professional background had prepared him to consider the difference between liberal democracy and social democracy—what the Bolsheviks were pursuing. His patronizing attitude about the "naïve" Russians may have also disarmed him to understand what was under way in their "backward" country. Unlike the Bolshevik leader, he knew nothing of the rich lessons Marx and Engels had distilled about the European Spring, lessons that Lenin nearly committed to memory. For Lenin, soviet democracy more faithfully represented the opinion of the toilers than the parliamentary arena of liberal democracy, especially when it came to the war question. The balance sheet that Marx drew on the Paris Commune of 1871, his *Civil War in France*, taught Lenin the significance of soviet democracy. No opinions of the toilers were more important for him than those of the workers and peasants in uniform. Obvious to everyone in that moment was that soviet governance, led by the Bolsheviks, and not liberal democracy led by the Provisional Government, extricated Russia from the slaughter.

Whether Wilson actually believed that the Bolsheviks at Brest-Litovsk were acting, as he put it in his Fourteen Points speech, in "the true spirit of modern democracy"—the only usage of the term in it (and virtually expunged in renditions today)—is probably unknowable. That he felt compelled, more importantly, to laud the Bolsheviks speaks volumes about how the world's toilers, the intended audience for his famous speech, viewed Russia's new rulers. Because the Bolsheviks took the initiative to begin the talks to end the bloodbath, they now occupied the moral high ground—setting the bar high. Wilson, until what the Bolsheviks did, was widely seen as the sole adult in the room. The speech was an attempt to retake that position. That meant having to call on all of Russia's "sister nations" to support "her own political development … under institutions of her own choosing"—in other words, soviet governance, the all-too-oft ignored point six. Little wonder that Lenin did all he could to publicize Wilson's speech. Compelled to echo in his speech the Bolshevik stance at Brest-Litovsk for no retributions for the warring parties, it's no surprise either that Berlin wanted Wilson to head up negotiations for a final peace based on his Fourteen Points.

Wilson's characterization of the Bolsheviks at Brest-Litovsk, in the "true spirit of modern democracy," is especially instructive. It's an instance of the unexpected finding of this real-time comparison—the image of the Russian Revolution amongst US rulers, one quite different from that which emerged during the Cold War. That, for example, the "forerunner of Citibank opened its Moscow branch 'nearly three weeks after the Bolshevik take over'" is only the most recent discovery for my revisionist claim.[12] A Wilson-era reading of the Soviet Union was more aware of the contrast between Bolshevik and Romanov rule than subsequent accounts. Soviet governance, effectively in place for about five or six years, was for many US elites as democratic, if not more so, as parliamentary democracy.[13] The process that Lenin led provided, in other words, more political space than had ever existed in Russia. Adam Tooze, no friend of the Bolsheviks, highlights that the first truly democratic elections in history, to the Constituent Assembly in November, 1917, took place under Bolshevik rule.[14] Western elites also knew that the Bolsheviks were more popular than what had existed before owing in large part to the fulfillment of their promise to extricate Russia from the slaughter of World War I. Wilson's point six in his Fourteen Points speech was an implicit recognition that they were indeed a breath of fresh air blowing through the "miasmatic gases of the past." The civil war's outcome was also a popular vote, with feet, on Bolshevik rule. The White Army, to whom Wilson had given support, lost to the Red Army mainly because its practices harkened back to Russia's monarchial past.

The only consistent opponent of Bolshevik rule in the Wilson administration had been his secretary of state Robert Lansing, but Lansing's objection that the Bolshevik call for the dictatorship of the proletariat meant the tyranny of the majority wasn't persuasive. In the context of a Europe where monarchial rule was still in place, the tyranny of the few, such a charge carried little weight. Wilson seems never to have embraced

Lansing's take on the Bolsheviks. Bullitt's sympathetic portrait of them—Colonel House's also—was probably more influential with him. Whatever the case, such contrasting views by Wilson's assistants likely explain his ambivalence about the Bolsheviks and why he could never fully commit to an effective US intervention for their overthrow. Bolshevik influence in America was, however, another matter; he didn't hesitate to try to stem the "poison."

Wilson seems to have been concerned more with the Bolshevik charge that he "represents a bourgeoisie which has made billions out of the war," thus enabling the American version of aristocracy, finance capital, as personified by J.P. Morgan. Arguably, the most consequential action of Wilson's presidency was the institution of the Federal Reserve Bank in 1913, the brainchild of Morgan and, not surprisingly, unaccountable to the electorate. Wilson's very last publication in 1924, a liberal/humanist/Christian critique of capitalism, shows that he was far from the confident Cold War warrior that typically assumed capitalism could do no wrong, especially after the collapse of the USSR and the other Stalinist regimes in Eastern Europe. The two recent mainstream accounts about these events I interrogate, specifically, Arthur Herman's *1917: Lenin, Wilson, and the Birth of the New World Disorder* ((2017) and Adam Tooze's *The Deluge* (2014), read the collapse, I contend, through the lens of the betrayal of the Bolshevik Revolution by the Stalinist counterrevolution—through hindsight. Given the horrors that later took place, the temptation is to assume that there must have been a smoking gun in place somewhere under Lenin's leadership to explain what unfolded. If it existed, it escaped the eyes of the key actors on the scene. Reading back into history from subsequent events, as real-time analysis shows, is always problematic. As for why the Stalinist counterrevolution occurred, that question is about to be addressed.

Max Weber accurately foresaw how Russia's monarchy would end: "Only in the tragic event of a *European* war would the autocracy finally be destroyed." Little did he think, however, that Nicholas's cousin, Germany's last monarch, would suffer a similar fate and usher in liberal democracy for the first time in Germany as it had been done in Russia. Lenin would not have been surprised at how Kaiser Wilhelm II's tenure ended, especially because he did all he could to make that happen—civil war in Germany, and what Weber the nationalist *bürgerlich* scholar so feared. Decisive in politics for Lenin as for his mentors was what took place outside the electoral/parliamentary arenas—on the streets, the barricades and the battlefields, the all-important lesson of the European Spring with which these four comparisons begin.

What are the lessons of these four comparisons for the advancement of the democratic quest? If the European Spring revealed, indisputably, that the democratic credentials of Marx and Engels were more deserved than those of Tocqueville—think, again, about his complicity in the slaughter of the Parisian proletariat in June 1848—what about the other liberal protagonists in this exposition? Mill, at least when it came to the U.S. Civil War, the decisive test for the nineteenth century, acquitted himself better than Tocqueville in 1848–1849. He had been on the right side of history unlike his French friend. But the Marx-Mill comparison shows that it's not enough to be well-intentioned when it comes to making democracy a reality. Putting in the requisite time and effort is the real test of commitment—what Mill for whatever reason was unwilling to do. On this essential criterion, Marx clearly outshone the other leading liberal light in the Atlantic world.

Weber, it might be objected, is an inappropriate candidate for the liberal cause. In the German context, however, he was indeed a liberal, desirous of at least a constitutional monarchy. His call for parliamentarization of the Reich in the midst of the Great War—yes, he vacillated—also qualifies him for membership in Germany's liberal milieu in that epoch. But in comparison to Lenin, especially in the lead up to and after Bolshevik ascent in the October Revolution, his democratic credentials were seriously wanting. Also important about Weber is that he remains a model for much of social science research, especially his fact/value distinction. But as this comparison reveals that distinction is problematic. It obstructed Weber's ability to see the reality in Russia, specifically, the appeal of the Bolsheviks—why he missed the most important political development in his lifetime. His self-admitted *bürgerlich* values meant that he could never, like Tocqueville—Mill too—and so unlike Lenin, envision "the mob" as the efficacious democrats. Weber, like Tocqueville and Mill, is another reminder that class and class orientation matter when it comes to the democratic quest.

What about Wilson, the author of the slogan, "making the world safe for democracy"? He too came up short in comparison to Lenin. In leading the fight to extricate Russia from the Great War, Lenin did more, objectively, to advance the democratic struggle in Russia than the liberals on the scene, the Cadets, and their cheerleader in the White House. Wilson tried unsuccessfully to keep Russia in the bloodbath. Soviet democracy, Lenin argued, represented mass opinion in Russia more faithfully than the parliamentary democracy promoted by the Provisional Government and that Wilson was banking on. Little wonder that the masses didn't shed any tears when the Constituent Assembly was sent packing in January 1918 at the initiative of Lenin. Even Wilson had to endorse in his Fourteen Points Speech Russia's right to the "independent determination of her own political development ... under institutions of her own choosing," that is, soviets. Whatever progressive content there was in the address was due to the high bar the Bolsheviks had raised with their peace proposals immediately made upon taking power, the massive first WikiLeaks dump shortly afterward, and the concessions they were willing to publicly make at the negotiating table in Brest-Litovsk. If the opponents of Lenin think there were better alternatives to Bolshevik hegemony for ending the slaughter, in real-time, they should make that case. Otherwise, their complaints are merely hindsight.

Maybe the most significant lesson of this inquiry is how the revolutionary process can push liberals to the left, toward the democratic cause. This was certainly true in the case of Tocqueville and Weber. Both were opponents of republican government and electoral reform until the toilers took to the streets and successfully confined to the proverbial dustbin of history the less than democratic constitutional monarchial regimes they supported. Both saw the light, in other words, because they felt the heat of the masses in the streets. Tocqueville instructively admitted as much in his support for the right to work provision in the draft constitution in 1848. Liberal democracy wasn't the default position of either Tocqueville or Weber but it was preferable to the tyranny of the majority or what Marx, Engels and Lenin called the "dictatorship of the proletariat." Mill could appear to be more enlightened because he was in support of a social revolution abroad, the fight to overthrow the slavocracy. It burnished his liberal image unlike anything before. But at home he could be as conservative as Tocqueville and Weber, particularly when it came to electoral reform. How he would have responded to an English version of France's February 1848 Revolution or Germany's November 1918 Revolution can only be speculated on. Indisputably, he acted as never before in July 1866, to make sure that he would not have to face such a scenario. As for Wilson, he's best known for a progressive international political perspective, specifically, the right of national self-determination, a basic democratic right. But that was in response to the Bolsheviks who first raised the demand immediately upon taking power in the October Revolution. His Fourteen

Points speech, the full version and not the usually abridged one, was an effort to retake the moral high ground away from the Bolsheviks. At home, Wilson, too, could be not only conservative but also reactionary. In sum, what Marx, Engels and Lenin stood for and/or promoted, the toilers in the streets, on the barricades or on the battlefields, is what compelled Tocqueville, Mill, Weber and Wilson to take more progressive democratic postures—however brief and contradictory. That lesson continues to have currency.

Twenty years ago, I wrote, again, that no two individuals did more to advance the democratic quest in the nineteenth century than Marx and Engels. I can now update the claim. No three individuals did more than Marx, Engels *and* Lenin—who stood on their shoulders—to advance the process in not only that century but also the first two decades of the twentieth, more than what any of the four most outstanding representatives of the different varieties of liberalism ever did. That a bloody counterrevolution overthrew Lenin's project within a decade of his death no more impugns its achievements than the counterrevolutions that overthrew the two prior breakthroughs—the two-and-a-half-month-long Paris Commune in 1871 and the decade-long experiment with Radical Reconstruction in the U.S. All were episodic ebbs and flows and glimpses into the future of the millennial-old democratic quest.

Two Consequential Moments in Twentieth-Century Politics

In route to the Paris peace talks in December 1919, Wilson, to repeat, shared with the press corps on board the *USS George Washington* his concerns about the parties with whom he would be negotiating. "'The only way I can explain susceptibility of the people of Europe to the poison of bolshevism, is that the Governments have been run for wrong purposes, and I am convinced that if this peace is not made on the highest principles of justice it will be swept away by the peoples of the world in less than a generation'."[15] Seldom in history have forebodings been so consequentially and tragically confirmed. Also revealed—and unacknowledged—is how much the Bolsheviks were on Wilson's brain when he went to Paris; his project, he hoped, would be a way to obviate the siren call of their appeal.

Lenin, too, was prescient. He charged in early 1917 that Wilson was making preparations for "a *second* great imperialist war." But that claim, I argue, was a probabilistic one that only the class struggle could decide if accurate. More immediately verifiable were his real-time claims about the negotiations Wilson was leading to end the Great War that Lenin disparaged even before the signing of the Treaty of Versailles. Nothing good could come of the talks given his basic premise about the predatory character of advanced capitalism. Imperialism precluded the making of a "democratic peace" based on "the highest principles of peace" amongst the parties at Paris, the perpetrators of the carnage. Had he known what Wilson told the press conference, that the regimes that made the war had "been run for wrong purposes," to serve the pecuniary interests of their capitalist classes, and exactly why the Bolsheviks could get a hearing from the victims of their venality, Lenin would have agreed. When the terms of the Treaty became public, he felt vindicated for having dismissed the negotiations. Predatory capitalists could only agree to a predatory peace and not a democratic peace—explaining why the Treaty would indeed be "swept away by the peoples of the world in less than a generation." In the end, Wilson, as Lenin accused, did aid and abet—inadvertently perhaps—the "*second* great imperialist war." That one of the participants in the Paris negotiations, John Maynard Keynes, also disparaged the outcome for similar reasons was perfect ammunition for Lenin.

Wilson left Paris thinking that something meaningful was in place, an agreement to ensure that there would never be another Great War. Why he thought so has been the subject of much discussion and debate that can't be judged here. The League of Nations, for certain, proved to be not up to the task. For whatever reasons, Wilson was unable to sell his project to both the U.S. public and its ruling class. Whether Washington's presence in the League would have made it more effective is too the subject of much speculation.[16]

Three factors are commonly agreed to have given birth to World War II—the problematic nature of the Treaty of Versailles, the rise of fascism and the Great Depression. But all too often ignored in that literature is Lenin's claim: again, only, if the working class overthrew their predatory ruling classes and took power could war be avoided. That goal, Lenin also claimed, depended on proletarian internationalism. If Wilson's internationalist project failed miserably, what about Lenin's alternative? Was it ever a viable option? In anticipation of the answer, know that the Communist International effectively ceased to exist by at least 1935, four years before the outbreak of World War II. In the middle of the war, in 1943, Stalin unceremoniously pulled the plug on it. To understand why, it's necessary to step back into history.

Owing to the intense research he was doing, including a reading knowledge of Russian, Marx concluded in 1882—in the "Preface" to the second Russian edition of the *Communist Manifesto*—that "Russia forms the vanguard of revolutionary action in Europe." Not advanced capitalist England, in other words—and contrary to what text book Marxism incessantly claims—but in overwhelmingly peasant and economically underdeveloped Russia is now where Marx and Engels set their sights on for the outbreak of Europe's socialist revolution. The opening of the social revolution in Russia, both now held, would spread westward, leading to "*radical change throughout Europe*." And in uncanny anticipation of 1917–1918, the "overthrow of Tsarist Russia … is … one of the first conditions of the German proletariat's ultimate triumph." When Marx party members inquired, also in 1882, about reestablishing a new international, Engels advised: "wait for this ["in Russia where the avant-garde of the revolution will be going into battle"] and its inevitable repercussions on Germany, and then the moment will also have come for a big manifesto and the establishment of an *official*, formal International, which can, however, no longer be a propaganda association but simply an association for action."[17] The fact that the Socialist or Second International, founded in 1900, wasn't the product of a revolution in Russia as Engels had advised may explain why it failed the test of proletarian internationalism when starkly posed in August 1914.

Engels's last pronouncement on Russia, about six months before his death in 1895, speculated on the likelihood of a revolution there. If it does happen, he opined, it would "give the labour movement of the West fresh impetus … hastening the victory of the modern industrial proletariat, without which present-day Russia can never achieve a socialist transformation."[18] "*Without*," and unequivocally, a proletarian revolution in the west Russia could "never achieve a socialist transformation." To their peril were those who thought otherwise. Engels, again, was remarkably and deadly prescient.

Ten years later, when 1905 erupted, Lenin reiterated, without necessarily knowing it—making even more significant what he said—Engels's point: "the Russian revolution can achieve victory by its own efforts, but it cannot possibly hold and consolidate its gains by its own strength. It cannot do this unless there is a socialist revolution in the West. Without this condition restoration is inevitable … Our democratic republic has no other reserve than the socialist proletariat in the West."[19] "Restoration," or the overthrow of the revolution, was "inevitable" without the proletariat in the west taking power—again, pathetically prophetic. Think Putin's Russia. Little wonder, then, why Lenin staked so much on the German revolution, the most likely place in the west where the working class could duplicate what their cohorts in Russia had done in October 1917. Three times the German proletariat tried doing so, suggesting that proletarian revolution in Germany was not a pipe dream on Lenin's part.

Missing again in Germany, however, was what existed in Russia—a party of the caliber that Lenin headed. The assassination of Luxemburg and Liebknecht in January 1919 marked the end, in hindsight, of Germany's first attempt at a socialist revolution. German fascism, a few years away, was bred on the ashes of the other two missed opportunities. Hitler's name for his party, the National Socialist German Workers Party, Nazis for short, testified to the depths of pro-socialist sentiment amongst Germany's broader population. Demoralized after three failures, many of them, especially middle-class layers, became easy prey for anything that paraded as socialism, with all the horrific consequences.

The failure of the Bolshevik example to spread westward enabled a conservative turn in Russia, a tendency to look inward for salvation, one of the factors Lenin offered in his final months of political activity to explain what he increasingly realized were problems with the revolution. Two other factors were also determinant in his opinion: the toll the civil war had taken—in which the Wilson administration had been complicit—and the backwardness of the country. A socialist Germany with a much more advanced economy could have provided essential assistance to overcome that legacy. Never did Lenin employ "socialist" to describe what was in place in Russia. Rather, as he put it in his final formulation, December 1922, in place was a "worker's state with bureaucratic distortions." The Soviet Union was, at best, a provisional model until "the victory of the proletarian revolution in at least one of the advanced countries."[20] About a recently drafted blueprint for a model communist party, it was "too Russian," wrote Lenin, and aspiring revolutionaries elsewhere "cannot be content in hanging it in a corner like an icon and praying to it."[21] Aware of what was developing, Lenin, from his sickbed in 1922–1923, mounted his last and ultimately unsuccessful fight against the increasing bureaucratization of the revolution led by Joseph Stalin whose removal from the post of secretary-general of the Bolshevik party Lenin had called for in his so-called Last Testament.[22] His final incapacitating stroke in March 1923 ended that hope.

Within half a decade of Lenin's death in 1924, it was obvious to most Russians that the process he saw under way had now calcified into a bureaucratically controlled state. Trotsky, increasingly isolated by Stalin and eventually exiled, offered an explanation, drawing on the kernels of wisdom Lenin had left. *The Revolution Betrayed*, his 1936 book, refuted Stalin's pronouncement that year that socialism had been realized in the Soviet Union. By then Stalin had had jailed or murdered virtually every other leading Bolshevik, as well as having mummified and iconized Lenin. Trotsky's thesis was that Stalinism, with all its deadly consequences, con-stituted a counterrevolution in which the bureaucracy usurped political power that had momentarily been in the hands of Russia's workers and peasants after October 1917. The dictatorship of the proletariat was replaced with the dictatorship of the bureaucracy with Stalin at its head, the last man standing. Determinant again were the three factors Lenin offered. For a contemporary analogy, consider Egypt's "Arab Spring," prematurely ended by a new military dictatorship.

Stalin had consolidated his rule in the Soviet Union by 1928. That was when the largest number of aspiring revolutionaries elsewhere, mostly fledgling parties, affiliated with the Comintern or Third International based in Moscow. That embrace meant, as Trotsky put it, they were "doomed to degeneration." Founded in 1919, the international having been until 1924 a venue for democratic discussion and debate became a rubber-stamp machine for Stalin's political twists and turns. Rather than "Marxism," or "Marxism-Leninism" as they assumed, the new affiliates actually imbibed Stalinism in one form or another with all the deadly con-sequences. Most consequential were the polices of the so-called Third Turn in 1928 which directed affiliates to denounce social democrats as "social fascists," thus preventing alliances with them to stem the tide of fascism. The outcome in Germany was truly disastrous, what allowed Hitler's party, which garnered less than a majority of the popular vote, to come into office. Except for the few nuclei that traced their origins to the Bolsheviks through Trotsky or before Stalin's counterrevolution, no other current in the world that claimed to be "Marxist" escaped the degenerat-ing influence of Stalinism.

The Bolsheviks at their Tenth Congress in 1921 made a fateful decision owing to the still precarious situation the revolution faced in the immedi-ate wake of the brutally debilitating civil war. The party overwhelmingly voted to temporarily suspend the right to form factions, giving more weight to centralism in the democratic centralist formula that the party had long operated under. Factions had allowed for organized challenges to the party leadership, an essential requirement for the "democratic" in the democratic centralist formula. The vast majority of the members feared that a factional fight would be an existential threat to the party and, thus, the revolution. Fifteen years later, with the advantage of hindsight, Trotsky acknowledged that the organizational means for the subsequent Stalinist counterrevolution had its origins in that decision. He too had voted for it and continued, despite hindsight, to defend the decision given the circumstances under which it was made: "one thing is absolutely clear: the banning of factions brought the heroic history of Bolshevism to an end and made way for its bureaucratic degeneration." The damage went beyond the USSR; the new norm was extended in 1923 to the new affiliates of Comintern, what Trotsky meant when he said in 1935 that they were "doomed to degeneration before they had time to grow and develop." When the international, by then moribund, no longer served as a pawn in Stalin's diplomatic maneuvers, he unceremoniously pulled the plug on it in 1943—a gesture of fealty to his new allies, Churchill and Roosevelt—three years after one of his many assassins had put an ice pick into Trotsky's brain.

All of the foregoing history suggests that historical contingency best explains the Stalinist outcome of the Russian Revolution. Rather than being foreordained owing to some kind of original sin or authoritarian flaw in Lenin's make-up, as opponents of the project usually claim, fortuitous factors are the likely reason.[23] Nothing in the history of either the original Marx-Engels project or that of Lenin would have predicted such an outcome. None of the real-time actors—except for one, maybe (and to be discussed below)—could see what hindsight wisdom claims to have discerned. Given the horrible consequences of the counterrevolution, which continue to resonate, the desire to find the proverbial smoking gun to indict the entire project is understandable.

If the rise of fascism was one of the three key factors in the making of World War II, then the crimes of Stalinism exacted a greater toll on humanity than usually recognized. That is especially true if looked at from a Leninist perspective. Lenin, to repeat, argued that only if the working class took political power could war be avoided. Fascism's success in Germany was the other side of the coin of working-class failure, more specifically, of proletarian internationalism. If the bloodletting of World War II was due not just to the predatory character of the Treaty of Versailles but to the triumph of fascism in Germany, then the utterly bankrupt policies of Stalin's Comintern were deeply implicated in the carnage. His "Third Turn" policy was also informed by the all so criminal claim that if the fascists came to power in Germany, they would make things so bad that the German public would welcome the communists as a replacement. It's hard to fathom—maybe the problem with hindsight—how such insane thinking could actually have been promoted by Moscow; sadly, it was.

Did proletarian internationalism perform any better than liberal internationalism when it came to World War II? An answer is now possible. Comintern had ceased to be the organization that Lenin once led. Whether the original organization would have been more successful than the League of Nations in preventing World War II is unknowable. What can confidently be said is that the policies of the Stalinized Comintern were an unmistakable obstacle to the working-class alliance needed to stop the Nazis from coming into office. The League of Nations, on the other hand, Wilson's solution for preventing wars, operated as it was designed—admittedly without the participation of Washington—in the lead-up to World War II. Proletarian internationalism in the embodiment of the Comintern, Lenin's alternative, had long ceased to operate as intended. The last congress organized on the basis of democratic debate and discussion was in 1928. Contrary to the original norm of annual congresses, the next one took place in 1935; by then totally under the thumb of Moscow. Most telling about Comintern is that only in the last few years has the history of its healthiest period, from 1919 to 1924, been fully recovered.[24] If the historically unprecedented carnage of World War II was due to the failure to heed Lenin's advice about the necessity of working-class ascent, then the Stalinist counterrevolution was as guilty of the crime as capitalist imperialism. Not the first betrayal of proletarian internationalism. The vote for war credits for the Guns of August of 1914 by the Socialist International's flagship German affiliate is forever a reminder. The second betrayal came with a price at least twice as costly to humanity; the toilers in the Middle East—think the national boundaries there and their consequences—continue to pay for both wars.

Yet it is sobering to contemplate that with all of the horrors of World War I, humanity could have paid an even dearer price. Only three decades later, nuclear weapons became a reality. Does anyone believe that the capitalist perpetrators of the bloodbath, driven, again, by greed, would have refrained from using them had they been in their arsenals?

Neither Lenin nor Wilson lived long enough to see the build up to and commencement of World War II, denying posterity a real-time comparison of their reading and responses to both events. Two figures who played key roles in the conclusion of the Great War did see the commencement of World War II—Trotsky and Keynes. A real-time comparison of them as is done in the four cases in this book might prove just as rewarding. Though both were aware of and commented on one another in the interwar period, a comparison may be limited in terms of issues to look at. Beyond their varying opinions on the Treaty of Versailles, a cursory reading of Keynes's collected writings via its detailed index suggests that that may be the sole issue upon which a meaningful comparison could be made. There is virtually little in Keynes's writings, for example, on the rise of fascism, one of the crucial interwar issues and to which Trotsky devoted considerable attention in words and actions.[25] That Keynes said so little about fascism might in itself be telling. Did he not perceive it to be the threat that Trotsky thought it was? If not, why? Perhaps combining Keynes with some other key figure on the liberal side of the class divide may be necessary. The influential liberal commentator Walter Lippmann? There may be others I'm unaware of who could also qualify.

One issue that in theory could make for an interesting comparison was the coming of the Great Depression and its role in the origins of World War II. Trotsky certainly had a lot to say about the course of world capitalism; his report to the Third Congress of Comintern in 1921 remarkably anticipated in many ways the crisis.[26] Keynes, a leading bourgeois liberal economist may also have been prescient but, again, a cursory reading of his collected writings via its index isn't revealing. A deep read into his writings is probably necessary.

Another issue could focus on the rise of Stalinism. This too would probably require some combination of leading liberal thinkers in the interwar period. Familiarity with some of them suggests that the Soviet Union was as perplexing as it had been for Wilson. Trotsky, by the way, is the only real-time protagonist in this story who could legitimately claim to say "I told you so" about the Stalinist outcome of the Russian Revolution—at first blush. It was he who initiated, in 1904, the Lenin-as-ogre accusation, specifically, Lenin the "Jacobin."[27] The more than decade-long enmity between the two had roots in the charge. Indeed, some of Lenin's modern-day enemies have tried to employ Trotsky to make their case. But the more informed ones are reluctant to do so exactly because of the reconciliation between the two communists in April 1917. Until his assassination in

1940, Trotsky continued to be a loyal defender of Lenin's project. About his original opposition to Lenin, "its profound erroneousness had been long ago demonstrated both in theory and practice," he wrote in his final months—making it difficult, then, for those to employ Trotsky in their Lenin-bashing campaign.[28]

Because World War II looms so large in modern history, understanding the lead-up to it would benefit from the kind of comparative real-time analysis as done in the four cases in this book—if possible. Trotsky, arguably, the next most able student of Marx and Engels after Lenin, would easily qualify as the figure for the Marxist side of the comparison. Some combination of liberal figures would most likely be necessary to make for a rewarding inquiry—a future research project, for someone.

If the Bolshevik Revolution impacted the twentieth century like no other event, the overturn that took place in Havana on January 1, 1959, is arguably its second edition—continuing to resonate into the twentieth-first century. Trotsky's point that Comintern "doomed to generation" all of the post-October 1917 revolutionary projects that, first, had not originated before Stalin's usurpation of power nor, second, benefitted from his efforts to forge an alternative to Moscow's agenda is all too soberly accurate. But Cuba, I claim, is the exception to the rule. It is the only revolution, independent of both developments, that escaped Moscow's deadly embrace. Precisely for that reason has it been so difficult for Washington to make sense of what transpires on the island—not unlike for Wilson regarding the Bolsheviks. US policy makers assumed that its various modus vivendi with Moscow that began in World War II, which combined a mix of carrots and sticks, would also work for Cuba. Never, however, in the annals of world politics has a major power—the most powerful for all that time—been so unable to dictate to a small power sitting virtually on its doorstep, six decades and counting. Historical contingency provides the best explanation.

There was indeed a Moscow affiliate in Cuba that Trotsky, who spent his final years in Mexico, likely knew about. But it, unlike any other "fraternal party" in Latin America, was distinguished by actually having occupied ministerial posts in a capitalist government—in fulfillment of Comintern's "popular front" policy—of none other than that of the U.S.-backed Fulgencio Batista, the dictator that Fidel Castro's revolutionary movement overthrew in 1959. Such class collaborationist policies of Moscow's Havana affiliate made it suspect in the eyes of radicalizing youth like Castro—why he never became a member. He organized, rather, in

1952 an alternative to the Stalinists, what later became his July 26th Movement. Moscow's sycophants actually denounced his bold attack on the Moncada army barracks in 1953—what established Castro's unrivalled revolutionary credentials for the first time.[29] Only when Castro's current was winning the armed struggle did the Stalinists conclude that it was time, in 1958, to get on his bandwagon. A merger between the two currents and a third one resulted in the Cuban Communist Party in 1965. But it was clear in fact and appearance that the Castro current was the dominant one in the marriage.

Despite the Stalinist baggage that came with the union—including the one with the Soviet Union—it wasn't a fatal attraction as was so often the case elsewhere. Radicalizing post-World War II youth were understandably attracted to what posed as the only revolutionary alternative to Washington, namely, "communism"; I include myself amongst that milieu. Our cohorts in Cuba were, luckily, more informed about the "communists," having seen them, first-hand, in bed with the local agents of US imperialism. Fortuitously, in other words, the Cuban revolution, headed by Fidel Castro, was able to resist the siren call of Stalinism and its deathly embrace unlike almost anywhere else exactly because of the realization of the popular front in Cuba. Castro came close to saying so in a major speech in 2005 in which he posed the question why Cuba's socialist revolution had not succumbed like Russia's.[30] His last request, as his brother Raúl read to the massive outpouring celebrating the leader's life shortly after he died in 2016, was quintessential Fidel. "After his death," he wanted that "his name and likeness never be used to designate institutions, plazas, parks, avenues, streets, or other public spaces, nor monuments, busts, statues, and other such tributes be erected." To the very end, Castro sought to make clear—tormenting once again his enemies who had boilerplate ready about the preparations for the latest Stalinist cult of personality—that what had taken place in Cuba was different from all that too often had been done elsewhere in the name of Marxism, Marxism-Leninism or some similar label. The frustration of his class enemies was palpable. One measure of the future course of the Cuban Revolution may be its fealty to Fidel's last wish.

The difficulty Washington has had in dealing with the Cuban revolution, due to its singularity, as I argue, was evident from the very beginning.[31] The Cold War templates Washington employed simply didn't work, reminiscent, again, of Wilson's conundrum with the Bolsheviks. A 1964 state department memo speculated on whether the then Johnson administration could reach the kind of accommodation with Havana as it had done with Moscow, some variant of "peaceful coexistence" or "détente." Even if it could, there was a deeper problem, the authors admitted. It lied "in the impact the very existence of [Castro's] regime has upon the leftist movement in many Latin American countries ... The simple fact is that Castro represents a successful defiance of the U.S., a negation of our whole hemispheric policy of almost a century and a half ... As long as Castro endures, Communists in other Latin American countries can, to use Stalin's words, 'struggle with good heard.'"[32] Washington had, to put it metaphorically, a Don Corleone problem; it was being dissed in its own backyard. Therein, I contend, is the axis around which the six-decade old bipartisan policy of Washington toward Havana orbits. Echoes of the discussions amongst Wilson and his operatives about the "poison" of Bolshevism easily come to mind. Therefore, a real-time comparative analysis of Castro's readings and actions vis-à-vis some combination of key actors in the Eisenhower and Kennedy administrations could make for a fascinating story, to see if indeed it was in any way a replay of the Wilson-Lenin diplomatic dance, another opportunity to test competing Marxist and liberal theoretical/political perspectives. It would also be interesting to see if there was any institutional memory at the state department about Wilson's Bolshevik dilemma and whether it would have made a difference. Another, therefore, possible research project. The Lenin-Wilson contest is also unlikely known in Havana. Arguably, the greatest crime of Stalinism was its falsification of the real Lenin. Aspirant and would-be revolutionaries around the world had to improvise and reinvent the revolutionary diplomatic wheel. Imagine if Fidel Castro had known about Lenin's "cheeky diplomacy" vis-à-vis Wilson and how much fun he would have had in employing it—much to the consternation of Washington and Wall Street.

At the beginning of the second year of the Donald Trump administration, Cuba is back in the cross hairs of Washington after what seemed to have been a brief respite under the Obama administration. But a resort to business as usual for Washington when it comes to Cuba shouldn't be surprising. Only with the Stalinist counterrevolution in Russia could US rulers feel confident they could engage Moscow in a nakedly quid pro quo dance that has marked their relations ever since World War II. Exactly because Fidel Castro's project is still in place, despite all the pressures on it to capitulate to its neighbor to the north, has Washington continued to see the need for its dismantlement in whatever form that might take—the Obama let's-play-nice version or perhaps now the Trump let's-play-hardball variant. As Castro—drawing on the kinds of Marxist lessons distilled here—explained in 1988: "Even if the day were to come when relations between socialist Cuba and the empire improve formally, that would not stop the empire from trying to crush the Cuban revolution ... that as long as the empire exists we will never be able to lower our guard." Given the historic crisis of global capitalism today—to be discussed shortly—Washington and Wall Street have even greater reason to fear the Cuban example. Hence, the claim here that the Cuban revolution continues to weigh as much on world politics as what Lenin initiated a little over a century ago.

To put what Fidel Castro led in perspective, and what this book traces, the first attempt of the working class to take power, Paris, June 1848, failed. The second, the Paris Commune in 1871, did succeed but lasted less than three months. The third, Bolshevik ascent, a qualitative advance, lasted, however, less than a decade, if that. Cuba's toilers, its working class specifically, have been in power for six decades. But as Lenin would have certainly understood, a socialist revolution in an economically underdeveloped country, Cuba's reality, can only be guaranteed if it is emulated by the toilers in more advanced settings. Thus, the need to consider the present moment.

THE CURRENT SITUATION AND LESSONS FROM THE PAST

When I first encountered the "Impeach Bush" movement in 2007, I responded: "if we don't impeach the system that gave us Bush, we'll have someone in the White House who'll make us long for Bush." No crystal ball informed my retort; only the kinds of lessons distilled from the four comparisons presented in this book.

Given all the talk in mainstream circles today about how democracy can be undermined, it is worth recalling the ignominious end to the Second Republic in France and its replacement with what Marx called "a grotesque mediocrity." As with all attempts to draw lessons from history, caution is required. It's indeed tempting to think about the present occupant of the White House in the indelible language Marx employed to describe Louis-Bonaparte. That Trump, also, is the first US president, as far as I can tell, to have mounted a campaign against "socialism" also tempts historical parallel-making.[33] Tocqueville, after all, enabled Bonaparte's coup d'état because of his own fear of "socialism." The provisional government that was overthrown was in fact the first iteration anywhere of what most of the chatter about "socialism" in the U.S. is really about, social democracy.

To claim, as some strident voices on the left do, that the inauguration of the Donald Trump administration in January 2017 constituted a similar kind of coup, the abortion of liberal democracy, is a dangerous but, fortunately, not yet fatal error. The more measured voices amongst this milieu allege that authoritarianism, and its more virulent fascist variety is now knocking at the door. To subscribe to such thinking is to risk prophecy self-fulfillment—why dangerous. The only actual similarity to that earlier moment was the attitude of most mainstream liberals in the lead-up to November 2016. Like Tocqueville, they couldn't countenance a social democrat, Bernie Sanders specifically, in the White House; think the editorial pages of the *New York Times*. They opted, rather, for a seriously flawed candidate, Hillary Clinton, risking, therefore, a Trump administration. Tocqueville, too, fearful of "socialism," was willing to take his chances with the "grotesque mediocrity." He was at least honest about his calculations.

Liberal democracy in 2016 in the U.S. was never threatened owing to the history and staying power of the prior democratic conquests on its terrain—liberal apocalyptic scenarios about a Trump presidency notwithstanding. Nevertheless, fear of the "deplorables," the "mob" for Tocqueville, is what animates "Trump derangement disorder" amongst much of liberal America. Rather than indict capitalism, which put Trump in the White House, liberal ire targets the minority of working-class workers who voted for a blatantly sexist and xenophobic capitalist candidate who they thought might ensure their jobs, or help pay their mortgages. They have equal disdain for the abstainers who chose none of the above, an even larger pool of workers—also victims of capitalism. Blaming the victims rather than the system that put Trump in the White House registers how much mainstream liberalism, especially the meritocracy, has a stake in, or thinks it does, in capitalism. Their assumption that voting is the end-all and be-all of politics—what I call "voting fetishism" (inspired by Marx's and Engels's "parliamentary cretinism")—and, thus, their contempt for the abstainers and "deplorables," makes them even more complicit in sustaining the system that produced a Trump presidency and all that it represents beyond just Trump. They consciously obscure the key lesson of history that only in the streets, on the barricades and the battlefields is where the oppressed advance themselves—what Tocqueville and Weber consciously denied and the former actively opposed. Contrary to what the mantra of the Occupy Wall Street movement suggested, the "one percent"—more accurately, the one-tenth of the one percent—is able to be efficacious precisely because of the assistance rendered by the approximately twenty percentile or more of the population right below it on the social ladder, particularly the meritocracy.

Most problematic and dangerous is the inclination of the meritocracy to think that a small group of well-intentioned and smart cohorts like themselves can defend liberal democracy without mobilizing the masses in their immense majority. Tocqueville and his comrades thought the same and, hence, were gobsmacked when the "grotesque mediocrity" outsmarted them. Especially dangerous, as was also the case with Tocqueville, is the assumption that placing limits on liberal democracy is the way to protect it, in the name of advancing "the resistance" to Trump. Applauding the FBI, whose headquarters is still proudly called The J. Edgar Hoover Building, or welcoming limits on free speech and similar other antidemocratic practices will redound to the disadvantage of those who most need political space, the oppressed. Though Tocqueville and his friends paid for their miscalculations with only a few nights in jail, the toilers in France were saddled with a Bonapartist dictatorship, with all the costs that came with it, for two decades.

Tocqueville in many ways was the prototype for all the other liberals in this study; thus, the importance of his all so trenchant point about socialism—again, as he understood it—and the course of human history. When it comes to social organization, that is, nothing is set in stone. The need to question the assumption that capitalist property relations were humanity's last word in how it organizes itself was central, obviously, to Marx's and Engels's project. In the context of the still unfolding global economic crisis, both the desirability and viability of capitalism are being questioned in ways not seen since the Great Depression in the 1930s. It is not a question if there will be another global capitalist crisis, but only when. A major article in today's *New York Times*, as this is being written, is about youth in Britain with the title, "Growing Up Lean and Giving Up on Capitalism." The digital copy headline is "Austerity, That's What I Know': The Making of a Young U.K. Socialist."[34] There should be no doubt that the capitalist crisis will breed social explosions. Uncertain is whether a leadership will be in place to channel all the anger that will come with it toward the only real solution, working-class ascent to power. Think the tragedy of Germany beginning in 1918.

Tocqueville was also prescient about revolutionary prospects in America. Three decades before the Civil War and Radical Reconstruction, he wrote in volume two of his *Democracy*: "If ever America undergoes great revolutions, they will be brought about by the presence of the black race on the soil of the United States; that is to say, they will owe their origin, not to the equality, but to the inequality of condition." Isn't "inequality of condition" at the heart of politics today in the U.S., what the Trump/Sanders and now the Alexandra Ocasio Cortez Democratic Socialist of America phenomena have tapped into? And isn't the likelihood of working-class realization of that reality, in all its skin colors and other identities, an even more frightening prospect for the ruling class and its "literary representatives," as Marx called them, today's punditocracy? Not surprising the need for all of them, both on the left and right, to play the identitarian card in order to head off proletarian consciousness. Owing to their unique place in America's system or class/race stratification, both historically and currently—think the "criminal justice" system—"the black race," or better, "workers in black skin," as Marx called them, will disproportionately be in the vanguard of the coming socialist revolution in the U.S.

That Tocqueville could be as perceptive as the Marx-Engels team revealed the key difference between the two sides. Politics is more than "just the facts ma'am." Smart people can agree, as in the case of all three, that revolutionary conditions exist and that a socialist alternative may be on the agenda. Politics is about what to do next, what to do with those facts. Tocqueville's class identification and orientation prevented him from doing what Marx, Engels and Lenin did. They, unlike him, had broken with their class origins and committed, as African revolutionary Amilcal Cabral once put it, "class suicide." Tocqueville, Mill, Weber and Wilson all identified in one way or another with the ruling elites of their nation states, the social unit they took as fundamental. All, for whatever reason, were unwilling to do what Marx, Engels and Lenin had done, to break with their class origins and adopt world humanity as their home and unit of analysis. Fear of the masses as Tocqueville was so transparent about—"I despise and fear mobs … I hate demagoguery, the disordered action of the masses, their violent and unenlightened intervention in public affairs"— explains what was and remains central to liberal politics, be it the social democratic, conservative, or social welfare variety. In the era, again, of near universal suffrage, Tocqueville's modern descendants cannot be so transparent.

In politics, then—the real world of politics—it is not just about the facts but in the end which side one takes in the class struggle, the willingness to embrace the toilers with every fiber of one's being. It means believing what Marx and Engels had concluded by 1844—that the proletariat "cannot emancipate itself without abolishing the conditions of its own life … without abolishing all the inhuman conditions of life of society today which are summed up in its own situation." Tocqueville and Weber, both known for being acute observers of social reality, were unapologetic about whose side they were on in the class struggle. And as the comparison with Mill reveals, it may mean having, if necessary, the courage to break with one's privileged class in order to realize that vision. Class orientation *and* political character, in other words, may be the key lessons to be distilled from these four comparisons.

All seven of the protagonists in this study came from privileged backgrounds of one kind or another. Do any of their examples offer an answer to the question, who is likely from such backgrounds to make the break to embrace the cause of the proletariat? After all, as the *Manifesto* argues, it is easier for those who have nothing to lose to reach and *act* on revolutionary conclusions.

Of the seven, Engels was the most privileged, at least materially. And therein may be the explanation for his decision to take the side of the oppressed. Had his family been some combination of wealth, on one hand, and intelligentsia origin on the other, such as Marx's, Mill's and Weber's families, perhaps he wouldn't have taken a revolutionary route. That he "married down," to an ardent working-class Irish nationalist was no doubt significant. Weber may have offered an explanation for Engels's trajectory. In a later introduction to his 1904 *Protestant Ethic and the Spirit of Capitalism*, he wrote that "the tendency which has existed everywhere and all times being quite strong in Germany today, for middle-class fortunes to be absorbed into the nobility, was necessarily checked by the Puritan antipathy to the feudal way of life, is evident."[35] Engels, in other words, was able to avoid seduction "into the nobility," despite his family's capitalist "fortunes," precisely because its Pietist Protestant origins inoculated him—three-quarters of a century earlier—from being enticed by what the feudal elite had to offer. His marriage choices, to first Lydia Burns and then later to her sister Mary after Lydia's death, testified to and reinforced the class choices Engels had earlier made.

What about Marx? He was on the road to upward mobility with his PhD in 1841, especially after having married a year later into the German aristocracy. Like Engels, he consciously chose to break with his expected class trajectory, clearly a minority amongst his cohorts. Burning bridges to the world for which he was being groomed forever earned him the respect and admiration of the organic proletariat with whom he collaborated—and why all attempts by rivals to class bait him never worked. In Lenin's case, his chances for upward mobility in increasingly unstable Czarist Russia—even if he had wanted to pursue that route—were circumscribed by his older brother's unsuccessful attempt on the life of Alexander II. That option, then, was probably never a viable one for him. He didn't, in other words, like so many of his cohorts, have much to lose, relatively speaking, in taking the revolutionary road. This pool of candidates is, no doubt, too small to answer the intriguing and all-important question about who of the more privileged layers of society decide to side with the oppressed. Were it to expand to include Trotsky, Fidel Castro and Che Guevara, it might make for a more fruitful inquiry into the question. But that's beyond what this project has set out to accomplish. Luckily, in the history of the quest for human emancipation, owing exactly to what capitalism has bequeathed, the oppressed, the working class specifically, are less in need of privileged layers of society for leadership. Lenin once said that the role of the intelligentsia in the revolutionary project is to make itself expendable. That's far easier today than when he made the point or when a group of confident class-conscious workers a half-century earlier directed Marx and Engels to write the *Manifesto*.

This in no way exhausts what I have to say about the current moment. Elsewhere I've opined.[36] What I pretend to do here is to employ the essential lessons of the four comparisons to make some sense of the historically unprecedented period in which we live and, more importantly, to know how to respond. Exactly because there is no precedent for today, caution is required about reading the past to understand the present. But if there is one historical constant, it is that the democratic quest can only be advanced—for those who truly want to do so—*outside* the electoral/parliamentary arenas by "the mob" that Tocqueville so feared—yes, including the "deplorables." For the impeach Trump crowd, and specifically those amongst them who, unlike Tocqueville, don't fear "the mob," I ask them to consider a variant of what I once said to an "Impeach Bush' activist: if you don't impeach the system that gave us Trump, someone will arrive in the White House who'll make Trump pale in comparison."

While US elites, especially their meritocratic mouthpieces, are fearful of the working class, owing to their awareness that there aren't any immediate and painless solutions to the capitalist crisis, it is not an existential fear—at least not yet. Democratic Party lesser/evil electoralism continues to ensure a docile labor movement. The teachers' strikes, as I write this, is the lone exception. The most exemplary of them, instructively, has taken place in West Virginia, a "red state." In the "blue states," the union movement and its misleadership remain pawns of the Democratic Party. Once the toilers do go into real motion—the deepening crisis will ensure that will happen—there will be enough modern-day Tocquevilleans, who, owing to their deep fear of "the mob," will be willing to hold their noses to accept whatever is needed to keep their class in power, including someone in the White House who'll make Trump look like a model of moderation. Only then will it be appropriate to talk about the fascist option in American politics.

Trotsky's analysis of fascism remains superior to any subsequent treatment of the subject precisely because it was done in real-time. Weimar Germany showed that the reactionary movement could only be defeated in the streets, its birthplace, not in the electoral/parliamentary arena through lesser/evil maneuvering. Mobilizing the masses in all their identities will, thus, be the only effective answer to its siren call—and why defending the political space that exists today is so crucial in order to prepare for that moment. The fight against fascism will be part and parcel of the decisive struggle, the one to elevate the working class to the ruling class for the first time—the real socialist project. That's not on the immediate agenda, fortunately. What Lenin advised in 1901 is, however. If the working class, again, doesn't have its own party in place, it will be too late to try to construct one when the proverbial "s—t hits the fan." All of humanity still pays for what was missing in post-World War I Germany—Lenin's unheeded advice and what he was so banking on. There's still enough time and space to not make the same mistake.

To return to the opening theme of this book, the current debate/discussion about "socialism," it is unlikely to go away any time soon given the circumstances that generate it, the still unfolding crisis of capitalism. There is nothing to suggest that those who pray at the altar of the market have figured out how to remedy what ails their beloved mode of production. The debate about its future, therefore, will only deepen. Missing in action so far in the debate is the working class. As this is being written, there are perhaps glimpses of what lies ahead; again the example of the teachers' strikes, with West Virginia in the leadership, and now, possibly, a successful echo in New England with the Stop and Shop workers. Such vanguard actions—that's exactly what they were—will have to generalize to the larger working class before it can be said that a new stage in the U.S. class struggle has commenced.

Until then, how to make judgments about the pontifications of the punditry in the media and their spokespeople in the academy about all of this? If there is one thing this exposition has revealed, the best that the academy, the liberal wing specifically, has to offer about how to read such potentially cataclysmic events and the overall moment in which we now live must be taken with a grain of salt. Tocqueville and Weber, certainly, Mill and Wilson to a lesser degree, were indeed keen observers and commentators on socio/political reality. But their class blinders prevented them from accurately representing reality. We should be wary of their current counterparts for the same reason when reading and listening to their pronouncements on the present moment. At the risk of sounding like a reductionist, class and class orientation matter. As for those who speak in the name of Marx, Engels and Lenin, they too should be subjected to the same standards. What's been their practice and track record? How aware are they of the evidence uncovered by this excavation about the historical Marxist project? The mistakes made and the acknowledgments Marx, Engels and Lenin made about those misjudgments? If not, we should be just as wary of that crowd's pronouncements.

Again, whither "socialism"? Like today, a debate ensued in the mid-nineteenth century about its meaning. The oft-neglected third part of Marx's and Engels's *Communist Manifesto* speaks directly to those disagreements. Tocqueville thought that the February 1848 Revolution in France had ushered in "socialism." Marx and Engels disagreed. Instituted, rather, they argued, was the first iteration of today's social democracy. A real socialist revolution, as Engels explained months before the February upheaval—thus, not hindsight—would "destroy not only the political, but the social power of capital that will guarantee their [the proletariat] social welfare, along with their political strength"; that didn't happen, a major reason for the revolution's demise. As long as the means of production remained in private hands, the "social slavery" of the working class, Marx argued, would persist with all the debilitating consequences; Tocqueville, from the other side of the class divide, came close to admitting as much. The destruction of the "social" as well as "political power of capital" was the criterion Marx and Engels employed for distinguishing between "bourgeois socialism" and "scientific socialism." For those who think the two founders of the modern communist movement are still relevant—

what this inquiry seeks to make a case for—the distinction is indispensable in not only explaining why and how the working class is adversely impacted by the continuing crisis of capitalism but in finding a solution.

NOTES

1. *MECW, 11*, p. 79.
2. See my *Marx and Engels*, chapter 4, for details.
3. Tocqueville continues to get an undeserved free pass for his all so consequential counterrevolutionary actions. In what is otherwise a good overview of the 1848–1851 events, Rosenblatt, pp. 129–41, makes not even a hint about how he enabled the overthrow of the Second Republic.
4. See Chap. 2 for details.
5. My "Marx and Engels on the US Civil War: The "Materialist Conception of History' in Action," *Historical Materialism*, vol. 19, no. 4 (2011), provides details.
6. Nimtz, *Marx and Engels*, p. 300.
7. Wells and Baehr, "Editor's Introduction," pp. 24–8, Max Weber, *The Russian Revolutions;* Mommsen, 1997. pp. 13–17; Mommsen, 1984, pp. 278–80; John Patrick Diggins, *Max Weber: Politics and the Spirit of Tragedy* (New York: Basic Books, 1996, p. 239; Paul Honigsheim, *The Unknown Max Weber* (New Brunswick, NJ: Transaction Books, 2000), p. 13.
8. See Tooze's chapter 3, "The War Grave of Russian Democracy" for details. Also, Herman, pp. 303–11.
9. John Reed's articles "How Soviet Russian Conquered Imperial Germany" https://www.marxistsfr.org/archive/reed/1919/conquered/conq2.htm is an insider's account of the Bolshevik efforts to either win or neutralize German soldiers and sailors. For an informative overview of the mood of German armed forces in the war see Steffen Bruendel's "Between Acceptance and Refusal: Soldiers' Attitudes Towards War (Germany)" https://encyclopedia.1914-1918-online.net/article/between_acceptance_and_refusal_-_soldiers_attitudes_towards_war_germany.
10. See Mommsen (1984), chapter 8, for details on Weber's complicated opinions on the monarchy and the final days of the regime.
11. See Herman, pp. 337–45, and Tooze, chapter 11, for details.
12. *Wall Street Journal*, Jan. 23, 2019.
13. Often forgotten today is that parliamentary democracy as the paragon of liberal democracy is largely a post-World War II phenomenon. James Bryce's 1923 classic *Modern Democracies* makes that clear in its final chapters—far from a celebration of the institution; uncertainty, rather, as if in anticipation of World War II, is the tone.

14. Tooze, pp. 84–6.
15. *PWW, 53*, p. 352.
16. For a useful and recent introduction to both questions, see Margaret Macmillan, "The Treaty of Versailles and Its Impact on WWII" https:// www.c-span.org/video/?455201-5/treaty-versailles-impact-world-war-ii.
17. *MECW, 46*, p. 198. See my Marx and Engels, pp. 245–8, for details.
18. *MECW, 27*, p. 433.
19. *LCW, 10*, p. 280.
20. *LCW, 31*, p. 21.
21. *LCW, 33*, p. 431.
22. For details, see V.I. Lenin, *Lenin's Final Fight: Speeches and Writings, 1922–1923.* New York: Pathfinder Press, 2010.
23. Again, see my two-volume *Lenin's Electoral Strategy* for details about his well-deserved democratic credentials.
24. See the five volume Comintern project of Pathfinder Press and the two volumes of Haymarket Press.
25. Trotsky's, *The Struggle Against Fascism in Germany*, New York: Pathfinder Press, 1971, collects his key writings on the topic.
26. Leon Trotsky, "Report on the World Economic Crisis and the New Tasks of the Communist International," *The First Five Years of the Communist International, Vol 1* (New York: Monad Press, 1972), pp. 174–237.
27. The most egregious rendering of that portrait has to be Bertrand Wolfe's utterly blatant sleight of hand in *Three Who Made a Revolution: A Biographical History* (New York; Stein and Day Publishers, 1984), a text—originally published in 1948—upon which generations of post-World War II graduate and undergraduate students were introduced to the Bolshevik leader. What he did to Lenin is unparalleled even in the annals of the Lenin-bashing enterprise. As I detail in my *Lenin Electoral Strategy*, vol. 1, pp. 190–3, he performed a cut and paste job on something Lenin wrote in 1904 that transformed it into its opposite; possibly the origins of the Cold War image of Lenin-the-ogre. Because Wolfe had once been a functionary in the Stalinized Comintern, it is hard to resist employing what Trotsky once wrote about its modus operandi—"the Stalinist school of falsification"—in explaining what he did to Lenin; in other words, Wolfe had been well trained to do his fabrication. Two subsequent and very influential text-book portraits of Lenin built off Wolfe's legerdemain: Alfred G. Meyer's *Leninism* (New York: Praeger, 1957), and Samuel Huntington's *Political Order in Changing Societies* (New Haven, Conn.: Yale U.P. 1968), specifically, "Leninism and Political Development," pp. 334–44.
28. Leon Trotsky, *Stalin: An Appraisal of the Man and His Influence* (New York: Harper and Brothers, 1941), p. 112.

29. Castro's younger brother Raúl had been a member of the youth wing of the Stalinist party—for reasons that seemed more opportunist than anything—but was expelled because he participated in the Moncada attack.

30. Read his multi-hour speech at the University of Havana, November 17, 2005, about half way into it: http://www.scoop.co.nz/stories/WO0512/S00120.htm.

31. For the most up-to-date details in a book, see William LeoGrande and Peter Kornbluh, *Back Channel to Cuba: The Hidden History of Negotiations between Washington and Havana* (Chapel Hill, N.C.: University of North Carolina Press, 2015).

32. Piero Gleijeses, *Conflicting Missions: Havana, Washington, and Africa, 1959–1976* (Chapel Hill, NC: The U of NC Press, 2002), p. 26.

33. "The Opportunity Costs of Socialism," October, 2018, is a seventy-page report of the White House Council of Economic Advisers (www.whitehouse.gov/cea) that informs Trump's diatribes.

34. https://www.nytimes.com/2019/02/24/world/europe/britain-austerity-socialism.html.

35. ebookcentral.proquest.com/lib/umn//reader.action?docID=242182), p. 158.

36. In chronological order: "A black socialist in Trump country," *Minneapolis Star Tribune*, July 29, 2016; "The Graveyard of Progressive Social Movements: The Black Hole of the Democratic Party," *MR Online*, May 9, 2017; "The Meritocratic Myopia of Ta-Nehisi Coates," *MR Online*, Nov. 17, 2019; "Why do Republicans behave the way they do?" *Minnpost*, January 26, 2018; "Bourgeois Fear of Revolution Means Disowning the Civil War," *MR Online*, April 3, 2018; "From a Constituent of Congresswoman Ilhan Omar on Anti-Semitism," *Tikkun*, May 8, 2019.

BIBLIOGRAPHY

PRIMARY SOURCES

de Beaumont, Gustave. 1835. *Marie, ou l'Esclavage aux États-Unis*. Paris: Gosselin.

Hamilton, Thomas. 1833. *Men and Manners in America*, 2 vols. Edinburgh: William Blackwood.

Lenin, Vladimir. 1976. *Collected Works*, 45 vols. Moscow: Progress Publishers.

Marx, Karl. 1972. *Capital*. Vol. 1. New York: International Publishers.

Marx, Karl, and Frederick Engels. 1975–2004. *Collected Works*, 50 vols. New York: International Publishers.

———. 2016. *The Civil War in the United States*. Ed. Andrew Zimmerman. New York: International Publishers.

Mill, John Stuart. 1963–1991. *The Collected Works*. Ed. J.M. Robson. Toronto: University of Toronto Press, 33 vols. https://oll.libertyfund.org/people/john-stuart-mill.

Tocqueville, Alexis de. 1945. *Democracy in America*. Ed. Phillips Bradley, Trans. Henry Reeve, Francis Bowen, and Phillips Bradley, 2 vols. New York: Vintage Books.

———. 1962. *Oeuvres Completes, III, 1*. Paris: Editions Gallimard.

———. 1985. *Selected Letters on Politics and Society*. Ed. Roger Boesche. Los Angeles: University of California Press.

———. 1987. *Recollections: The French Revolution of 1848*. Eds J.P. Mayer and A.P. Kerr. New Brunswick, NJ: Transaction Books.

Weber, Max. 1989a. *Gesamtausgabe*, I/10. Tübingen: J.C.B. Mohr.

———. 1989b. *Gesamtausgabe* Bd. II/4, Briefe, 1903–1905. Tübingen: J.C.B. Mohr.

© The Author(s) 2019
A. H. Nimtz, *Marxism versus Liberalism*, Marx, Engels, and Marxisms, https://doi.org/10.1007/978-3-030-24946-5

———. 1994. *Political Writings*. Ed. Peter Lassman and Ronald Speirs. New York: Cambridge University Press.

———. 1995. *The Russian Revolutions*. Ed. Gordon C. Wells and Peter Baehr. Ithaca, NY: Cornell University Press.

———. *The Protestant Ethic and the Spirit of Capitalism*. https://ebookcentral. proquest.com/.

Wilson, Woodrow. 1966–1994. *The Papers of Woodrow Wilson*, 69 vols. Princeton, NJ: Princeton University Press. https://rotunda.upress.virginia.edu/founders/WILS.

SECONDARY SOURCES

Acemoglu, Daron, and James Robinson. 2000. Democratization or Repression? *European Economic Review* 44 (4–6).

Aldenhoff-Hübinger, Rita. 2004. Max Weber's Inaugural Address of 1895 in the Context of the Contemporary Debates in Political Economy. *Max Weber Studies* 4 (2).

Altman, Roger. 2018. The Markets Will Stop a Trade War. *Wall Street Journal*, July 26.

Aminzade, Ron. 1993. *Ballots and Barricades: Class Formation and Republican Politics in France, 1830–1871*. Princeton: Princeton University Press.

Anievas, Alexander. 2014. *Capital, the State, and War*. Ann Arbor: University of Michigan Press.

Ascher, Abraham. 1988. *The Revolution of 1905: Russia in Disarray*. Stanford, CA: Stanford University Press.

Atanassow, Ewa, and Richard Boyd, eds. 2013. *Tocqueville and the Frontiers of Democracy*. New York: Cambridge University Press.

Bailey, Stephen. 1980. The Berlin Strike of January 1918. *Central European History*. 13 (2).

Barbalet, J.M. 2001. Weber's Inaugural Lecture and Its Place in His Sociology. *Journal of Classical Sociology* 1 (2).

Berman, Sheri. 2019. *Democracy and Dictatorship in Europe: From the Ancien Régime to the Present Day*. New York: Oxford University Press.

Boesche, Roger. 1987. *The Strange Liberalism of Alexis de Tocqueville*. Ithaca, NY: Cornell University Press.

Boyd, Richard. 2004. Review of Nimtz, *Marx, Tocqueville, and Race in America*. *Perspectives on Politics* 3 (2).

Brogan, Hugh. 2006. *Alexis de Tocqueville: A Life*. New Haven: Yale University Press.

Brooks, David. 2018. Understanding Student Mobbists. *New York Times*, March 9.

Bruendel, Steffen. 2014. Between Acceptance and Refusal: Soldiers' Attitudes Towards War (Germany). https://encyclopedia.1914-1918-online.net/article/between_acceptance_and_refusal_-_soldiers_attitudes_towards_war_germany.

Bryce, James. 1923. *Modern Democracies*, 2 vols. New York: Macmillan.

Bullitt, William C. The Bullitt Mission to Moscow. https://www.masterandmargarita.eu/estore/pdf/eren004_bullitt.pdf.

Cairns, John. 1991. Mill and the Revolution of 1848. In *The Collected Works of John Stuart Mill*, vol. 20. Toronto: Toronto University Press.

Calhoun, Craig. 1989. Classical Social Theory and the French Revolution of 1848. *Sociological Theory* 7 (Fall).

Campbell, Duncan Andrew. 2003. *English Public Opinion and the American Civil War*. London: Royal Historical Society.

Capaldi, Nicholas. 2004. *John Stuart Mill: A Biography*. New York: Cambridge University Press.

Cooper, John Milton, Jr. 1982. Woodrow Wilson: The Academic Man. *VQR* 58 (1). https://www.vqronline.org/essay/woodrow-wilson-academic-man.

———. 2009. *Woodrow Wilson*. New York: Alfred Knopf.

Council of Economic Advisers. 2018. Report: The Opportunity Costs of Socialism. October 23. https://www.whitehouse.gov/briefings-statements/cea-report-opportunity-costs-socialism/.

Diggins, John Patrick. 1996. *Marx Weber: Politics and the Spirit of Tragedy*. New York: Basic Books.

Dobbs, Farrell. 1980. *Revolutionary Continuity: The Early Years—1848–1917*. New York: Monad Press.

Doyle, Michael W. 1997. *Ways of War and Peace*. New York: W.W. Norton.

Doyle, Dan. 2015. *The Cause of All Nations: An International History of the American Civil War*. New York: Basic Books.

Draper, Hal. 1977. Marx and the Economic-Jew Stereotype. https://www.marxists.org/archive/draper/1977/kmtr1/app1.htm.

———. 1986. *Karl Marx's Theory of Revolution: Volume III*. New York: Monthly Review Press.

———. 1994. *The Adventures of the Communist Manifesto*. Berkeley, CA: Center for Socialist History.

———. 2005. *Karl Marx's Theory of Revolution*, Volume 5: War and Revolution. New York: Monthly Review Press.

Duncan, Graeme. 1973. *Marx and Mill: Two Views of Social Conflict and Social Harmony*. New York: Cambridge University Press.

Eccarius, J.G. 1866–1867. A Working Man's Refutation of some Points of Political Economy Endorsed and Advocated by John Stuart Mill. *The Commonwealth* Nos. 192–195, 198, 200, 203, 204, 206–211, November–March.

Emmons, Terence, and Wayne Vucinich, eds. 1982. *The Zemstvo in Russia: An Experiment in Local Self-Government*. London: Cambridge University Press.

Figes, Orlando. 1996. *A People's Tragedy: A History of the Russian Revolution*. New York: Viking.

Foglesong, David S. 1995. *America's Secret War Against Bolshevism: U.S. Intervention in the Russian Civil War, 1917–1920*. Chapel Hill, NC: University of North Carolina Press.

Foot, Paul. 2005. *The Vote: How It Was Won and How It Was Undermined*. New York: Viking.

Fraser, Antonia. 2013. *Perilous Question: Reform or Revolution? Britain on the Brink, 1832*. New York: Public Affairs.

Gabriel, Mary. 2011. *Love and Capital: Karl and Jenny Marx and the Birth of a Revolution*. New York: Little, Brown.

Gargan, Edward T. 1955. *Alexis de Tocqueville: The Critical Years, 1848–1851*. Washington, DC: Catholic University Press.

Glatthaar, Joseph. 1993. Black Glory: The African American Role in Union Victory. In *Why the Confederacy Lost*, ed. Gabor Boritt. New York: Oxford University Press.

Gleijeses, Piero. 2002. *Conflicting Missions: Havana, Washington, and Africa, 1959–1976*. Chapel Hill, NC: The University of NC Press.

Guess, Raymond. 2008. *Philosophy and Real Politics*. Princeton, NJ: Princeton University Press.

Hayward, Jack. 1991. *After the French Revolution: Six Critics of Democracy and Nationalism*. New York: New York University Press.

Herman, Arthur. 2017. *1917: Lenin, Wilson, and the Birth of the New World Disorder*. New York: Harper, Collins.

Honigsheim, Paul. 2000. *The Unknown Max Weber*. New Brunswick, NJ: Transaction Books.

Holzer, Harold. Lincoln an Immigration. https://www.c-span.org/video/?418240-2/abraham-lincoln-immigration.

Huntington, Samuel. 1968. *Political Order in Changing Societies*. New Haven, CT: Yale University Press.

Jardin, Andre. 1988. *Tocqueville: A Biography*. New York: Farrar, Straus, Giroux.

Kahan, Alan S. 1992. *Aristocratic Liberalism: The Social and Political Thought of Jacob Burckhardt, John Stuart Mill, and Alexis de Tocqueville*. New York: Oxford University Press.

Kaledin, Arthur. 2011. *Tocqueville and His America: A Darker Horizon*. New Haven: Yale University Press.

Kelly, George. 1992. *The Human Comedy: Constant, Tocqueville, and French Liberalism*. Cambridge: Cambridge University Press.

Kloppenberg, James T. 2016. *Toward Democracy: The Struggle for Self-Rule in European and American Thought*. New York: Oxford University Press.

Kulikoff, Allan. 2002. Revolutionary Violence and the Origins of American Democracy. *The Journal of the Historical Society* 2 (2).

Lenin, V.I. 2010. *Lenin's Final Fight: Speeches & Writings, 1922–1923*. New York: Pathfinder Press.

LeoGrande, William, and Peter Kornbluh. 2015. *Back Channel to Cuba: The Hidden History of Negotiations Between Washington and Havana*. Chapel Hill, NC: University of North Carolina Press.

Levin, Alfred. 1940. *The Second Duma: A Study of the Social-Democratic Party and the Russian Constitutional Experiment*. New Haven: Yale University Press.

Losurdo, Domenico. 2011. *Liberalism: A Counter-History*. London: Verso.

MacIntyre, Alasdair. 1983. The Indispensability of Political Theory. In *The Nature of Political Theory*, ed. David Miller and Larry Siedentop. Oxford: The Clarendon Press.

Mahoney, Daniel. 1993. Tocqueville and Socialism. In *Tocqueville's Defense of Human Liberty: Current Essays*. New York: Garland Publishing.

Manela, Erez. 2007. *The Wilsonian Moment: Self-Determination and the International Origins of Anti-Colonial Nationalism*. New York: Oxford University Press.

Mayer, Arno. 1959. *Political Origins of the New Diplomacy, 1917–1918*. New Haven: Yale University Press.

Mayer, J.P. 1960. *Alexis de Tocqueville: A Biographical Study in Political Science*. New York: Harper & Brothers.

Macmillan, Margaret. The Treaty of Versailles and Its Impact on WWII. https://www.c-span.org/video/?455201-5/treaty-versailles-impact-world-war-ii.

McDonald, Bradley J. 2015. Review of Nimtz, *Lenin's Electoral Strategy*. *Perspectives on Politics* 13 (4).

McPhee, Peter. 1974. The Crisis of Radical Republicanism in the French Revolution of 1848. *Historical Studies* 16 (162).

Meyer, Alfred G. Meyer. 1957. *Leninism*. New York: Praeger.

Mommsen, Wolfgang J. 1984. *Max Weber and German Politics, 1890–1920*. Chicago: University of Chicago Press.

———. 1997. Max Weber and the Regeneration of Russia. *Journal of Modern History* 69 (1).

Montgomery, Scott L., and Daniel Chirot. 2015. *The Shape of the New: Four Big Ideas and How They Made the Modern World*. Princeton, NJ: Princeton University Press.

Nimtz, August H. 2000. *Marx and Engels: Their Contribution to the Democratic Breakthrough*. Albany, NY: State University of New York Press.

———. 2003. *Marx, Tocqueville, and Race in America; The 'Absolute Democracy' or 'Defiled Republic*. New York: Lexington Books.

———. 2010. "Violence and/or Nonviolence in the Success of the Civil Rights Movement." *New Political Science*, "Marx's and Engels's Electoral Strategy: The Alleged versus the Real". *New Political Science* 32 (3).

———. 2011. "Violence and/or Nonviolence in the Success of the Civil Rights Movement." *New Political Science*, "Marx and Engels on the US Civil War". *Historical Materialism* 19 (4).

———. 2014. Violence and/or Nonviolence in the Success of the Civil Rights Movement. In *New Political Science, Lenin's Electoral Strategy From Marx and*

Engels Through the Revolution of 1905, and Lenin's Electoral Strategy From 1907 to the October Revolution of 1917. New York: Palgrave Macmillan.

———. 2016a. Marx and Engels on the Revolutionary Party. In *Socialist Register 2017*, ed. Leo Panitch and Greg Albo. London: The Merlin Press.

———. 2016b. Violence and/or Nonviolence in the Success of the Civil Rights Movement. *New Political Science* 38 (1).

———. 2017. 'The Bolsheviks Come to Power': A New Interpretation. *Science & Society* 81 (4).

Nolte, Ernst. 1966. *Three Faces of Fascism: Action Française, Italian Fascism, National Socialism*. New York: Holt, Rinehart and Winston.

O'Connor, Harvey. 2009. *Revolution in Seattle*. Chicago: Haymarket Books.

Phillips, Michael M. An American Tragedy in Russia. https://www.wsj.com/articles/the-one-time-american-troops-fought-russians-was-at-the-end-of-world-war-iand-they-lost-1541772001.

Pipes, Richard. 1955. Max Weber and Russia. *World Politics* 7 (3).

Pitts, Jennifer. 2000. Empire and Democracy: Tocqueville and the Algeria Question. *Journal of Political Philosophy* 8 (3).

Porshneva, Olga. World War I Russian Soldiers and the 1917 Revolution. https://www.c-span.org/search/?searchtype=All&query=Olga+Porshneva.

Price, Roger. 1988. *The Revolutions of 1848*. Atlantic Highlands, NJ: Humanities Press.

Proudhon, Pierre-Joseph. 1840. *Qu'est-ce que la propriété?* [What Is Property?] https://www.marxists.org/reference/subject/economics/proudhon/property/index.htm.

Rabinowitch, Alexander. 2007. *The Bolsheviks in Power: The First Year of Soviet Rule in Petrograd*. Bloomington, IN: Indiana University Press.

Reed, John. 1919. How Soviet Russia Conquered Imperial Germany. https://www.marxists.org/archive/reed/1919/conquered/conq1.htm.

Reeves, Richard. 2007. *John Stuart Mill: Victorian Firebrand*. London: Atlantic Books.

Rehmann, Jan. 2015. *Max Weber, Modernisation as Passive Revolution: A Gramscian Analysis*. Chicago: Haymarket Books.

Richard, Carl J. 2013. *When the United States Invaded the Soviet Union: Woodrow Wilson's Siberian Disaster*. New York: Rowman & Littlefield.

Riddell, John, ed. 1986. *The German Revolution and the Debate on Soviet Power: Documents: 1918–1919*. New York: Pathfinder Press.

Rosenblatt, Helena. 2018. *The Lost History of Liberalism: From Ancient Rome to the Twenty-First Century*. Princeton, NJ: Princeton University Press.

Service, Robert. 1985. *Lenin: A Political Life*. Vol. 1. Bloomington: Indiana University Press.

Spence, R.B. 2017. The Voyage of the *Shilka*: The Bolshevik Revolution Comes to Seattle, 1917. *American Communist History* 16 (1–2).

Tilly, Charles. 1986. *The Contentious French*. Cambridge: Harvard University Press.

Tooze, Adam. 2014. *The Deluge: The Great War, America and the Remaking of the Global Order, 1916–1931*. New York: Viking.

Traugott, Mark. 1985. *Armies of the Poor: Determinants of Working-Class Participation in the Parisian Insurrection of June 1848*. Princeton, NJ: Princeton University Press.

Trickey, Eric. 2019. The Forgotten Story of the American Troops Who Got Caught Up in the Russian Civil War. *Smithsonian.Com*, February https://www.smithsonianmag.com/history/forgotten-doughboys-who-died-fighting-russian-civil-war-180971470/.

Trotsky, Leon. 1941. *Stalin: An Appraisal of the Man and His Influence*. New York: Harper and Brothers.

———. 1971. *The Struggle Against Fascism in Germany*. New York: Pathfinder Press.

———. 1972. Report on the World Economic Crisis and the New Tasks of the Communist International. In *The First Five Years of the Communist International*, vol. 1. New York: Monad Press.

Tuchinsky, Adam-Max. 2005. 'The Bourgeoisie Will Fall and Fall Forever': The 'New-York Tribune', the 1848 French Revolution and American Social Democratic Discourse. *Journal of American History* 92 (2).

Valverde, Sergio. 2017. *A Speculative Theory of Politics: Logic of the Party Form*. Dissertation. University of Minnesota.

Varouxakis, Georgios. 2013. 'Negrophilist' Crusader: John Stuart Mill on the American Civil War and Reconstruction. *History of European Ideas* 39 (5).

Weber, Marianne. 1988. *Max Weber: A Biography*. New Brunswick, NJ: Transaction Books.

Welch, Cheryl B. 2003. Colonial Violence and the Rhetoric of Evasion. *Political Theory* 31 (2).

Weyland, Kurt. 2012. The Arab Spring: Why the Surprising Similarities with the Revolutionary Wave of 1848? *Perspectives on Politics* 10 (4).

Williams, James H. 1917. From Russia with Love: Lenin's Letter to American Workers. *New Politics*, August 23.

Wolfe, Bertrand. 1984. *Three Who Made a Revolution: A Biographical History*. New York: Stein and Day.

Zeitlin, Irving M. 1971. *Liberty, Equality, and Revolution in Alexis de Tocqueville*. Boston: Little, Brown.

Zimmerman, Andrew. 2010. *Alabama in Africa: Booker T. Washington, the German Empire, and the Globalization of the New South*. Princeton, NJ: Princeton University Press.

Zinoviev, Gregory. 2017. Wars: Defensive and Aggressive. In *3 Study Guides on Lenin's Writings*. New York: Pathfinder Press.

Index[1]

[1] Note: Page numbers followed by 'n' refer to notes.

© The Author(s) 2019
A. H. Nimtz, *Marxism versus Liberalism*, Marx, Engels,
and Marxisms, https://doi.org/10.1007/978-3-030-24946-5